ILLUSTRATED GREEN GUIDE

ILLUSTRATED

GREEN GUIDE

The Complete Reference for Consuming Wisely

FOREWORD BY
MERYL STREEP

BY THE
EDITORS OF
THE *GREEN GUIDE*
MAGAZINE

WASHINGTON, DC

Contents

Foreword

BY MERYL STREEP

THIS IS IT. This is the book we've all been wishing would be written for years. It's the ultimate green living reference, a go-to guide for practical, ready-to-apply solutions to the most pressing environmental problems facing us today at home, in our communities, and around the world.

And there is no one more qualified to write it. The editors of the *Green Guide* have been researching and reporting on sensible ways for consumers to care for themselves and their families since the early 1990s. I know this, because I was a co-founder of the organization Mothers & Others, which published the first *Green Guide* in 1994. The original *Green Guides* were short — just four pages — and frequent — biweekly. They were intended to be read in just minutes, with ideas easily put into action. Whether you were concerned about hormones in milk and poultry or emissions of greenhouse gases from the burning of fossil fuels, *Green Guide* made the latest scientific issues understandable and the remedies easy to implement.

Those same good-sense solutions have been the hallmark of the *Green Guide* throughout the past decade and a half. A website was added in 2002, providing concerned consumers 24/7 access to a dynamic database, replete with regularly updated product reports, smart shopping tips, and step-by-step guides to greening their homes. And then, in 2007, the National Geographic Society bought the *Green Guide*, eager to make it the "mother of all resources" for consumers wanting to live a greener life. It was National Geographic's idea to convert the *Green Guide* from a short-form newsletter into a magazine, the only mainstream periodical devoted 100 percent to green consumer information.

National Geographic was also quick to jump on the idea of a *Green Guide* book, chock-full of simple, useful ideas broken down into achievable steps. Good thing, too, as I like books — particularly books like this that bring it all together, covering so much that matters in our lives, from the food we choose to put on our tables, to the way we heat our homes, even how we dress up our children for Halloween. That's what I value about the *Green Guide*, that's why I turn to it when I need advice. It helps us to see how even the most mundane decisions, from our choice of coffee to how long we shower, matter a lot.

I was a mother of young children when I joined with Wendy Gordon to create Mothers & Others. Our aim then was to protect our kids from trace levels of harmful pesticides in common fruits and vegetables. We were responding to reports by the Natural Resources Defense Council and the National Academy of Sciences showing that young children were exposed to levels of pesticides above those the federal government considered safe. My neighbors and I lobbied our supermarkets to begin to offer organic and sustainably grown produce and to buy from local growers. (Hard to believe, but 15 years ago these products were simply not available in most stores!) We worked with other concerned citizens to change the regulations to take into account the particular eating patterns and vulnerabilities of very young children.

What we learned in those early years was that while government reform can take years to bring about, concerned consumers wanted to know what they could do now. What choices did they have? Could they make a difference? These direct questions from everyday consumers—how do I safeguard my kids, what can we do to live more responsibly—inspired Mothers & Others, and a couple of years later, the *Green Guide* was launched. Our mission from the outset was to make living in an environmentally aware way understandable, practical, and immediate. It wasn't about the actions of others, about big institutions or government agencies, but about us, what we do, how we do things, the way we live our lives. And sure enough, what we do does count. By voting with our dollars—demanding products that are more intelligently made, from toothpaste to wind turbines—we have provided much of the impetus for manufacturers and governments to do the right thing, too, now and for the future.

The *Green Guide* has been my source all these years, and I'm grateful. I encourage you to make it yours and to use this book as it was intended to be used. Mark in it, turn down the corners, and put tabs on those pages you'll go back to over and over again. It's that sort of a book: a reference, a workhorse, a companion for all of us making extraordinary things happen in the most ordinary of ways.

Introduction

BY SETH BAUER
EDITORIAL DIRECTOR, *GREEN GUIDE*

"SO, WHAT CAN I DO?"

It's the question we hear from readers all the time, and it underlies all the work we do at National Geographic's *Green Guide*. Asking what you can do shows that you've recognized the kind of stress that human activity puts on the planet—on natural resources from trees, water, and soil, to minerals and ancient deposits of oil and coal, to the delicate balance of gases in our atmosphere that lets life exist on Earth. It shows that you realize that it's not just up to others—scientists or businesspeople or governments—to deal with the issues; that every day, each of us makes decisions that worsen or lessen the stress on the planet; that widespread individual action could make a tremendous difference (and in some ways already has). And best of all, it shows that you're ready to act. You're ready to go green.

MYTHS ABOUT GOING GREEN

There are a lot of myths about going green. The first is that going green requires a lot of sacrifice. But living green doesn't mean returning to a 19th-century lifestyle of manual labor and living in the dark. It doesn't mean forgoing all that new technology has to offer. In fact, the newest technologies—efficient alternative energy production, better recycling capacity—will allow us to live greener than any time since the industrial revolution. In many ways, it's the leftover technology from the second half of the 20th century that has led to global concerns about climate change and dwindling resources. Going green means replacing that generation of manufacturing, energy production, and goods with a whole new wave of approaches to the resources that we use and the gases that we create. It means doing a lot more with a little less, and in that way it could not be more cutting-edge—or important.

The second myth is that going green is expensive, that it's only for the rich. There's a small element of truth in the latter assertion, but it's not because going green costs a lot of money. It's because in some ways the less

well-to-do tend to be green already. When your electricity and heating bills directly affect how much money you have to spend on food and clothing, you tend to conserve. You are not quick to dispose of things, repairing or reusing rather than replacing. You don't have more space to live in than you need. You use public transportation. You don't waste food. Green ideas, all. But, as the ideas in this book show, everyone can find ways to conserve. And in nearly every case, going green means saving green.

The third myth is that going green is a political statement. Somehow over the years environmentalism, which should have been the concern of people of every political stripe, got swept up in the tornado of politics and precariously set down on one side of the political aisle. Yet the bottom line is that every organism on Earth has an interest in preserving its ecosystem, and humans are no different. Take a step back, and it's easy to see that we're all in this together. Going green means looking at your consumer choices through a new lens, but it's not the lens of politics.

LIFE THROUGH THE LENS OF LIFE CYCLE

So what is that lens? The primary green lens is the lens of life cycle. Every product we buy and use, from the food we eat, to the cars we drive, to the energy we purchase to heat and light our houses, has a life cycle of its own. It's grown or manufactured from natural resources, or from chemicals made from natural resources. There is energy and waste involved in the manufacturing process. It's packaged in some way. It's transported to market. It's used by you, the consumer. Then it's disposed of in some way, poured down the drain or recycled or sent to a landfill or even given away. Each of these steps affects how green the product and process might be. And each has a cost, either to the manufacturer, to you as a consumer, or to you as a citizen of the planet.

Take a seemingly simple example: orange juice. Orange juice comes every which way—frozen, in concentrate, reconstituted from concentrate, packaged in cartons or in plastic containers. As a conventional consumer, you might have several reasons to choose a particular kind of orange juice: its price, its nutritional value, its taste, whether you mind stirring it from concentrate, and maybe the way it has been advertised.

But look again at buying orange juice, this time through that green lens. Now you think about how and where the oranges were grown: Did the grower use pesticides that leached into the soil or streams nearby? Was there plenty of natural water for the orange trees, or was it diverted from other sources? And the manufacturing of the juice: Is it energy-intensive to turn it into concentrate? It can't be efficient to turn juice into concentrate, then reconstitute it before sending it to market. The packaging: Clearly the concentrate takes less packaging; on the other hand, the plastic might be recyclable. The transportation: It takes much more energy to truck full gallons of the stuff than it does to truck concentrate.

Now orange juice sold in concentrate is starting to look like the smarter choice. Add back in the factors you would have considered anyway (concentrate preserves nutrients, and tends to be cheaper, too), and you have a whole new way of making your choice. What did it take? A few seconds of logical thought. What did it save? Well, it saved you some money, first of all. It may be better for your health. And over the course of your lifetime as a consumer, it may save hundreds of gallons of fuel in trucking costs and hundreds of pounds of paper or plastic for cartons, along with space in landfills. Choose organic juice and it will also save hundreds of pounds of pesticide use over your consumer lifetime, though it may cost more. And that's just from one consumer— you— making one greener choice.

Fortunately, you're not the only one making such choices. Millions upon millions of people around the world are looking for ways to lower the stress they put on the planet. The science behind the recognition of global climate change and limits to natural resources has begun to change behavior in many countries. Citizens and leaders of the world's most rapidly growing countries, like China and India, are aware that with an improving living standard come global responsibilities. And those in high-consuming regions, like the United States, Japan, and Europe, are becoming greener every day.

THE THIRD WAVE OF ENVIRONMENTALISM

Going green on an individual basis represents a new wave of environmental action. Environmentalism, as a social movement, has entered its third major phase. The first, when national and state parks were created and open land preserved, centered around land conservation. The second, which began to take hold in the 1960s, was a phase of activism as scientific inquiry and the broad-scale recognition of the health impacts of pollution and chemical use led to legal and administrative oversight—and our food supplies, waterways, and skies began to get cleaner. Now the third wave—call it consumer or personal environmentalism—brings all the personal choices we make every day into play: Do we recycle? Conserve? Waste? Recognize that every drop of rain is precious, that every chemical we pour down the drain goes somewhere, and that every time we raise the thermostat, make an extra trip in our cars, or buy something that's been shipped long distances, we're adding unnecessary carbon to the atmosphere and hastening global warming?

The *Green Guide* is here to help make personal environmentalism easy. That's what it's always been about. The *Green Guide* was started in 1994 by Wendy Gordon, who had been a research scientist at the Natural Resources Defense Council. As she raised her two sons, she became alarmed at the chemicals children were exposed to in their food, around their houses, and in nearly every part of their lives. She saw simple solutions: nonchemical cleansers, pesticide-free foods, household products that did not release gases. Wendy established the *Green Guide* newsletter, which has been helping ever increasing numbers of consumers make better-informed choices. In 2007, the *Green Guide* joined the National Geographic Society and its mission of inspiring people to care about the planet.

Under Wendy's guidance, the *Green Guide* has always been practical, simple, and grounded in science. Each assertion we make about potential hazards or benefits of products and practices has been documented in peer-reviewed scientific journals. Our writers are painstaking in their research and held to a high standard of fact-checking. The team that created this book was overseen by a panel of outside experts who volunteered to review each chapter. For us, making green easy means making sure that the ideas presented are worthy of your time and effort.

So, what can you do?

Go green. We're here to help.

1

PRODUCE
MEAT • POULTRY
SEAFOOD • DAIRY
COOKING OILS
HERBS & SEASONINGS
SNACKS & SWEETS
WATER • COFFEE & TEA
BEER & WINE
COOKWARE • BOTTLES
STORAGE CONTAINERS
WRAPS & BAGS
LUNCH BOXES
RESTAURANTS

EAT GREEN

Healthy, Sustainable Meals

THERE'S NO DOUBT ABOUT IT: FOOD IS THE FUEL THAT YOUR body needs to make it through each day. It keeps your body running smoothly, from the minute you wake up until the moment that your head hits the pillow. But just as you want the fuel you put in your car to be as safe for the environment as possible, it makes a difference what types of food you eat—and where that food comes from.

In today's world, with busy schedules at work and at home, the option to fuel your body with convenient foods is tempting. Quick and prepacked food, whether a hamburger and french fries, a bag of potato chips, or a candy bar, is readily available and easy to grab on the go. These foods may give you a burst of energy at the start, but the boost they provide is temporary.

Instead, your best choices are fresh, whole foods that are chock-full of antioxidant compounds, vitamins, minerals, and other nutrients. Study after study has revealed the health-protective benefits of foods and beverages like fruits, vegetables, whole grains, and tea, with moderate amounts of fish, poultry, and other lean meats. And eating this way isn't just good for your body. Foods and beverages such as these are also delicious and can be simple to prepare.

So you're ready to start eating a healthier diet. But open any newspaper these days and you're bound to feel alarmed. You may see stories about pesticides in produce, *E. coli* bacteria in meat, and mercury in seafood. Dig a little deeper, and you'll uncover concerns regarding how food is grown, harvested, and manufactured: Your coffee could be helping destroy the rain forest, and your chocolate bar may have helped support child slave labor. Even the containers, bags, and wraps that you use may contain toxic chemicals that can migrate into the foods and beverages that they hold.

It's all enough to make you second-guess your healthy diet. But don't give up on wholesome foods and beverages yet. With a little research and some simple changes, you can enjoy a diet that's healthy for you in every way. Although some environmentally friendly foods may cost more than their conventional counterparts, the good they can do for you—and the planet—is worth the investment. Plus, many ecologically sound foods and products cost the same or even less.

So where should you start? You'll want to follow some basic guidelines: Choose fruits, vegetables, and other foods that are as fresh as possible, particularly those that are locally grown and produced. Learn which foods are most likely to be contaminated with pesticides, fertilizers, and other toxic chemicals, and select varieties that have been labeled as being certified organic. And research where your food comes from, and how the workers, animals, and environment involved in its production were treated. Once you've got these and a few other tricks described in this chapter up your sleeve, you'll have the tools you need to eat healthy, green, and sustainable meals for life.

Produce

A ripe, juicy peach... a crunchy ear of sweet corn... a perfectly crisp leaf of spinach. With choices like these, it's easy—and delicious—to get your five to nine recommended daily servings of fruits and vegetables. But even fresh produce raises questions we need to ask and answer intelligently.

OPTING FOR ORGANICS They're meant to protect fruits and vegetables from insects, fungi, and other pests, but pesticides are poisons, and their

toxic effects are hardly safe for anyone. Some pesticides have been linked to health problems such as cognitive difficulties, cancer, and Parkinson's disease. And the pesticides don't disappear when the produce hits your plate: It's estimated that conventionally grown fruits and vegetables can contain the residues of more than a dozen different pesticides.

So what should you do?

The obvious answer is to buy organic varieties, which contain about one-third the level of pesticide residues compared with conventionally grown produce. Research shows that eating more organic foods can significantly lower levels of pesticides in our bodies: In one 2006 study of children ages 3 to 11 who ate an organic diet for five days, scientists noted a "dramatic and immediate protective effect" against two common pesticides until the kids resumed their conventional diets. While the children were consuming organic foods, for example, the metabolite of the pesticide malathion was undetectable in most of the children's urine samples. Once they returned to their conventional diets, however, the average malathion metabolite concentration returned to 1.6 parts per billion, about the same concentration as that found before the children adopted the organic diet.

Even though prices for organic foods are dropping as consumer demand increases, purchasing only organic produce can still be pricey. The most cost-effective solution is to pinpoint the fruits and vegetables that are most likely to be contaminated with pesticides and buy organic varieties of them. Identifying organic produce has gotten easier than ever, thanks to the federal organic standard. In effect since 2002, the law specifies that in order to be labeled as organic, a food must have been certified as having been produced without synthetic pesticides or fertilizers, genetic engineering, antibiotics, hormones, sewage sludge, or irradiation. Organic fruits and vegetables that qualify may carry a label that reads "Certified Organic." Organic certification also implies that the farmer is promoting biological diversity by rotating crops, conserving and renewing the soil, and protecting water sources.

ECO-TIP: WHEN TO GO ORGANIC

The Environmental Working Group has compiled a list of the top 12 fruits and vegetables most often contaminated by pesticides. When possible, buy organic versions of these foods:

peaches	cherries
apples	lettuce
sweet bell peppers	grapes (imported)
celery	pears
nectarines	spinach
strawberries	potatoes

BUYING LOCAL Neighborhood farmers markets offer colorful bounty, freshly picked and brought to market. It looks beautiful and tastes even better, but looks and flavor aren't the only differences between local produce and the produce offered at the supermarket. Opting for locally grown fruits and vegetables can have larger benefits, too.

First, buying locally or regionally grown produce sold at farmers markets, farm stands, natural-foods stores, and farmer-friendly supermarket chains helps support area farmers. Small farms are a dying breed: According to the U.S. Department of Agriculture (USDA), since 1960 farmland has been converted to nonagricultural use at a rate of 1.5 million acres annually.

Second, there are definitely nutritional benefits to buying local produce. Produce that is shipped long-distance is usually picked before it ripens, and treated, possibly with fungicides, so that it can travel and be stored. On the other hand, farm-fresh fruits and vegetables are typically picked at their peak, making for ripe, ready-to-eat produce.

Third, choosing locally grown produce can often help ease the burden on our environment. On average, domestically grown produce sold in conventional supermarkets has traveled some 1,500 miles from farm to table. Even organic produce can use up fossil fuels and contribute to pollution during its transport: One 2007 Canadian study pointed to the environmental cost of greenhouse gas emitted to transport organically grown produce, since it was being shipped so much farther than the conventional fruit and vegetables.

You can support local farmers—and reap the rewards of their harvest—by joining a community-supported agriculture program (CSA). These local farms allow you to purchase shares of each season's harvest. Investing in a CSA operation trains you to eat seasonally, since what you receive each week depends on the growing season, weather, and harvest of specific crops. In spring, for example, you might receive

strawberries and greens; summer brings peas and string beans; autumn yields squash and root vegetables.

CSAs are one organized way of getting local produce efficiently. The energy equation that describes the production and transportation is a complex one. Recent studies show that in a situation of uncoordinated local production, with every farmer and every consumer driving a vehicle to the central market, more fuel may be consumed than in a more organized regional food system.

GREEN DICTIONARY

CSAs

Community-supported agriculture programs (CSAs) are farms that sell shares of their harvest to local residents. Members pay a fixed fee, typically $300 to $600, and In exchange they receive weekly shares of the farm's bounty, which varies depending on the season, weather, and specific crops grown.

The equation gets more complicated when considering the international produce market. Fruits and vegetables that were once strictly seasonal are now available year-round, thanks to vast shipping networks. Out-of-season produce can be expensive, because transport uses so much energy. It's also more likely to have been imported from a country with looser pesticide regulations. Yet vegetables traveling to New York City from China by boat actually require less transport energy than vegetables shipped across the continent by truck from California to New York.

What to do? Emphasize quality over quantity, and do all you can to become aware of the larger implications of every food purchase you make.

GENETICALLY MODIFIED FOOD Genetically modified organisms (GMOs) are created by inserting a gene from one organism into another organism. This alters the recipient's genetic makeup to produce new and different traits, such as pest resistance or faster growth. Available since the early 1990s, GMOs are now present in more than 60 percent of processed foods found on supermarket shelves in the United States.

GMOs may represent remarkable scientific accomplishments, but they may also have harmful effects on human health and the environment. Traces of GMO DNA have been found in traditional seed supplies of corn, soybean, and canola. The health risks posed by GMOs are still unknown but may include allergies and increased cancer risk. Although the environmental impact of GMOs cannot be predicted, scientists worry that genes for herbicide resistance could jump from GMO crops to wild plants, creating "superweeds" immune to herbicides. Another concern is that multiple foreign genes could accumulate in wild plants and spread unchecked into ecosystems, threatening biodiversity. To best avoid foods that contain GMOs, look for those that are labeled "Certified Organic."

ECO-TIP: LEARN YOUR LABELS

When shopping for food produced in ways that best benefit the environment, your first step should be to look at the label. But don't let appearances fool you: Labels and logos mean very little if they aren't backed up by strong standards. The following labels can be trusted, since each one indicates certification by an independent third party.

1. **Bird Friendly:** protects tropical bird habitats
   FOODS CERTIFIED: coffee
2. **American Humane Certified:** assures humane care of livestock, no use of growth hormones or nontherapeutic antibiotics
   FOODS CERTIFIED: meat, poultry, eggs, dairy
3. **Demeter Biodynamic:** designates no synthetic pesticide use, no genetic engineering, no crops grown in areas subject to strong electromagnetic fields, agriculture timed with planetary rhythms
   FOODS CERTIFIED: wine, cheese, eggs, fruit, meat, vegetables
4. **Fair Trade Certified:** ensures farmers receive fair prices
   FOODS CERTIFIED: coffee, tea, chocolate, tropical fruit, rice, sugar
5. **Food Alliance Certified:** indicates sustainable farming practices, soil and water conservation, fair treatment of workers
   FOODS CERTIFIED: milk, frozen food, fruit, wheat, meat, vegetables
6. **Free-Farmed:** means that animals had access to clean food and water and were raised without antibiotics to promote growth
   FOODS CERTIFIED: meat, poultry
7. **Grass-Fed:** guarantees livestock receive continuous access to natural outdoor forage during growing season
   FOODS CERTIFIED: dairy, beef, lamb
8. **Marine Stewardship Council:** signifies well-managed fisheries
   FOODS CERTIFIED: farmed, wild-caught fish
9. **Rainforest Alliance:** protects rain forests
   FOODS CERTIFIED: bananas, coffee, orange juice, chocolate, tea
10. **Salmon-Safe:** protects watersheds
   FOODS CERTIFIED: wine, dairy, fresh produce

Meat

Beef, chicken, pork, lamb—despite the growing inclination to eat vegetarian, meat is often still at the center of many a meal on the American dining table. While some may argue that the entire cycle of meat production and processing drains the environment, new methods of animal husbandry are being developed that respect both the animals and the land that they graze.

THE FACTS

According to the Center for a New American Dream, if just 1,000 Americans ate one fewer beef meals a week, over 70,000 pounds of grain, 70,000 pounds of topsoil, and 40 million gallons of water would be saved each year.

When animals are raised for meat in settings of intensive rotational grazing, gathering their own food and spreading their own manure, that weed-strewn pastureland may be more environmentally beneficial than the vegetable farmland next door, where seasonal crops are being grown and cultivated fields lie fallow for long parts of every year. Once again, it's a complicated equation; once again, the conscientious consumer looks as clearly as possible at all parts of the picture.

It's true that meat is a good source of protein, but so are soybeans and other legumes. And it's quite possible to eat a healthy, balanced diet with little or no meat in it. If the link between meat consumption and cancer isn't reason enough to cut back, consider the other risks. Meat can be a breeding ground for *E. coli* and other bacteria responsible for foodborne illness. Industrial animal husbandry practices are hardly kind to animals—or the people who work in slaughterhouses. And the meat industry contributes significantly to air and water pollution. But there are ways for even the most dedicated meat eaters to reduce their contributions to these problems.

COMMON CONTAMINANTS Modern feedlot and slaughterhouse practices have lowered the cost of meat, but they've also increased the risk of foodborne illness from pathogen-tainted meat. Manure from feedlot cows—fattened on an unnatural diet of corn, fed antibiotics routinely, and raised in close quarters—makes a perfect breeding ground for infectious disease. When these animals are slaughtered and processed, the bacteria can mix with the meat. The result: meat that's contaminated with pathogens such as *Campylobacter, Salmonella, E. coli,* and *Listeria monocytogenes.* Ground meat—which is derived from more than one animal—is especially likely to be tainted. Another concern is bovine spongiform encephalopathy, also known as mad cow disease. Although the European Union has banned the practice of feeding animal products to other animals (a common route of infection), the United States still allows cattle feed to contain remnants of dead animals, cattle blood, and restaurant waste.

THE FACTS

Routine industrial meat and dairy production practices today mean that an estimated 70 percent of all antibiotics and related drugs in the United States are fed to cows, pigs, and chickens that are not sick.

If you're not ready to give up meat altogether, there are healthier meat choices. The first step is to look for organic meat. A "Certified Organic" label on meat means that the animal was given organic feed grown from plants that were not genetically engineered and were not treated with pesticides or sewage sludge. The animal was not given antibiotics or hormones and was not genetically modified, and it had access to the out-of-doors, including pasture for grazing. Meat from organically raised animals is processed according to strictly defined standards that restrict the use of chemicals and irradiation. (See "Green Dictionary: Irradiation," opposite.) Look for meat labels marked "100 Percent Organic"; products that are at least 95 percent organic may be labeled "Organic," and those with more than 70 percent organic ingredients may be labeled "Made with Organic Ingredients."

Meats labeled "Grass-Fed" are also a good choice. Grass-fed cows, sheep, goats, and bison are raised exclusively on pasture and stored grasses; supplements must be free of grain and animal products. Meats from grass-fed animals are also lower in total fat and saturated fat, and higher in healthy omega-3 fatty acids.

As with produce, so with meat: Buying from small local farms may be the best environmental solution. Once again, it's a complicated equation.

MEDICATED MEAT? Animals raised for meat are often fed antibiotics routinely, not to fight active illness but to promote growth. The problem is, these are the same antibiotics that we need to fight disease ourselves. The overuse of these drugs in animal husbandry has contributed to antibiotic resistance in humans. Hormones are also used to speed growth in cattle and lambs in the United States, and residues of them may remain after processing.

The European Union has banned the use of hormones in livestock, citing concerns about their effects on developing children and cancer risk.

To avoid meat from animals that received antibiotics or hormones, choose varieties labeled "Organic." Grass-fed meat is another good option. Animals that have been grass-fed tend to be healthier, have less need for antibiotics, and have lower rates of *E. coli* infection. Don't assume that meat products labeled "Free Range," "No Antibiotics Administered," "No Hormones Administered," or "Natural" are always better. These claims are approved by the U.S. Food and Drug Administration (FDA) but aren't verified by third parties.

A DIRTY JOB Factory farming doesn't just pose risks to your health. In most cases, it also damages the environment, causes undue harm to the animals, and creates unsafe working conditions.

Nitrates, ammonia, and other pollutants from animal waste threaten ecosystems and our water supply. Hormones used in livestock (which come through in their manure) have been found downstream from factory farms and are linked to altered sexual traits in fish and other wildlife. The methane gas released in the flatulence and manure of livestock and the carbon monoxide produced during animal transport and processing also contribute to greenhouse gas pollution.

Cows, chickens, turkeys, pigs, and lambs can suffer severe stress and pain when raised industrially—and that's even before they are brought to slaughter. Animals are often confined to cramped quarters, surrounded by waste, and fed an unnatural and unhealthful diet. Humans aren't immune either: Workers in slaughterhouses hold some of this country's most dangerous jobs. According to the Bureau of Labor Statistics, 12.6 out of every 100 meatpackers suffered a job-related injury or illness in 2005, twice the average for all manufacturing jobs.

You can support farmers, promote animal welfare, and protect the planet with the choices you make at the grocery store. In addition to choosing organic and grass-fed varieties—which tend to be raised on small family farms and require less fossil fuel for their production—be on the lookout for "free-farmed" products.

Meat that is "free-farmed"—a term synonymous with the official designation "American Humane Certified™"—comes from animals that have been raised with adequate space and comfort and without hormones and

GREEN DICTIONARY

IRRADIATION

This process uses electron beams or radioactive substances to kill pathogens, retard sprouting or spoiling, and otherwise prolong transit time and shelf life in meat, eggs, grain, produce, and spices. The U.S. FDA, the American Medical Association, and the World Health Organization consider irradiated foods safe to eat, but critics argue that irradiation destroys vitamins and other nutrients, hurts small farms by inviting importation, and improperly addresses contamination concerns. Steer clear of irradiated foods by reading labels.

antibiotics, in accordance with American Humane Association standards. You might also consider purchasing meat that has been certified humanely raised and handled, which means that it meets verifiable standards for the treatment of livestock that exceed current laws.

Meat labeled "Food Alliance Certified" comes from animals that were raised on ranches that preserve soil and water quality, were not given antibiotics or hormones, and were given access to fresh air, pasture, and clean living quarters.

All these indicators help you find the meat products that are healthiest for your family and for the environment.

Poultry

Chicken and turkey are often viewed as healthier alternatives to red meats such as beef or pork. They are generally lower in fat and cholesterol, not to mention less expensive, than red meat. But modern methods of poultry husbandry and processing raise the risk of pathogen contamination, increase antibiotic resistance, and contribute to environmental pollution.

PATHOGENS & POLLUTANTS With some careful label reading, you can safely eat poultry. The problem begins with the way that chickens are raised en masse, both those that lay eggs and those that are destined for the meat counter. Poultry and egg processing practices sometimes allow the growth of bacteria responsible for foodborne illness, including *Salmonella, Listeria monocytogenes, Campylobacter jejuni,* and *E. coli,* which is why safe handling and thorough cooking are essentials for those who eat chicken and turkey.

But such pathogens aren't the only unhealthy substances associated with poultry. Processing methods use chlorine or chlorine dioxide to reduce pathogen loads, and these chemicals may be absorbed, especially by the bird's skin. To control infections and boost growth, the feed eaten by chickens typically contains arsenic, a heavy metal and a known

carcinogen that is excreted into their manure and released into the environment. Poultry also often receives frequent doses of insecticides aimed at killing lice, roaches, and other pests common to their living quarters. Although there are legal limits set for pesticide residues in poultry products, testing is infrequent.

THE FACTS
According to some surveys, 96 percent of chickens processed for meat conventionally in the United States are contaminated with *Campylobacter* bacteria.

As with meat, your best bet is to choose poultry and eggs that are labeled "100 Percent Organic," indicating that the birds were given organic feed, were not given antibiotics, and were not genetically modified or irradiated. Organic chickens also show much lower levels of *Salmonella* and *Campylobacter* bacteria. Furthermore, no matter what kind you're buying, to ensure that the poultry you and your family eat is safe, be certain to cook it thoroughly.

ANTIBIOTIC ISSUES On average, a chicken raised industrially in the United States receives four different antibiotics, all used to hasten growth. The overuse of these medications in poultry has contributed to resistance in humans, particularly to a class of antibiotics called fluoroquinolones, which are used to treat infectious diseases like anthrax. A 2006 study found that hospital patients who ate poultry were more likely to be resistant to an antibiotic than healthy individuals who were vegetarians.

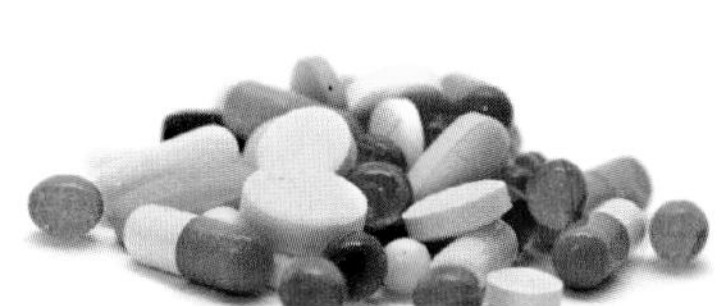

Fluoroquinolones are now banned from use in poultry farms in the United States, and many mainstream poultry producers and retailers say they have cut back on or stopped purchasing birds raised with antibiotics, although these claims are difficult to verify. You can reduce your risk of contracting antibiotic-resistant bacteria from poultry by choosing to buy organic and free-farmed varieties.

Since the United States has made hormone treatments illegal in poultry farming, they do not present a health risk for U.S. consumers.

AN UNPLEASANT ENVIRONMENT Mass poultry farming creates unsafe conditions for animals and humans and can have troubling consequences for the environment. Manure generated by poultry farms pollutes our water supply and soil. Runoff washes massive amounts of chicken waste into the Chesapeake Bay, threatening fish and wildlife habitat. And the production, processing, and transport of mass-produced poultry squanders valuable ecological resources, including soil, water, grain, and fossil fuels.

Increasing consolidation in the poultry industry means that farmers are often forced to work through contracts with huge companies, which produce up to 90 percent of this country's poultry. Most contract poultry farmers earn poverty wages for their efforts; their chicken catchers also earn poor wages and endure unhealthy air quality from ammonia, pesticides, and particulates in the chicken houses. And workers at poultry plants suffer one of the highest injury rates in the United States.

Poultry and eggs marked "Free-farmed" come from birds that were raised in adequate space and comfort and without the use of antibiotics, as verified by third parties, and meet standards set by the American Humane Association. You may also see products labeled "Raised without Antibiotics," "No Antibiotics Administered," "Natural," and "Cage Free." These claims may or may not be accurate—they are not third-party-verified. Similarly, although the label "Free Range" implies that the bird was free to roam, it only means that it was allowed some access to the out-of-doors. There is no standard for the use of the term "Free Range" in eggs, rendering it nearly meaningless. "Grass-Fed" or "Pastured" birds may live more comfortably and naturally than conventional poultry—and their eggs may contain higher amounts of healthy omega-3 fatty acids. But because the claims aren't verified by outside observers, you cannot know exactly how the chicken was raised.

ECO-TIP: A HEALTHIER TURKEY

They may sound like tasty time-savers, but turkeys labeled "Basted" or "Self-basted" aren't the best choice. These birds are typically filled with added fat, broth, water, and flavor enhancers, which can constitute up to 3 percent of the turkey's weight. Likewise, choose fresh rather than "processed" turkeys, which may contain unhealthy additives such as monosodium glutamate (MSG), salt, and other preservatives.

Best of all, choose fresh, organic turkeys—or go one step further and look for vegetarian turkeylike products made from wheat gluten, tofu, or other vegetable ingredients.

Seafood

The omega-3 fatty acids found in fish help our hearts and brains, yet contamination with heavy metals and pollutants increases the problems in eating seafood. Meanwhile, the oceans are being fished out, making seafood a matter of conscience as well as health. It's a complicated equation.

THE FACTS

According to a computer model generated in 2006, the ocean's fisheries are in such a state of decline that nearly a third of all fish species have reached collapse, defined as a population now at 10 percent of its original level. The study predicts all species of wild seafood to reach collapse by 2048.

WILD ONES Fish caught in the wild raise many concerns. The most well-known dangers are mercury and polychlorinated biphenyls (PCBs). Mercury from polluted waters can contaminate fish, particularly larger species near the top of the food chain such as swordfish, tuna, shark, king mackerel, and tilefish.

Once a fish is contaminated, there's little you can do. Mercury builds up in the fish's muscle meat rather than in its fat, so it cannot be trimmed away. Canned light tuna usually contains less mercury than bluefin or albacore, but a 2006 study in *Consumer Reports* found that 6 percent of it contained levels just as high as those found in albacore.

Mercury is known to harm developing brains and nervous systems, so childbearing women and children are especially at risk from eating too much mercury-laden fish. Women who are pregnant or nursing are advised to avoid predator species like swordfish and shark altogether and eat no more than 12 ounces of other species, including canned tuna, per week. Children can safely consume one-half to one full can of tuna per week. ▸For more information and a list of other mercury-heavy fish, see "Eco-Tip: Safer Seafood," pages 26-27.

PCBs are industrial pollutants that can persist in waterways for decades. They are probable carcinogens and have been found to cause problems with cognitive and immune systems in the body, making them a threat to both children and adults. PCBs accumulate in fatty fish like salmon, as well as in oysters and other shellfish.

ECO-TIP: SAFER SEAFOOD

Use this chart the next time you're at the fish counter. Some dilemmas still arise, when species resilient to overfishing pressures show high mercury or PCB levels.

SAFE FOR EATING:

Abalone (farmed)

Anchovies

Arctic char

Barramundi (U.S., farmed)

Catfish (U.S., farmed)

Caviar (U.S. or France, farmed)

Clams, soft-shell and steamers (farmed)

Crab, Dungeness (U.S., trap-caught)

Crab, imitation (AK, wild-caught)

Crab, stone (FL)

Crawfish (U.S., farmed)

Cuttlefish

Herring

Hoki

Lobster, spiny/rock (U.S., Australia, N. Amer. Baja coast)

Mackerel, Atlantic (purse seine-caught)

Mussels (U.S., farmed)

Octopus (HI, Gulf of California, wild-caught)

Oysters (Pacific, farmed)

Pollock (AK, wild-caught)

Prawn, spot (BC, wild-caught)

Salmon (AK, wild-caught)

Sardines (Pacific)

Scad, big-eye and mackerel (HI)

Scallops, bay (U.S., farmed)

Shrimp, pink (OR, wild-caught)

Squid, longfin (U.S. Atlantic)

Striped bass (farmed)

Sturgeon (farmed)

Tilapia (U.S., farmed)

Trout, rainbow (U.S., farmed)

Tuna (troll-caught Pacific albacore)

Turbot, halibut (Greenland)

EAT ONLY OCCASIONALLY:

Bluefish

Calamari

Clams (wild-caught)

Cod (Pacific)

Crab, blue (Gulf Coast)

Crab, king (AK)

Crab, kona (HI, Australia)

Crab, snow (AK, Canada)

Flounder (Pacific)

Haddock (hook and line)

Hake, silver, red, and offshore (wild-caught)

Halibut (Pacific, wild-caught)

Jacksmelt

Lobster, Maine

Mackerel, king and Spanish (Gulf of Mexico)

Mackerel, Spanish (Atlantic)

Mahimahi (troll-caught)

Marlin

Octopus (trawl-caught)

Opah

Oysters, eastern (Gulf Coast)

Perch, yellow

Pomfret, big scale

Prawn, spot (U.S., wild-caught)

Sablefish/black cod

Salmon (CA, OR, WA, wild-caught)

Sand dabs

Scup/Porgy

Shrimp (U.S. Atlantic, U.S. Gulf of Mexico, farmed or trawl-caught)

Shrimp, northern (Canadian and U.S. Atlantic, wild-caught)

Sole (Pacific)

Squid, jumbo (Gulf of California)

Tilapia (Central America, farmed)

Trevally

Tuna (canned light)

AVOID EATING:

Basa (China, farmed)
Bass/sea bass
Catfish (China, farmed)
Catfish (wild-caught)
Caviar (Russian/Iranian)
Chilean sea bass
Cod (Atlantic)
Conch, queen
Crab, king (imported)
Crawfish (farmed, imported)
Croaker
Dace (China, farmed)
Eel (China, farmed)
Flounder (Atlantic)
Grenadier
Grouper
Gulf corvina (white sea bass)
Haddock (trawl-caught)
Hake, white
Halibut (Atlantic)
Lobster, spiny (Caribbean)
Mahimahi (longline-caught)
Monkfish
Orange roughy
Pompano, Florida
Rockfish (Pacific red snapper; trawl-caught)
Salmon (Great Lakes, farmed)
Scallops, sea (U.S. mid-Atlantic)
Sea turtles
Shark
Shrimp (imported)
Skate
Snapper (red or imported)
Sole (Atlantic)
Sturgeon (wild-caught)
Swordfish
Tilapia (China, Taiwan, farmed)
Tilefish
Totoaba

Pesticides, antibiotics, and other contaminants have been found in shrimp. Between the time they're caught and the time you buy them, nearly all shrimp are treated with such preservatives as sodium bisulfite and sodium tripolyphosphate, substances that can cause allergic reactions such as hives and wheezing in some people.

The choices that you make at the fish counter have an impact on your family's health—and on the ocean and waterway environments as well. Your consumer choices can go a long way toward supporting safe, sustainable seafood. There *are* other fish in the sea; you just need to know what to look for. Since 2005, seafood sold in grocery stores must include its country of origin—as well as whether it is farmed or wild—on its label. Country of origin does matter: Research has shown that farmed salmon raised in Europe have significantly higher levels of PCBs and other contaminants like dioxin, toxaphene, and dieldrin than those from farms in Chile, Canada, and the U.S. (The studies also show that farmed salmon in general have significantly higher PCB levels than wild salmon, regardless of origin.)

Fishing operations may also upset the delicate balance of ocean ecosystems. Just as modern industry has greatly contributed to polluted waterways, commerical fishing, in response to consumer demand, has skyrocketed, to the point that the oceans are suffering. An estimated 75 percent of the world's fish species are either being caught at maximum levels or are near collapse from overfishing. Large fish have been most affected: Populations of tuna, swordfish, cod, and halibut have been reduced by some 90 percent worldwide. Their natural habits are also being damaged by industrial fishing techniques such as bottom trawling, which destroys deep-sea coral beds. Shrimp harvesting can also result in "bycatch," meaning that other marine wildlife, including endangered sea turtles, become caught in the shrimp nets and die.

To ensure that you are not contributing to the global problem of overfishing, look for seafood that has been certified by the Marine Stewardship Council, an organization created by the World Wildlife Fund and Dutch-based multinational Unilever, one of the largest commercial buyers of fish in the world. Its "Fish Forever" seal ensures that the product comes from a well-managed fishery with healthy populations that are captured without damaging ocean ecosystems. One such sustainable fish is wild Alaskan salmon. Since fish farms are not allowed in Alaskan waters, you can be sure that any salmon labeled "Alaskan" is also wild.

FARMED FISH Nearly half of the world's fish supply originates in fish farms. Raising fish in a controlled environment may seem like the answer to overfishing and contaminants. But in fact, fish farming—in which fish are reared in confined "net pens" or cages—is rife with problems. Farm-raised fish may live in crowded conditions requiring the use of antibiotics and antiparasite pesticides; these, along with spilled food and feces, can pollute surrounding waterways. Fish farming also has the potential to destroy nearby wild fish populations. Farmed fish can escape and spread disease, compete for food, and dilute the gene pool by interbreeding. In Scotland, for example, areas with fish-farm pens are now devoid of wild salmon runs; wild Atlantic salmon, not caught commercially in North America, has become an endangered species.

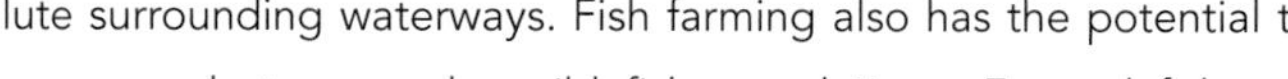

ECO-TIP: ORGANIC VERSUS NONORGANIC FISH

Some salmon farms have recently begun reducing densities of fish in pens, switching to organic and contaminant-free feed, and avoiding antibiotics and dyes. But is organic really a better choice?

Some organic fish farms are "certified" under foreign standards like those of the United Kingdom's Soil Association, a nonprofit that campaigns for organic food and farming. But the Soil Association allows feeding organic salmon a mix including fish oil from fish not fed an organic diet themselves. And organic salmon farms in the United Kingdom can use the synthetic pyrethroid pesticide cypermethrin to rid fish of sea lice, so "organic" fish may also be treated with veterinary medicines. (There is no comparable organic standard for seafood in the United States.)

Your best option: Choose salmon from sustainable fisheries in Alaska and California, which are a seasonably available fish. When you can't find fresh, wild salmon, look for healthier, more environmentally friendly and better-tasting alternatives to organic salmon, try other species such as herring and sardines, or choose canned wild salmon.

TASTY TUNA Tuna, processed so extensively that we almost forget it comes from the ocean and not from a can, presents a complicated situation for those who want to make wise food choices. Three major issues arise. First, some tuna species are being overfished to the point that their populations are endangered. Second, many tunas are harvested by longline technology—multiple lines up to 50 miles long with thousands of hooks each. The bycatch is wasted, thus disturbing other ocean species. Third, mercury levels in several different tuna species reach disturbing levels, leading some watchdog agencies to post health alerts.

If you still want to keep tuna on the menu, take these precautions. Ask for troll-caught or pole-caught tuna, if possible, avoiding longline-caught fish altogether. Avoid bluefin tuna, the most endangered of the tuna species. Choose "chunk light" canned tuna, which is usually yellowfin or skipjack, known to reproduce faster than other tuna species.

Dairy

If you eat animal products, milk, cheese, and yogurt can be healthful additions to your diet, especially if you choose low-fat varieties. But the use of hormones and possibly carcinogenic chemicals in cows' milk makes seeking certified organic dairy products a must.

THE FACTS

The hormone rBGH is currently used in an estimated one-third of U.S. dairy cows, according to its manufacturer.

HEAVY ON THE HORMONES Recombinant bovine growth hormone, shortened to rBGH, is also sometimes referred to as recombinant bovine somatotropin (rBST). It's a genetically engineered hormone that is injected into dairy cows to increase their milk production. The hormone was approved by the Food and Drug Administration in 1993 for use in dairy cows and introduced as a commercial product in 1994 by the Monsanto Company, which sells rBGH to dairy farmers under the brand name Posilac.

Concerned experts and consumer groups have cited a number of reasons for worry. First, rBGH never underwent any safety testing for long-term health effects before it was introduced into the milk supply. Although the FDA claimed that milk from cows treated with the hormone was "safe for human consumption," this statement was based on a 90-day study of rBGH—in rats. In fact, FDA did not require the human safety assessment typically required of veterinary drugs intended for use in food-producing animals. Even more alarming, when Canada's equivalent of the FDA delved further into that study as part of its own approval process, it found that some of the treated rats had been affected by the hormone: Up to 30 percent of rats in the study had developed antibody responses to rBGH, suggesting that the hormone was being absorbed into the bloodstream, and some male rats had developed cysts on their thyroid glands. As a result, rBGH was not approved for use in Canada. Spokespeople from the FDA later admitted that they had never actually read the study but instead relied on a summary of results provided by Monsanto.

Second, rBGH stimulates a cow's liver to produce another hormone, insulinlike growth factor-1 (IGF-1), which ends up in the cow's milk. Amounts of IGF-1, which is absorbed when ingested, are from 25 to 74 percent higher

GREEN DICTIONARY

HIGH-FRUCTOSE CORN SYRUP

High-fructose corn syrup (HFCS), a modified form of corn syrup with increased amounts of the sugar fructose, is made when cornstarch is treated with acids or enzymes. That process breaks down the starch into sugars, thus enhancing sweetness and making a syrup that dissolves at lower temperatures. Low-cost HFCS is used in many processed foods, and experts cite a number of concerns about it. It may trigger the liver to release more fat into the bloodstream, actually increasing appetite—and thus contributing to the U.S. obesity epidemic. It also often comes from genetically modified corn.

in milk from cows that have been treated with rBGH, according to a summary of studies by Consumers Union. Why worry? Some studies have shown that IGF-1 can cause cell division and tumor growth, and IGF-1 has also been associated with the growth of colon, breast, and smooth muscle cancers.

Finally, the use of rBGH can actually increase the use of antibiotics in dairy cow feed. That's because cows that are treated with rBGH suffer from higher rates of infected or inflamed udders (mastitis), and their milk may contain higher somatic cell counts (or pus) as a result. To treat these infections, dairy farmers give the cows antibiotics—a practice that very likely contributes to the development of bacteria resistant to these lifesaving drugs. This development ultimately affects humans, who may fall prey to the antibiotic-resistant bugs. The use of rBGH can harm the health of cows in other ways, too. Since the hormone was introduced to the market in February 1994, the FDA has received numerous reports from dairy farmers complaining of reproductive problems, digestive disorders, injection site reactions, and foot or leg problems in treated cows.

The United States is one of the few countries whose dairy farmers use rBGH: The hormone is not approved in Canada, the European Union, New Zealand, and Australia, so dairy products from those nations are rBGH-free. All dairy products made from sheep or goat milk are also rBGH-free, because rBGH cannot be used on these animals.

Of course, your best bet is to choose milk and other dairy products labeled "100 Percent Certified Organic." This guarantees that the product is not produced with milk from cows injected with rBGH or treated with antibiotics. Some nonorganic dairy farms operate rBGH-free—and will usually proudly say so on the label.

CHEMICAL CONTAMINANTS Milk and dairy products are often fortified with vitamins to make them more nutritious. But what else is in your milk or cheese that you don't know about? The main ingredient in rocket fuel, perchlorate, has been found in some milk samples. The chemical is believed to originate from runoff from defense plants and military bases, and it has been shown to increase the risk of thyroid disorders, especially in infants and fetuses. According to the Environmental Working Group, half of 32 samples of milk from central California tested by the state's agriculture department contained perchlorate levels deemed unsafe in drinking water. Dairy cows have absorbed perchlorate from alfalfa grown with contaminated water from the Colorado River. Perchlorate has also been identified in drinking water from 22 states.

Dioxins can be another cause for concern in some regions. These toxic chemicals—which have been linked to an increased risk of cancer, birth defects, and reproductive damage—tend to concentrate in animal fat, including milk fat. Through industrial processes, dioxins enter the air and then fall onto pastureland, where they are ingested, along with grass, by grazing animals. You can avoid consuming this contaminant by drinking skim milk, which contains virtually no dioxins because it contains no fat.

Cooking Oils

Cooking and salad oils add flavor—and fat—to meals, but could they be adding something else? It depends in large part on the food from which the oil was derived.

Conventional oils made from corn, canola, and soy are likely to be made from seeds that were genetically modified. These products have been genetically engineered to resist insects or to be immune to herbicides, allowing large-scale farmers to produce more per acre. Genetically modified organisms (GMOs) are troubling for several reasons. They threaten Earth's genetic and biological diversity, and their long-term effects on the health of those who consume them are not yet known. For more on GMOs, see page 17.

Fortunately, concern over genetically modified organisms has inspired a growing array of organic oil alternatives in the marketplace.

Look for those oils that are marked "Certified Organic," which is a sign that these products were made from ingredients that were not sprouted from genetically engineered seedstock and were, furthermore, grown without pesticides. From a health perspective, the best choices are organic olive, canola, and walnut oils, which are higher in healthy monounsaturated and polyunsaturated fats.

GREEN DICTIONARY

ACRYLAMIDE

Acrylamide is a chemical produced when carbohydrate-rich foods are baked, fried, or grilled to a golden brown. It has been found to cause birth defects, neurological problems, and cancer in laboratory animals. To reduce exposure, limit your intake of such foods as potato chips, french fries, and toasted marshmallows.

Herbs & Seasonings

Compared with meats and vegetables, the quantity of herbs, salt, sweeteners, and other culinary seasonings that we consume is small. But that doesn't mean they shouldn't be chosen with care, as some may contain pesticides or unsafe additives, and others cause damage to the environment. Here's what to look for.

SALTS AND SWEETS Industrial salt production can be environmentally unsound: Artificial ponds used to process salt can pollute nearby waterways with toxic brine. Limit your contribution to this eventuality by choosing to buy organic sea salt or artisanal "single origin" salt, which is made by traditional, not industrial, methods. Purchasing this type of salt also supports small businesses.

Sugar and other sweeteners can be problematic, too. Recent reports show that industrial sugar production has contributed to the destruction of primary forest habitat and erosion and degradation of soils in the tropics. Because sugar cultivation requires intensive irrigation, it has diverted water from Hawaiian streams through tunnels and ditches, drying out natural ecosystems and farms. Nutrient-rich runoff from sugarcane fields in the Florida Everglades—together with artificial alterations in water levels—have led to the invasion of natural sawgrass prairie by cattails. And sugar has contributed to the global slave trade more than any other crop. As for artificial sweeteners, aspartame, saccharin, and acesulfame potassium have all been linked to cancer and other illnesses in laboratory animals.

Organic sugar, which is grown without synthetic fertilizers or pesticides and uses production techniques that conserve the soil, is increasingly available, even from large manufacturers such as Domino; fair-trade sugar, certified by TransFair USA, is also increasingly available. ▸See "Green Dictionary: Fair Trade," page 36. If you prefer natural sugar alternatives, honey is a healthy choice, especially when you choose locally grown honey, of which there are more than 300 distinct types in the United States alone.

Honey contains traces of vitamins C and B-complex, amino acids, enzymes, and minerals. It's also environmentally friendly: Purchasing local honey helps protect bees and their habitats, which are under threat from pesticides, nonnative parasitic mites, and disappearing woodlands and fields. Other sweet alternatives include pure maple syrup, agave nectar, date sugar, and Sucanat, the brand name for organically grown, dehydrated cane juice, which has no added chemicals.

HEALTHIER HERBS Herbs add zest, flavor, and even healthful compounds to your meals, but they can also add contaminants. As with conventionally grown produce, nonorganic herbs are often grown using pesticides and may contain chemical residues. Look for fresh or dried herbs that have been certified organic—or grow your own on the windowsill or in your garden.

Snacks & Sweets

Bread, cakes, cookies, and candy all are tempting treats, but their ingredients often aren't so appetizing. From unhealthy fats to artificial sweeteners to carcinogenic compounds, you'll want to keep an eye on the ingredients list of your favorite snacks.

BAKERY TREATS Potassium bromate, used by some commercial breadmakers as a flour additive, may leave traces of the carcinogenic chemical bromate in baked goods. It has actually been banned in many countries. And trans fats, made from liquid oils that have been solidified through hydrogenation, have been shown to raise levels of LDL cholesterol (the "bad" cholesterol). Trans fats are common ingredients in packaged cookies, crackers, and other baked goods.

Breads and other carbohydrate-rich foods may also contain acrylamide, a carcinogenic chemical produced during baking. ▸See "Green Dictionary: Acrylamide," page 32. It's close to impossible to eliminate acrylamide, but breads with the lightest crusts and cookies that are chewy rather than crispy tend to contain lower levels. Reconsider toast: The longer bread

THE FACTS

A 2001 Iowa State University study found that food grown by participating Iowa farmers traveled an average of 44.6 miles to reach consumers in the state; if sourced from conventional national producers, the same groceries would have traveled 1,546 miles.

is toasted, the more acrylamide it contains. Choose organic breads, which are made only with grains and other ingredients that are organic. Thanks to recent rules, avoiding trans fats in foods is easier than ever. The FDA now requires that amounts of trans fat greater than 0.5 gram per serving be listed on the ingredient label, making it easier to choose what foods to buy and prepare for your family.

SWEET TEETH High-fructose corn syrup, artificial sweeteners, and artificial colors (which may contribute to cancer risk and hyperactivity in children) are often main ingredients in baked goods and candy. In fact, a 2007 study published in *The Lancet* found that kids who consumed high amounts of artificial colors and flavors also had higher levels of hyperactivity. Companies that offer cakes, cookies, and candy that are organic, free of preservatives, HFCS, and artificial colors and flavors are increasingly easy to find.

SNACK ATTACK They may give you an energy boost between meals, but snacks can raise health concerns similar to those raised by baked goods. Potato chips, fries, and pretzels contain acrylamide. Granola bars can be made with HFCS and trans fats. Research has shown that microwave popcorn may be contaminated with perfluorooctanoic acid (PFOA), a likely carcinogen found coating the inside of the popcorn cooking bags—the same ingredient that is generated when Teflon cooking pans overheat. Even nuts—typically recommended as a healthy snack—can be problematic: Pesticides are abundant in commercially produced nuts. Luckily, the growing number of responsible manufacturers has made healthier snacks a reality, with green choices that include organic trail mix and granola bars, chips, pretzels, dried fruit, nuts, and soy nuts. (Keep in mind, though, that even organic brands of chips and pretzels can still contain acrylamide.)

CHOCOLATE Made from the fruit of the cacao tree, chocolate was called the food of the gods by early Aztecs. Recent studies have shown that chocolate, particularly darker varieties, is rich in antioxidants. Health food or a heavenly treat, however, chocolate's production techniques are not so sweet.

Cacao evolved to grow naturally in the rain forest; cacao farms are traditionally planted under a thinned canopy of towering rain forest trees in the African nations of Ivory Coast, Ghana, Nigeria, and Cameroon; in Indonesia;

and in Brazil. Man-made cacao groves have become the next best thing to natural rain forest; they are supplemental habitats for migratory songbirds and other rain forest–dwelling birds, mammals, insects and reptiles, many of which are declining due to habitat destruction.

But this type of farming is currently threatened. High demand for chocolate has led to the need for higher cacao bean yields, which farmers are meeting by growing cacao in full sun. Although this practice produces more beans, it also causes the plants to be more susceptible to disease, insect infestation, and damage due to stress from heat and dryness. Sun-grown cocoa also requires high amounts of pesticides and fertilizers—including toxic chemicals such as paraquat and lindane. These are widely used by growers to kill insect pests and fungi on cacao crops. Paraquat is extremely hazardous to workers and potentially carcinogenic; lindane, which is banned for agricultural use in the United States, can cause neurological damage and disrupt hormone functions and reproduction, and it is believed to increase cancer risk. Inevitably these pesticides will spread to nearby air and groundwater. Residues of pesticides have also been found to be present in the chocolate itself.

It's easy to find healthier, environmentally friendly chocolate these days. Choose chocolate products labeled "Certified Organic"—these contain cocoa grown without the use of synthetic pesticides and fertilizers. Products marked "Rainforest Alliance Certified" are made from cacao plants that were grown in shade—preserving wildlife habitat—rather than in full sun.

GREEN DICTIONARY

FAIR TRADE

"Fair trade" products come from importers who ensure that farmers receive a minimum set price, that workers receive fair wages, and that growers follow fair labor and sound environmental practices.

PLAYING FAIR In recent years, overproduction and market deregulation have forced the nearly six million small cacao farmers worldwide to cut back on expenses to survive. As a result, workers are paid lower wages—or not at all. Investigations by UNICEF and other international organizations over the past decade have uncovered forced child labor on cacao farms. Boys as young as age nine have been found working for no pay on plantations in the Ivory Coast, the African nation responsible for more than 40 percent of the world's cocoa. Children are typically sold to traffickers by their destitute parents, who are unaware that they'll be forced to work for nothing. Allegations of beatings and abuse by cacao plantation owners are widespread. Some U.S. candy manufacturers still buy cocoa from the Ivory Coast, where evidence suggests that cocoa plantations still depend on the labor of children.

A "Fair Trade Certified" label ensures that chocolate farmers were paid a fair price for their cocoa. On average, certified fair-trade growers are paid 80 cents a pound—twice as much as other growers. TransFair USA certifies companies in the United States; TransFair Canada and the United Kingdom's Fairtrade Foundation are two other national certifiers.

THE FACTS

According to a Euromonitor report cited by Dagoba, organic chocolate sales in the United States total about $70 million a year.

Water

Just because water is plentiful doesn't mean that it's safe. In fact, our water supplies can be contaminated with everything from heavy metals and pesticides to bacteria and pharmaceutical drugs. Before you take a sip of that tap or bottled water, consider what could be lurking in plain sight.

IS BOTTLED BETTER? Bottled water isn't necessarily safer than tap—and it may be worse. The truth is, bottled water is not regulated as strictly as tap water. In fact, unlike tap water, bottled water can contain some contamination by *E. coli,* or fecal coliform bacteria, and still comply with health regulations. Nor do regulations require disinfection for *Cryptosporidium* or *Giardia,* common waterborne pathogens that can cause intestinal problems, including diarrhea. Tests have also shown that unhealthy chemicals can migrate from plastic into the water. See "Bottles and Storage Containers," page 55. And don't let the scenic mountains and pristine-looking springs depicted on those bottles fool you: In some cases, bottled water may actually *be* tap water. According to the landmark 1999 study sponsored by the Natural Resources

Defense Council (NRDC), 25 to 40 percent of bottled water actually comes straight from a tap somewhere.

The NRDC study confirmed that tap water is often better regulated than bottled water and has to meet more stringent standards at both the federal and local levels. For example, while cities must test their water for chemical contaminants at least once a quarter, bottlers must test only annually. Most city water systems test routinely for *E. coli, Cryptosporidium,* and *Giardia.* City tap water must also be filtered and disinfected, but there are no federal filtration or disinfection requirements placed on the bottled water industry. Tap water must also meet standards for toxic chemicals such as phthalates (hormone disruptors that can leach from some plastics), but the bottled water industry is exempt from these regulations. In fact, the 1999 study included chilling findings: Among the thousand bottles tested by the NRDC, about one-fifth contained chemicals such as toluene, xylene, or styrene, known or possible carcinogens and neurotoxins.

Bottled water raises another major environmental concern. It is estimated that as many as 1.5 million tons of plastic are manufactured from petrochemicals in order to package handy, disposable containers of drinking water each year. In locations that lack plastic recycling programs, most of those plastic bottles will be incinerated or will end up in already overcrowded landfills. According to the Environmental Protection Agency, plastics are the fourth largest category of municipal solid waste, after paper, yard trimmings, and metal. Besides consuming nonrenewable natural resources like petroleum, bottled water also contributes to pollution, noise, and overcrowded highways and streets as it gets transported from bottling plant to store to home or gym.

THE FACTS

According to the Natural Resources Defense Council, contaminated tap water sickens an estimated seven million Americans annually.

And bottled water doesn't just harm the environment in the form of waste. The plastic manufacturing process used to make bottles is also associated with toxic byproducts, such as dioxin and benzene, which are released in the air and cause not only pollution, but respiratory problems as well. They may also cause cancer. If the environmental cost of bottled water doesn't make you pause, consider the financial implications: According to calculations by the Natural Resources Defense Council, bottled water can cost from 240 to up to 10,000 times more per gallon than water from the faucet.

If you must choose bottled water, read the label for the source of the water. Try to find brands from sources closest to your area. The farther away the water source, the more nonrenewable fuel was used to transport it.

FRESH FROM THE FAUCET? There are many different sources of possible contamination all along water's journey to your glass, from river to reservoir to tap. The biggest culprit is development around reservoirs, whether agricultural or urban. Runoff from agricultural fields and industrial livestock facilities can carry pesticides and manure into the water supply, while urban development can contribute pollutants from topsoil, lawn pesticides and fertilizers, human and animal waste, roadway oil, soot, and salt, as well as landfill runoff. Water supplies near urban areas have been found to contain bacteria like *E. coli, Giardia,* and *Cryptosporidium* and to have high levels of turbidity, or cloudiness, in the water, which reduces the effectiveness of chlorine treatments.

Even more alarming, a May 2002 study by the U.S. Geological Survey of the nation's stream water discovered chemicals in public water supplies that are found in drugs, detergents, disinfectants, insect repellents, plastics, and personal care products. Although contaminants vary depending on the individual water supply, common pollutants in reservoirs include the following:

ARSENIC. This element can enter water through natural soil deposits or industrial and agricultural pollution. Arsenic causes skin problems as well as bladder, lung, kidney, and skin cancer. It may also cause damage to the heart and nervous system. Even very low levels of arsenic have been found to disrupt hormone functions.

TRIHALOMETHANES. Also known as THMs, these chemicals are formed when chlorine used to disinfect water reacts with organic matter, such as animal waste, treated sewage, or leaves and soil. THMs can increase the risk of cancer and may damage the liver, kidneys, and nervous system; high levels can increase rates of miscarriage and birth defects.

ATRAZINE. A weed killer used on most corn crops, atrazine can cause organ and cardiovascular damage and is a suspected hormone disruptor.

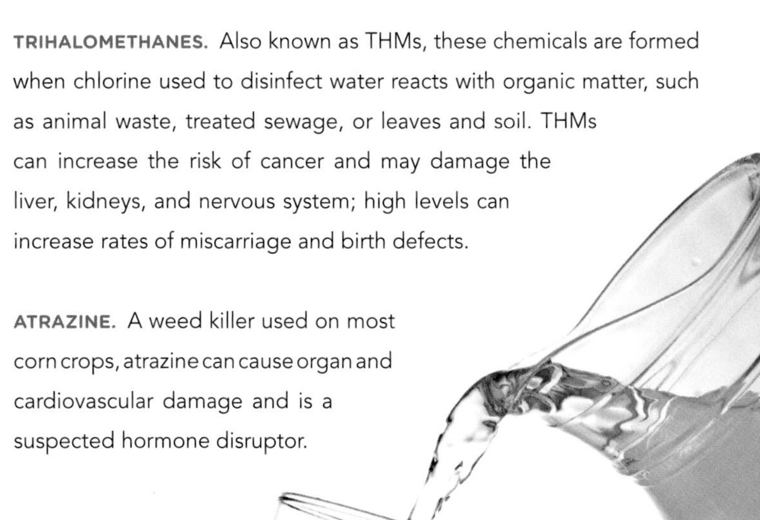

COLIFORM BACTERIA. Although not harmful in themselves, coliform bacteria may indicate the presence of dangerous microbes such as *Cryptosporidium,* which can be life-threatening to people with weak immune systems.

LEAD. This toxic heavy metal can damage developing brains and nervous systems. Lead may not be present at the source, but it can leach into drinking water from lead-containing pipes in your home and in public water mains.

Not all local water companies are thoroughly screening for these and other pollutants. To determine the healthfulness of your tap water, check your water report, which your water utility is required to send you annually. You can request one from your water supplier, or visit the Local Drinking Water Information website of the Environmental Protection Agency. ▸See "Resources."

Tap water is still your best bet, however. At just 10 to 20 cents a gallon, it is not only more cost-effective than bottled water, but it also gives you control over what's in—and what's not in—the water you drink. You do not need to assume that you should be using a water filter. Plenty of areas have tap water that is naturally clear, clean, and contaminant-free.

If your drinking water comes from a private well, test it every two to three years for nitrates and other contaminants such as volatile organic compounds, annually for coliform bacteria, and more frequently for radon or pesticides, if those are problems in your area. (To find out, check with your local health department or contact National Testing Laboratories or state-certified water laboratories, listed on the EPA's Drinking Water website as well.)

THROUGH THE FILTER If your water is contaminated—or if you simply don't care for the way it tastes or smells—you may want to consider buying a water filter. Water filters are classified according to the specific contaminants they can remove. There are many different types, ranging from simple carafes that are readily available to complex whole-house systems that cost a thousand dollars or more and need to be installed by a plumber.

Before you make your choice from the wide array of water filters, ask yourself some basic questions to help guide your decision.

ASK THE EDITORS

Q **How can I tell where my bottled water comes from?**

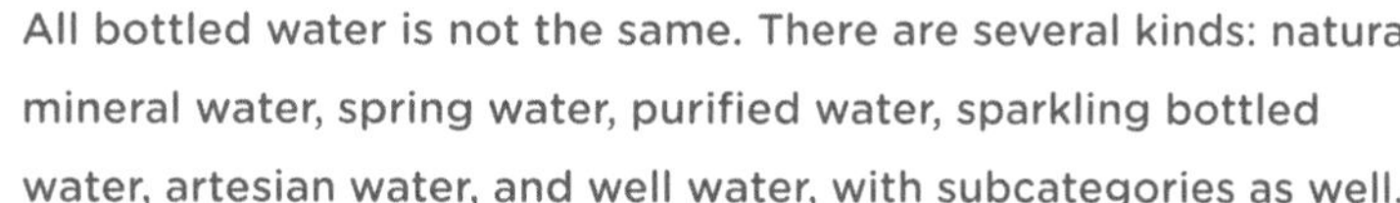

A All bottled water is not the same. There are several kinds: natural mineral water, spring water, purified water, sparkling bottled water, artesian water, and well water, with subcategories as well.

The European Union defines natural mineral water as "microbiologically wholesome water, originating in an underground water table or deposit and emerging from a spring tapped at one or more natural or bore exits." The sources of natural mineral water are protected from pollution, but the water is not disinfected and can contain microflora. In the United States, natural mineral water is defined as having at least 250 parts per million total dissolved solids, according to the International Bottled Water Association, and comes from springs or boreholes drawing from a protected underground water source.

Spring water does not have to have a constant mineral composition. Purified water comes from lakes, rivers, or underground springs and has been treated to rid it of minerals and contaminants, so it is almost identical to tap water. Sparkling water often comes from a spring and is treated to replicate the carbonation at its source. Artesian water originates from a tapped source whose level stands above the aquifer. Well water comes from a hole bored to tap an aquifer directly.

Other subcategories of water include fluoridated water and soda water or seltzer. Fluoridated water contains added fluoride and is marketed as a product to help prevent tooth decay. Soda water or seltzer, often made from tap water, is regulated by the FDA as a soft drink, following standards different from those for bottled water.

- ✓ Is the filter certified to remove the particular contaminants in your water?
- ✓ Is an expensive model really worth the money?
- ✓ Is it easy to install, change, and clean?
- ✓ Will it provide a steady rate of flow throughout its life span?
- ✓ Does it waste water?
- ✓ Does it take out beneficial minerals along with pollutants?

Once you've answered these questions, you're ready to start shopping. Here are common types of water filters you might encounter.

CARBON FILTERS. These water filters typically work by passing tap water through a granular carbon filter built into a carafe or pitcher. They are the least expensive filter type and are sufficient for most needs. They contain a carbon-activated filter that adsorbs lead, chlorine by-products, pesticides, some organic chemicals, and some other heavy metals, along with intrusive odors and tastes. They won't remove dissolved inorganic contaminants or metals such as arsenic, fluoride, or mercury, nor will they pick up nitrates, bacteria, or sediments.

CERAMIC FILTERS. Often combined with carbon filters, ceramic filters will remove bacteria, asbestos, and sediments.

FAUCET-MOUNTED FILTERS. These can be attached to kitchen sink faucets or refrigerator water dispensers and filter water as it flows through. They must be changed periodically, following the manufacturer's instructions.

DISTILLERS. These filters boil water into steam and then condense it back into water in a separate chamber, separating out particles, chemicals, microbes, and dissolved solids. Distillers eliminate virtually all pollutants from water, but some consider the technique overkill, since they also eliminate substances in water that can have beneficial effects, such as fluoride.

REVERSE-OSMOSIS SYSTEMS. Typically expensive and difficult to install, reverse-osmosis systems operate by pushing water through a membrane, then flushing away a few gallons of contaminated water for every gallon purified. These systems are regularly used on boats to create fresh water

from salt water. They effectively remove industrial chemicals, heavy metals, nitrates, and asbestos, but not radon, certain volatile organic compounds, or certain pesticides. They do waste enormous amounts of water, though, so they are not a sustainable solution to water contamination.

ULTRAVIOLET LIGHT FILTERS Some filters work by passing water through ultraviolet (UV) light, which kills bacteria, viruses, molds, cysts, and other biological contaminants. This is a supplemental treatment to filtration and should not be used alone, because it does not remove heavy metals, chlorine, or volatile organic compounds.

Every solution carries its own complicated set of environmental implications. Discarded plastic cartridges contribute to landfill overload, and the plastic used to make them and the carafes themselves derives from petroleum, a nonrenewable resource.

ECO-TIP: SAFER TAP WATER

Everyone who drinks tap water needs to be aware of certain water safety precautions. Address concerns about water purity by taking these steps to reduce contaminants.

- ✓ Always cook with and drink cold water, never hot, from the tap. When fecal coliforms are found in drinking water, water suppliers must issue a Boil Water Notice. In this event, you should boil water vigorously for one minute to kill any bacteria and parasites.
- ✓ Let water run for at least one minute in the morning before you use or drink it. This helps any accumulated cast-off ingredients from the pipes in which it has been sitting all night.
- ✓ Investigate the piping material where you live. Old homes and apartments can have lead piping. Boiling does not remove heavy metals like lead from water: It concentrates them.
- ✓ Leave an open container of tap water in the refrigerator for a few hours. Doing so helps chlorine, sometimes used by water treatment plants, to evaporate.

Coffee & Tea

If you're like most Americans, your morning cup—or three—of coffee or tea is a necessary wake-up ritual. Indeed, $60 billion worth—500 billion cups—of coffee and more than 1.5 billion cups of tea are consumed worldwide each day. It's important to pause and think how that coffee or tea got to the table.

COFFEE PICKS Like cocoa, vanilla, and bananas, coffee is produced almost exclusively in the developing world, but it is consumed by the developed world. The coffee plant is a rain forest shrub laden with bright red berries that grows mainly in the tropics of Africa and Latin America. The berries are picked by hand, the green beans inside removed before shipping.

Coffee plants, which thrive in shade, have traditionally been grown under the rain forest canopy. Such shade farms are a welcome alternative to natural rain forest for migrating birds and the many species of insects, mammals, and reptiles that call them home. But full-sun coffee plants can produce almost five times as many beans as shade coffee plants. In fact, since the 1970s, almost half of all Latin American coffee cultivation has taken place on full-sun farms instead of shade farms. As a result, habitats have been decimated for countless numbers of birds and other wildlife. Studies have found up to 97 percent fewer bird species in sun coffee farms than shade farms.

Sun-grown coffee plants require large amounts of pesticides and chemical fertilizers to thrive. Pesticide residues on the coffee beans are mostly burned away during the roasting process, so they aren't a big problem for consumers, according to the FDA, but farmers and workers on coffee plantations are exposed to these toxic chemicals on a daily basis.

In 1995 an insecticide, Miral 500 CS, was recalled after two Colombian coffee workers died and five others got sick from exposure to it. Another insecticide, endosulfan, is widely used against the coffee berry borer beetle. But endosulfan is also known to be toxic to mammals, birds, and fish—and it can remain in the environment for months if it binds to soil particles.

Coffee farms have been called "sweat shops in the fields." The coffee market tends to fluctuate, and so growers are often forced to sell their harvest

below production costs during slow cycles, which can put them in debt. Coffee retailers receive the beans at an enormous discount—but they don't pass that discount on to consumers. Instead, the disparity between debt-ridden growers and profitable retailers is only getting larger. In the early 1990s, coffee producers received 30 percent of total coffee income, but since then their share has dropped as low as 8 percent or less.

Coffee may be brewing with problems, but it is possible to enjoy safe, environmentally sound beans. Start by looking for coffee labeled "Certified Organic," which means that it was grown without synthetic pesticides by growers who protect their laborers, wildlife, and waterways from toxic chemicals. "Fair Trade Certified" coffee has been assessed by TransFair and purchased directly from growers or their cooperatives for a price substantially higher than they might receive in the standard coffee market.

It's also a good idea to buy coffee that is marked "Shade Grown," which means that it was raised under the rain forest canopy rather than on full-sun farms. There are currently two certification programs for shade-grown coffees. The Smithsonian Migratory Bird Center certifies coffee as "Bird Friendly" if it is organically grown under shade conditions. The "Rainforest Alliance" program run by the Sustainable Agriculture Network guarantees that the coffee is sustainably shade-grown and that the coffee workers were paid a fair wage and treated well.

ECO-TIP: BETTER DECAF

Diehard coffee drinkers may have their reasons for requesting decaffeinated cups later in the day, but the chemical solvents used to remove most of the caffeine, particularly methylene chloride and ethyl acetate, can pose health hazards. Methylene chloride is a suspected carcinogen, and ethyl acetate may cause skin problems. If you enjoy decaf, look for organic brands made with the Swiss water, the carbon dioxide, or the sparkling water process, which treat beans by soaking them in water or carbon dioxide.

TEA TIME Pesticides are widely used on tea plantations. But in the case of tea, unlike coffee, pesticide residues can linger in products, creating health risks for consumers. China-grown green teas, for example, are praised for their antioxidant properties, but tests have shown high levels of both lead and the pesticide DDT—long banned in the United States but still used in many developing countries—in Chinese green tea. Pesticides such as chlorpyrifos, ethion, dicofol, paraquat, and dalapon are also still widely used on many of India's tea plantations. Workers often apply pesticides without proper protective masks or clothing, and they may drink from pesticide-tainted streams.

Less is known about the environmental impact of tea production, but it does share some similarities with coffee. Tea plants yield the best quality leaves when they are grown on cool, damp mountain slopes. Unfortunately, such mountain slopes are particularly prone to erosion during the planting and pruning of the tea plants. As a result, landslides have occurred on tea plantations located in the mountains of India's Darjeeling district. And studies have found lower bird diversity in tea monoculture systems, where vast crops of tea have replaced the diverse forests that grew there originally.

Tea production is rife with labor concerns, from poor wages to unhealthy working conditions. Most of the tea consumed in the United States comes from China, India, Kenya, Sri Lanka, and Turkey, in order of the amount these countries produce. As with coffee, tea production has skyrocketed, outpacing demand. As a result, prices have dropped over the years. Between 1970 and 1998, for example, tea prices dipped an average of 41 percent among major tea trading companies. Financial woes mean low wages, long hours, and poor living and working conditions for many tea workers. Tea pickers in India, most of whom are women, earn less than two dollars a day on average and face unsanitary housing conditions for their families. Because of low wages, many of their children must quit school to join family members at work on tea plantations. While India's Bonded Labour System Act and other laws are meant to protect workers, these well-intentioned laws suffer from loopholes and lack of enforcement. In Uganda, meanwhile, tea pickers make less than half of the country's average annual wage, which is roughly $300.

Although their popularity is steadily growing, fair-trade and organic teas still represent a small fraction of overall tea sales. Just seven transnational companies

control approximately 90 percent of the Western tea market; Unilever alone now owns brands Lipton, PG Tips, Brisk, Salada, and Red Rose. But there are some changes afoot.

Teas that are certified as both fair trade and organic are increasingly finding their way into the marketplace, through health-food stores, co-ops, and Internet and mail-order shops. "Fair Trade Certified" tea is also more available than ever in this country, thanks to growing ranks of fair-trade plantations in India, Sri Lanka, Africa, and China. Companies that import fair-trade tea are responsible for sending the price premium to local communities of tea workers, who use the money to fund nutrition, sanitation, and family planning services for their community. Fair-trade certification requires that local labor and wage laws are obeyed, such as those restricting the use of child labor. It maintains the rights of workers to organize and requires that workers who handle pesticides first receive education and protection. Fair-trade certification also requires the tea plantations to follow more sustainable environmental practices.

Beer & Wine

An occasional drink of beer or wine can be relaxing and enjoyable, and moderate drinking has even been found to have a positive influence against cardiovascular disease. There are health and environmental issues, however, that make a glass of wine or a bottle of beer a complicated pleasure.

The U.S. Department of Health and Human Services has warned that "consumption of alcoholic beverages is causally related to cancers of the mouth, pharynx, larynx, and esophagus." Laboratory research has suggested that there are possible connections between the consumption of alcohol and breast, liver, and colorectal cancers. And diseases such as cancer aren't the only concern. Conventionally produced alcoholic beverages may contain residues of pesticides and other toxic contaminants, contribute to the overuse of fossil fuels, and harm and sicken workers.

BEER BLUES Although the exact amounts and their actual effects on human health are still unknown, it's clear that alcoholic beverages contain substances carcinogenic to humans. According to the U.S. Department of Health and Human Services, wine, beer, and spirits may contain "components and contaminants" besides ethanol that are known or suspected human carcinogens, including acetaldehyde, nitrosamines, aflatoxins, ethyl carbamate (urethane), asbestos, and arsenic compounds.

ECO-TIP: ORGANIC FOR SURE

An easy way to double-check whether a piece of produce is truly organic is by consulting the Price Look-Up (PLU) code number on its label. The PLU code on an organic product should start with the number 9 and be five digits long; non-organic items have PLUs that are just four digits long.

The pesticides and other toxic chemicals used to produce beer are of concern. Beer is made primarily from barley, hops, and yeast, whereas some wheat is used to make wheat beers. Commercial production of these grains involves the use of herbicides, insecticides, and fungicides, as well as fossil fuel–derived fertilizers. Hops are particularly susceptible to fungus, which conventional growers treat with large amounts of fungicide. These chemicals pose threats to human health and ecosystems.

Organic beer is an environmentally conscious choice. Making beer with organic grains supports a farm system that enhances soil fertility, increases species diversity, conserves water, and produces fewer greenhouse gases. "Certified Organic" beers are made with 95 percent organic ingredients following all the standards set by the USDA. Beers "made with organic ingredients" have been brewed with 70 percent organic ingredients. To earn the organic label, both types of beer must be processed in breweries that are cleaned without using harsh acids or chemicals. Both are made with products supplied by organic farmers.

Organic beer is attracting interest: U.S. sales increased by 40 percent in 2005 to $19 million. Even Anheuser-Busch, the nation's largest beermaker, has jumped into the market, rolling out two organic brews in 2006.

Local beer is another good choice. Buying local beer reduces the amount of fossil fuels used in shipping, and supports smaller, local businesses. Microbreweries have become popular over the past few decades, as beer may be brewed in small vats even in confined urban spaces. Many restaurants have their own microbreweries on premises, and most regions now have regional beermakers.

WINE WOES The fumigants, insecticides, fungicides, and herbicides used in conventional wine production are harmful to the environment. The pesticide methyl bromide, for example, has been used to kill nematodes, insects, and weeds prior to the planting of vines in vineyards, and sterilizes soil—killing everything in it. Methyl bromide, acutely toxic, has harmful effects on the respiratory, neurological, and reproductive systems; it has also been found to contribute to ozone layer destruction. The California Winegrape Pest Management Alliance says methyl bromide has not been used on wine grapes since 2005, but wines bottled earlier were produced with it. Workers producing alcoholic beverages may be exposed to other toxic chemicals, too. According to the Pesticide Action Network, the majority of cases of occupational pesticide exposure reported in California in 2004 were in vineyards.

The production and distribution of alcoholic beverages also requires fossil fuels. Typically encased in heavy glass bottles and often shipped across country or from overseas, alcohol can eat up energy. It has been estimated that the average domestic case of wine consumes more than a gallon of gasoline to reach its final destination. And chilled wine, beer, and other beverages consume additional energy as they sit in refrigerators awaiting purchase.

Wine drinkers need to learn to read labels carefully. Bottles marked "100% Organic Wine" are made from organic ingredients and do not have any added sulfites (although small amounts of sulfites occur naturally in wine). "Organic Wine" is made from 95 percent organic ingredients and may have added sulfites up to 100 parts per million. Wine "Made with Organic Grapes" is made from 70 percent organic ingredients and may contain added sulfites up to 100 parts per million.

Some wines are organically processed as well, meaning that no synthetic agents are used in the clarifying process and that the equipment and tanks are sterilized with hot water or steam rather than chemical agents. Further, little or no manipulation of the wine occurs during the winemaking process in the way of reverse osmosis, excessive filtration, or added flavoring.

The advantages of organic wine are clear. Making wine with organic grapes supports a farm system that enhances soil fertility and increases species diversity. Organic growers also claim that it helps produce flavorful wines: Flourishing soil microorganisms and careful attention to the health of the vines, they claim, make a great contribution to taste. In fact, many also possess a richer sense of *terroir* (qualities of the area in which vines were grown) than ordinary wines. Organic wine is easier to find than ever. It's growing in popularity, and producers aren't just small boutique wineries anymore: Fetzer, one of the largest premium wineries in the United States, recently transitioned its entire 2,000-acre operation to organic.

You may also find wines that are labeled "biodynamic." Similar to organic wines, they are produced without exposure to synthetic inputs, animal by-products, or genetic modification. Biodynamic farming also avoids electromagnetic fields and considers lunar and solar cycles in meshing agriculture with the planet's natural rhythms. Look for the Demeter Biodynamic certification.

Locally grown wines are also making inroads as interest in regionally produced food and beverages grows. Look for them at farmers markets, or ask your local wine store to sample and offer local options.

Cookware

What you eat isn't the only thing to consider when it comes to food. The pots, pans, and other cookware that you use to heat that food are equally important. Although many of us may not give a second thought to cookware, it's worth a look.

Research shows that the compounds found in some cookware can migrate into the food cooked in it. And the chemicals used to manufacture modern conveniences such as nonstick pots and pans can pose real health threats to both animals and humans. Here's the lowdown on the types of cookware most commonly found in kitchens.

NONSTICK COOKWARE First introduced about 50 years ago, nonstick cookware quickly became popular because it is lightweight and incredibly easy to clean, and because cooking in it requires less fat or oil. According to the Cookware Manufacturers Association, more than half of cookware sold today is nonstick. Teflon is the brand name for the high-performance plastic coating that has become synonymous with nonstick cookware, but all nonstick coatings are made the same way, and all present the same environmental issues.

GREEN DICTIONARY

PFOA

Perfluorooctanoic acid, or PFOA—one of the synthetic chemicals known as perfluorochemicals (PFCs)—is used to manufacture fluoropolymers, including Teflon, the coating used on nonstick pots and pans. It is also used in stain- and soil-resistant coatings for carpets and clothing and in grease-resistant films for food packaging, including the bags containing microwavable popcorn.

So what's the problem? DuPont tests have shown that fumes from Teflon heated above 660°F can cause flulike symptoms in humans. Environmental Working Group tests show that when Teflon pans are heated above 680°F, toxins are produced, including the animal carcinogens tetrafluoro-ethylene and perfluorooctanoic acid (PFOA). Fumes from overheated Teflon have proved fatal to pet birds, which have sensitive respiratory systems.

In 2006, science advisers to the U.S. Environmental Protection Agency deemed PFOA "likely to be carcinogenic." PFOA has shown up both in the environment and in human blood. In laboratory rats, it has been shown to cause liver and pancreatic tumors and other adverse effects. In manufacturing plants that make or use it, workers seem to be experiencing some negative health trends. And a 2007 study found that babies exposed to PFOA in the womb were more likely to have a lower birth weight and small head size. PFOA lingers in the environment; it shows up in the blood of people and animals around the world.

The DuPont Company, which uses PFOA to make Teflon, has announced its commitment to eliminate the need to make, buy, or use PFOA by 2015 as well as to develop new products and processes that offer the same cooking convenience but are more environmentally sustainable.

Meanwhile, environmentalist consciousness has made a difference. A 2007 study released by the U.S. Centers for Disease Control and Prevention (CDC) reported "significant reductions in human blood concentrations of PFOS and PFOA" between 1999-2000 and 2003-2004. The CDC credited the efforts of government agencies and industry, but consumer concern and purchasing decisions certainly entered into the equation.

So should you toss the Teflon? Fifteen years ago, the U.S. Food and Drug Administration said that consumers could safely use Teflon and other nonstick cookware and that eating tiny flakes of Teflon and other nonstick coatings that chip off of pots and pans did not appear to pose a health risk. No new government warnings have been published since. DuPont recommends using Teflon cookware only on low or medium heat. Do not use it for broiling, which reaches temperatures between 500° and 550°, and don't leave empty cookware on a hot stove or in a hot oven. Nonstick cookware isn't your best choice from a culinary point of view anyway. Chefs usually prefer stainless steel, cast-iron, and enameled cookware, all widely available, more durable, and less risky for your health.

ABOUT ALUMINUM Aluminum is a safer cookware material than you might imagine. Although studies in the 1960s and 1970s revealed elevated levels of aluminum in the brains of some Alzheimer's patients, subsequent research has not produced any evidence proving that food cooked in aluminum pans causes the disease. In fact, more recent studies suggest a reverse scenario: Aluminum may in fact accumulate in the brain of those suffering from Alzheimer's because of tissue damage inflicted by the disease.

Although aluminum cookware can corrode slightly into very salty or acidic foods, such as tomato sauce, the amount you ingest is minute compared with that from other sources, such as antacids and buffered aspirins. When shopping for aluminum pots and pans, you may come across varieties that have been anodized. This means that the metal has been bathed in electrically charged chemicals, which alter the molecular structure of the aluminum surface. The result is a thicker oxide coating that is harder, smoother, and less likely to corrode aluminum into food.

COPPER CUES Serious chefs prefer copper cookware because of its ability to conduct heat, but all-copper pots and pans can leave residues in foods, which can trigger nausea, vomiting, and diarrhea. To prevent this, choose only copper cookware that is lined with stainless steel or tin.

SUPERB STAINLESS Pots and pans made from stainless steel are shiny, highly durable, and by and large dishwasher safe. On the other hand, stainless steel does not conduct heat as evenly as copper or other materials, and cooks using it need to add more oil to keep food from sticking to the pan. One benefit of stainless steel cookware is that it is widely available in a range of prices, some fairly inexpensive.

OLD-FASHIONED IRON Cast-iron pans may seem old-fashioned, but they're actually the original nonstick cookware. That's because, over time, cast-iron pans develop nonstick properties as the oils and fats used in cooking fuse with the surface of the pan.

It's best not to soak the pan or clean it with soap; instead, just wipe it with a cloth to leave a thin grease coating in the pan. The older a cast-iron pan, the more nonstick its surface will be.

For best results, season cast-iron pans before their first use: Warm the pan briefly to make sure it is completely dry, then coat it with lard, shortening, or vegetable oils like canola or safflower, and bake it in the oven at 300°F. Resist the temptation to use olive oil, which will leave a sticky surface and can smoke during cooking. After baking the pan for 15 to 30 minutes, remove it to pour off excess oil, then return it to the oven to continue baking for two hours at 300°F. (Make sure that the handle does not have a plastic coating that could melt in the oven.)

Be aware that new cast-iron pans have a protective coating that must be removed prior to using them to cook food; use a scouring pad, soap, and hot water to do this. Enameled varieties of cast-iron cookware are also available.

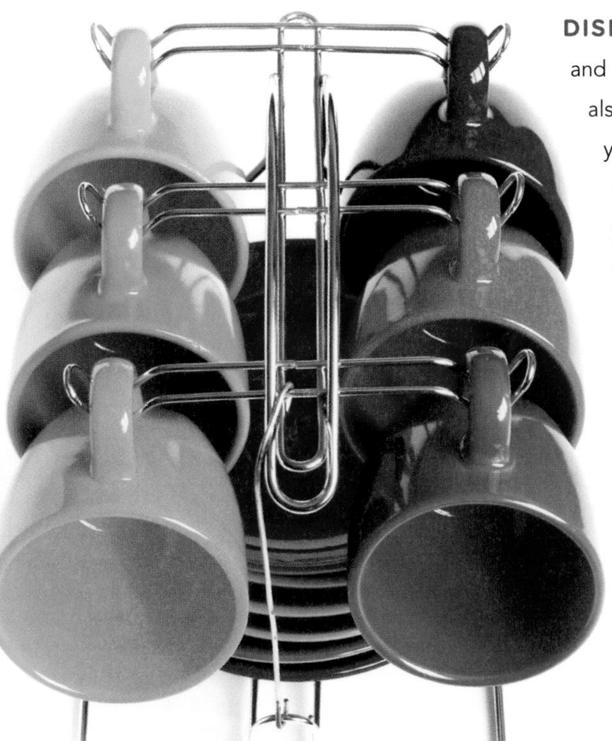

DISHES AND GLASSWARE Using family heirlooms and antiques isn't just a way to connect with the past. It's also a form of recycling. But don't start sipping wine from your grandmother's crystal glasses or serving your family with the vintage pottery you found at a flea market just yet. Such dishes and glassware can be contaminated with lead. Ceramic tableware made in some foreign countries can also contain this heavy metal. Fortunately, there are simple ways to detect lead, and plenty of appealing, environment-friendly alternatives with which to set your table.

CRYSTAL AND CHINA While glazed ceramic dishes and crystal glassware once typically contained lead, many product lines, such as Fiesta, now specify that their dishware is lead-free. It's a good thing, too. Lead can damage the nervous system, including the brain; the kidneys; and the reproductive system. It accumulates in the body and poses the number one environmental health threat to children. More than 300,000 children under the age of 5 in the United States are found to have unsafe levels of lead in their blood every year.

Since 1980, the U.S. FDA has begun regulating the amount of lead and cadmium, another toxic heavy metal, in dishes made in this country. It has no jurisdiction over imported dinnerware or lead crystal, but the crystal industry has set voluntary limits.

The FDA's standards require that plates contain no more than 3 parts per million (ppm) lead; bowls contain no more than 2 ppm; serving dishes contain no more than 1 ppm; and pitchers, cups, and other containers that hold liquid have no more than 0.5 ppm. The state of California requires a warning label on (but does not ban the sale of) plates that contain more than 0.226 ppm of lead, and all other dishes that contain more than 0.1 ppm of lead.

Because major dinnerware manufacturers sell their dishes in California as well as the rest of the country, they generally meet the California regulations, which are stricter. Still, it's smart to take precautions. First, you can test your current ceramics and crystal with strips found at many hardware stores. It's best not to use products that test positive for lead.

In particular, be sure not to store or drink juices and wines in lead-crystal decanters or other containers that could have lead in them. Acidic foods such as tomatoes and citrus also leach out the lead.

Lead can also be found in the glazes on some pottery, especially those that are bright red in color. To ensure that pottery you purchase is free of lead, choose dishes from the online list of lead-free china patterns maintained by the nonprofit Environmental Defense Fund. When in doubt, ask sellers if the glazes on the dinnerware you are considering are lead-free.

RECYCLED AND RENEWABLE MATERIALS Reusing antiques isn't the only way to keep your place settings easy on the environment. A number of both attractive and eco-friendly recycled dinnerware options are now available.

You can choose from plates and bowls handcrafted from seaglass, goblets made from recycled wine and beer bottles, and even dishes fashioned from old windows. Dishes made of renewable bamboo and finished with food-safe lacquer are another environment-friendly choice.

Bottles & Storage Containers

In the world of storage containers, one material reigns: plastic. Whether you're pouring water or juice from a jug or packing up Thanksgiving leftovers, plastic containers have become the number one choice for most people. Plastic is cheap, popular, convenient—and everywhere.

These days, most of the food we buy comes in contact with plastic, including most dairy products (milk, yogurt, cream cheese, and ice cream), frozen foods (prepackaged dinners on plastic trays, frozen vegetables in plastic bags), and fluids (juice, water, and oil in plastic bottles). In fact, since 1976 plastic has been the most widely used material in the world.

Not all plastics are created equal, however, and some are safer to use than others, especially when it comes to food packaging and storage. Indeed, the health risks and environmental concerns associated with many types of plastic can make them a less than attractive choice for home kitchens.

CHEMICAL COMPOUNDS Plastic containers are light, easy to carry, and can form an airtight seal that keeps the contents from drying out or spilling, but the chemicals used to manufacture them can be anything but healthful.

Chemicals of concern include:

ANTIMONY. Research has shown that #1 polyethylene terephthalate (PET) plastic water bottles can leach antimony into the water they hold. See "Eco-Tip: A Plastics Primer," page 57. A 2006 study conducted at the University of Heidelberg, Germany, found that antimony levels in PET water bottles were higher than the levels where the water was sourced, confirming that antimony was leaching into the water from the containers. According to the researchers, the levels found in the water were within safe drinking standards and consumers should not be concerned about drinking water bottled in PET plastic. Keep in mind, however, that storing water in any plastic bottle for a prolonged period of time allows chemical leaching to occur.

BISPHENOL A. Manufacturers began using this chemical, also known as BPA, in the 1950s. You can find BPA in many #7 polycarbonate bottles (including baby bottles), microwave ovenware, eating utensils, and plastic coating for metal cans. BPA can leach into food from the epoxy linings in cans or from polycarbonate bottles as they age. Many studies have evaluated BPA as a hormone disruptor. Research suggests that BPA simulates the action of estrogen when tested in human breast cancer cells and can significantly decrease testosterone in male rats.

DIOXINS. These chemicals are produced by waste incineration, chemical and pesticide manufacturing, and pulp and paper bleaching. Highly toxic even in low doses, dioxins can have a wide range of adverse health effects. The EPA estimates that the average American's risk of contracting cancer from dioxin exposure may be greater than 1 in 1,000. Dioxins can also interfere with the body's natural hormone signals. Short-term exposure to dioxin can cause chloracne, a severe skin disease; skin lesions and discoloration; and liver dysfunction. Long-term exposure can damage the immune, nervous, and reproductive systems and affect development.

PHTHALATES. Also known as plasticizers, these toxic chemicals are added during production of #3 PVC to make it soft and pliable. One such plasticizer, di(2-ethylhexyl) phthalate, has been shown to cause damage to the liver, kidneys, and reproductive systems of animals. Its effects on humans remain unclear. Phthalates can leach from PVC plastics into foods, especially those that are hot and fatty.

STYRENE. Found in #6 polystyrene, this chemical can leach from products like foam containers and cups. It is considered a possible human carcinogen and may also disrupt hormones or affect reproduction.

PLASTICS AND THE PLANET The first plastics were developed during the 1860s, but not until after the Second World War did plastic become the ubiquitous material that it is today. Polyvinyl chloride, polyvinylidene chloride (commonly used in plastic food wrap), and polyethylene were accidentally discovered in the petroleum industry during the 1930s, but all

soon found uses in the modern world. According to the American Chemistry Council, in 1976 plastic became the world's most widely used material. With it came serious environmental problems.

First of all, the manufacturing process used to form plastic resin creates toxic emissions. Producing a 16-ounce PET bottle generates more than 100 times the toxic emissions to air and water than making the same bottle out of glass. The plastic industry contributes to some of the most toxic chemical releases into the air, including styrene, benzene, trichloroethane, sulfur oxides, nitrous oxides, methanol, ethylene oxide, and other volatile organic compounds.

ECO-TIP: A PLASTICS PRIMER

The different types of plastic are identified by numbers, which indicate the types of resin used to produce them. Each plastic has different uses—and different risks.

 # 1 polyethylene terephthalate (PET or PETE) FOUND IN: Soda bottles, peanut butter jars, microwavable trays

 # 2 high-density polyethylene (HDPE) FOUND IN: Trash bags, grocery store bags, cereal box liners, and bottles for milk, water, detergent, shampoo, motor oil

 # 3 polyvinyl chloride (PVC) FOUND IN: Clear food packaging, shampoo bottles, medical tubing, plumbing pipe

 # 4 low-density polyethylene (LDPE) FOUND IN: Shrink-wrap, squeezable bottles for condiments, toys

 # 5 polypropylene (PP) FOUND IN: Syrup bottles, yogurt tubs, diapers, medicine bottles

 # 6 polystyrene (PS) FOUND IN: Coffee cups, clamshell take-out containers, egg cartons, grocery store meat trays

 # 7 other (usually polycarbonate) FOUND IN: Medical storage containers, some reusable water bottles, oven baking bags

Plastic polymers never fully biodegrade: They photodegrade into dust that, when in bodies of water, can absorb other toxins such as PCBs and the pesticide DDT. The toxins are concentrated even more strongly in the dust, which is consumed by the fish that humans eventually eat. It's best to use containers made with #2 HDPE, #4 LDPE, and #5 PP, since research has not shown these plastics leaching carcinogens or endocrine disruptors. Unfortunately, #4 and #5 plastics are not as readily recyclable.

Plastics are made of petroleum, a nonrenewable resource, and plastic waste is a mounting problem. According to the EPA, plastics are the fourth largest category of municipal solid waste. While plastic recycling is on the rise, the volume of new plastic manufacturing is on the rise, too, which keeps the rate of plastic recycling about the same: about 25 percent. Often consumers don't know which plastics can be recycled, mistakenly believing that the chasing-arrows symbols mean the item is recyclable when, in fact, they only identify the resin base of the plastic—not all of which are accepted by all recycling programs.

So when you use plastic containers, whether once or repeatedly, be sure to select those that are accepted for recycling in your area. One easy way to tell if a container is recyclable is by its shape: A container that has a neck, like a jug, is likely to be made of #1 or #2 plastic and therefore readily recyclable, while a tub, like a yogurt container, is not. When you shop, look for products bottled in #2 HDPE, readily recyclable. Stay away from liquids bottled in #3 PVC, dangerous both to health and environment. Purchase canned fruits and vegetables in safe glass jars, and opt for soups, milk, and soy milk packaged in cardboard cartons.

Greener food packaging may be on the way. An expanding number of commercial plastic storage containers now use the corn-based biodegradable material polylactic acid (also called polylactide, or PLA). A number of food purveyors have begun to use PLA for bulk food packaging, and the U.S. FDA has

approved PLA for use as disposable drink receptacles. PLA appears not to leach any toxic chemicals as it biodegrades, which gives it an advantage over some plastics commonly used for holding liquids, such as polycarbonate, which can leach bisphenol A, a polymer additive that may disrupt hormone activity, and polystyrene, which can leach styrene, a possible human carcinogen. Another bonus: Cups made from PLA biodegrade completely, require 50 percent less fossil fuel than regular plastics to produce, and are not toxic to burn.

Because the type of PLA currently in use can only withstand temperatures of up to 105°F, it is used only in the manufacture of cold disposable cups. Several companies, however, manufacture and distribute hot-beverage cups made entirely from corn.

ALTERNATIVES TO PLASTIC Keep your food chemical-free by storing it in nonplastic containers made from these materials:

GLASS, CERAMIC, AND STONEWARE. These materials do not leach questionable chemicals when they're in contact with food, making them the safest options for food storage. Plus, glass recycling is more environmentally friendly than plastic recycling, which produces toxic chemicals. Ceramic thermoses are a safe, sturdy way to carry liquids on the go, particularly hot or acidic liquids, which can encourage the leaching of higher amounts of plasticizer from plastic bottles.

ALUMINUM. Food storage containers made from aluminum can be recycled, are relatively inexpensive, and can be used for reheating in the oven. In fact, it's a good idea to reuse aluminum containers , since aluminum extraction is so energy-intensive. Aluminum can sometimes react with certain foods or leave behind a metallic taste, so use it for storing foods that are not acidic or salty.

STAINLESS STEEL. Containers made from stainless steel are an environmentally friendly choice, not only because the material is 100 percent recyclable but also because stainless steel is easy to clean without any harsh chemicals: Just use warm water and a cloth. Stainless steel is also inexpensive, attractive, and will not react with foods during cooking.

ECO-TIP: SMART REUSE

Cleaning and reusing food containers is a great way to cut down on waste. Glass mustard and mayonnaise jars can be reused as containers for salad dressings, for example. Yogurt tubs are great for storing leftovers (but not for reheating). Not all containers can be reused safely, however. Here's what to keep in mind when reusing containers.

- ✓ Only reuse containers that can be washed thoroughly.
- ✓ Never reuse containers that have contained chemicals, such as those used for cleaning or pest control.
- ✓ To reduce the risk of bacterial poisoning, do not reuse any packing that came into contact with meat or dairy products unless it has been thoroughly sterilized.
- ✓ Don't use plastic food tubs (like from yogurt, margarine, or takeout) for reheating in the microwave, because chemicals in plastics can migrate into hot, fatty foods.
- ✓ Never reuse #1 plastic bottles: Their design doesn't lend itself to proper cleaning, and the bottles can harbor bacterial growth.
- ✓ If you already own #7 bottles, keep an eye out for cracks or cloudiness in their plastic. Wash them by hand with mild dishwashing soap, not in the dishwasher, to avoid degrading the plastic and increasing leaching of BPA.

Wraps & Bags

Wraps and storage bags may protect food against outside bacteria, but they also harbor potential to harm. Plastic wraps and storage bags contain chemicals that can leach into food, especially when heated, and plastic shopping bags are wasteful and hard on the environment.

WRAPPED IN CHEMICALS Like their container counterparts, wraps and food storage bags made of plastic can leach toxic chemicals into food. Research suggests that #3 PVC, commonly used in some forms of plastic wrap, is an endocrine disrupter and may mimic or interfere with hormones in the body. To soften #3 PVC plastic into its flexible form, manufacturers add various toxic chemicals known as plasticizers, including one called di(2-ethylhexyl) adipate, or DEHA. Traces of such chemicals, known as adipates and phthalates, can leak out of PVC when it comes in contact with foods.

Most cling-wrapped meats, cheeses, and other foods sold in delis and grocery stores are wrapped in #3 PVC. In one study by the nonprofit Consumers Union, pieces of cheddar cheese wrapped in #3 PVC by supermarket deli departments were tested. Most of the DEHA that was an ingredient in the wrap ended up in the cheese. A 1995 Danish study found that 44 to 58 ppm of DEHA leached into cheese within just two hours of being packaged in PVC.

Another study by Consumers Union found that only one of seven brands of plastic wrap contained DEHA, however. The Food and Drug Administration says that DEHA is safe, but some studies have shown that the chemical may interfere with male reproductive function and can cause birth defects and liver cancer in lab animals. In the absence of certainty, it's best to avoid DEHA.

With some careful shopping and storage techniques, you can greatly reduce your exposure to DEHA and other plasticizers. When you purchase cling-wrapped food from the supermarket or deli, slice off a thin layer where the food came into contact with the plastic and store the rest in a glass or ceramic container, or non-PVC cling wrap.

If you purchase meat, do so from a butcher and ask for it to be wrapped in paper. Try to purchase deli cheeses coming directly from a cheesemaker, and request that they be wrapped in paper, too. And take care when you reheat food in the microwave: According to the FDA, microwave-safe plastic wrap should be placed loosely over food so that the steam can escape and should not directly touch your food. Better yet, cover your food with another dish—or microwave your food uncovered.

When you wrap food at home, choose butcher paper or wood-based cellulose bags, waxed paper and waxed paper bags (made of unbleached paper thinly coated with petroleum-based paraffin or wax, which is approved for food storage use by the FDA).

ECO-TIP: MICROWAVE-SAFE?

Labels reading "microwave safe" or "microwavable" only ensure that the containers won't melt, crack, or fall apart in the microwave. It is no guarantee that the containers won't leach chemicals into foods when heated. To be safe, don't heat foods in plastic. Especially steer away from microwaving food in containers not intended for that purpose, such as take-out platters and margarine tubs. Use ovenproof glass or ceramic containers instead.

TRASHED BAGS Americans use an estimated 100 billion plastic shopping bags each year, representing about 12 million barrels of oil. Less than one percent of those plastic bags is ever recycled. The rest photodegrade, breaking down into tiny bits of plastic that can contaminate soil and waterways and harm animals that ingest them. Hundreds of thousands of marine animals die annually, entangled in plastic debris or eating plastic bags that they mistake for food. Plastic bags are top items found during coastal cleanups.

Paper bags come with their own problems. It takes an estimated four times as much energy to manufacture a paper bag as it does to manufacture a plastic one, and more than ten times as much energy to recycle a paper bag as a plastic one. Paper mills can contribute toxic chemicals to our air, soil, and waterways. And paper bags do not degrade substantially faster than plastic.

If you already have a stash of paper or plastic bags at home, it makes sense to reuse them as long as they'll hold up. Most groceries these days sell reusable bags made of nonwoven polypropylene that are lightweight, durable, and recyclable. They're also washable and can be reused multiple times.

If you live in San Francisco, plastic shopping bags may not even be an option: In 2007, the city's government voted to ban plastic shopping bags at large supermarkets and chain pharmacies. The stores are allowed to offer shoppers bags made of cornstarch or recyclable paper instead.

THE FACTS

Australia, Bangladesh, Ireland, Italy, South Africa, and Taiwan, along with the cities of San Francisco and Mumbai, India, have all enacted legislation to ban or otherwise curb the use of plastic shopping bags.

Consider investing in one or more sturdy, reusable bags made of nylon, cotton, and other materials. Organic cotton canvas bags are the most eco-friendly alternative, but their material can stain and isn't always water-resistant.

Sea Bags, shopping bags made from old sailboat sails, are another option. The material used in the sails is Dacron, a polyester fiber. While the material's production isn't exactly Earth-friendly (petroleum-based polyester contributes to the depletion of nonrenewable fossil fuels and increases our dependence on foreign oil), Sea Bags are strong, water-resistant, machine-washable—and reusable. Their handles are made of rope that is spliced by hand.

Or consider reusable nylon grocery bags. Their production requires the same amount of energy as 50 disposable plastic bags, but they last much longer, hold up to 25 pounds, and can be folded into their own mini-pouch. Finally, you may want to seek out plastic bags made from polylactic acid, or PLA. ▸For more on PLA, see pages 58-59. Bags made of PLA look, feel, and smell like normal plastic bags, but a PLA bag breaks down within weeks, unlike conventional plastic bags, estimated to take up to a thousand years to decompose.

Lunch Boxes

Lunch brought from home is often a healthier alternative to what's served at workplace and school cafeterias. But you need to take care when packing on-the-go meals. Traditional plastic lunch boxes, thermoses, and utensils can add something extra to packed lunches—toxic chemicals.

BOXES, SACKS, AND THERMOSES Chemicals in plastic lunch boxes and sacks, thermoses, and other travel containers can leach into foods—especially those that are hot or fatty. Common culprits include products made with #3 PVC (which contains hormone-disrupting phthalates), #6 polystyrene (a possible human carcinogen), and #7 polycarbonate (which contains hormone-disrupting BPA).

Another problem is lead. In September 2007, the state of California's Department of Public Health warned parents to toss imported Chinese canvas lunch boxes, because testing revealed that some contained significant levels of lead. There are commercially available home lead-testing kits that you can purchase to test your child's lunch box.

Fortunately, there are plenty of fun, fashionable, and environmentally friendly alternatives. Traditionalists may prefer lunch boxes crafted from sturdy, reusable tin or stainless steel. Certified organic cotton canvas lunch sacks are another attractive option. You can even find Free Trade Certified lunch boxes—or make your own lunch bag out of a piece of cloth and a drawstring. Reusable, nonleaching thermoses and plastic cups can be cleaned easily and give your child an alternative to soft drinks and bottled water. There are also a number of safe, environmentally friendly varieties from which to choose.

UTENSILS AND PLATES Plastic flatware, plates, and cups clog landfills with extra waste. Choose reusable utensils whenever possible. If you must use disposable items, seek out biodegradable utensils, plates, and cups. Some made from corn are dishwasher-safe and degrade in your compost pile. Other biodegradable tableware is available, including those made from recycled paper, corn or potato starch, sugarcane or sustainably harvested trees.

Restaurants

Recent books and movies have detailed the artery-clogging nature of fast food and the toll that the industry takes on our air, water, and soil, not to mention our health and longevity.

FAST-FOOD CHANGES—TO GO Morgan Spurlock's film *Super Size Me* and Eric Schlosser's book *Fast Food Nation* signaled a growing public awareness of the health issues surrounding fast food. McDonald's and other restaurants began offering more salads and other items described as low-carb or heart-friendly. But are fast-food restaurants really as healthy as they claim? Nutritionists note that McDonald's salads can actually be higher in fat and calories than a Big Mac when you add the salad dressing, and that the salads lack substantial amounts of fiber and other nutrients. Arby's salads can be high in fat—the Santa Fe salad contains 520 calories and 29 grams of fat with salad dressing, 45 percent of the FDA's recommended daily intake of fat. Fast-food salads and other "healthy" choices are expensive, too: Pricing still favors buying calorie-heavy foods and larger portions.

If you must head to a mass-market chain, ask the hard questions. Restaurants may advertise food as 50 percent less fat—but less than what? Is it 50 percent less than something like a Burger King Whopper? An original Whopper without cheese has 39 grams of fat; a Double Whopper with cheese has 64 grams. The reduced-fat versions of both are still high in fat. Refer to nutrition charts, and keep your fast-food meals to a minimum.

FINE DINING A growing number of fine restaurants offer local, seasonal, organic—healthier—food and drink. They have banded together to form Chefs Collaborative, a nonprofit dedicated to sustainable, environmentally responsible and health-conscious food preparation for the public. The Green Restaurant Association, in harmony with the Chefs Collaborative, is a nonprofit aimed at building environmental sustainability in the restaurant industry. Certified restaurants follow guidelines for energy

efficiency, recycling and composting, sourcing of sustainable foods, and cleaning products that are non-toxic. For pointers to locate chefs and restaurants who serve local and organic foods, consult the Chefs Collaborative and Green Restaurant websites. ▸See "Resources."

Take Action

- ✓ Buy "Certified Organic" fruits and vegetables when possible.
- ✓ Buy local produce or join a community-supported agriculture program.
- ✓ In meat and poultry, look for brands marked "100 Percent Certified Organic" and"Grass Fed."
- ✓ Buy organic cooking oils made without genetically modified ingredients.
- ✓ Use organic sugar or experiment with sweet alternatives such as honey.
- ✓ Choose snacks low in trans fats and without high-fructose corn syrup.
- ✓ Buy chocolate that is labeled "Certified Organic" and "Fair Trade Certified."
- ✓ Minimize your use of bottled water. Test your tap water and use a water filter to remove the contaminants specific to your water supply.
- ✓ Buy coffee and tea labeled "Certified Organic," "Fair Trade Certified," or "Shade Grown."
- ✓ Avoid cookware coated with Teflon and other nonstick materials.
- ✓ Test your crystal and tableware for lead; use plates and glasses shown to be lead free or made from recycled or renewable materials.
- ✓ Choose plastic containers that are recyclable and safest: #2, #4, and #5.
- ✓ Favor glass, stoneware, ceramic, metal, and biodegradable storage containers.
- ✓ Remove plastic wrapping from food as soon as possible.
- ✓ Invest in reusable or biodegradable shopping bags.
- ✓ Avoid lunch boxes and thermoses made from #3, #6, and #7 plastic. Choose metal, cloth, or recycled materials instead.
- ✓ Eat at restaurants that offer organic, sustainable meal choices. Ask your favorite establishments where their food comes from.

The Energy in a Hamburger

The average quarter-pound hamburger patty begins its existence in a calf born on a private cattle farm. For the first few months of life, the calf nurses from his mother, and then he begins to graze on pastureland. Grass is the natural diet of cows and other ruminants, animals that have evolved to extract nutrients from the hardy cellulose plant matter that humans find indigestible.

After about nine months, the cow boards a tractor trailer and journeys to a cattle feedlot, where he will spend the rest of his life, eating from a trough, in an enclosure roughly half the size of a football field. Until the 1950s, cattle were grazed on pastureland until big enough to slaughter, a process that took two to three years. In concentrated feedlots, cattle can be fed high-nutrient diets that allow them to grow to maturity—roughly 1,100 pounds—in as little as 14 months.

They receive a high-nutrient diet of corn flakes mixed with other grains like sorghum and barley plus measured amounts of liquefied fat, protein mixture, vitamins, synthetic estrogen, and antibiotics. Antibiotics promote growth and prevent and treat disease. Estrogen works as a growth promoter. Other ingredients help the cow's rumen, fine-tuned to grass, digest corn instead.

More than a quarter of all corn grown worldwide is fed to cattle, primarily in the United States. Each 1.2 pounds of corn-based feed translates into a quarter pound of marbled muscle tissue, which will be ground into hamburger. Growing all this corn takes resources: nitrogen fertilizers, gasoline and diesel to power the farm machinery, and irrigation water. Intensive corn agriculture also requires pesticides such as atrazine, a hormone-mimicking chemical that runs off fields and has been detected in water wells throughout the Midwest.

Raising one cow requires 35 gallons of oil. Most of this energy is used to produce synthetic fertilizers made from fossil fuels, and the rest is used for milling and transportation. One-fourth of all fertilizer used in the United States goes to grow corn fed to cattle and other livestock. One-fifth of the petroleum consumed in the United States goes to crop production and transportation. All told, the amount of energy that it takes to create a single quarter-pound hamburger patty equates to the energy in one cup of gasoline.

That quarter-pound hamburger also requires 600 gallons of water, most of it to grow the corn feed and the rest to water the cattle and to cool down and reduce dust in the feedlots. Some 40 percent of all beef cattle in the United States are fattened on corn grown with water drawn from the dwindling Ogallala aquifer, an underground store of water lying under the states of Colorado, Kansas, Nebraska, and Texas.

Since the cattle are confined, they stand in piles of their own manure. Manure harbors microorganisms, including the deadly strain of *E. coli* bacteria known as 0157:H7. About 40 percent of feedlot cattle carry this strain in their gut. If the manure is not washed off the cattle prior to slaughter, this microbe can easily enter the food supply.

Small farms may recycle manure as fertilizer, but large feedlots bulldoze it into lagoons, where it slowly decomposes, posing a threat to water supplies. The high level of nutrients in manure can cause harmful algae blooms in surface waters and contaminate well water. These manure ponds also release methane, a greenhouse gas more potent than carbon dioxide. These emissions, combined with the carbon dioxide spewed from the tailpipes of farm machinery and the fertilizer plants, mean that a single quarter-pound burger creates about eight pounds of carbon dioxide, the same amount of greenhouse gases emitted on an eight-mile drive in an SUV.

Once matured, the cow is ready for the slaughterhouse and packing plant. The carcass is butchered and some of the meat ground into hamburger. Ground bits of beef from one cow combine with meat from others, making it difficult to track individual cows in the meat supply—so beef recalls must be massive. The meat from a single diseased cow can end up in several hundred packages of ground meat distributed throughout the nation.

Given the effects of its life cycle on the environment and the potential for deadly microbes to enter the food supply, the modern American burger clearly costs more than 99 cents.

BETTER HOUSEKEEPING

Clean & Green

IT'S BEEN SAID THAT CLEANLINESS IS A VIRTUE. YOUR appliances gleam, your windows are spotless, and everything smells fresh and airy. But clean doesn't always mean healthful—not if you've relied on conventional disinfectants, detergents, and other cleansers for the task. Yes, they get the job done, but what's lurking inside those liquids, scrubs, and sprays is hardly good for you. In fact, those bottles hide a dirty little secret.

Most of us equate cleanliness with health. But most conventional cleaning products are anything but safe: By the numbers, they're downright toxic. In 2005 alone, cleaning products were responsible for about 9 percent of poisonings in adults and almost 10 percent of poisonings in children younger than age six, according to the American Association of Poison Control Centers. The most immediately hazardous cleaning products are corrosive drain cleaners, oven cleaners, acid toilet bowl cleaners, and anything that contains chlorine or ammonia.

Cleaning products aren't just poisonous. Fumes created by the chemicals in cleaning products also greatly contribute to indoor air pollution. The U.S. Environmental Protection Agency (EPA) found that levels of about a dozen common organic pollutants were two to five times higher inside homes than outdoors, including homes located in both rural and industrial areas. A major source of this pollution is a class of irritating chemicals called volatile organic compounds (VOCs), which evaporate or "off-gas" from many cleaning products. Not only do people using products that contain VOCs expose themselves—and others who are in the vicinity—to elevated concentrations of these chemicals, but the remaining fumes can linger long after the cleaning is completed, according to EPA studies.

The health effects of VOCs vary depending on the chemical and length of exposure to it. Acute, immediate concerns include eye and respiratory tract irritation, headaches, dizziness, nausea, visual disorders, loss of coordination, and memory impairment. Over time, exposure to some VOCs can damage the kidneys, liver, and nervous system, and may cause cancer.

A growing body of evidence highlights the continuing threat that VOCs and other chemicals in cleaning products pose to our health. In one November 2003 study of more than 4,000 women, researchers found that 25 percent of asthma cases could be attributed to domestic cleaning work. And a 2002 report detailed the negative effects of cleaning products on the health of janitors. The study also suggested that reducing the use of products that contain VOCs could protect health and improve indoor air quality.

More recently, large studies have pinpointed the health impact of specific VOCs on people. Human population research conducted by the National Institute of Environmental Health Sciences (NIEHS), and published in *Environmental Health Perspectives* in 2006, found that a VOC called 1,4-dichlorobenzene (1,4-DCB) may harm lung function. This chemical is commonly found in air fresheners, toilet bowl cleaners, mothballs, and other deodorizing products. The NIEHS researchers found modest reductions in pulmonary function with increasing blood concentrations of 1,4-DCB.

A 2006 study by researchers at the University of California, Berkeley, and Lawrence Berkeley National Laboratory looked at the health risks posed by VOCs in household cleaners such as ethylene-based glycol ethers and terpenes. Ethylene-based glycol ethers are water-soluble solvents found in many cleaning products that have been classified as toxic air contaminants by the EPA. Terpenes are a class of chemicals found in pine, lemon, and orange oils that are used as solvents and fragrances in cleaning products. Although terpenes themselves are not toxic, studies suggest that

they may react with ozone and form toxic compounds, including very small particles similar to those found in smog and haze, and formaldehyde, a respiratory irritant that is classified as a known carcinogen by the International Agency for Research on Cancer. The researchers found that, of 21 household cleaning products tested, 12 contained terpenes and other ozone-reactive compounds and 6 contained ethylene-based glycol ethers. Three out of four air fresheners studied contained substantial quantities of terpenes.

Further research showed that people could be exposed to dangerous levels of pollutants when cleaning with these products. For instance, a person who spends 15 minutes cleaning a shower stall could inhale three times the "acute one-hour exposure limit" set for ethylene-based glycol ether by the California Office of Environmental Health Hazard Assessment. And a person who uses a moderate amount of a terpene-containing product to clean a kitchen on a day when outdoor ozone levels are high—and then remains in the room for two hours afterward—would inhale about one-quarter of the total daily guideline for particulate matter.

Other toxic chemicals found in household cleaning products include:

ALKYLPHENOL ETHOXYLATES (APES). These chemicals, found in some detergents and cleaners, are hormone disruptors shown to mimic estrogen. In a test-tube study, an APE called p-nonylphenol caused estrogen-sensitive breast cancer cells to multiply.

AMMONIA. Found in floor, bathroom, and tile cleaners and some glass cleaners, this chemical is poisonous when swallowed, irritating to respiratory passages when inhaled, and potentially caustic to skin on contact.

ANTIBACTERIAL AGENTS. Compounds called triclosan and benzalkonium are used in soaps, sprays, and other cleaners to kill germs, but they may also contribute to antibiotic resistance. Triclosan forms dioxin, a toxic chemical, when exposed to sunlight; it forms chloroform, a probable human carcinogen, when exposed to chlorinated water. Recent studies conducted at the Columbia University School of Nursing found that antibacterial products are not necessarily any more effective at killing germs than regular cleansers.

BUTYL CELLOSOLVE. *(also known as butyl glycol or ethylene glycol monobutyl ether).* Found in glass cleaners and all-purpose cleaners, this chemical is poisonous when swallowed and acts as a lung tissue irritant.

CHLORINE BLEACH. This disinfectant can contribute to the formation of ozone-damaging organochlorines.

DIETHANOLAMINE (DEA) AND TRIETHANOLAMINE (TEA). Found in sudsing products, including detergents and cleansers, these substances can combine with nitrosomes (preservatives or contaminants whose presence is often not cited on the label) to produce carcinogenic nitrosamines that can penetrate the skin.

THE FACTS

Of the roughly 17,000 chemicals used in household products, including those used for cleaning, only about 30 percent have been adequately tested for their effects on human health.

PETROLEUM. Found in many detergents, solvents, and polishes, common cleaning products derived from petroleum include paraffin, mineral oil, diethylene glycol, perchloroethylene, and butyl cellosolve. Petroleum is a nonrenewable resource whose extraction and refinement contribute to air and water pollution.

PHOSPHATES AND ETHYLENEDIAMINETETRAACETIC ACID (EDTA). These agents are commonly used in detergents to soften the water and enhance cleaning power, but they encourage growth of aquatic weeds and algae in waterways, which can kill off fish populations. Phosphates have largely been phased out of many cleaning products, but they still can be found as ingredients in some laundry and dishwasher detergents. EDTA, a phosphate substitute, degrades slowly.

PHTHALATES. Used to prolong the fragrance of cleaning products, these chemicals are hormone disruptors and have been shown to cause liver, kidney, and reproductive diseases in animals.

SODIUM HYDROXIDE (LYE). Found in drain, metal, and oven cleaners, this chemical is extremely irritating to eyes, nose, and throat and can burn those tissues on contact.

ECO-TIPS: LABEL LINGO

How toxic is your cleaner? Although products don't always list specific ingredients, you can still learn much by reading their labels. To stay safe, follow these steps.

1. Watch for words that signal a product's toxicity. Products that are labeled "Danger" or "Poison" tend to be the most hazardous. Those that are marked "Warning" or "Caution" are moderately or slightly toxic. Also avoid products that warn "may cause skin irritation," "flammable," "vapors harmful," and "may cause burns on contact."

2. Avoid products that contain chlorine or ammonia as their main ingredients. They can cause respiratory and skin irritation and create toxic fumes if accidentally mixed together.

3. Don't be fooled by "greenwashing." Labels like "natural" and "eco-friendly" and even "nontoxic" often mean nothing. Instead, look for more specific terms such as "solvent-free," "plant-based," "no phosphates," and "no petroleum-based ingredients." Cleaning products cannot be certified organic, so a reference to "organic" may mean no VOCs but not environmental friendliness.

   Watch for claims regarding degradation. Those that offer specific time periods (e.g., "biodegradable in five days") are more apt to break down effectively. To be considered biodegradable, a product should break down completely within weeks or, better yet, within days.

4. Ventilate your rooms during and after cleaning. Promptly remove cleaning supplies from occupied spaces once you have finished using them.

   Don't use ozone generators or ionizing air cleaners at all if you can help it, since the ozone generated by these devices is harmful to health—but be especially careful not to use them in the same space as cleaning products that contain terpenes: Used together, they produce toxic compounds.

Household Cleaners

Keeping your home clean is important for your health and comfort, but household cleaners, meant to kill germs, can contain toxic ingredients. Choosing environment-friendly options is critical not just for your health but for the sake of the planet.

ALL-PURPOSE CLEANERS Whatever they may save you in time and money, all-purpose cleaners can cost you in health. Some contain the sudsing agents DEA and TEA. When these agents come in contact with nitrites—often present as undisclosed preservatives or contaminants—they react to form nitrosamines, carcinogens that can easily penetrate the skin. All-purpose cleaners made with ethoxylated alcohols can also contain 1,4-dioxane, another probable carcinogen. Other all-purpose cleaning products contain butyl cellosolve (also known as butyl glycol or ethylene glycol monobutyl ether), which is easily absorbed through the skin and may cause damage to the kidneys, liver, and reproductive system. Fumes from ammonia-containing cleaners may cause respiratory irritation. Sodium hydroxide (lye) and sodium hypochlorite (bleach) are highly caustic, and sodium hypochlorite should never be mixed with any product containing ammonia or quaternium compounds: They create toxic gases when combined.

Instead of using conventional all-purpose household products, go natural. Making your own all-purpose cleaner is safe, inexpensive, and easy: Simply dissolve four tablespoons of baking soda in one quart of warm water, or use a vinegar-and-salt mixture or liquid castile soap and a sturdy scrubber sponge to attack grease and grime. If you prefer to purchase prepared products rather than do it yourself, several safe and effective all-purpose cleaners are available in natural-foods stores and online or by mail order.

ECO-TIP: HOMEMADE CLEANERS

Effective and easy "green" cleaning can be as simple as stocking your cabinet with a few tried-and-true products. Pick up empty spray bottles at the hardware store, save old rags and used toothbrushes for scrubbing, and keep the following on hand:

- ✓ **Baking soda: provides grit for scrubbing and reacts with water, vinegar, or lemon by fizzing, which speeds up cleaning times.**
- ✓ **Borax: disinfects, bleaches, and deodorizes; especially useful in laundry mixes (should not be used around children or pets or during pregnancy).**
- ✓ **Distilled white vinegar: disinfects and breaks up dirt; choose white vinegar over apple cider or red vinegars, which can stain surfaces.**
- ✓ **Hydrogen peroxide: disinfects and bleaches.**
- ✓ **Isopropyl alcohol: disinfects, although it may irritate skin.**
- ✓ **Lemons: cut grease; bottled lemon juice also works well, although you might need to use a bit more to get the same results.**
- ✓ **Olive oil: picks up dirt and polishes wood; cheaper grades work well.**
- ✓ **Vegetable-based (liquid castile) soap: nonpetroleum all-purpose cleaner.**
- ✓ **Washing soda: stain remover, general cleaner, helps unblock pipes; should be handled with gloves due to its caustic nature. Washing soda (sodium carbonate) is usually found in the laundry aisle of grocery stores and drugstores.**

DISINFECTANTS You probably wouldn't spray your home's countertops with pesticides, yet that's just what most conventional disinfectants are. Disinfectants that claim to kill *E. coli* and *Staphylococcus* are regulated by the EPA as pesticides because they kill bacteria. But they may not be as effective as you think: Although they can kill germs on surfaces, no surface treatment will completely eliminate bacteria. Plus, disinfectants can't kill germs in the air and they do not provide long-lasting protection against bacteria. As for

antibacterial soaps, they are no more effective than ordinary soap and warm water at preventing the spread of infection.

Also, some disinfectant cleaners have been found to contain APEs, hormone disruptors that don't readily biodegrade. Triclosan, a commonly used germ-killer in disinfectants, is structurally similar to dioxins. According to one study, triclosan reacts in sunlight to produce DCDD, a dioxin harmful to human health; triclosan also can react with chlorinated water to form chloroform, a probable human carcinogen. After it washes down your drain, triclosan persists in the environment for months. It can even promote antibiotic-resistant bacteria: A 2004 study found that *E. coli* bacteria repeatedly exposed to triclosan quickly acquired resistance to triclosan and other antibiotics.

Unless you have a compromised immune system or illness that increases your susceptibility to infection from microbes and bacteria, you probably don't need a disinfectant for most household tasks. Take steps to avoid foodborne illness instead. Wash all foods thoroughly before preparation, and be sure to soak leafy greens, rinsing at least three times. Cook meat and eggs thoroughly to 160°F (no rare beef or over-easy scrambles). Eat only fresh fish, and thaw frozen meats in the refrigerator instead of on the countertop, to inhibit growth of bacteria on the surface of the meat as it thaws. Wash all cutting boards, dishes, knives, and other surfaces that touch raw meat or eggs in hot, soapy water before you use them for other foods that will not be cooked. Refrigerate foods within two hours of cooking. Keep cold foods cold (in the refrigerator at 40°F or the freezer at 0°F), and hot foods hot (at 140°F—or heat them to 165°F if reheating).

THE FACTS

The chemical triclosan, a common ingredient in antibacterial soaps and disinfectants, was detected in almost 58 percent of stream water samples from across the United States, according to a May 2002 study by the U.S. Geological Survey.

To clean household surfaces, hot, soapy water usually does the trick. Or mix half a cup of borax into a gallon of hot water to disinfect and deodorize (but be aware that borax is toxic to humans; keep it away from children, pregnant women, and pets, and don't use it around food). Isopropyl alcohol is an excellent disinfectant, but use gloves and keep it away from children. White vinegar is also effective.

GLASS CLEANERS You don't need bottles of unnaturally blue liquid to make your windows gleam. Many common window cleaners contain butyl cellosolve, a petroleum-based solvent that can damage your liver, kidneys, and red blood cells and can irritate mucous membranes. This chemical is also a neurotoxin, which means that it can damage nerves, and is poisonous when swallowed. Window cleaners often also contain ammonia, which may irritate airways and will release toxic chloramine gases if accidentally mixed with chlorine-containing cleaners.

Plain water is often just as effective as some commercial glass cleaners. You can also make your own glass-cleaning spray from a cup of water plus a quarter cup of white vinegar or a tablespoon of lemon juice.

FURNITURE POLISH Furniture polishes may remove smudges, but they can also be hazardous to your health: Many brands of both furniture and metal polish can contain nerve-damaging petroleum distillates, which are flammable and dangerous if swallowed. Contact with furniture polishes can cause skin and eye irritation, whereas aerosol spray furniture polishes are easily inhaled into lung tissue. Some formulations of furniture polish may also contain formaldehyde, a known carcinogen. Metal polishes may contain lung-irritating ammonia, which can irritate eyes, skin, or airways during use.

For dusting and polishing, combine one-half cup of white vinegar and a few drops of olive oil. (If you find that this ratio leaves your wood furniture too oily, use less olive oil.) Or look for solvent-free products that use plant oils as the active polish. To remove tarnish, try scrubbing silver with ordinary toothpaste. For copper, dissolve salt in white vinegar or lemon juice and rub on with a cloth, then rinse with water. Polish unlacquered brass with a paste of one teaspoon of salt, one cup of white vinegar, and one cup of flour.

BATHROOM CLEANERS You might find it surprising, but the bathroom actually isn't the most bacteria-laden room in your home—it's the kitchen. Still, bathrooms naturally harbor their fair share of germs, found both in places you'd expect (the toilet) and lurking in less obvious locations such as showerheads, faucets, and drains. Clearly, your first instinct is to decontaminate the room with plenty of antibacterial products. But you could be doing more harm than good: Bathroom cleaning products can be acutely toxic. Follow these tips to get your bathroom sparkling without nasty side effects.

TOILET CLEANERS Toilet bowl cleaners contain corrosive ingredients that can irritate your eyes, skin, and respiratory system. Some contain sodium bisulfate, which may trigger asthma attacks. And bathroom cleaners containing sodium hydroxide, sodium hypochlorite (bleach), or phosphoric acid can irritate lungs, burn eyes and skin, and, if ingested, harm internal organs.

Instead, use a paste of baking soda and water to scrub toilet bowls. Lemon juice will remove stains from porcelain, while isopropyl alcohol is an effective disinfectant. For tougher toilet jobs, you can use borax, as long as it doesn't come into contact with infants, pets, or pregnant women. Borax, a naturally occurring mineral, is water-soluble and can remove stains, deodorize, inhibit growth of mold and mildew, and boost the cleaning power of other gentle soaps. Pour one cup of borax and one-quarter cup of distilled white vinegar or lemon juice into the toilet bowl. Let it sit for a few hours and then scrub with a toilet brush and flush.

DRAIN CLEANERS Most commercial drain de-cloggers contain corrosive ingredients such as sodium hydroxide and sodium hypochlorite that can permanently damage eyes and skin. Some can be fatal if ingested.

Still, since drains have been shown to be the germiest parts of most bathrooms, it's important to keep them clean. Regularly dispose of hair that collects in and around shower or sink drains. When clogs do occur, use a "snake" plumbing tool to manually remove blockage, or try suction removal with a plunger. To disinfect drains, pour a cup or two of vinegar down them twice a week. Ordinary vinegar can kill up to 99 percent of bacteria.

SCRUBS AND CREAM CLEANSERS Scouring powders, scrubs, and cream cleansers are effective at eliminating tough stains, but the abrasive ingredients that they contain can be hazardous to your health. Some scouring powders contain silica as their abrasive scrubbing agent, a chemical that is harmful when inhaled. Others use chlorine bleach, which irritates skin and airways and forms toxic gases when combined with ammonia or acidic cleaners.

Instead, to scour away grease and grime, use a paste of baking soda and water. For grease, try this mixture from cleaning expert Annie Berthold-Bond: Combine one-half teaspoon of washing soda, two tablespoons of distilled white vinegar, one-quarter teaspoon liquid soap, and two cups of hot water in a spray bottle. Wear gloves when working with washing soda.

ASK THE EDITORS

Q **Are enzyme cleaners safe and effective, or are they just as bad as other conventional cleaners?**

A It seems as if enzymes are everywhere these days: They're now a prominent ingredient in many so-called environmentally friendly cleaning products that claim to be nontoxic to plants and animals, harmless if ingested, and completely free of VOCs and other dangerous chemicals.

According to green cleaning experts, enzymatic cleaners are relatively safe and effective, although more research is needed.

Enzymatic household cleaners break down dirt and grime, using specific enzymes designed for specific targets: Protease enzymes break down protein stains; lipolases break down fat, or lipid, stains; and amylases break down starch-based or other carbohydrate-based stains. Enzyme cleaners are definitely a better alternative to petroleum-based, chemical-laden cleaners, but they come with a few caveats: Some enzymes are riskier than others.

Continually inhaling protease enzymes can trigger asthma and other respiratory allergies, for example, so they shouldn't be used on carpets, where they'll remain and get stirred up by vacuuming. Also, ready-to-use enzyme cleaners require preservatives, and many companies use harsh chemicals like propylene glycol, a skin and eye irritant, or other neurotoxic glycol ethers such as butyl cellosolve.

You can avoid harsh preservatives by purchasing enzyme concentrates, which, because of their lower water content, require fewer preservatives. Do be aware that, as a general rule, enzyme cleaners have a relatively short shelf life, as little as three months, depending on the formulation. As for biodegradability, look for products with vegetable-based, not petroleum-based, surfactants and cleaning agents The enzymes themselves dissolve dirt and grime particles, essentially reducing those particles to water, and then are washed down the drain, where they are eaten by other living matter.

Soaps & Detergents

Take a good look at the cleaning soaps and detergents that you use. While soaps and detergents get things plenty clean, they may have side effects that aren't so easy to detect: on your home, your clothing, your family's health, and on the environment.

THE PETROCHEMICAL PROBLEM Petrochemicals occur in everything from polyester to plumbing pipes to household cleaning products. Manufacturers claim that petrochemicals are cheaper and more effective than their plant-based counterparts, but they also have detrimental effects on your health. Petrochemical solvents like benzene and formaldehyde emit harmful volatile organic compounds (VOCs) that trigger asthma and other respiratory problems, can mimic hormones in your body, and can cause liver damage. In extreme cases, petrochemicals can cause cancer. Alkylphenol ethoxylates (APEs), petroleum-derived surfactants used in detergents, can mimic the hormone estrogen and have caused breast cancer cells to multiply in test tubes. APEs don't biodegrade and eventually end up in waterways, where they're absorbed by fish and can impact the survival of fish embryos. Plus, petroleum is a nonrenewable resource that increases our dependence on foreign oil and contributes to global warming.

DISHWASHING LIQUIDS Most conventional dishwashing detergents and liquids are petroleum-based, which means that their manufacture has contributed to the depletion of this nonrenewable resource. Powdered detergents for use in automatic dishwashers can contain phosphates, which overnutrify rivers and streams, causing excessive algae growth that deprives fish of oxygen. Those made with chlorine can release steamy chlorine fumes into the air when the dishwasher is opened at the end of the wash cycle.

Colored dish detergents get their bright orange, yellow, and green hue from dyes, which can be contaminated with heavy metals such as arsenic and lead, and may penetrate the skin during washing and leave impurities on

dishes. To avoid dyes, choose detergents that are clear, not colored. While it can be difficult to find products that are entirely free of petrochemicals, look for those that contain plant oils instead.

GREEN DICTIONARY

PETROCHEMICALS

Petrochemicals are the many chemical products derived from petroleum and natural gas. They are made when petroleum is broken down and its building blocks are combined with other chemicals.

LAUNDRY SUPPLIES They may smell like a breeze of fresh air, wildflowers, or a mountain stream, but there's nothing safe or natural about many commercial laundry detergents and other supplies. Manufacturers often use decidedly unnatural ingredients, like nonrenewable petroleum, synthetic fragrances, and chemical whiteners that can pollute your laundry room and the rest of your home. Fragrances added to many laundry detergents and fabric softeners may cause respiratory irritation, headache, sneezing, and watery eyes in sensitive people or those with allergies and asthma. Other chemicals they contain are even more threatening: They may be hormone disruptors, or they may contribute to poisoning, neurological problems, and cancer.

Our environment takes a hit from laundry supplies, too. Detergents, bleaches, and fabric softeners go down the drain and can enter the groundwater, seeping into drinking water supplies. Laundry also eats up a lot of energy, which in turn produces greenhouse gas emissions. And the plastic bottles used to contain laundry detergents and other products contribute to the large quantities of solid waste that must be sent to a landfill, incinerated, or recycled.

DETERGENTS AND SOAPS Laundry detergents aren't just soap. In fact, they contain a number of chemical ingredients that can pose varying amounts of risk to people and to the environment. Phosphates have been phased out, due to their damaging environmental impact. Most commercial laundry detergents are still far from benign, however. Many contain nonylphenol ethoxylates (NPEs)—chemicals surfactants, which means that they make surfaces more susceptible to water, allowing cleaners to easily penetrate stains and wash them away. These surfactants are derived from petroleum, a nonrenewable resource, which increases our dependence on foreign oil. They break down in the environment into nonyl-phenol, which harms the reproductive abilities and survival of fish.

Used instead of or along with NPEs, linear alkylbenzene sulfonate (LAS) isn't much better. It's another surfactant used in laundry powders and liquids and is often listed among ingredients as an "anionic surfactant." LAS has been found to causes contact dermatitis, respiratory irritation and, if ingested, nausea, vomiting, and diarrhea. It can also be corrosive to the eyes. Like phosphates, LAS can deprive water of oxygen, disrupt the reproductive abilities of fish, and kill aquatic organisms.

Some laundry detergents contain alcohol ethoxylates in place of LAS, NPEs, and other APE surfactants. Although they are derived from plant and vegetable oils and are readily biodegradable, alcohol ethoxylates are created by a process called ethoxylation that produces as a by-product the probable human carcinogen 1,4-dioxane, which can penetrate skin. Present in very small amounts in the final product, dioxane may be a human carcinogen. Detergent manufacturers have yet to find a perfectly healthy replacement for LAS, NPEs, and other surfactants.

THE FACTS

The kitchen sink is one of the germiest places in the home, according to researchers at the University of Arizona. It typically contains more bacteria than the bathroom floor or even the toilet seat.

Surfactants aren't the only concern regarding laundry detergents. Petroleum-based synthetic dyes, fragrances, and other chemicals are often added to detergents. Synthetic fragrances may contain hormone-disrupting phthalates, which prevent the scent from dissipating but also trigger asthma and other respiratory problems and may damage the lungs, liver, and kidneys. Fragrances can also cling to fabrics for weeks after washing and may cause stuffy nose, sneezing, headache, and other allergic symptoms.

It is possible to have clean clothes *and* protect your health and that of the environment. First, look at labels. If laundry product labels don't list specific ingredients, watch for words such as "Danger," "Warning," or "Caution" on labels: They provide some indication of a product's toxicity. Don't be fooled by claims like "Nontoxic," "Hypo-allergenic," or "Natural." These claims aren't verified by third parties and are therefore meaningless. A label that says "Biodegradable" is meaningful only if a time period is provided.

To reduce packaging waste, buy the largest size available. Select products in bottles made with at least some recycled plastic or in cardboard boxes made with 100 percent recycled content. And choose concentrated formulas, which require less packaging and fuel for shipping.

When purchasing laundry detergents, avoid harsh fragrances, choosing those that are labeled "Fragrance-Free." Also look for detergents that are vegetable-based (corn, palm kernel, or coconut oil), rather than petroleum-based. If you're using detergent made with citrus oil, take care: The scent of such products can be irritating to allergic or sensitive people, so sniff-test a small amount (from a safe few feet away) before using it. And pass up antibacterial detergents. A Columbia University study of 238

Manhattan households, published in 2004, found virtually no difference in the rate of viral infectious disease symptoms (such as runny nose, cough, sore throat, and fever) in homes using antibacterial products—including laundry detergent—and those that did not.

If you're feeling truly industrious, try making your own laundry detergent: Combine either liquid castile soap or plain soap flakes with either washing soda to cut grease (it is caustic, so always wear gloves when handling) or borax to remove stains (keep away from pets and children, as it can cause vomiting if ingested, and don't use it if you are pregnant).

ECO-TIP: HAND WASH OR DISHWASHER?

You believe that washing dishes by hand is more effective and easier on the environment, but your spouse swears by the automatic dishwasher. Who's right? The jury's still out, although one European study found that dishwashers use only about half of the energy, one-sixth of the water, and less soap than does a human washing an identical set of dirty dishes by hand. Automatic dishwashing machines also got dishes cleaner. On the other hand, the top-quality German dishwashers used in this study were more energy-efficient than the average American model, and the human dishwashers were not advised to be as sparing of resources as possible—just to get the dishes clean.

- ✓ **Instead of prerinsing dishes under a running faucet, scrape food into the garbage or rinse the dishes in a pan of water in the sink. Prerinsing adds an extra 20 gallons per load on average, canceling out any water-saving efforts you've achieved with your dishwasher. You can save energy by air-drying or hand-drying dishes rather than using the washer's drying function. And, of course, only run the dishwasher when it's full.**
- ✓ **If you're in the market for a new dishwasher, choose an Energy Star-rated model. They do cost more, but highly efficient models can reduce total water use by one-third, which translates to an annual savings of $30. They also use 40 percent less energy.**

BETTER WAYS TO BLEACH It may get your whites whiter, but bleach containing chlorine (sodium hypochlorite) hardly gets a clean bill of health. Chlorine bleach is highly caustic and may cause skin irritation and redness. Its fumes can irritate eyes, nose, and airways. It can be fatal if swallowed. In 2005, chlorine-based bleaches caused 19,581 poisonings in children under six in the U.S., reports the American Association of Poison Control Centers.

Chlorine can also react with other cleaners to form toxic gases. Mixed with cleaners containing ammonia, chlorinated cleaning products form chloramine gases; mixed with acids, such as in some toilet bowl cleaners, chlorinated products can form toxic chlorine gas: Both can cause respiratory damage. When released to waterways, chlorine bleach can create organochlorines, suspected to be carcinogens; reproductive, neurological, and immune system toxins; and the cause of developmental disorders. Another bleach commonly used in detergents is sodium perborate, which is a skin, eye, and respiratory irritant. Ingestion of products containing sodium perborate can result in vomiting, nausea, and diarrhea.

Natural and safe whitening is as close as your kitchen cabinet, thank goodness. To boost your detergent's cleaning power and remove odors, add one-half cup of baking soda or washing soda—two related minerals—to your wash. (Wear gloves when handling washing soda; it can irritate skin.) Remove stubborn stains by soaking fabrics in water mixed with borax, lemon juice, hydrogen peroxide, or white vinegar. When choosing store-bought whiteners, look for products labeled "non-chlorine bleach." These bleach alternatives are made with hydrogen peroxide or sodium percarbonate, which breaks down into oxygen, water, and soda ash.

GENTLER FABRIC SOFTENERS They can make laundry feel soft and smell nice, but most commercial fabric softeners also use harsh chemicals, and can emit, among others, the neurotoxins isopropylbenzene and trimethyl benzene, styrene (a possible carcinogen), the respiratory irritants phenol and xylene, and thymol, which can cause abdominal distress. Chemicals known as phthalates, found to harm hormonal systems and reproductive organs in animals, are used in fragrance formulas to make the

scent last longer. But fragrance residues on clothes can cause skin irritation and provoke allergies. Furthermore, fabric softeners can build up on clothing, making the fabric appear dull. They also reduce the ability of towels to absorb moisture.

Try making your own fabric softener at home with baking soda or white vinegar: Add one-quarter cup of baking soda or white vinegar, which will soften clothes and eliminate static cling. If you prefer to purchase fabric softener, look for vegetable-based, essential oil-scented alternatives.

Dryer sheets may be treated with the same harmful chemicals as those in liquid fabric softeners. They are also made from synthetic, petroleum-based chemicals that don't biodegrade in landfills. Some companies have introduced reusable products, but don't be fooled. Dryer balls are made from polyvinyl chloride (PVC or vinyl), which releases carcinogenic dioxin during production and may release hormone-disrupting phthalates.

You can eliminate static cling in the dryer by drying natural-fiber clothes and synthetic-material clothes separately, or add one-quarter cup of white vinegar to the wash cycle. Even better, dry synthetic fabrics on a clothesline for all-natural anti-cling.

IRONS, IRONING BOARDS, AND BASKETS It's something most of us probably never consider, but ironing can be a substantial drain on energy. Irons can consume up to 1,800 watts of energy. And that's not the only concern: Irons and ironing-board covers may be treated with perfluorooctanoic acid (PFOA), which is used to prevent sticking and stains. Also used on clothes that claim to be stain- and wrinkle-repellent, PFOA is a persistent chemical that has been detected in the blood of virtually all Americans. It was found in 2004 to cause cancer in lab animals. The one U.S. manufacturer of PFOA has disputed those findings—and agreed to stop making the chemical by 2015.

Line-drying clothes, drying them with cold air, or removing them promptly from the dryer will minimize wrinkling. When transporting and storing laundry, look for nonsynthetic, petroleum-free baskets and hampers.

Home Fragrances

They may smell good, but many commercial air fresheners, deodorizing sprays, scented candles, and potpourri products are adding more than aromas to your home.

FRESHEN UP Fragrance products often contain alcohols, aldehydes (like formaldehyde, a common indoor air pollutant and known carcinogen), and aromatic hydrocarbons, which can irritate the eyes and respiratory system. Fragrances can also release hormone-disrupting chemicals known as phthalates, as well as ethyl alcohol, limonene, and camphor, which are irritants. Paradichlorobenzene (also used in mothballs) is a known allergen that has caused neurological and kidney damage and may be a carcinogen.

The real key to a great-smelling home lies in removing the root cause of offensive odors, rather than merely disguising them. Freshen the air by ventilating your home: Open windows and doors for a short period and use fans if necessary. To remove unpleasant cooking odors, place a few partially filled dishes of vinegar around the kitchen. Baking soda is also good for removing odors, as is borax. To inhibit mold and bacteria growth that can cause odors, sprinkle one-half cup of borax in the bottom of garbage and diaper pails—but remember to keep pets and children away from borax, and don't use it if you are pregnant.

AEROSOL SPRAYS Aerosol spray air fresheners may be the worst of the bunch. They produce tiny droplets that are easily inhaled and absorbed into the body, and their propellants, usually butane and propane, are flammable and toxic to nerves at high levels. Aerosol air fresheners may also be linked to other health effects. In a September 1999 study in *New Scientist*, researchers at Bristol University recommended caution in using aerosols and air fresheners after finding that they might be making pregnant women and children sick. In their survey of 14,000 pregnant women, they found that women who used aerosols and air fresheners suffered from 25 percent more headaches and 19 percent more postnatal depression, and infants under six months in these homes had 30 percent more ear infections and a 22 percent higher incidence of diarrhea. Another worry is that small children might be tempted to taste air fresheners that smell like fruit or candy. If you like spray scents, look for essential oil mists instead.

BURNING SCENTS Candles and incense also pose problems. Their smoke contains fine particulate matter, which can trigger allergies and asthma. And researchers have found high levels of polycyclic aromatic hydrocarbons (PAHs)—carcinogenic by-products of combustion that have been linked to lower birth weights in babies of exposed mothers—in temples and churches where incense is burned frequently. Instead of traditional paraffin candles, look for soy or beeswax candles scented with essential oils. Avoid incense as much as you can.

ECO-TIP: NATURAL SCENTS

Try these all-natural solutions for home fragrance.

- ✓ **Boil cinnamon and cloves in a pan of water to add a delicious aroma to your home.**
- ✓ **Wooden cedar blocks and sachets of natural dried flowers or herbs also add fragrance.**
- ✓ **Try pure essential oils, which are distilled from flowers (lavender, jasmine), woods (sandalwood, cedar), leaves (basil, eucalyptus), and resins (frankincense, myrrh).**
- ✓ **Use essential oils with caution, since they are highly concentrated, flammable, and can exacerbate allergies or asthma.**

Wiping Up

Whether you're using them to wipe up a spill or wipe your child's nose, paper products are hard to avoid. But they're also a drain on the environment. Investigate just what goes into creating that paper towel in your hand, and the ecological costs become clear.

Nearly half of the trees cut in North America are made into paper. And wood pulp and virgin paper (nonrecycled) products are increasingly sourced from other parts of the world, such as South America and China. The manufacture of paper products from virgin timber results in deforestation, which destroys wildlife habitats and damages ecosystems by increasing erosion, silting, and flooding. Widespread tropical deforestation also has damaging effects on climate, altering rainfall patterns and increasing the release of carbon to the atmosphere. Even when trees are replanted or harvested from tree plantations, the effect is to replace native forests, which support a variety of species, with single-species "tree farms" that have little value as habitat for native plants and animals. Processing paper from virgin trees also sucks up energy. In 2000, the pulp and paper industry contributed an estimated 9 percent of total manufacturing carbon emissions in the United States. And much of that paper just ends up in landfills: In 2006 alone, the U.S. produced 251 million tons of municipal solid waste—over a third of which was paper.

Paper processing also consumes resources and creates pollution. To make paper, wood is ground, pressure-cooked, and dried before being treated with whitening agents. The process is energy-intensive and releases wastewater effluent containing pollutants as well as creating a by-product called black liquor. To avoid all the ills of virgin paper products, try these greener solutions.

RAG TIME The most environmentally friendly choice for your kitchen is to eschew paper products in favor of cloth, which can be washed and reused over and over. If you're in the market for new kitchen towels, dish towels, or napkins, consider those made from organic cotton, hemp, or linen.

THE FACTS

The average American uses an estimated 50 pounds of tissue paper (such as toilet paper, paper towels, and facial tissue) a year. Each American also uses about seven trees' worth of wood and paper products every year.

BUY RECYCLED Purchasing recycled paper products also goes a long way toward preserving the Earth's forests. They're increasingly easy to find—just take a look at the label. First, choose paper products that have the highest post–consumer waste (PCW) content. The percentage of PCW in a recycled product refers to the amount of pulp derived from paper that was used by consumers and then recycled, which saves trees and promotes the use of recycled paper.

Also opt for products that are labeled "Processed Chlorine Free" (PCF). This means that no additional chlorine or chlorine derivatives have been used to bleach the final recycled product. "Elemental Chlorine Free" (ECF) may also appear on labels of recycled products, meaning that a chlorine derivative has been used to bleach the paper instead of chlorine gas itself. Paper processed in this way produces wastewater with virtually no dioxins or bioaccumulating toxins.

Take Action

- ✓ Read labels on all cleaning products; stop using any with toxic ingedients.
- ✓ Use natural ingredients, such as vinegar, baking soda, and lemons, to make your own household cleaners whenever possible.
- ✓ Use fragrance-free, vegetable-based laundry detergents.
- ✓ Line-dry your laundry.
- ✓ Avoid brightly colored dish detergents.
- ✓ Avoid artificial home fragrances; eliminate odors by addressing the root cause of the problem.
- ✓ Use washable cloth rags or buy recycled paper towels and other paper products.

Down the Drain

The soft sound of the flush assures us that our wastes are whisked safely and sanitarily away from our homes. Where does that water—and our waste—go?

The reassuring answer: the wastewater treatment plant, where soiled water is transformed into fairly clean effluent and discharged into streams or other water bodies. At the plant, the water is treated in three stages: 1) primary removal of easily collected filth and large objects, 2) secondary treatment with beneficial bacteria, and 3) tertiary removal of disease-causing bacteria, nutrients that promote harmful algal blooms, and toxins.

In most homes and apartment buildings, the toilets, sinks, showers, and water-using appliances such as dishwashers and washing machines drain into a single pipe that exits the building and shunts wastewater into a common sewer pipe. The sewer pipe joins with larger pipes under the streets of the town or suburb, leading to the water treatment facility.

At the plant, the sewage flows through coarse screens that remove debris. The wastewater also may run through a channel designed to allow sand, coffee grinds, and other grit to fall to settle out for removal. Some plants also shunt the water through a series of large primary sedimentation tanks that allow heavy organic matter to sink to the bottom and light materials like oil and grease to rise to the top for removal by giant mechanical rakes.

After the large, easily collected items have been removed, the water shuttles into the heart of the plant for the secondary treatment. Although there are many different plant designs, this step harnesses the bacterial appetite for fecal matter and other organic refuse and uses the bacteria to break down material in the water being treated.

Bacteria and protozoa love to consume carbon-rich materials such as sugars and fats. These waste-eating bacteria live their lives either stuck to sludgy particles in suspended growth systems or on large filters in fixed film systems. The filter may move through the water in some fashion, such as on a rotating disk in the center of the tank. As the bacteria and protozoa consume organic materials, they bind them into clumps of solids called flocs.

Bacteria thrive on organic matter, but they also need oxygen. Giant propellers on the surface of the tank scoop air and drag it underwater to supply aeration to the bacteria. As the bubbles course toward the surface, they disrupt the sewage and cause dirt and other particles to settle to the bottom. The streaming bubbles also facilitate the escape of dissolved gases that form from the decomposition of rotting organic matter. One of these gases, hydrogen sulfide, gives the treatment plant its characteristic rotten-egg smell.

After the aeration tank, the flocculent water flows into a secondary sedimentation tank. Here, the clumpy organic particles sink down to the bottom, where they are periodically siphoned off and sent to a digester. Over a period of one month, the solids break down in the airless, heated digesting vat. Bacteria in the vat consume the organic matter, shrinking the amount of refuse and reducing odors. The heat kills off disease-causing organisms. Slowly but surely waste material, even at the microscopic level, is removed from the water.

In some communities, the water next undergoes tertiary treatment, a final cleansing step needed if it will be discharged into environmentally sensitive areas. In this stage the water may flow through a sand filter, which removes bacteria and odor and reduces the amount of iron and other minerals in the water. An activated carbon filter may be employed to remove toxins. Phosphorus and nitrogen, two nutrients that can spur harmful aquatic algal blooms, can be removed with a combination of bacterial and chemical treatment. Additionally, the water may be treated with chlorine, ozonation, or ultraviolet light to kill any remaining harmful microorganisms. If treated with chlorine, the water may then be dechlorinated to protect against toxicity to fish and aquatic species. Finally, the treated water flows into a river or the ocean.

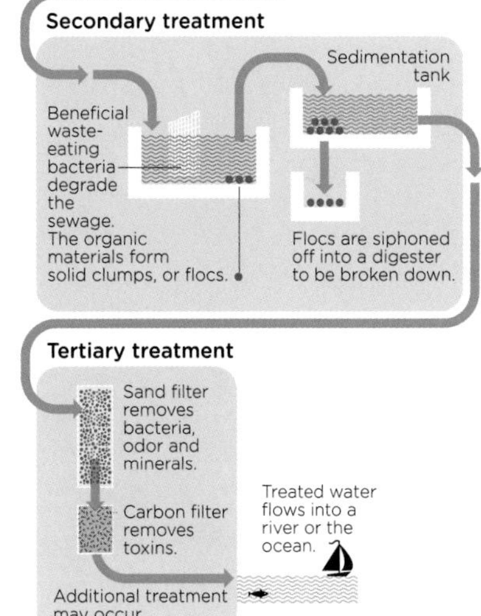

WASTEWATER TREATMENT Water flows down the drain, out through the pipes, and into a municipal water treatment system before being released back into the environment.

POWER DOWN

Appliances & Electronics

CALL IT THE DIGITAL AGE, THE ELECTRONIC AGE, THE AGE OF convenience. These days, there's hardly a single home or public space where you won't find some sort of electronic device or electrical appliance—refrigerators to chill our food, machines to clean our dishes and clothes, air conditioners to provide respite from the summer heat. While these conveniences do well to keep us productive, comfortable, and entertained, we rarely consider how they impact our environment and our health.

The U.S. Department of Energy's International Energy Outlook predicts that worldwide electricity use will increase by 50 percent between 2005 and 2030. To keep our homes, businesses, and the public infrastructure whirring along, power plants burn large amounts of fossil fuels, such as coal and crude oil. Coal plants now produce an estimated 57 percent of U.S. electricity and, in the process, emit ghastly amounts of greenhouse gases, including the most notorious one of all, carbon dioxide. If greenhouse gases continue to deplete our planet's protective ozone layer and global temperatures continue to rise, global warming could mean the loss of our polar ice caps and rising sea levels, with devastating climatic and biological consequences.

Contrary to popular belief, crowded freeways are not the main source of CO_2 emissions; in fact, it's the generation of electricity to power our homes and industry. The average American household produces 9,900 pounds of carbon dioxide a year, which means that the energy we use in our homes is responsible for more greenhouse emissions than running our daily errands.

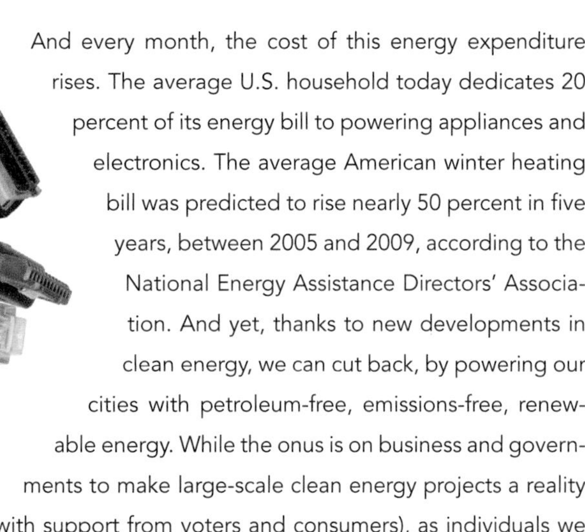

And every month, the cost of this energy expenditure rises. The average U.S. household today dedicates 20 percent of its energy bill to powering appliances and electronics. The average American winter heating bill was predicted to rise nearly 50 percent in five years, between 2005 and 2009, according to the National Energy Assistance Directors' Association. And yet, thanks to new developments in clean energy, we can cut back, by powering our cities with petroleum-free, emissions-free, renewable energy. While the onus is on business and governments to make large-scale clean energy projects a reality (with support from voters and consumers), as individuals we can help by reducing our power burden.

One way is to buy green power from your local utility company, an increasingly viable option. Consumers can designate a certain amount of their electricity bill to green power, and the utility company will either purchase or produce green power to fuel their homes or to supply the national energy grid. The Department of Energy's Green Power Network can help you determine if you have a green power program in your area, and offers tips on supporting clean energy projects nationwide.

Not sure how much power you're using, or how much is too much? Perform an energy audit on your home. It will detect which appliances are costly for you and the planet, and help you prioritize which appliances to upgrade or replace. Some utility companies offer free audits; for a do-it-yourself solution, the Alliance to Save Energy offers a free online checkup to follow on your own. By answering questions related to your home and energy usage, you can instantly find out the savings—both financial and environmental—of switching to more energy-efficient appliances and electronics.

Ultimately, successfully reducing your family's impact requires a four-pronged approach: finding ways to reduce power loss through appliances you're not using, eliminating the use of appliances you can do without, gradually replacing old electronics with more energy-efficient ones, and choosing models made with less resource-intensive materials and fewer polluting chemicals. Combined with the purchase of greener power from your utility company, these steps add up to a significantly greener existence.

ECO-TIP: GREEN POWER CHOICES

Depending on where you live, your power provider may offer certain options for buying green power. Some offer green pricing, a program by which consumers pay a premium but are assured that a larger proportion of their power comes from renewable resources. Some consumers can actually switch to green power suppliers that use wind, solar panel arrays, hydropower, or other technologies for generation. Renewable energy certificates (RECs; also called green tags) are occasionally available, allowing consumers to purchase a specific amount of renewable energy to be added to the national energy grid, even when green power isn't available locally. The Green Power Network's website lists REC marketers, most of which are certified by the independent Green-e certification program.

Air Conditioners

As the temperatures start to rise outside, air conditioners start pumping inside. If your house isn't designed to cool down the rooms naturally, it's likely that you rely on the comforts of an air-conditioning system.

Most household air conditioners (both room and central AC units) use cooling agents, or refrigerants—chemicals that easily convert from cool, low-pressure gases to hot, high-pressure gases, then to liquids, and back to cool gases. As this heat transfer process takes place inside an air conditioner, air that circulates through the unit is cooled, producing those enjoyably chilly drafts we savor come late August. Unfortunately, the environmental effects of those refrigerants are far less pleasant. Though they're less common now than they once were, chlorofluorocarbons (CFCs) are the most troublesome air-conditioning chemicals used for home cooling; in 1930, DuPont began producing CFCs under the name Freon, and for many years the inexpensive and versatile chemical was considered the gold standard. (CFCs are used in other substances as well, including aerosol propellants and cleaning solvents.) Eventually, however, the use of CFCs was linked to an increase in air pollution and the depletion of Earth's ozone layer—a troubling realization, considering the atmospheric ozone layer protects our bodies from potentially cancer-causing ultraviolet rays. Depletion of the ozone layer also damages agricultural crops, kills marine organisms, and worsens smog. Though scientists had suspected CFC- and emissions-related changes in atmospheric ozone in the late 1970s, it wasn't until a team led by British researcher Joseph Farman discovered an ozone hole over the Antarctic in 1985 that the effects of human activities on ozone became a widespread concern. Farman's team recorded a 40 percent ozone loss over the South Pole, and his data began showing ozone depletion as early as 1977.

What does that mean for the average consumer? According to the UN Environment Programme, losing just 10 percent of global ozone could result in enough additional radiation to cause 300,000 additional cases of squamous cell cancer and basal cell cancer, and up to 9,000 additional cases of melanoma worldwide each year. Depending on the type, CFCs can linger in the air for decades, and are a major contributor to smog and ozone depletion. Fortunately, the U.S. enacted a phaseout of CFC use with the Clean Air Act amendments of 1990, and after 1996 no longer allowed the use of these ozone-depleting refrigerants. Hydrochlorofluorocarbons (HCFCs) are now used in most systems, which deplete 95 percent less ozone than the once common CFCs. But they're not perfect, and a booming demand for air-conditioning—especially in hot climates such as India and China, where CFCs banned in the U.S. are still allowed—nearly negates the positive effect of switching over from CFCs to the less harmful HCFCs. By 2030 the U.S. will no longer produce or import any HCFCs, and manufacturers must find an ozone-safe alternative to use in air conditioner systems. In the meantime, follow these guidelines to get the most out of your AC with the fewest environmental consequences.

ROOM OR CENTRAL AIR? If you're set on having an AC but aren't able to install a central cooling system, an inexpensive solution is to install a room air conditioner. These units usually sit in windows, but some are installed in the wall, with a vent to the outside of the home. Others are portable floor models. The room air conditioner, like a central system, contains a heat transfer system consisting of compressor and condensing and evaporating coils, as well as

ASK THE EDITORS

Q How does electricity use affect carbon emissions?

A These days, it's not uncommon to hear appliance and electronics manufacturers talk about how much more or less carbon you'll generate by using certain products, or how large a company's (or individual's) "carbon footprint" is. This is understandably confusing for consumers, since it's not our TVs and dishwashers themselves that emit carbon dioxide into the atmosphere. Rather, the strategy is used to illustrate how much power a person or device consumes, and how much carbon dioxide gas is released into the atmosphere as a side effect of generating that power.

How are these numbers calculated? That can vary according to where you live and who provides your energy, since the amount of carbon dioxide released depends on the type of fuel sources your energy provider uses. Power plants that burn coal, oil, petroleum, or gas emit CO_2 in the course of power generation, while hydroelectric and nuclear power plants do not (although they have other environmental problems). Energy from renewable sources, such as wind turbines and solar panels, emits no CO_2 and is the best choice.

According to the Energy Information Administration (EIA), the U.S. national average is 1.34 pounds of CO_2 per kilowatt-hour of energy consumed, but you can find the multiplier for your state at the EIA website. If you know the wattage of an appliance or electronic device, you can calculate the annual CO_2 emissions using this formula: (watts x hours used daily x 365 days)/1,000 x 1.34 pounds. Or use your state's carbon coefficient, found on the EIA website. See "Resources."

a fan. The difference is that a room air conditioner cools only a small space, while the central unit can distribute air to the entire house.

Room air conditioners can be a great, cost-effective choice if you only need to cool certain rooms at a time—the bedroom, for example. But be sure to choose a system with an Energy Efficiency Ratio (EER) of at least 10 (see "Green Dictionary: EER," opposite) and one that is just big enough to cool the size of your room. Buying a system that is too big will not be as energy-efficient. The Air Conditioner Contractors of America sells a manual to guide you through calculating the correct size, and an online search will bring up a wide selection of sizing calculators.

THE FACTS

U.S. power plants emit 140 million tons of carbon dioxide each year just to cover the energy used by home air conditioners.

There are many factors involved—number of occupants, heat-generating equipment, position of windows and doors, type of flooring, room/house size. For an easy, cost-effective solution, you can use this equation to get a general idea of how big or small your air conditioner should be: Multiply the room's square footage by 10 and add 4,000. The result will be the approximate number of British thermal units (Btu, a measure of heat) per hour necessary to cool your space.

If you have a larger space to cool down, you might want to consider a central air system. This type of unit works by passing cooled air through a blower and duct vents to distribute it throughout the entire house. Although more expensive—and complicated—to install and run than room AC units, central AC is more efficient, since it can reach more rooms at once, and because the cooled rooms aren't constantly losing heat to non-cooled rooms.

Central systems are most effective if the indoor and outdoor coils are kept clean, and if the system is not competing with heat-generating appliances such as ovens, dishwashers, and space heaters. Other measures, such as closing the blinds on the east and west sides of the house and turning off the AC when you leave your house for a long time, can also maximize efficiency. Architectural and landscape features can help economize in your use of AC: Roof overhangs, awnings, and nearby deciduous trees can reduce the sun exposure coming from the south or west and still allow low-angle sunlight to enter during the winter months. And rethink room temperature: For every degree above 78 that you set your system, you can reduce your cooling costs by 6 to 8 percent.

EVAPORATIVE COOLERS Instead of air conditioning, those who live in dry, hot climates might consider using an evaporative cooler. These "swamp coolers" cost less to install and run than an AC and require less maintenance. They function by using evaporation in the same way that human sweat cools the body. With a fan blowing the air from outside through a wet pad, the air becomes more humid and about 20 degrees cooler when entering the house. An even cooler fact is that these evaporative coolers use 75 percent less energy than AC.

If you're looking to install an evaporative cooler, you will most likely have three choices: portable, fixed-room, and whole-house. For smaller rooms or spaces, a portable unit can be transported throughout the house to cool specific areas. To cool a larger space, a fixed-room model would be more appropriate. These fit into a window or wall and can circulate cool air in an entire room. Whole-house coolers are usually set up with a network of ducts that directly and/or indirectly transport cool air throughout the house.

One drawback to evaporative coolers is that they can collect sediment and dirt in the water pad and filter during use. You may have to clear the buildup yourself whenever necessary (more often during high usage), but newer models are set up to automatically flush and drain the system. And be prepared to pay a bit more on your annual water bill, since these systems require between 3.5 and 10.5 gallons of water per hour—which makes them a less attractive choice in settings where water is at a premium. You may also find that they turn the air in your house more humid.

GREEN DICTIONARY

EER

The Energy Efficiency Ratio (EER) rates air conditioners according to how much heat is removed per hour for each watt of energy used, expressed in British thermal units (Btu) of heat per hour per watt. Today, the federal standard rating is at least 13, and Energy Star ranking requires a rating of at least 14. (See "Green Dictionary: Energy Star," page 109.) Central air conditioners use a seasonal energy efficiency ratio (SEER) as a measure of performance.

ENERGY-SAVING MOVES Looking to score major eco-points? Try not using air conditioning at all. Install an Energy Star fan instead, which burns 90 percent less electricity than AC. The most popular are ceiling, floor, and window-box fans, but if you live in a dry region, a whole-house fan would be a great choice, too. Whole-house fans are located between the attic and living spaces of your home; the fan utilizes outside air and functions in the evening through the morning. It pulls in cooler air through open windows low in the house and pushes out hotter air through attic vents, keeping your home comfortable in a more energy-efficient way than a room or central air conditioner.

There are ways to use AC carefully, so that you keep your cool but still conserve energy. If warm air is entering your home, or the cool air is leaking outside, an air conditioner will consume more energy in an attempt to keep your rooms comfortable. To prevent this from happening, check to make sure all windows and doors are kept closed and are tightly sealed with caulk and weather stripping. There may also be leaks in your system's ducts. Use duct mastic to patch up any cracks or possible spots where air is leaking from the system, and be sure to insulate ductwork that passes through any portion of your house that is not receiving air-conditioning. Also think about your thermostat setting. The higher you set it, the better for the environment (and your electricity bill). Set it at about 78 degrees and leave it there. Turning it lower in an attempt to cool your house quickly doesn't work.

Another easy step to give your AC a break is to prevent heat sources from excessively warming up the rooms. Installing home insulation, closing doors, and keeping window shades drawn where the sun shines in during the hottest parts of the day can cool down your rooms and take some pressure off a running AC. Keep windows on the southern or western side of your home shaded, either with window treatments or shade-giving trees. Finally, think about the type of lighting and appliances you use during the day. Choose energy-efficient lights and limit the amount of time you run the oven, dishwasher, or dryer during peak sun hours.

ECO-TIP: WHEN YOU'RE NOT HOME

As you rush out the door to run your daily errands, you may wonder if switching your AC to "off" will help you save energy and money. When you're not around for hours at a time, you can save energy by turning off the AC. If you're in and out of the house, though, it's best not to turn the system on and off for short periods of time throughout the day—frequently powering it up and turning it off puts too much stress on the air conditioner, and can wear the unit down over time.

Another way to save energy? Set your thermostat to cycle a regular schedule of high and low settings, depending on your needs throughout the day. You can also turn the AC to a warmer setting, or off, during peak hours when electricity costs are higher. And if you have a central air unit, close vents in rooms that do not need to be cooled.

Refrigerators

Along with air conditioners, refrigerators are one of the highest energy consumers in a home. Since the average life of a refrigerator is 14 years, the benefits and savings from an energy-efficient model are worth the switch.

Today's Energy Star–approved refrigerator consumes at least 40 percent less energy than a conventional model sold in 2001. Making the switch can reduce your energy bill up to $70 a year. Even among Energy Star models, you can compare energy usage and choose the refrigerator with the lowest kWh listing: That stands for kilowatt-hours, a standard unit of measure representing the amount of electricity consumed by the appliance in an hour.

Efficiency isn't the only matter of concern, though. To keep food cold, some refrigerators use problematic chemicals. As with air conditioners, refrigerators employ a heat transfer system in which gaseous cooling agents, or refrigerants, are converted between gaseous and liquid states, cooling the surrounding air in the process. With refrigerators, however, the refrigerants are contained within the insulated interior of the fridge and freezer compartments. Prior to 1996, CFCs like Freon were the common refrigerants used; HCFCs are often used today, although these, too, must be phased out. While we must rely on manufacturers to choose better cooling chemicals, there are measures you can take as a consumer to make your fridge a little greener, from choosing an energy-efficient model to maintaining it properly.

FINDING YOUR FIT When it's time to browse for a new unit, look for the style, size, and features that will best fit your energy saving goals. A top-mounted freezer is the most energy-efficient type (it uses 10 to 30 percent less energy than a side-by-side style), and these models usually have a lower initial cost. Reconsider the automatic icemaker and water-dispensing features; the American Council for an Energy-Efficient Economy, a watchdog nonprofit, reports that these add-ons increase refrigerators' energy use.

Be sure to purchase a refrigerator that is appropriately sized for the amount you plan on storing. If you plan on cooling only milk and eggs, opt for a smaller model, but if you're feeding a large family, one bigger model may be more efficient than numerous smaller ones.

FRIDGE DISPOSAL Once you've settled on a new, energy-efficient fridge, dispose of the old one properly. About eight million refrigerators and freezers are thrown away in the U.S. each year, and since most appliances are composed of 75 percent steel, recycling the old ones adds up to a lot of reusable metal (and a lot less landfill waste). Check with the Steel Recycling Institute for a recycling location near you. Your municipality's waste department can inform you of the standard disposal procedures in your area, and tell you whether they offer scheduled pickup or require appliances to be taken to a local recycling center. Some even offer rebates to pick up old machines.

THE FACTS

About 125 million refrigerator units are in use in the U.S. today.

Recycling ensures that your old refrigerator's steel content will be salvaged and that the cooling chemicals will be appropriately captured and recycled. Approximately four million pounds of ozone-depleting chemicals escape from appliances during disposal each year, the EPA reports.

ECO-TIP: KEEP YOUR COOL

No matter what type of refrigerator is running in your home, here are a few ways to be a wise energy consumer:

✓ Help the machine do what it does best. Maintain cleanliness of the coils by vacuuming behind and under the refrigerator. Keep the top of the unit clear of items likely to hold in heat. If it's a manual defrost machine, perform routine defrosts. Keep the door tightly sealed. (Test it by closing it on a dollar bill; the bill should be nearly impossible to remove without tearing.)

✓ Set the temperature on your fridge between 35°F and 38°F and your freezer at 0°F.

✓ Do not place your refrigerator next to heat sources (sunlight, oven, dishwasher, etc.). The hotter the surroundings, the more energy your unit will use to cool its contents down.

Air Purifiers

Suffering from allergies or asthma? Looking to clear your indoor air of toxins? Then you may have considered investing in an indoor air purifier.

Some air purifiers may help reduce biological and particulate pollutants, such as dust, pollen, and animal dander, but they don't trap unhealthy gases such as VOCs or cigarette smoke. ▸For more on VOCs, see pages 69-71. Some "ionizing" and electrostatic purifiers even emit unhealthy amounts of ozone, which could potentially cause lung damage. Here are things to consider.

INDOOR AIR POLLUTANTS Three types of microscopic pollutants in your home can take a toll on your well-being: biological, chemical, and gas/combustion by-products.

Biological particles such as dust, dust mites, mold, mildew, pollen, and animal dander are very much alive in your home. They can spring from pets, pollen (coming in not only through doors and windows but also on clothing and shoes), or, in the case of dead skin cells, even our own bodies. This organic matter collects as dust and can silently affect your health, triggering allergic reactions and respiratory problems.

Making matters worse, our lungs now have all manner of man-made air pollutants to contend with, too. Through chemicals in products brought into the home—furniture, dry-cleaned clothing, household cleaning or personal care products, for example—levels of chemical pollutants in the air can be about two to five times higher indoors than outdoors, according to the U.S. EPA. Some of the most problematic indoor air pollutants are the endocrine-disrupting compounds (EDCs), which have been found looming in vacuum dust in many U.S. homes; these compounds complicate reproductive functions, may lead to certain cancers, and can cause lasting damage to the nervous and respiratory systems. Common EDCs include phthalates, pesticides, and polybrominated diphenyl ethers (PBDEs), and many of these are also VOCs. ▸For more information on PBDEs, see page 137. Some air purifiers may reduce organic particulates and chemical pollutants in your home. Read up on the basics to consider which technology fits your needs.

FILTER TYPES High-efficiency particulate air (HEPA) filters are the most effective in trapping smaller particles (0.3 micron), and they remove 99.97 percent of these particles. HEPA filters must be replaced every few years. Employing a paperlike filter material, usually made from fiberglass, HEPA filters are pleated accordion-style in order to increase the surface area. These filters do not emit ozone and trap some indoor pollutants. They are especially effective against mold. When installed inside air ducts, the reusable or disposable filters can be used in ventilation systems, but they can also be used in stand-alone room filtration units. Less expensive filters marketed as "HEPA type" or "high efficiency" may not provide the same relief for allergy and asthma sufferers, but for the general population, these filters can be very effective and offer a good value. Often called pleated media filters, these are made by combining various fibers and metals and, like HEPAs, have a large surface area on which to trap particles.

More effective than HEPA filters at removing the tiniest particles, ultra-low penetrating air (ULPA) filters are more expensive and less commonly used. They are rated to remove particles as small as 0.12 micron from the air. They are made from glass fibers that are spun into hooks and rolled out to resemble a material similar to paper.

Two other commonly available filter types include activated carbon filters, which are based on the same technology as many water-purifying pitchers, and electrostatic filters. The first two are affordable, but they require frequent replacement, as often as once a month. Similarly, electrostatic filters, which use an electric charge to attract and trap particles, must be cleaned often, sometimes monthly as well. Also, they often don't remove gaseous pollutants from the air. Compared with the ease and effectiveness of HEPA or pleated media filters, these filter types are generally less desirable.

Finally, your search for purer inside air may also lead you to "ionic" or "ionizing" air purifiers and ozone air purifiers. Consumers may want to avoid these machines, which may not do much to clean the air and may actually increase ozone levels indoors, not a good solution. Ozone is desirable in the upper atmosphere and is often used as an effective way to disinfect water, but it can have harmful health effects at ground level, causing lung damage and aggravating asthma sufferers' symptoms. While the biggest offenders are ozone purifiers, some ionic air purifiers also produce

Q I'd like to clear the air in more than one room in my house. So what is better: Should I buy numerous air filters or invest in a whole-house air purifier?

A In general, room purifiers appear to be more effective—at least according to in-depth reviews of air filters conducted by the Consumers Union. The reason? Built-in filters in forced-air heating and cooling systems work only when the air is being blown, and indoor pollutants can build up during seasons when the system isn't used as frequently. Portable, single-room units allow you to continuously filter the air in your home, regardless of whether the heating or cooling systems are on. When choosing a room filter, avoid purchasing any ozone-producing models.

If you already have a central filter installed in your air-handling system, there are a few measures you can take to maximize its effectiveness. Start by replacing the existing filter in the air duct with a HEPA or pleated media filter. These are relatively inexpensive and easy to install. Then, remember to wash or replace the filter on a regular basis per the manufacturer's instructions, as a clogged filter can block airflow and actually worsen air conditions inside your home.

And finally, don't forget that the ultimate solution for cleaner indoor air is source control. Regular cleaning and vacuuming, as well as avoidance of toxic household chemicals, paints, and other products in your home, will reduce the number of pollutants you'll need to filter out in the first place.

ozone by adding an electric charge to the air, but to a much lesser degree. Ionic systems, which are often portable and less expensive, may be tempting, but they still have the potential to release ozone. Used incorrectly in a too-small space, they can build ozone to questionable levels.

ESTIMATING EFFICIENCY Look for the Clean Air Delivery Rate (CADR) certification rating on an air purifier to find your best fit. The Association of Home Appliance Manufacturers, a trade association, created the CADR system for stand-alone units. It is a rating system that compares how many cubic feet of air per minute will be cleansed of small particulate matter by a given air purifier at its highest setting. According to *Consumer Reports*, a worthwhile purifier will have a rating of at least 350.

To reap the greatest benefits from air purifiers, be sure to maintain a regular cleaning schedule in the house. By vacuuming, dusting, and avoiding the release of harmful gases or toxins in your home, you can reduce the amount of irritating particles, allowing you to breathe more easily during allergy season.

Vacuum Cleaners

Despite air filters, dirt and other particulate matter accumulates on floors, carpets, shelves, window sills, furniture, and drapery. We could dust, dry-mop, scrub, sweep—but most of us plug in, switch on, and vacuum.

The fact is, air purifiers just can't remove most dust and pollutants from our homes. What we mean by "deep cleaning" is getting down to these invaders, which not only are unsightly but can also be unhealthy, too.

Vacuuming, therefore, seems inevitable. Unfortunately, not all vacuums are either particularly energy-efficient or environment-friendly. Since about 18 million vacuum cleaners are purchased in the U.S. every year, choosing a more eco-conscious model is a smart move that can make a difference.

Bagless-style vacuums reduce waste, but models with bags are better for allergy sufferers whose symptoms may be triggered by the act of emptying the vacuum canister. The filtration system is an important factor to consider when selecting your appliance. There are different ways a vacuum can filter out dust, including HEPA and HEPA-type filters, ULPA filters, and even cloth bag filters. Here's a rundown of your options.

BETTER FILTRATION HEPA-filtered vacuums may be your best bet, and they're relatively easy to find. These popular air filters can capture 99.97 percent of particulate matter, and you won't have to worry about cleaning through a cloud of dust because the filter covers the back vent, preventing particles from kicking back into the air. HEPA filters are most popular for those prone to allergies and asthma. They may also reduce levels of chemical pollutants that have entered your home via furniture, clothing, cleaning and personal care products, and the like.

When buying HEPA-filtered vacuums, exercise caution. Products labeled as "HEPA-type" or "high-efficiency" may not actually contain a true HEPA filter. This distinction is especially important for consumers who suffer from allergies and asthma, because even the tiniest particles can still trigger reactions. But if your home is not occupied by anyone with these health issues, a lower efficiency filter could be a thrifty choice. If you have moderate to severe allergies or asthma, though, a HEPA may not be thorough enough. If this is the case, a ULPA filter (see page 106) may be more suitable.

You may not need to buy a new vacuum to get the benefit of HEPA filters. A few companies sell HEPA filter bags to fit older canister vacuums.

ECO-TIP: VACUUM ADVICE

Vacuums can help improve the health-friendliness of your indoor environment, but they can also be energy-sucking, waste-producing purchases. Follow these steps to increase the efficiency and life cycle of your vacuum:

- ✓ **Purchase a vacuum with a longer warranty. If your vacuum breaks down and repairs aren't covered, it won't be long before the thing ends up in a landfill. Buy a model that is protected from defects and can be repaired by the manufacturer.**
- ✓ **Repair, don't replace. If your vacuum is on the fritz, don't assume you need a new one. Call the manufacturer for parts or for recommendations about local repair shops.**
- ✓ **Keep up with maintenance. Change bags and air filters regularly, and keep vacuum tubes and brushes clear of clogs and**

obstructions. Vacuums perform more efficiently when they're clean and clear, so you won't have to vacuum as long.

- ✓ Ready to move on? Donate your old one to a charity or thrift store, which will extend the appliance's life cycle.
- ✓ Opt out of vacuuming altogether. To eliminate or reduce your need to vacuum, consider forgoing carpets in favor of tile or hardwood flooring. ▸For information on eco-friendly flooring, see pages 138-140. Choosing an alternative floor covering can also prevent excessive buildup of irritating particles such as dust and dander.

Dishwashers

At the end of a long day, who doesn't appreciate the dishwasher? But this convenience comes at a price: In the U.S., 300 million gallons of water are used each day for dishwashing.

In regions where drought is common, this excess of water usage is especially concerning. Help solve the problem by purchasing an Energy Star dishwasher, which will use only about 6 gallons each cycle—a significant improvement over older models (built before 1994), which can use up to 15 gallons of water per cycle. Read the label and make comparisons, even between Energy Star models. An energy-efficient machine can save you about $40 in utility costs each year.

THE FACTS

The U.S. EPA estimates that by 2013 at least 36 states will be facing local, regional, or statewide water shortages.

THE DISH ON EFFICIENT WASHING Ever wonder which saves more energy and water when it comes to dishes: washing by hand or using a machine? According to recent studies at the University of Bonn, Germany, newer dishwashers can be more efficient than washing by hand, provided you don't prerinse your dishes and you only run a full machine.

Relatively new dishwashers use about half as much energy and one-third of the water as washing the dishes by hand. That means that by using an Energy Star–rated machine, you can save 5,000 gallons of water each

GREEN DICTIONARY

ENERGY STAR

The Energy Star label signifies that an appliance has met rigid guidelines set by the U.S. EPA and the Department of Energy in an effort to reduce greenhouse gas emissions and save money and energy.

year. To maximize efficiency, try to select a machine that's appropriate for the number of dishes you regularly wash, and only run a cycle when the machine is full. Most of the machine's energy is expended to heat the water, so the smaller the dishwasher is, the less hot water will be required to complete a cycle.

Some circumstances still warrant washing dishes by hand — perhaps you do not own a dishwasher, or you have so few dishes and want to get them clean right away, for example. In those cases, there are practices you can follow to minimize your use of energy and water. As mentioned earlier, using two separate sinks or tubs, one for detergent washing and one for rinsing, has proven to require less water than letting it run out the tap.

ECO-TIP: DISHWASHER TRICKS

When dishes pile up, a dishwasher can be your savior after a long day. Keep in mind these tips before loading up and running the cycles:

- ✓ Skip the prerinse step in your dishwashing routine. You can save up to 20 gallons of water per load and receive the same cleaning effects just by scraping the food off the plates before you put them in the dishwasher.
- ✓ Run the wash cycle only when the machine is full.
- ✓ Let the dishes air-dry instead of using the dry cycle on the machine.

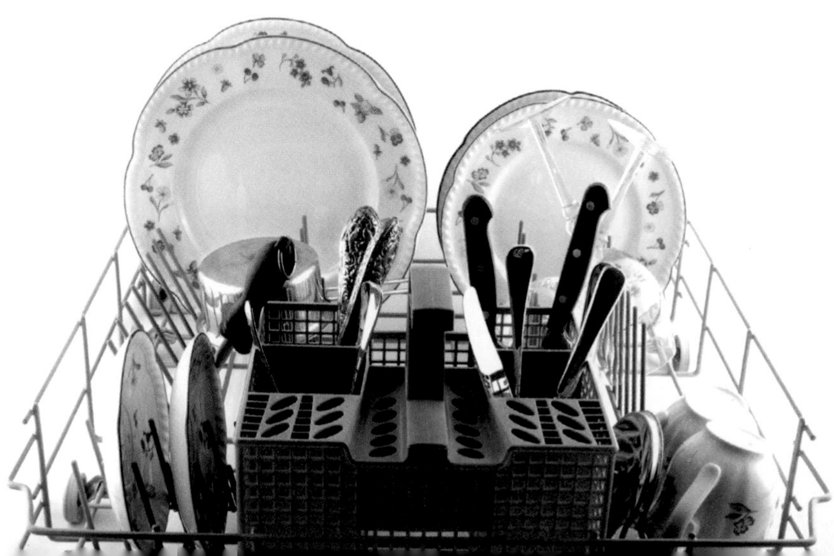

Washing Machines

Clothes washing machines are big water and energy sappers. That is why the U.S. Environmental Protection Agency, in assessing machines and their eligibility according to the Energy Star rating system, created two measures, the Water Factor and the Energy Factor.

THE FACTS

Cold-water cycles can clean your clothes while saving 100 pounds of CO_2 and about $64 on your energy bill annually.

The Water Factor (WF) measures gallons used per washing cycle per cubic foot of machine capacity. As of January 2007, Energy Star–rated machines measured 8.0 or lower. The Energy Factor correlates the energy required for mechanical action and water heating with machine capacity. This equation was modified in 2004 to include the energy required to dry the washed clothes as well. The higher the value of this Modified Energy Factor (MEF), the more efficient the machine. As of January 2007, Energy Star–rated top- or front-loading machines measured 1.72, while federal standards required 1.26. These calculations suggest all the energy use that goes into one load of laundry. If 1 out of every 100 homes in the U.S. switched to a more efficient washing machine, we could save up to 75,000 pounds of greenhouse gases a year from being released. On average, Energy Star machines use 7,000 gallons less water per year than nonrated machines.

Get the most out of the energy spent running your washer by using it only for full loads and selecting cold-water cycles. Not only does this save on energy and therefore reduce carbon emissions, it's also gentler on your clothes, prolonging their life so you don't have to keep buying new threads.

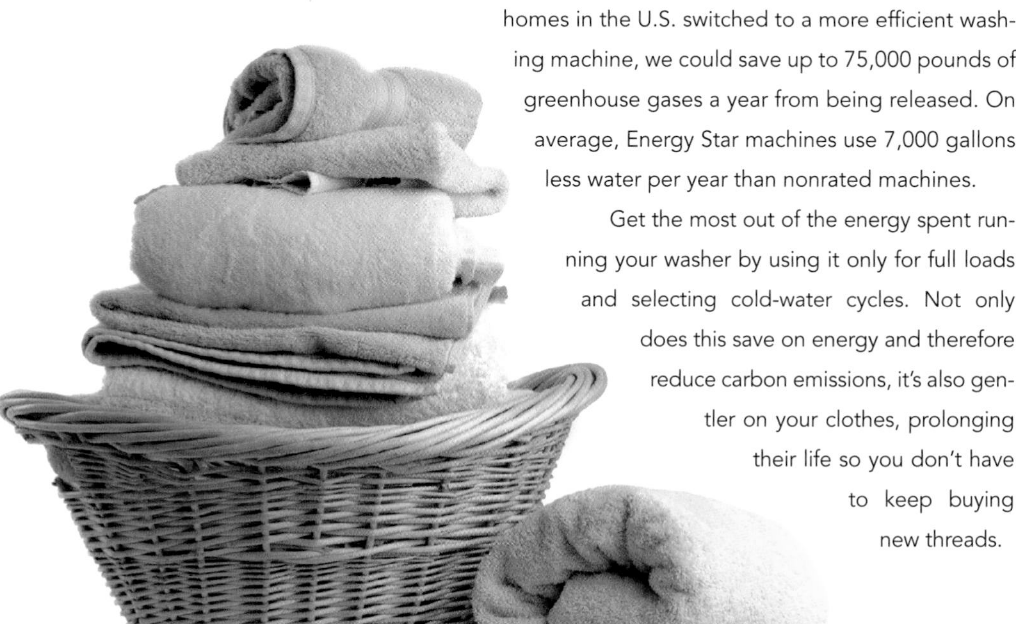

ASK THE EDITORS

Q **Which would be my better choice: a front- or top-loading washing machine?**

A In times past, the answer might have been a front-loading machine, but these days manufacturers are making efficient, environment-friendly washing machines of both designs.

The most important thing to look for when shopping for a new clothes-washing machine is MEF—Modified Energy Factor—and WF—Water Factor. These equations give you a quick, quantitative analysis of the energy efficiency of the machine. When comparing models, look for a higher MEF and a lower WF. You can learn more about these measures by going to the EPA's Energy Star website.
▸See "Green Dictionary, Energy Star," page 109.

Clothes Dryers

Drying your clothes the old-fashioned way—on a clothesline or drying rack—is the most environment-friendly option. Even hanging one load up a week can make a difference and change a few habits. Second best is to find an energy-efficient machine.

DRYER OPTIONS Investing in a more efficient model and using your machine wisely will help reduce the carbon dioxide released into the atmosphere—and help bring down your fuel bill. Unfortunately, no Energy Star–rated clothes dryers are available at present. According to the Energy Star program, though, there is not a lot of difference between dryer models in the energy they consume. If you're in the market for a new dryer, you can also look for energy-efficient features, such as a moisture sensor that will turn the machine off automatically when clothes are dry, instead of spinning them mindlessly for a pre-set amount of time. An air-dry option will save energy by tumbling your clothes in cold air while reducing wrinkles.

There are also some energy-saving moves that don't require the purchase of a new dryer. The simplest way to reduce drying time is to make sure you've spun out all of the excess water during the washing cycle; using a high-speed spin cycle can take care of that. Another simple step to save energy is to clean the machine's lint filter after each load and regularly check the exhaust to ensure that it's clear and working properly, with an unobstructed flow of exhaust air coming through. When lint builds up or your vent is clogged, the dryer has to work harder and longer in an attempt to get the moisture out of your clothes. The accumulated lint also becomes a potential fire hazard. Keep your dryer well maintained and it'll reward you with faster, safer drying cycles.

THE FACTS

Dryers might shrink your clothes, but they definitely don't shrink your ecological footprint. As power consumers, dryers rank high on the list of household appliances that cause the most impact; each year, they're responsible for 2,224 pounds of carbon dioxide emissions per U.S. household.

Kitchen Ranges

Stoves and ovens are not yet given Energy Star ratings, but there are ways to cook more efficiently, environmentally speaking. Heed the following advice while cooking, or review your options for a replacement unit.

STOVE TYPES Although there are an increasing number of options available, from professional grade to ceramic-top, most cooking appliances fall into one of two categories: gas or electric. Gas stoves tend to be fueled by natural gas or propane, piped into the appliance; you can guess what electric stoves run on. If you're presented with a choice between the two, the greener option tends to be gas, provided it has an electric ignition. (A pilot light, which was once the standard ignition system in gas stoves, is a less attractive option, since it continues to burn and consume gas at all times.)

What gives gas stoves the edge? For most houses, an electric range depends on electricity coming from the power grid. This means that cooking requires the conversion of gas and other fuels into electricity at a power

plant, with an average conversion rate of three or four units of fuel to one unit of electricity and significant losses in power transmission and distribution as well. (The case is different for houses equipped with photovoltaic cells or with other private generating capacity.)

Gas ranges, on the other hand, use fuel that is supplied directly to the home from the plant, or even from tanks near the home, so more energy is derived from the fuel that powers your cooking. Just be sure that your home is sufficiently ventilated to clear the indoor air of the gaseous pollutants—carbon monoxide, sulfur dioxide, nitrogen dioxide—that are released when a gas flame burns.

If you're leaning toward electric, consider the newer halogen or magnetic-induction stovetop heating technology instead of traditional coils. Halogen ceramic glass tops are heated by quartz-halogen lamps, while magnetic induction sends heat directly to the cookware by magnetically reacting with the metals. (Oddly enough, an induction cooktop remains cool to the touch, even when the pans are heated to very high temperatures.) Ceramic and induction stovetops do tend to be more expensive than coil ones, and induction tops are effective only with iron or steel cookware, but both stove types are better than coils in terms of energy efficiency.

OVEN OPTIONS The large conventional ovens that are standard in modern kitchens devote more energy to heating the steel and surrounding air than actually cooking your food. And when the air in your house heats up from the oven during the warmer months, it can force your air conditioner to work overtime, expending more energy. Unless you're cooking a big meal, smaller appliances are more environmentally friendly.

Electric convection ovens, for example, circulate heat throughout the oven using a fan, which allows food to cook more quickly and evenly. Food typically cooks in about 25 percent less time in a convection oven than in a conventional one. Although these are on the pricier side, the time and energy savings that result make them a worthwhile purchase.

A self-cleaning oven is also a better choice than a conventional version, not because of the cleaning capability itself, but because these types of ovens are designed to insulate heat extremely well. (However, the energy savings add up only if you do not run the high-heat cleaning cycle more than once a month.)

SMALLER SOLUTIONS Currently, there aren't a lot of options for more energy-efficient cooktops and ovens. But if you want to save energy and still put a hot meal on the table, it pays to think outside the range. Other appliances can cook and heat just as effectively and at a lower cost to you and the environment.

A pressure cooker can speed up cooking time and reduce your energy use up to 75 percent. If you're making a one-pot meal such as a soup or stew, try an energy-efficient slow cooker, such as a Crock-Pot. Just heating water for a cup of tea? Turn on the electric kettle and save about one-third of the energy compared with a conventional tea kettle. Just want to reheat that leftover piece of pizza? Plug in the toaster oven and save up to half the energy of a larger oven.

ECO-TIP: SMARTER COOKING

To keep your energy use down while whipping up a meal, follow these steps:

- ✓ **Choose the right size. On electric stoves, use the smallest pot that accommodates what you're cooking and a burner size that matches. It takes more energy to heat a large pan than it does to heat a small one.**
- ✓ **Turn down that flame. Don't turn the flame up too high on a gas stove; any flame that doesn't hit the pan is wasted. Just high enough to heat the bottom of the pan will suffice.**
- ✓ **Put a lid on it. Enclosing the heat in a stovetop pot or pan can save up to two-thirds of the energy.**
- ✓ **Use high-quality cookware. Heavyweight stainless steel, copper, cast-iron, and anodized aluminum pots and pans are known for their ability to heat evenly and thoroughly. Because they're such good heat conductors, they require less energy to heat up and keep warm. Bonus: They'll last years longer than cheap cookware, too.** **▸For more on cookware, see pages 50-54.**

Batteries & Chargers

They power our cell phones, flashlights, portable music players, and cars. How they are made and where they go after we're done with them merit our attention, especially given that billions of them are sold each year.

All batteries—from the standard alkaline type to rechargeable cell phone batteries—contain a combination of electrolytes and heavy metals. The inclusion of the toxic metals cadmium, lead, mercury, lithium, and nickel qualifies most batteries as hazardous materials, and simply tossing spent batteries (and battery-containing devices, such as cell phones and radios) into the trash can lead to dangerous health and environmental conditions. Buried in landfills, those metals—toxic to humans in large amounts—may leach into the ground and groundwater; during incineration, the heavy metals may be released into the air. There are better ways of saying goodbye to batteries.

BATTERY DISPOSAL Batteries can be classified into two basic types: wet-cell and dry-cell. The former are most often used in cars, and most are recycled by automotive retailers and mechanics. Reclaimers crush batteries into nickel-size pieces, separate the plastic to be reprocessed, and deliver the purified lead back to battery manufacturers and other industries. A typical wet-cell, lead-acid battery contains 60 to 80 percent recycled lead and plastic. Wet-cell batteries used for industrial purposes—equipment, emergency lighting, and alarm systems—are generally recycled the same way.

Dry-cell batteries include the everyday alkaline type used in personal electronics and the round button-cell type found in items such as watches. While each of these small batteries contains far less toxic material than an industrial wet-cell battery, their use and handling merit concern, since it's up to the consumer to dispose of them properly. Each person in the United States discards an average of 8 dry-cell batteries per year—that's 2.4 billion batteries.

For regular alkaline batteries, the best bet is to contact your local waste department to find out about disposal procedures in your area. These may entail taking batteries to a hazardous waste disposal facility, waiting for the next household hazardous waste pickup day, or simply placing them in a sealable plastic bag before throwing them in the garbage. Since button-cell batteries contain toxic heavy metals such as cadmium and lithium, they are often classified as hazardous waste and should not be thrown out with the garbage; you'll likely be advised to take them to a local drop-off location for proper recycling or disposal. On a positive note, manufacturers are making an effort to green up their product selections, removing some of the most hazardous components from their batteries. Since the 1980s, mercury levels in alkaline batteries have dropped by about 97 percent, but metals such as nickel, lithium, and cadmium are still used.

THE FACTS

For every rechargeable battery sold, 500 to 1,000 single-use batteries will be saved from entering the waste stream.

TAKE CHARGE A second way to battle the battery problem is to recharge. New technologies allow you to recharge traditional alkaline batteries several times before having to discard them. You can also start with rechargeable batteries and a charger specifically made for them. These still rely on heavy metals for power, but because they can be reused over and over, they're far less wasteful than single-use varieties. And luckily, many of today's most popular electronics—cell phones, personal organizers, and the like—rely on rechargeables to function. Still, eventually these batteries do lose their juice and need to be disposed of properly. For this reason, the Rechargeable Battery Recycling Corporation (RBRC), a nonprofit public service organization, targets four kinds of rechargeable batteries for recycling: nickel-cadmium, nickel metal hydride, lithium ion, and small sealed lead. Its "Charge Up to Recycle!" program offers various recycling plans for communities, retailers, businesses, and public agencies.

Of course, the battery chargers required to power up your batteries do consume electricity, so it's wise to look for the most energy-efficient system. An Energy Star-certified battery charger will use up to 35 percent less energy than a conventional model. And unplugging your chargers when they're not in use will prevent them from sucking energy unnecessarily.

Cell Phones & Mobile Devices

If you've ever lost a cell phone, you know how accustomed to constant contact we've become. But mobile phones and organizers require more electricity than we realize, and they're powered by batteries containing toxic metals. Learning how to charge and dispose of them is essential.

CHARGING UP Most cell phones and mobile communication devices come equipped with a rechargeable battery (often lithium-ion or nickel-cadmium). This type of battery needs to be plugged in frequently to retain a charge. Many people tend to leave their cell phones on the charger overnight, even though it only takes a few hours to charge most devices. Even when it's not attached to your phone, a plugged-in charger is still consuming power.

The energy drawn by an unused charger is just one factor in the so-called phantom energy drain created by many office and household electronics left on while not in use. It's best for the environment to disconnect and even unplug all such devices. In the case of your cell phone, unplug the charger as soon the phone is fully charged. Furthermore, try to charge your phone during the day instead of while you are asleep.

To save even more energy, choose an Energy Star–certified external power adapter. These chargers will save you one-third of the energy that comparable conventional models would use, and they are often smaller and lighter to transport.

THE FACTS
Electronics make up about one percent of municipal waste, according to the EPA.

OPTIONS FOR THE OBSOLETE Cell phones are manufactured using toxins and harmful chemicals, such as brominated flame retardants and heavy metals. Keeping these substances out of our landfills and our groundwater is crucial, as they have been linked to serious health effects including reproductive and neurological disorders and kidney and liver damage. Adding to the waste issue is the alarming rate at which the average person goes through phones, replacing them every 18-24 months. You don't need a new phone just because there's a new model out. Reconsider upgrading if the one you have works just fine.

When it's finally time to purchase a new model, one waste-preventing option is to hand your old phones over to be reused. Many organizations (such as the nonprofit Eco-Cell) accept donations of retired functioning phones. And when you buy a new phone, some phone service providers now accept old phones at the time of purchase. The used phones are refurbished and passed along to schools, community groups, and low-income households. (By law, all cell phones are able to call 911, even without a cell phone plan, making them a useful emergency tool for folks in need.) Just be sure to erase all personal information from the memory card before handing your phone over.

In 2005, approximately 30,000,000 cell phones were replaced or thrown away. That's a lot of steel, plastic, glass, and metals that could be recycled into new products. Search online or contact your phone manufacturer to find a reuse and recycling program near you. The U.S. EPA website offers information on recycling electronic products and lists participating partners in the "Plug-In to eCycling" program.

ECO-TIP: GREENER BILLS

Are your cell phone bills more like novellas mailed to you each month? Consider all the paper and fuel used to receive and pay your bills. You could save precious natural resources by requesting paperless online billing. Most cell phone providers and utility companies now allow you to manage your account and send payments via the Internet. By viewing and paying bills online, you reduce your consumption of paper (the use of which contributes to deforestation) and your contribution to global climate change (since fossil fuels are burned during mail delivery).

Computers

Computers are a valuable part of our modern lives, but, like many other electronics, they can also have detrimental effects on the environment, your health, and your energy bill. They eat up electricity, and most consumers find them tough to dispose of.

Some environmental challenges posed by computers arise because of the substances they contain: lead, cadmium, mercury, and brominated flame retardants. If these materials end up in landfills they can leach into our groundwater, and if they end up incinerated they can pollute the air. Lead, cadmium, and mercury are highly toxic metals that have been known to cause lasting health complications; brain damage, cancer, and kidney and liver malfunctions have been linked to frequent exposure to these toxins.

THE FACTS

In 2005, an estimated 55 million obsolete computers ended up in landfills.

The most threatening flame retardants found in computers are polybrominated diphenyl ethers (PBDEs), used in the manufacturing of circuit boards and other electronics components in order to prevent electrical fires. The highest levels have been found in the blood of people who work closely with the chemical; people using computers or living near factories or waste sites are at risk of exposure as well. Wise computer users consider which is the right computer to start with, and what is the right way to dispose of it when it reaches the end of its life cycle.

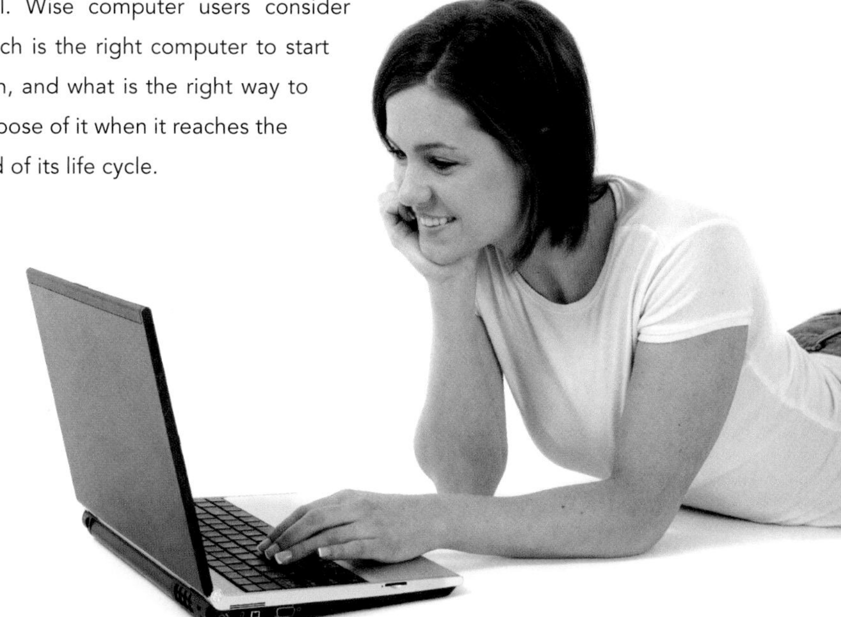

LOOK AT LABELS The Green Electronics Council's Electronic Product Environmental Assessment Tool (EPEAT) was created by IEEE, the electrical engineering trade association, to help consumers review computers' environmental standards before making a purchase. Features that earn products extra points include a high percentage of post-consumer recycled plastic, lower amounts of mercury and other heavy metals, Energy Star certification, manufacturers' takeback programs, and strong corporate environmental standards.

Do such things really matter? The Green Electronics Council evaluated the environmental effects of six months of computer users' behavior and found that by going green, in six months Americans saved 13.7 billion kilowatt-hours of electricity and prevented more than a million tons of greenhouse gases from escaping into the atmosphere. That matters.

COMPUTER DISPOSAL Usually a small fee is required to recycle your computer, but given the eventual cost of not recycling (on our health and the environment), the expense is well worth it. A quick search on the Web can help you locate the nearest participating drop location for your computer parts; your local waste management department, as well as some computer companies, may also arrange for home pickups. Or donate your old computer to a local school or charity organization. As an added benefit, your donation may qualify for tax incentives.

GREEN DICTIONARY

E-WASTE

Electronic waste is made up of electronics no longer in use—broken, obsolete, or discarded. Consider donating or recycling e-waste to avoid sending the toxic materials to a landfill or incinerator. Many local schools or nonprofit groups will accept your electronics, or you can find an e-waste recycling center on the Earth 911 website. Some manufacturers and retail stores also accept old electronics via takeback programs, so check with local companies for another way to properly let go of old items.

SLEEP OR SHUT DOWN? When you're not using your computer, you have a few power-down options for saving energy. The most efficient? Turning the computer completely off. It's true that a surge of energy is used when you turn the computer back on, but that surge is not large enough to outbalance the energy you save by leaving the computer turned off.

Only stepping away from the computer for about 20 minutes? Send your computer into its "standby" mode. If you use power-down features such as "sleep" or "standby," you'll consume 70 percent less electricity than you would if you left your computer on. Standby or sleep modes are also much more efficient than a screen saver. The bouncing geometric shape may be interesting to look at, but screen savers can actually use as much energy as an active screen.

Televisions

A full 99 percent of U.S. households own at least one television set, turned on for an average of seven hours per day, putting huge demands on power plants. Bigger screens and plasma TVs put even more pressure on the energy grid and emit even more air pollution.

THE FACTS
Plasma TVs can eat up about 849 kwh of energy per year.

STANDARD CRTS Older television sets most likely contain cathode ray tube (CRT) technology. These TVs, which tend to use the least amount of energy, bring you a picture by sending electrons to a screen coated with the chemical phosphorus; the best vantage point for their viewers is directly in front of the screen.

CNET, an online technology guide, reviewed the power consumption of various televisions and found that the CRT models averaged about 146 watts, although the actual amount of energy used depends on the size of the screen. For the biggest energy savings, use the smallest screen suitable for your needs.

FLAT SCREEN TVs A lightweight alternative to a standard CRT television would be a liquid crystal display (LCD). These TVs function by using a fluorescent backlight or bulb that either shines through an LCD panel with three color filters or bounces off of miniature mirrors and a color wheel. These sets use a bit more energy, according to CNET reviews, and average 193 watts. To save power, turn the backlight down to make the picture less bright.

GREEN DICTIONARY

CRT
Cathode ray tubes (CRTs), used in computer and television monitors, contain hazardous constituents—lead, mercury, cadmium, phosphorous, barium—that can leak if the tube breaks.

In terms of material content, an LCD screen will be the most Earth-friendly option, since it contains lower amounts of lead than a standard CRT model. While sleek new plasma TVs are becoming more popular, they consume more energy than LCDs or CRTs. Plasma screens create clear pictures by sending ionized gas to color millions of pixel ("picture element") cells. These were the least energy-efficient according to the CNET study, requiring an average of 328 watts. Plasma TVs provide the brightest picture, and therefore use the most electricity.

ECO-TIP: PULL THE PLUG

Unplug your television when it's not in use. Some models may consume more electricity in 20 hours of being off than they do in 4 hours of being on. In other words, "off" isn't really off. Most TVs remain in low-energy standby modes when turned off, so that they can instantly respond to remote controls. If you have more than one item to plug in for power, such as a TV and DVD player, use a power strip. This makes it easier to turn off all items at once when not in use, saving energy.

Pocket Players & Cameras

Like other electronics, MP3 players are manufactured with harmful substances such as mercury and lead—so keep in mind what you're buying, and make good decisions about what happens to it when you discard it.

OUT WITH THE OLD Compact disc manufacturers made millions in the U.S. every year. Now, replaced by digital audio technologies, those CDs are being discarded, and the materials in them—aluminum, polycarbonate, lacquer, dyes—can leach into the ground or pollute the air if incinerated. Just as harmful are the plastic CD cases. Most are made with polyvinyl chloride (PVC), which contains lead and is fairly hard to recycle so it isn't accepted by most city recycling programs. Only about one percent of PVC plastic is recycled in the U.S., according to the EPA. So when you trade in your CDs for an MP3 player, do so carefully.

You could donate them to a library, school, or local organization. Some music stores buy old CDs for cash or store credit. Those that are scratched can be reused for holiday ornaments or drink coasters. As a last resort, check with the National Recycling Coalition for companies that recycle or remanufacture CDs.

IN WITH THE NEW An environmentally conscientious shopper of audio electronics considers what the player is made of, how energy-efficient it is, and how one will eventually dispose of it. The European Union (EU) has started a Restriction of Hazardous Substances (RoHS) program for their electronics, to minimize the toxins and metals used in their manufacture. Some states have similar laws, but the U.S. has not yet developed a federal program, and so consumers may difficulty finding green options.

Also, be aware of your MP3 player's accessories. Many holders are made with plastics and rubber that do not degrade in a landfill. As an alternative, look for products made from recycled materials or buy used products when possible. And search for an external power adapter with the Energy Star label. By choosing a more energy-efficient model, you could save up to 30 percent in energy expenditure.

But what happens to the music player once the owner is ready to move on to a new one? Heavy metals in the devices pose a threat to the environment if not properly discarded. Check to see if your MP3 player's manufacturer offers a takeback program or incentives to recycle the product. Along with the other major electronics, obsolete MP3 players are often accepted as nonprofit donations, at thrift stores, or at electronics stores for resale.

DIGITAL DEVELOPMENT With the rise in digital camera use, the use of rolls of film is slowly fading—a good thing, given all the waste created by film canisters, packaging, the paper used to print bad shots that will be discarded, and the actual roll of film—not to mention the transportation involved in moving the film from camera to print shop and back to the photographer. In other words, digital cameras make sense for the environment.

Being able to store hundreds of pictures in one place and printing only the most important photos cuts back on much waste. What should you do with your old camera when you switch to a new model? Since cameras are manufactured using heavy metals and chemicals, these will be returned to the ground if they're sent to the landfill or cause air pollution during incineration. Check online at Earth 911 for a recycling center near you that accepts cameras. Even some disposable one-time-use cameras are recyclable. And as with other electronics, consider donating old cameras to community groups and schools.

Flashlights

No house is complete without a flashlight. These handheld tools can be lifesavers during a power outage. There are many different models available—battery-operated, rechargeable, and solar-powered.

BRIGHT IDEA Incandescent lightbulbs, which heat a filament to produce light, are being replaced by the more efficient light-emitting diodes (LEDs) in flashlights. LEDs light up when electricity is passed through a chemical compound; as the compound becomes excited, it generates light. LEDs require 90 percent less energy and produce far less heat than incandescent bulbs. They remain cool to the touch, making them a safer option. And unlike traditional incandescent bulbs, LEDs are mercury-free and can last up to 20 years. See "Lighting," pages 144-47, for more information on lightbulbs. With an LED bulb, you won't have to replace batteries as often. To reduce even more waste, though, power your flashlight with rechargeable batteries.

MODEL FLASHLIGHT Batteries contain heavy metals that can impact the Earth and human health when disposed of improperly. If you are using a flashlight that requires batteries, switch to rechargeable batteries to help cut back on toxic solid waste. See "Batteries & Chargers," pages 115-17, for more details.

Two new options may prove useful in emergencies. Solar-powered flashlights require sunlight to give them juice. Solar-powered lights will only shine for a few hours, so some models require an alkaline battery as back-up. Hand-crank flashlights are also available: The user generates power by cranking a lever on the flashlight; when the power runs low, a few more cranks will restore it. These are a great option for camping trips where extra batteries and power outlets may not be available. Whatever your reason for keeping a flashlight within reach, a model that does not run on single-use batteries will be your best bet. Although the initial cost may be higher, the savings come in the long run from less energy consumption, longer product life, and a cleaner environment.

Take Action

- ✓ Choose Energy Star products and appliances whenever possible.
- ✓ Avoid the use of an air conditioner by installing a fan.
- ✓ Purchase a refrigerator unit with a freezer on top, and keep it sufficiently full.
- ✓ Defrost your refrigeration unit on a regular basis.
- ✓ When you replace your AC or refrigerator, dispose of the hazardous chemicals properly.
- ✓ Check to make sure your air purifier is not the type that emits ozone (common offenders are ionic and electrostatic purifiers).
- ✓ If using a dishwasher, don't pre-rinse; just scrape to prepare dishes.
- ✓ Wash your clothes using cold-water cycles.
- ✓ Dry your clothes on a clothesline or drying rack.
- ✓ Choose a clothes dryer with a moisture sensor or air-dry feature.
- ✓ When possible, skip the big oven and rely on smaller cooking appliances.
- ✓ Use rechargeable batteries.
- ✓ Recycle old batteries.
- ✓ Use your cell phone as long as you can before buying a new one.
- ✓ Donate your old computer to a nonprofit.
- ✓ Turn your computer off instead of using the screen saver to conserve energy.
- ✓ Use a power strip in rooms where you have more than one item to plug in.
- ✓ Unplug appliances and electronics that are not in use.
- ✓ Dispose of e-waste properly; reuse or recycle.
- ✓ Look for an MP3 player made with fewer heavy metals and toxic materials.
- ✓ Choose a smaller television screen for bigger energy savings.
- ✓ If buying a single-use camera, choose one made of recycled materials.
- ✓ Use LED, solar-powered, or hand-cranked flashlights.

What Is Wind Power?

Modern wind turbines look like airplane propellers on poles that reach hundreds of feet into the air. Another model looks like a rapidly rotating eggbeater. Each is designed to be as efficient as possible at its job: turning wind into electricity.

Wind is an attractive source of renewable energy because it is clean, inexhaustible, and can reduce dependence on imported fuels. Wind energy currently produces more than 10,000 megawatts (MW) of electricity in the United States, enough to supply roughly 2.5 million average American homes. Eventually, industry experts predict that wind energy could supply 20 percent of U.S. energy needs.

Wind turbines convert wind energy into mechanical energy and then into electrical energy. Each wind turbine contains the rotor, consisting of the blades and shaft; an enclosure or nacelle that holds the parts of the turbine that make electricity; and electronic equipment that monitors and controls switches, valves, and motors.

The most prominent feature is the rotor. The blades turn due to the same physical laws that allow airplanes to fly: As air flows over the blade, a pocket of low-pressure air forms directly behind the blade, creating a vacuum-like force that pulls the blade toward it. This force is called lift. At the same time, the wind is pushing directly on the front of the blade, creating a weaker force called drag. The combination of lift and drag drives the blades to rotate like a propeller.

Turbine blades rotate at a speed of roughly 30 to 60 rotations per minute (rpm). For the sake of generating electricity, a series of gears in the gearbox ramps the speed up to between 1,000 and 1,800 rpm. The gearbox is one of the heaviest parts of the turbine, so an active area of research is the creation of "direct-drive" generators that can operate at lower speeds.

Inside the generator, the rotating shaft turns a copper wire inside a large magnetic steel cylinder, generating electrical current due to the property of electromagnetic induction. The electricity produced can be added to the electricity grid, stored in a battery, or used directly at a farm or rural home.

Turbines can either operate upwind (facing into the wind) or downwind (facing away from the wind). Upwind turbines require sensors and motors that detect

the wind direction and move the rotor accordingly. In downwind turbines, the wind itself blows the rotor into the optimal position. Turbines come in various sizes, with rotors ranging from about 165 feet to 300 feet in diameter. Offshore turbines can be even larger, whereas turbines for residential or farm use may have rotor diameters of roughly 30 feet.

To produce electricity, the wind speed needs to be at least 9 miles an hour for small applications, and at least 13 miles an hour for utility-scale wind power plants. Most turbines have an electronic controller that keeps the turbine operating when the wind speeds are between 8 miles an hour at a minimum and a maximum of about 55 miles an hour. Speeds greater than 55 could damage the turbine.

Wind turbines typically stand atop towers that are more than 100 feet tall, where the winds are stronger and less turbulent. Depending on the location, wind may blow intermittently or die back during certain times of the day—for example, after dusk. The timing may not coincide with peak demand times for electricity, so researchers are exploring ways to store wind energy. Batteries can be used but are expensive for large-scale storage. One idea is to use the electricity to compress air into underground storage containers. Releasing the air later would drive turbines that regenerate the electricity when it is needed.

The strongest winds are often in areas where few people live, for example, through mountain passes where it may not be efficient to make electricity due to losses during long travels through power lines. One place where large populations and high wind speeds coincide is along the coast. Offshore wind farms could generate large amounts of electricity quite close to where it will be used. Although today's wind turbines don't have the same charm as traditional windmills, many people find beauty in their sleek design and comfort in the fact that wind power won't produce air pollution to ruin the view.

WIND POWER Wind turbines transform the energy of the wind into electricity.

4

FURNITURE
FLOORING
WALLS & WINDOWS
LIGHTING
BEDS
LINENS
ACCESSORIES
SCENTS & CANDLES
HOUSEPLANTS

GREEN BY DESIGN

Environmentally Friendly Home Decor

WHETHER YOU'RE A HOMEOWNER, AN APARTMENT-DWELLER, OR a dorm room resident, chances are you've spent plenty of time—and no small amount of cash—furnishing and decorating your living space. And with good reason: There's no place on Earth that defines you more than your home.

Most interior design choices are based on factors like personal style, color, quality, and cost, and rarely does a product's environmental impact come into play. But why shouldn't it? After all, home is the place where we eat, sleep, relax, entertain, and generally spend most of our time outside of work and school. By and large, we have more contact with the items in our home than we do the great outdoors. So why would you allow them to contain harmful fumes, unsafe finishes, or hazardous materials? Just as purchasing natural, sustainable food nourishes our bodies from the inside out, inhabiting more natural, less toxic living environments supports well-being from the outside in. By choosing greener home goods, you'll be able to reduce your exposure to potentially damaging chemicals as well as lessen your impact on the planet as a whole.

So why haven't more of us gone green at home? First, there's the issue of aesthetics. For many, the expression "environment-friendly decor" conjures up images of unsightly, uncomfortable furniture, mud-colored walls, and home accents that are about as exciting as a pile of rocks. But fortunately, that paradigm is old, outdated, and ready to be recycled. These days nearly every large retailer of home goods offers myriad choices that are easier on the Earth. Better yet, "green" is a concept more and more design professionals truly understand, and a growing number of environmentally aware products and services are available to residents of almost every city and country. From mod side tables crafted from recycled magazines to indigo-dyed, natural fiber hallway rugs, today's options are extensive.

Second, many consumers assume green home goods are all costly, which couldn't be further from the truth. While there are a good number of green-oriented home furnishings stores and services that cater to the deep-pocketed, spare-no-expense crowd, there are just as many sustainable options that cost no more than your average rug, desk, or sofa. Organic cotton bed sheets—arguably the most important organic fabric purchase you can make, considering we spend a third of our lives in bed—are often available at prices comparable to conventional cotton sheets. And some budget-minded retailers have launched initiatives to lessen the environmental and health impact of their products.

THE FACTS

Around 32 million acres of natural forest are lost each year, according to the World Wildlife Fund. Once spread over half the Earth, forests now cover only a quarter of the planet's land surface. Two of the main causes? Unsustainable and illegal logging.

Many green options even result in cost savings. For hundreds (if not thousands) of dollars less than purchasing new living-room furniture, you can reupholster older sofas, chairs, and love seats using organic cotton or a natural-fiber material such as linen. And lest you think your color choices are limited, a simple Internet search will turn up a wide array of attractive organic fabric options. Other green home choices cost more to purchase but save you money over time. Take environment-friendly lighting, for example. Though new compact fluorescent light (CFL) bulb choices may require a slightly larger initial investment (in the neighborhood of a few more dollars per bulb), the resulting energy savings and the product's longer life quickly offset the difference. A CFL bulb can save $30 in electricity costs over the course of its lifetime. ▸For more information on lightbulbs, see pages 144-147.

So you're sold on green decor. Where do you begin? It's tempting, of course, to want to start with a fresh slate, especially if you're furnishing a new house or seeking a new aesthetic. But there's a strong case for taking things slowly: Throwing out still functional furniture so that you can replace it with newer stuff defies the fundamental logic of going green. As bad as it sounds to have an irresponsibly harvested, petroleum-lacquered, rapidly off-gassing wood table in your living room, sending that table to the landfill in order to

make more room for your brand-new bamboo one is hardly an improvement, environmentally speaking. Instead, follow this simple rule of thumb: Upgrade your choices only when an item is actually due to be replaced, unless you find out it's so terribly toxic or energy-inefficient that you just can't bear to have it around anymore. Follow the rules in spirit, which ultimately means finding creative, stylish ways to consume less and reuse more. When you do head to the store, let this chapter be your Earth-friendly guide.

Furniture

Heavy, durable, and easy to care for, wood is the stuff we depend on, but the journey from lush forest to furniture store can be an ecological nightmare. Unsustainable logging has contributed to the destruction of billions of acres of forest. The U.S. consumes about one-fifth of the world's wood supply.

BETTER WOOD CHOICES One simple solution to the problem is to buy only wood products certified by the Forest Stewardship Council (FSC), a nonprofit organization created in 1993 to promote responsible, sustainable forest management. The FSC accredits certifiers (such as the Rainforest Alliance's SmartWood program) whose auditors inspect forests according to environmental, social, and economic principles. Furniture and other wood products may carry the FSC label only if the manufacturer proves that the item was indeed produced with FSC-certified wood. When you buy an FSC-certified product, you know exactly what you're getting: Information on the wood's origins and a report for each certified logging operation is available to the public. Backed by groups such as the National Wildlife Federation, Greenpeace, the World Wildlife Fund, and the Sierra Club, the FSC is widely viewed as the most independent and credible global forest certification system.

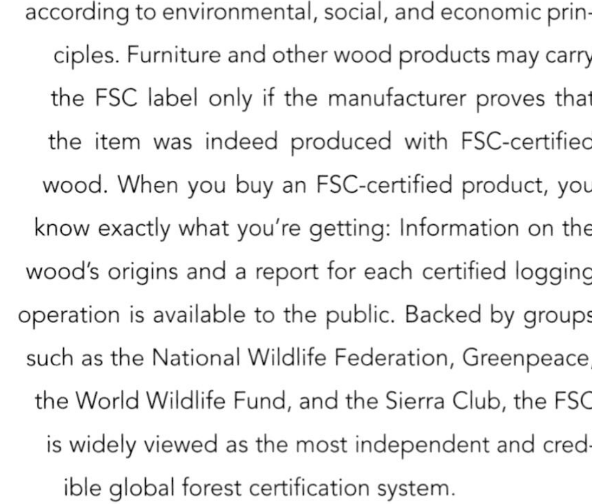

Another organization that offers certification is the Sustainable Forestry Initiative (SFI), a program first established by the American Forest & Paper Association (AF&PA), a forest industry trade group. The AF&PA created SFI to compete with the Forest Stewardship Council's certification system and to help counter the industry's bad publicity. While it has had its share of critics—in 2001, when the FSC and SFI certification systems were compared by three environmental groups, the SFI program was found to be sorely lacking—it has made strides to improve its assessment practices. In early 2007 it became a fully independent forest certification program with an advisory board that included several CEOs of nonprofit and conservation organizations, and it has since received endorsements from the Nature Conservancy and the Pacific Forest Trust. Outside the U.S., the Canadian Standards Association (CSA) and the international Programme for the Endorsement of Forest Certification (PEFC) offer green certifications based on third-party research.

THE FACTS

The U.S. Environmental Protection Agency (EPA) has found levels of about a dozen common pollutants to be two to five times higher inside homes than outside, regardless of whether the homes were located in rural or highly industrial areas.

You can also help protect forests by becoming familiar with endangered tree species. Pay a visit to the website of CITES, the Convention on International Trade in Endangered Species of Wild Fauna and Flora, to find updated listings. Species are divided into three appendixes according to the degree of protection they need. You can also opt for furniture made from "secondary" species—less well-known wood species like California oak and sweetgum, which are often harvested to make room for more popular species such as mahogany. Not only is the quality comparable to (or better than) the mainstream options, but purchasing these types of woods takes pressure off overused species and encourages more diverse forest ecosystems.

Another smart move is to choose products made with lower grades of wood. Color-streaked, knotted wood is considered less desirable, even defective, by many manufacturers, but that's largely an issue of taste and tradition. To many, these individual markings are things of beauty, both aesthetically and environmentally. Choosing lower-grade wood products takes the pressure off trees that contain a high percentage of homog-

enous, straight-grain, knot-free wood (usually those found in old-growth forests), and it creates a demand for materials that might otherwise be considered scrap.

Finally, explore the growing trend of reclaimed, recycled, or rediscovered wood furniture. Salvaged from demolished homes, ancient barns, out-of-commission railroad tracks, factories, and even garbage dumps, this approach focuses on responsible—and artful—reuse. Fans of reclaimed wood appreciate the material's history as well as its quirky, weathered look, using it for furniture as well as flooring. It's often a great idea, but it's not without its caveats.

Even if you are purchasing reclaimed wood as an alternative to newly harvested wood products, you still need to find out where and how the wood was obtained. Try to purchase furniture made from local wood instead of material that had to be shipped great distances, using fossil fuels in the process. Although many companies recover their wood from landfills or demolition sites without impacting the environment, there are some who retrieve logs from lakes and rivers, which can harm freshwater ecosystems if done incorrectly.

EARTH-FRIENDLY FINISHES Once you know what type of wood furniture you want to bring home, the next step is to consider its finish, which will both protect and enhance its beauty. Unfortunately, many finishes and furniture adhesives are made with harmful ingredients that not only pollute the environment but also contaminate the air inside your home. Due largely to their solvent content, many finishes emit formaldehyde, heavy-metal drying agents, and biocides (pesticides intended to ward off mold and fungi) in a process known as off-gassing. Many of these chemicals, called volatile organic compounds, or VOCs, are known carcinogens; others are neurotoxins. In high concentrations or with prolonged exposure, all can cause respiratory irritation, dizziness, and headaches. ▸See "Green Dictionary: Low-VOC," page 134. While off-gassing diminishes significantly over time, the chemicals can continue to seep into the air for a year or two after a finish is applied. So how can you avoid them? If you want to buy your wood furniture finished, your best bet is to contact the manufacturer directly and ask about products with low-VOC paints or stains. Better yet, consider unfinished hardwood furniture, which allows you to apply a low- or no-VOC finish of your choice. For the most natural finish of all, look for products made from linseed oil or beeswax.

THE FACTS

In homes with significant amounts of new pressed-wood products, air levels of formaldehyde gas can be greater than 0.3 part per million (ppm), says the EPA. That's ten times the amount normally found in outdoor air.

GREEN DICTIONARY

LOW-VOC

Labels identifying paints and finishes as "low-VOC" indicate that these products contain low levels of volatile organic compounds (VOCs), as defined by the U.S. EPA. VOCs are breathable gases that vaporize at room temperature. While some have no known health effects, others are highly toxic. Always choose painting and finishing products marked low-VOC.

WOOD ALTERNATIVES Of course, hardwood isn't the only furniture material. One common, more affordable alternative is pressed wood: plywood, particleboard, and MDF (medium-density fiber board). Much lower-priced furniture on the market today is constructed from this material, which consists of wood strips or particles bonded together with formaldehyde-based glues. Although far cheaper than wood, these products carry a different kind of cost: Formaldehyde becomes a gas at room temperature, and so pressed wood can release fumes, polluting your home's indoor air for years after purchase. While many pressed-wood products are covered by a plastic laminate layer that limits the release of formaldehyde, the chemical can still escape from exposed edges.

If you do choose furniture made from pressed-wood products, first contact the manufacturer and inquire about the product's formaldehyde levels and about whether it enforces any limits on the chemical. Or shop at stores that have demonstrated their concern about the issue. You can also find retailers of formaldehyde-free pressed-wood furniture through the FSC website. Once home, you can reduce emissions by letting furniture off-gas in a separate space like a garage for a few weeks before bringing it into the living space, and by coating unfinished pressed-wood surfaces with a low-VOC sealant purchased at a hardware store. And inspect your furniture thoroughly: A desk or table may look like it's hardwood, but thin wood veneers are often used to obscure pressed wood underneath.

Last thought on furniture: Don't forget to explore other Earth-friendly options! Furniture made from bamboo, increasingly available, earns kudos for sustainability and durability. You can always find furniture made from metal and glass, which won't leach any chemicals into the air. And if your style sensibility includes antique and retro furniture, check out local flea markets and online listings for pre-owned pieces. Doing so saves natural resources and benefits your family as well, since the longer a wood or pressed-wood item's been around, the less of a health risk it will pose.

UPHOLSTERY The beauty of upholstered furniture is its cushiony softness and versatile style. But sofas, love seats, padded chairs, and ottomans can contain more than plush padding. Pesticide residues, irritating dyes, unsafe fabric treatments, and potentially carcinogenic compounds come standard in many upholstered pieces. Given the amount of time most people spend lounging

ASK THE EDITORS

Q **I love the look of reclaimed wood—driftwood tables, stools made from old railroad ties, tables made from used wine barrels. But given their weight, I'm worried that shipping them cross-country isn't environmentally friendly. Should I be concerned?**

A Reclaimed furniture is becoming more prevalent in the marketplace—a good thing, since it theoretically extends the life cycle of the wood and prevents new trees from being cut down to produce new items.

That said, all furniture is fairly costly, environmentally speaking. Because of its size, it takes a great deal of energy to transport a solid wood dresser, reclaimed or not, across continents or oceans. And not all reclaimed wood is what you think; not all pieces labeled as such come from torn-down houses or pre-loved furniture. There's no regulation of the term in the furniture industry. Just as recycled paper may be made of leftover wood pulp from lumber mills, "reclaimed" wood may simply be construction scrap.

Ultimately the question is not whether reclaimed wood itself is good, but whether the item beats out your alternatives. If you're choosing between a reclaimed wood table from a salvage site 100 miles away and a conventional wood table made across the globe, then the reclaimed one wins hands down. If the reclaimed wood is coming from France and you're in California, however, you would be better off choosing an item made closer to home, using FSC-certified wood from a local forest.

around and watching prime-time TV, that adds up to a whole lot of chemical exposure. If you're in the market for new furniture, the guidelines on the following pages will help you turn up plenty of environmentally friendly options.

NATURAL FABRICS Cotton is a popular choice for covering furniture, affordable and fairly easy to care for. But cotton fields are often heavily sprayed with synthetic pesticides and fertilizers, a practice that both harms the soil and can compromise your health if you're sensitive to chemicals. Though most of the chemicals are removed during the fabric milling process, residues may remain. ▸For more on cotton, see pages 211-13. A few niche companies use organic cotton for upholstery, and you can also have older pieces reupholstered in organic cotton fabrics you've purchased in stores or online.

You can also opt for furniture upholstered with natural fabrics like wool, hemp, or linen, which typically use few (if any) pesticides in processing. Wool and linen may be the most convenient and easiest to find. Hemp furniture is rare, but an Internet search can turn up a few sources. Keep in mind, though, that a piece upholstered in chemical-free fabric may still contain chemicals in its wood frame, in the cushions, and in the dyes. Contact the manufacturer to inquire about the toxicity of these materials. When possible, look for natural fabrics that are either undyed or dyed using plant-based pigments. ▸For more on ecologically sound fabrics, see pages 216-18.

SYNTHETIC FABRICS Artificial materials such as acrylic, polyester, rayon, olefin, nylon, and microfiber are commonly used in upholstery as they are generally cheaper and more stain- and wrinkle-resistant than natural fibers. Many synthetic fibers are derived from petroleum products, however, so to avoid both carcinogenic residues and the depletion of our dwindling oil reserves, steer clear of them.

STAIN TREATMENTS When you have upholstered furniture you love, you want to keep it spotless. But before you treat it against stains, consider the cost to your health. According to the Environmental Working Group, the chemicals in stain-protecting products, perfluorochemicals (PFCs), are some of the worst chemical contaminants ever produced. Toxicity research performed in the 1990s, combined with the confirmation that these synthetic chemicals never biodegrade, led the EPA to remove one type, PFOS, from the market in 2000.

Use of a related chemical, PFOA, became highly regulated. Commerical

manufacturers of fabric protectors have largely phased out PFCs from their products, but PFOA may still be used in manufacturing. Considering the history and the science, it may be best to avoid using any sort of stain-resistant treatments altogether.

GREEN DICTIONARY

PBDEs

Polybrominated diphenyl ethers, commonly called PBDEs, are a class of chemicals used in the production of furniture, upholstery, and consumer electronics. Their chemical composition makes them slow to ignite. The consumer value of this feature is that, should a fire start in a home, objects treated with PBDEs will not burst into flame so quickly, giving residents more time to escape. Unfortunately, these chemicals may cause damage to the liver or thyroid and may hinder neurodevelopment.

INSIDE THE CUSHION You may not be able to see what's inside your couch cushions, but that's no reason to ignore their contents. The foam padding inside most upholstered furniture is often treated with a class of flame retardants called polybrominated diphenylethers, or PBDEs, which contribute to a host of human and environmental health problems.

PBDEs, which can represent up to 30 percent of a foam cushion's weight, are easily released into the air and inhaled. PBDE levels in Americans are the highest in the world, and traces have also been found in fish and aquatic birds in Europe, Asia, North America, and even the Arctic.

Why all the worry? PBDEs, chemical cousins to the banned neurotoxins PCBs, appear to have the potential to slow brain development, disrupt thyroid hormone levels, and cause liver damage. They may be carcinogenic. The European Union has banned these substances in upholstery, and several U.S. state legislatures have voted to follow suit. Want to ban PBDEs from your home? Find cushions made with untreated foam, foam treated with PBDE-free fire retardants, or all-wool stuffing, naturally fire-resistant.

LESS TOXIC LEATHER Leather looks and feels good, but extensive processing is required to make it so supple and durable, and leather tanning has historically been a polluting industry. Modern tanneries use many toxic substances, including formaldehyde, coal-tar derivatives, and cyanide-based dyes and oils. More than 95 percent of leather produced in the U.S. is chrome-tanned, as is most of the world's leather. All wastes containing chromium are considered hazardous by the EPA.

There are new, environmentally friendly ways of preparing leather on the horizon. One approach, for example, uses biological enzymes rather than chemicals to remove the hair. But these methods haven't fully caught on in the marketplace. For now, your best bet is to buy used or vintage pieces, which don't increase the demand for new materials. For more information on leather, see pages 222-23.

Flooring

Green home decor starts from the ground up—on the floor, to be exact. Compared with other design decisions, none can make as big an impact on your health as your choice of flooring.

CARPET CONCERNS Long-lasting, easy on the feet, and available in a vast array of colors and textures, wall-to-wall carpet is an ever popular option in today's homes. But it definitely has a downside: Those plush fibers that serve to cozy up your living quarters can also house many types of natural and chemical pollutants. For starters, carpets are constructed of several components: the textured pile, often made from nylon, polyester, or wool fibers; a backing, which gives the fiber its structure; and a layer of mixed-foam padding, which provides cushioning. Often these components are glued together, and the chemicals in the adhesives can release fumes into indoor air for weeks or even years after the carpet installation. Off-gassed chemicals can number in the hundreds, and often include harmful substances such as formaldehyde, toluene, and xylene. Not all carpets are toxic, but it can be difficult to tell which ones will be.

Once the carpet is in your home, it quickly begins to accumulate contaminants: soil tracked in from the outdoors, pesticides from the garden, pet dander, fungal spores, bacteria, and dust mites and their droppings. Because carpets are so thick, tightly woven, and insulating, it can be tough to remove these particles even with regular vacuuming. Adding to the "ick" factor, researchers have found an average of 67 grams of dust per square meter of carpet—far more than most people would tolerate on a tile or hardwood floor. Then, once a carpet is due to be replaced, there's the issue of waste. Carpeting adds a mind-boggling amount of mass to our landfills, and if it

contains glued-on polyurethane backings it can release chemicals as it slowly breaks down.

How can all this be avoided? In a new home, forgoing carpet altogether is smart, as hardwood and tile surfaces are far easier to clean. In older homes, check to see if there are hardwood floors hiding under your carpet, as they often can be refinished fairly easily. For more on wood flooring, see pages 307-308. If you choose to trade your old carpet for a new one, make your choice a healthy and environmentally friendly one. First, look for rugs and padding that have the Carpet and Rug Institute's Green Label Plus, which identifies products with low emissions of VOCs. (After the regular Green Label was criticized for setting arbitrary standards, the industry developed the Green Label Plus designation, signifying that the products meet or exceed California indoor environmental quality standards for low-emission products used in commercial settings.)

THE FACTS

About 1.75 million tons of carpet are thrown out each year in the U.S.—2 percent of the municipal solid waste stream by volume.

Second, opt for natural fibers such as cotton, wool, or even hemp instead of polyester or nylon. And try to avoid synthetic backings—the standard product is a matrix made of styrene-butadiene rubber—especially those that are glued on rather than sewn, because they may off-gas harmful chemicals. Greenpeace also recommends limiting the use of polyurethane, another standard backing, because it introduces many hazardous substances into the environment, including pigments, flame retardants, phosgene, isocyanates, toluene, diamines, and the ozone-depleting gases methylene chloride and chlorofluorocarbons. Backings made of jute or other natural plant fibers are less likely to off-gas *and* they're biodegradable. In lieu of foam padding, you can also look for felt or recycled-rag pads. Dyes and carpet treatments such as insecticides, pesticides, or fungicides may also off-gas.

Last, explore the trend of modular carpet tiles. Many of these are made with recycled materials and can be sent back to the manufacturer, which will reuse the tiles instead of throwing them away. You can replace stained or worn-out tiles as necessary, which creates less waste than a carpet that needs to be scrapped and replaced all at once.

ECO-TIP: FRESHER FLOORS

- ✓ Install new carpets with tacks, not glue, if possible. See if your carpet retailer has a takeback program to recycle your old carpet.
- ✓ To reduce tracked-in dirt, pesticides, and other pollutants, remove your shoes when entering the house.
- ✓ If your carpets contain synthetic components or finishes, avoid exposing them to direct sunlight or heat above 80°F, which makes them emit more fumes.
- ✓ Many carpet shampoos contain toxic, irritating solutions. Select natural carpet shampoos, and keep children away from newly cleaned carpet for several hours.
- ✓ Vacuum twice weekly, preferably with a machine that contains a HEPA filter, which traps tiny allergens.
- ✓ After steam-cleaning carpets, use a dehumidifier to speed drying and remove excess moisture (which can lead to mildew).

RETHINKING RUGS Area rugs are an excellent alternative to wall-to-wall carpeting, as they require no adhesives and can be cleaned or aired out. When you select a new rug, follow the same rules as with carpet: Choose natural fibers such as wool, cotton, jute, hemp, or sisal, and avoid products treated with chemical flame retardants or pesticides. Look for small, washable rugs that are stitched, not glued, to backing or that use low- to no-VOC glues.

There are also social concerns in the rug industry. Although efforts are under way to put an end to child labor in India, Pakistan, and Nepal, it still exists in the rug industry. To avoid inadvertently supporting this practice, seek out rugs certified by Rugmark, an organization that sends trained inspectors to randomly inspect the looms of companies that have agreed not to use child labor and partners with nongovernmental organizations to monitor rug production. Every Rugmark label has a number that can be tracked back to the loom on which it was woven.

Walls & Windows

Wall coverings and window treatments are increasingly in vogue and offer an easy way to add some drama to your interior decor.

Available in a vast array of patterns, today's wall coverings are a far cry from Grandma's flowery living-room border, and they're enjoying a resurgence in both commercial and residential spaces. The trouble is, most of today's options are also more toxic than those of the past. Long ago, wall coverings were made from natural materials—rice, papyrus, paper, leather, bamboo, linen—whereas today's products are often created from fume-emitting vinyl. The green solution? Get back to basics.

GREENER WALLPAPER Most wallpaper on the market is made with vinyl, specifically polyvinyl chloride or PVC, which is a petroleum product, thus presenting environmental concerns. In addition, soft vinyl usually contains plasticizers called phthalates, which have been shown to be detrimental to our health. For more on phthalates, see page 72. Vinyl production also releases dioxin, a known carcinogen and possible hormone disruptor, and vinyl products can contain heavy metals, such as lead and cadmium. Once it's applied, vinyl wallpaper generally off-gasses less than wall paint, but that doesn't make it safe. In the event of a house fire, incinerated vinyl can release high amounts of dioxin into the air.

Opt instead for wallpapers made the old-fashioned way: from paper, linen, bamboo, or other plant materials, and without any pre-applied adhesives. Another approach is to seek out antique and vintage wallpapers, which have historic charm as well as being environment-friendly. (Vinyl wallpaper was introduced in 1947, so papers made before that date are a good bet.)

Regardless of material, keep in mind that wallpaper has a tendency to retain moisture between itself and the wall, promoting mold and mildew. In kitchens, bathrooms, and any other rooms where moisture is present, low-VOC paint is a better bet. For more on VOCs, see page 134.

SAFER ADHESIVES Most commercial wallpaper adhesives are a cocktail of VOC-emitting chemicals. Look for low-VOC adhesives, which can be used to hang most types of wallpaper. If you're hanging actual paper (not vinyl) or lightweight cloth wall coverings, you may be able to use wheat-based adhesive paste, an all-natural mixture of wheat powder and water that was standard before the advent of chemical glues. For that, some wallpaper and hardware stores do carry bags of wheat powder; it's also available from online retailers. For a truly retro solution, you can make your own paste from scratch; recipes are available online. (Search for "wallpaper paste recipe.")

WINDOW TREATMENTS Beautiful window treatments offer practical benefits—sun protection, insulation, and privacy. In fact, you can cut your heating and cooling costs significantly just by covering your windows. But finding safer, more Earth-friendly window coverings can be tricky, though, because even the seemingly healthy choices come with caveats. Some products, even ones made of nontoxic materials, harbor allergens such as dust and mold spores. Others begin to break down into toxic substances almost as soon as they're installed. The solution is twofold: Choose the right products and give them the proper care.

THE FACTS

In warmer climates, unshaded windows can account for a quarter of total air-conditioning costs.

CHOOSING CURTAINS Like upholstery, drapery fabrics can be made of either natural fibers like cotton, linen, silk, and wool, or petroleum-based synthetics like polyester, nylon, and rayon. Avoid the latter whenever you can, both for environmental reasons and to avoid coming into contact with any chemical residues. If you're willing to do some legwork, it's possible to purchase organic cotton fabric and make custom drapes. Choose fabrics that have been colored with less toxic, "low-impact" dyes, or opt for naturally pigmented fabrics such as "color-grown" cotton. It's also wise to avoid curtains coated with stain treatments and flame retardants, which can contain toxic PFCs and PBDEs. If you're concerned about the fire risk posed by untreated fabrics, choose wool, naturally resistant to fire and staining.

To make the most of your curtains' energy-saving benefits during the summer months, look for styles that have a light-colored backing, which will deflect the sun's rays and help reduce summer cooling costs. (If your chosen curtains don't have backings, they can always be added later by a skilled seamstress.) On hot, sunny days, be sure to close the curtains on windows

that face the sun—doing so will help keep things cool and ease your air conditioner's workload. In winter, close the curtains in rooms you're not using in order to keep chilly drafts out and precious heat in.

Finally, regardless of what your drapes are made of, it's important to maintain them properly, as the layers of fabric can gather and trap lots of indoor air pollutants such as dust, mold, and any chemicals that may be floating in the air, all of which can lead to respiratory problems. Vacuum curtains weekly using a vacuum with a HEPA filter to remove loose particles. Dirty drapes made of cotton, linen, and wool can often be hand-laundered and hung to dry; even delicate fabrics like silk can sometimes be washed at home. (Check the care label to be sure.) Avoid dry-cleaning your drapes, as freshly dry-cleaned items can contain residues of perchloroethylene, a potentially carcinogenic solvent used by most dry cleaners. If you must dry-clean, allow your drapes to air out on a clothesline for a day before bringing them back into your home.

FINDING BLINDS Either in conjunction with cloth window coverings or as a streamlined alternative, window blinds are a popular choice for reducing the sun's glare and adding privacy. But certain construction materials come with an extra set of precautions. In the mid-1990s, PVC (or vinyl) mini-blinds came under intense scrutiny because of their connection to lead poisoning in children. As it turned out, several types of PVC blinds made in Indonesia, China, Taiwan, and Mexico contained lead as a stabilizer, and when they were exposed to light and heat, the materials began to break down. This led to the formation of lead dust on the surfaces of the blinds, which could easily be transferred to little ones' hands and mouths.

The lead exposure was due to the gradual breakdown of the PVC. The U.S. Consumer Product Safety Commission (CPSC) found that on certain blinds, lead levels were so high that if a child ingested the dust from less than a square inch of blinds each day for 15 to 30 days, his or her blood levels of lead could exceed ten micrograms per deciliter, the level the CPSC considers dangerous. While most manufacturers agreed to reformulate their blinds to be lead-free, there's no premarket testing to determine whether the new blinds are safe, even if they bear a "lead-free" label. Your best bet is to remove any blinds that were purchased before 1997 from your home, and replace them with either curtains or non-PVC blinds.

A great alternative to PVC *would* be FSC-certified, low-VOC finishes, but such products are still relatively rare in the marketplace. Roll-down or Roman shades woven from fast-growing bamboo, reeds, and grasses may be the best choice, as they're sustainably harvested and readily available. Whatever type of blind you choose, be sure to wipe them down often using a damp or dust-trapping cloth, which will help reduce your daily exposure to allergens and contaminants.

Lighting

Take a good look at the environmental impact of your home's lighting as well, beginning with the lightbulbs you choose. A few bulbs can add to a big impact, on the planet and on your wallet.

The U.S. Environmental Protection Agency estimates that the average household spends close to 20 percent of its annual electricity bill on lighting. And while generating electricity to light up our homes and workplaces, power plants release soot and other pollutants into the atmosphere. That's in addition, of course, to the physical waste of cheap lighting: dorm room halogen lamps that get tossed at the end of the year, and low-quality desk lamps that get discarded with the old office furniture. If you want to reduce both your energy bills and your environmental footprint, consider the following factors.

BETTER BULBS Traditional incandescent lightbulbs are incredibly inefficient. For every watt of energy consumed, only 10 percent is used to produce light—the remaining 90 percent is released as heat. Not only is this a waste of power, but it also is a fire hazard because of the heat generated. For these reasons, compact fluorescent light (CFL) bulbs are finding their way into homes and commercial spaces. Essentially miniature versions of the large overhead fluorescent lights

often found in office buildings and schools, most CFL bulbs can last 8 to 12 times longer than incandescents, at a quarter the cost per hour. If the word "fluorescent" makes you cringe, rest assured: Today's CFLs are designed to emit a softer and more flattering light than their predecessors, and they no longer flicker or buzz. They also produce 70 percent less heat than incandescents.

CFLs do come with a few caveats, however. First, they cost an average of $5 to $15 per bulb, significantly more than the typical two-for-a-dollar incandescent bulbs. But given their extended life and the energy savings they provide, the investment quickly becomes worthwhile. (Look for the Energy Star label on the package to ensure you get what you pay for.) Second, selecting the appropriate brightness level can be tricky. Start by taking a close look at CFL and incandescent bulbs' packaging side by side. A bulb's energy use is denoted in watts, while its light output is measured in lumens. If you want the same brightness from a CFL bulb, look for one with a lumen output comparable to that of the bulbs you normally use. Or just pick one that is about a quarter the wattage of the incandescent bulb you are replacing.

The EPA's Energy Star offers the following equivalencies:

COMPARABLE LIGHT OUTPUT

CFL (WATTS)	INCANDESCENT (WATTS)
9-13	**40**
13-15	**60**
18-25	**75**
23-30	**100**
30-52	**150**

Also, not all CFL bulbs can be used with dimmer switches, so if you'd like dimmable lights, be sure to check the label and verify that the bulbs are approved for this use. Likewise, you'll need to buy special three-way CFL bulbs if you want to use them in three-way lamps.

The most common CFL bulbs are shaped like a tight spiral coil of tubes. You may also see two or three horseshoe-shaped tubes that taper into the bulb's screw base. Whatever the shape, consider the light fixture you'll be using and make sure the bulb not only will fit in the base, but also will avoid touching the surrounding shade. Also note that certain types of lampshades clamp directly onto the bulb, so if that is the type you are furnishing, you'll need to buy a covered CFL.

Finally, just as incandescent bulbs come in a variety of light variations (such as daylight, soft white, and subtle rose hues), CFL bulbs can emit a range of light colors based on their Kelvin temperature, a number that should be printed on the packaging. Kelvin temperatures of about 2700 produce warmer, redder light; temperatures of around 6500 mean cooler, whiter light.

Another—albeit less popular—option is to choose fixtures that employ the newer light-emitting diode (LED) technology instead. Though they're still fairly hard to come by and are significantly more expensive ($40 for a single bulb), you can find LED-outfitted wall fixtures, ceiling fixtures, and even LED bulbs that fit into standard bulb sockets. With LEDs, energy savings are comparable to those for CFL bulbs, but LEDs can last ten times as long as CFLs, or up to 60,000 hours. Another advantage is that LEDs contain no mercury. The light from LEDs is also thought to resemble sunlight more closely than light from fluorescent or incandescent bulbs.

THE FACTS

If every household replaced just three 60-watt incandescent bulbs with compact fluorescent lightbulbs, the pollution savings would be equal to taking 3.5 million cars off the road, according to the nonprofit group Environmental Defense.

LAMPS & SHADES Options are fairly limited when it comes to environment-friendly light fixtures—not that lamps are notoriously harmful to the planet, but there are few standout products in the marketplace. It is possible to find lamp bases that are made from sustainable materials such as bamboo or FSC-certified wood, and a few online retailers sell lamps made with recycled glass and other found materials.

But in general, you have two options: buy classic-looking, high-quality glass, metal, or ceramic lamps that you'll use for years, or go vintage. Antiques shops, thrift stores, yard sales, and estate sales are great places to pick up pre-loved floor and table lamps, often of much higher quality than you'll find in big-box stores. In doing so, you'll be extending the life cycle of something otherwise destined for the dump. Lamps needn't even be in working order when you buy them; an electrician or a lamp-repair shop can easily rewire an old fixture for you, or you can do it yourself with a little guidance from do-it-yourself handbooks or websites.

To maximize the energy efficiency of any light fixture, choose the right shade. Pale colors that allow lots of light to pass through are preferable to heavy, dark lampshades; with task lamps, look for those with a white or metallic shade interior, which helps reflect the bulb's light onto your work or reading space. On sconces and chandeliers, avoid using dark-colored

ASK THE EDITORS

Q **What should I do with burned-out lightbulbs?**

A **Unfortunately, all types of lightbulbs contain a small amount of hazardous materials. The otherwise environmentally friendly CFL bulbs contain mercury; incandescent bulbs and LED lights contain lead. For this reason, avoid tossing any burned-out lightbulbs in the garbage can; these toxic substances are best kept out of our landfills. Instead, treat the bulbs as hazardous waste—dispose of them at your local hazardous waste site, or seek out recycling centers in your community that will accept used lightbulbs. (The Earth 911 website can help you locate one.)**

glass shades; opt instead for a frosted or etched clear or white glass. All of these choices will provide the maximum amount of light for the least amount of power.

LEAVING LIGHTS ON It's commonly believed that turning lights on and off requires a "surge" of power, and that it uses less energy to leave them on. For standard incandescent lightbulbs, this idea is just not true. They burn so much energy (mostly as heat, not light), they should be turned off anytime they are not needed, advises the U.S. Department of Energy (DOE). And while it's true that fluorescent lights require extra power to get going, the relatively higher "inrush" current lasts for only 1/120th of a second, according to the DOE, and the electricity consumed equals a few seconds of normal light operation. So unless you plan to leave the room and return in less than five seconds, you'll save energy by turning off fluorescent lights, too.

What these comparisons don't take into account is the wear caused by turning lights on and off. For all types of bulbs, operating life decreases each time with every on/off switch, meaning you'll need to replace them sooner. For maximum cost and energy efficiency, only turn on the lights you really need, and don't leave on the ones you don't.

Beds

You nestle into bed each night to rest your body and restore your spirit. Beds should be pure, safe places. Here's how to make them the healthiest possible, from frame to foam mattress, on top, underneath, and in between.

BETTER BED FRAMES With wooden bed frames, as with other wooden furniture, choose FSC-certified wood whenever possible to avoid supporting the irresponsible harvest of old-growth or endangered forests. Less expensive beds may be made of wood veneers over pressed-wood surfaces instead of wood solids; if this is the case, ask if the pressed wood contains formaldehyde, which can off-gas carcinogenic and irritating fumes. Likewise, avoid products coated with higher-VOC finishes, as these, too, can off-gas. ▸For more on wood, pressed wood, and finishes, see pages 131-33. Metal bed frames are an excellent option, durable and less likely to release chemicals.

If the vintage aesthetic appeals to you, look for antique beds made from metal or solid hardwoods. Although vintage wood products may have been treated with chemical paints or finishes, older products will have significantly off-gassed in years gone by and therefore will emit considerably lower amounts of VOCs than brand-new, just-painted furniture. They also don't require the harvesting of new trees, making them an Earth-friendly option.

THE FACTS

Most manufacturers suggest replacing your mattress every eight to ten years. For the average person, that means buying eight to twelve mattresses over the course of a lifetime.

SELECTING BOX SPRINGS Box springs provide additional support to the mattress of your choosing. Though they typically consist of a wood frame covered by a fabric layer, they can also incorporate pieces made of pressed wood and fume-emitting formaldehyde glues. To avoid any chemicals in your box springs, look for ones made from natural, untreated solid wood, preferably sourced from an FSC-certified forest. Or, look for a bed frame that doesn't require a box spring at all, such as the increasingly popular platform-style bed. Just double-check that your platform alternative doesn't contain pressed wood and formaldehyde glues.

SOFT, SAFE MATTRESSES Despite what most mattress commercials might have you believe, there's more to selecting a healthy sleep surface than just choosing between soft and firm, innerspring and memory foam—and there's more to it than just one number! Consider the health effects of the materials in your mattress, remembering the constant contact between your body and your bed.

There may be harmful chemicals lurking right under your nose. Many mattresses are stuffed with polyurethane foam, a synthetic product that can release the neurotoxin toluene. And, in accordance with U.S. federal fire safety regulations, all mattresses must meet standards for "cigarette ignition resistance," meaning that when a lit cigarette is applied to its surface, the fabric will not ignite or show more than a two-inch char. As a result, most are treated with flame-retardant PBDEs, the same harmful chemicals used to make upholstery and drapes fire-resistant. See "Green Dictionary: PBDEs," page 137.

The key to finding a mattress that's nontoxic *and* fire-safe is to choose the right materials. If you want a mattress with a foam core, look for mattresses made from natural latex foam—it's made from the rubber tree, and can be sustainably sourced. Some mattresses use a blend of natural and synthetic latex, as the latter substance is cheaper; even though chemicals can be added in the manufacturing process, both types are preferable to polyurethane.

If you prefer a mattress with an innerspring system, choose one padded with organic cotton, which is grown without pesticides, or better yet, go with wool, which is naturally fire resistant. In fact, wool is quickly becoming the go-to material for manufacturers of less toxic bedding, as it meets federal safety regulations without the addition of chemical fire retardants. (All-cotton mattresses lacking any type of fire-preventive material are available only to consumers with a doctor's prescription verifying that they have chemical sensitivities.)

A last note on mattresses: In recent years, one increasingly popular mattress option has been viscoelastic foam, aka memory foam. These types of cushions are made entirely from polyurethane, which may release toluene. Manufacturers generally advise airing these mattresses out before use, but if you're sensitive to chemicals (or just chemical-averse), you may prefer to avoid them entirely.

ECO-TIP: FABRIC FINISHES

Permanent-press, crease-resistant, shrinkproof, and water-repellent fabrics are likely to have been treated with chemicals and may release formaldehyde, PFCs, and PBDEs. Avoid these if possible, and to be safe, wash all new bedding in hot water at least once before use. A 1999 study showed that a single washing of permanent-press fabrics could reduce formaldehyde emissions by 60 percent.

BLANKET OPTIONS Two extremely common materials used in blankets and comforters are polyester and acrylic—they are popular choices for both the outside fabric and the fluffy white filler material of quilts and coverlets.

Unfortunately, popular doesn't always mean safe. Since polyester's raw material is petroleum—it's made by breaking down crude oil into petrochemicals and converting them into polyethylene terephthalate (PETE), a plastic that's used to make both soda bottles and polyester fibers—the fabric contributes to the depletion of our nonrenewable fossil fuel supply and to our reliance on imported oil. Polyester production also releases lung-damaging pollutants such as nitrogen and sulfur oxides, particulates, carbon monoxide, and heavy metals into the environment, as well as the greenhouse gas carbon dioxide.

Acrylic fabric, which is also petroleum-based, has a similarly detrimental effect on the environment. And it carries another cause for concern: It's made using the industrial chemical acrylonitrile, a probable human carcinogen. Workers who make acrylic fiber face a probable cancer risk, and we do not know what effect sleeping on or under it might have.

The good news: There's no shortage of healthy alternatives for blankets. Cotton may be the next easiest material to come by, and as a natural fiber it's certainly preferable to petroleum-based synthetics.

And if you can, take it one step further and go organic. Conventional cotton crops are sprayed with tons of synthetic pesticides and fertilizers each year, which inevitably run off into groundwater and, potentially, into drinking water. Of the top 15 pesticides used on cotton crops, 7 are considered possible, likely, probable, or known human carcinogens, according to the U.S. Environmental Protection Agency. Additionally, over three-quarters of all U.S. cotton is currently genetically engineered. These varieties inherently endanger the environment, wildlife, and potentially human health. Finally, cotton consumes enormous amounts of water.

By contrast, organic cotton is grown without synthetic pesticides or genetically engineered seed stock, and an increasing

number of national retailers now stock organic cotton blankets alongside conventional. If you can't find organic, the next best choice is cotton that is minimally processed. This cotton may not be organically grown, but it is usually processed without dyes, bleaches, and other chemical finishes. (Conventional cotton cloth is often bleached, sometimes with sodium hypochlorite, which releases toxic dioxin during manufacturing. It can also be treated with dyes and color fixers—heavy metals such as chromium, copper, and zinc. Read labels and ask manufacturers for information on any fabric treatments used.)

Another natural fiber to look for is wool. Naturally fireproof, it alleviates the need for treatment with chemical fire retardants, which are often applied to cotton and synthetics. It's not moth-resistant, however, and is usually treated with mothproofing insecticides. And depending on how the sheep were raised, wool may also contain other insecticide residues from dipping sheep in chemical baths to rid them of parasites. To avoid these, look for certified organic wool, or California "Pure Grow" wool, which comes from ranches that do not treat their sheep with chemicals. For more on wool, see pages 212-14.

THE FACTS

Cotton crops account for 10 percent of all pesticides and 25 percent of all insecticides used worldwide, according to the Sustainable Cotton Project. An average of a third of a pound of chemicals and synthetic fertilizers goes into the process of making a T-shirt from conventional cotton.

COMFORTERS AND DUVETS In winter months and in cooler climes, many people like to top—or replace—blankets with fluffy comforters and duvets. As with blankets and sheets, these bed toppers can be made using any number of fabrics, some better than others, and the same rules apply. For the exterior, opt for natural fibers like certified organic or Pure Grow wool, organic cotton, and naturally processed cotton instead of synthetics like polyester and nylon, and avoid anything treated with mothproofing insecticides and chemical fire retardants. As for the filling (also called batting) that gives comforters and duvets their characteristic loft, choose wool, feathers, and down rather than polyester.

PILLOW PICKS Pillows are designed to provide your head, neck, and shoulders with support. But what about supporting your overall health, or that of the planet? Conventional pillows are often filled with petroleum-based polyester or polyurethane foams, which deplete nonrenewable resources and compromise your indoor air quality. These synthetic fillings also absorb moisture, creating a breeding ground for dust mites—bad news for allergy sufferers. Even natural, breathable cotton pillows will contribute to land and water pollution if the fibers aren't produced organically. So there's good reason to seek out healthy alternatives, and they're plentiful.

The most readily available are pillows filled with feathers or down; if you decide to go this route, look for ones with an organic cotton exterior and be sure to cover the pillows with a washable fabric encasement so that stray feathers stay confined. If potential animal cruelty issues associated with down concern you, consider a pillow filled with kapok instead. The seedpods from the kapok tree are traditionally gathered as they fall to the ground, and the soft fiber around the seeds is used for stuffing pillows, making them a sustainable option.

THE FACTS

If it's made of conventional cotton, one queen-size sheet set requires 1.25 pounds of petroleum-based pesticides and fertilizers. Often, these run off into nearby waterways where they harm or kill aquatic life.

As with comforters, wool is an excellent choice for stuffing pillows, especially the Pure Grow or certified organic types, which are free of insecticide residues. Naturally fire- and water-resistant, wool wicks moisture off your skin, repels dust mites, and doesn't require treatment with fireproofing products. (It may be treated with moth repellent, however, so read labels and contactthe pillow's manufacturer for details.)

Natural latex is a fourth alternative to synthetic pillow filling. It's sustainably derived from tapped (not logged) rubber trees, and purchasing natural latex helps support responsible rain forest management. Because it's relatively firm compared with down, wool, and kapok, natural latex is a good choice for those seeking more neck support, and latex pillows don't encourage dust mites; on the other hand, those with latex allergies will certainly need to steer clear.

Finally, consider taking a cue from Japanese tradition and resting your head on a buckwheat pillow. The hulls are a by-product of the grain milling process, and make for a body-conforming filling that many doctors recommend to patients dealing with neck pain and insomnia. As buckwheat is typically grown without pesticides, it's very environment-friendly, and the hulls are naturally resistant to dust mites, a benefit for allergy sufferers.

There is one caveat, however: Before buying a buckwheat pillow, ask the retailer or manufacturer whether the hulls have been thoroughly cleaned, as lingering dust can trigger asthma attacks and allergies. (Some bear a label stating that the hulls have been "triple cleaned.")

ASK THE EDITORS

Q **I'm a vegetarian and want to avoid animal products in other areas of my life. Are down and feather bedding animal-friendly?**

A Given your principles, you should probably not use anything containing down or feathers.

In general, goose and duck down is collected from dead fowl as a by-product of the poultry-meat industry. Still, that doesn't mean that the process is cruelty-free. Down is commonly gathered from factory-farmed ducks and geese, whose living conditions are less than ideal. Factory farms are crowded and dirty, and even "free-range" fowl sometimes have little to no access to the outdoors. Worse yet, live plucking of geese and ducks still occurs in China, Poland, and Hungary, and possibly in France and Israel. For these reasons, many vegetarians, vegans, and those concerned about animal welfare choose not to use down or feather bedding and clothing.

If you prefer to avoid down, seek out alternative, environmentally friendly filler materials, such as certified organic or Pure Grow wool. Kapok (a fiber that comes from the seedpods of the tropical kapok tree), which has a fluffy texture similar to that of down, is an excellent insulator, and is very water resistant, making it inhospitable to mites and mildew.

But read labels closely, because some products in this category may contain bird down added in with other materials. And remember that many down alternatives are made of acrylic, polyester, and other petroleum-based synthetics; likewise, conventional wool can contain pesticides. Given all of these competing factors, weigh your options in terms of your priorities. The "right" decision is ultimately a personal one.

Linens

We use the term "linens" to refer to any number of fabric products—sheets and towels, napkins and tablecloths. The name comes from one of the most environmentally friendly materials around, but rarely is it used anymore.

Woven of fiber from the flax plant, linen is an all-natural product. But most of today's so-called linens don't live up to their namesake material's healthy standard. Synthetic fabrics and insecticide-laden cotton abound in the bed-and-bath aisles these days, adding up to a serious risk of toxic chemical exposure.

ECO-TIP: GOT ALLERGIES?

For allergy sufferers, chemicals aren't the only troublesome thing hiding in the sheets. Certain filler materials, such as down, can trigger symptoms. No matter how tidy your home or how perfect your hygiene, bedding and mattresses frequently accumulate dust and dust mites, microscopic insects that feed on dead skin cells. Most people suffer no ill effects from their presence, but for those with a dust mite allergy, they can cause bothersome symptoms. The following measures can help ease the sneezing.

✓ **Use protective covers. Several companies sell "allergen barrier" encasements for both pillows and mattresses. While dust mites can still gather on the surface, these cases will keep them from getting inside your bedding. Choose fabric encasements rather than vinyl, as the latter can emit other problematic air pollutants.**

✓ **Launder often. Wash sheets, blankets, and protective coverings in hot water (130°F to 140°F) every two weeks to kill dust mites and remove their allergenic droppings. Freeze nonwashable bedding overnight.**

✓ **Filter your air. A bedroom air purifier with a HEPA filter can help capture dust mites before they settle into your bed, and can reduce seasonal allergy triggers such as pollen.**

✓ **Ditch down. If you're allergic to duck or goose down, skip the feathery fills. Even if the filling seems securely encased in a quilt or pillow, allergenic particles can still escape.**

✓ **Vacuum frequently. A model with a built-in HEPA filter will help eliminate dust on the floor, which easily makes its way into your bed via your feet.**

BETTER BEDSHEETS For consumers who are just starting to go green, switching to organic cotton sheets is often the next logical upgrade after opting for organic groceries. It makes sense—our bedsheets are in constant contact with our skin, and organic sheets are now easier to find than ever, with options available in every price range. National retailers now carry basic organic sheets for the budget-conscious buyer, while boutiques carry ultra-luxe, high-thread-count sheet sets.

The advantages of organic cotton sheets over conventional cotton ones are twofold: They reduce your daily exposure to pesticide residues, and they support more sustainable farming methods. There are, however, no restrictions on what can be added to organic cotton sheets during the dyeing and finishing processes, so avoid potentially toxic dyes and fabric treatments by choosing unbleached, dye-free sheet sets without any anti-wrinkling or fire-resistant treatments. Admittedly, these all-natural bedsheets come with fewer style and pattern options than their chemical-treated counterparts, but they are more certain to be free of potentially carcinogenic residues.

GREEN DICTIONARY

HEAVY-METAL DYES

Heavy metals such as chromium and copper fix dyes in fabrics. Roughly half the chemicals used end up in rivers and soil, however. Minute amounts of these elements are good for your health, but larger quantities may be toxic. Look for fabrics that are unbleached and undyed; for color variety, look for "colorgrown" cotton, which is naturally pigmented and comes in shades of tan, green, and brown.

Another approach: Go back to basics. Centuries ago, linen was the favored material for bedsheets, and the material is coming back into vogue today. Breathable and durable, linen sheets soften with use and get better with every wash. While significantly pricier than cotton, their long-lasting nature, all-season comfort, and timeless elegance make linen sheets a worthy investment. Your neighborhood department store may not carry them, but they're often found at shops specializing in fine linens or by mail order from specialty catalogs. Italian and Belgian linen are often held as the gold standard, but you can also find linen sheets made domestically.

If you prefer to dress your bed in something a little more showy, opt for silk rather than synthetic polyester satin, which is petroleum-derived. Better yet, choose wildcrafted silk if you can find it. Still produced primarily by worms in China, silk traditionally involves extensive use of synthetic pesticides and fertilizers; the pesticide methoprene and the plant-based steroid hormone phytoecdysone are often used in concert to lengthen the worms' lifetime and synchronize readiness of cocoons for harvest. Many consumers are also troubled by the treatment of the worms. Traditionally, the pupae are killed—either by baking or drowning—before emerging from their cocoons, which breaks the long silk threads. Wildcrafted silk, on the other hand, is produced organically and without killing the pupae, making it a better choice. After the pupae hatch, wildcrafted silk is spun to combine the threads.

TONY TOWELS Most people don't give much thought to their towels beyond choosing a color that matches their decor. But towels present the same challenge as other fabrics: On the journey from cotton field to towel bar, they typically encounter tons of pesticides, bleaches, and dyes. Choosing organic cotton towels instead is an excellent idea, but don't overlook all the other fabric options. For small hand towels and dish towels, linen is growing in popularity because it's extremely absorbent yet dries quickly between uses. For full-size bath towels, ultrasoft bamboo fiber is becoming increasingly common, as it comes from the fast-growing, usually pesticide-free bamboo plant and has natural antibacterial properties. Hemp is another sustainable fabric choice, as it's grown with very few pesticides, is naturally mold- and mildew-resistant, and can absorb 150 percent of its weight in water; for now, though, it's still a bit tougher to come by than organic cotton or bamboo.

ASK THE EDITORS

Q **I've heard that plastic shower curtains are full of chemicals. What's the problem, and what are my alternatives?**

A Most plastic shower curtains are made of polyvinyl chloride, aka PVC or vinyl. It's among the most environmentally unfriendly plastics around, as it's tough for consumers to recycle and some varieties can release both lead and phthalates into the air you breathe (hence the potent "new shower curtain smell" when one is first pulled out of the packaging). Disposal of vinyl is particularly problematic given that, if incinerated, it will release dioxins and other contaminants into the environment.

If you're due for a bathroom remodel, consider installing a shower door, which will eliminate your need for curtains and is easy to keep mold-free. If that's not an option, look for fabric curtains made of hemp, which is washable, sustainably grown, and naturally mold resistant. Cotton curtains work too, but they're mold-prone and you may need two (one as a liner and one as a decorative curtain). Synthetics such as polyester are a less toxic option than vinyl, but proceed with caution, as they're petroleum-derived. If you do stick with vinyl, do yourself a favor and hang it outside to off-gas for a few days before using it. Your nose—and the rest of your body—will thank you.

LESS TOXIC TABLE LINENS Pure and natural beats cheap and processed when it comes to the surfaces on which meals are served, too. Convenience products like paper napkins and disposable plastic or vinyl tablecloths are less than ideal choices—used once, they're tossed in the trash en route to the landfill. Paper products are often bleached, a process that releases dioxin into the environment, and plastic or vinyl table coverings may release hormone-disrupting phthalates into your indoor air.

Instead, seek out higher quality table linens. Since it's reusable, cotton fabric is better than any disposable product, and organic cotton trumps conventional, because it avoids problematic pesticide use. Linen is an excellent alternative, too, given the typically lower chemical use on the flax crops from which it's derived. Choose unbleached, undyed cotton and linen whenever possible, since heavy-metal dyes are often used in the processing of colored table linens. As with bedsheets and other household linens, skip the special fabric treatments that resist staining and wrinkling, as they may contain carcinogenic formaldehyde.

Another approach is to avoid table linens altogether, opting instead for placemats and table runners made from woven reeds, straw, and bamboo; these sustainably grown materials don't deplete natural resources and are easy to clean and maintain.

Accessories

It's the little things that make a house into a home—framed photos and favorite artwork hanging on the wall, beloved vases filled with fresh flowers. With a little effort, you can find decorative items for every room of your house without compromising your health or the environment.

PICTURE PERFECT Picture frames aren't the worst evil in the world, but it's better to choose frames that won't contribute to deforestation or leach chemicals into the air. It's exceedingly difficult, though, to find new frames that aren't made of plastic or finished with VOC-emitting paints or finishes. Your best bet is to go vintage, heading to thrift stores, antiques stores, and yard sales. You not only prevent further damage to the environment, but you reduce waste by keeping old frames out of landfills. And you'll probably end up with pieces far more unusual than those you'd get at a big-box store. If sorting through others' castoffs isn't your style, keep an eye out for picture frames made using recycled—in other words, reclaimed—materials such as glass, tin, and wood.

KNICKKNACKS & ACCENTS Small accent pieces are another relatively minor issue compared with home decor choices like paint, carpet, furniture, and bedding, but that doesn't mean you shouldn't look for more planet-friendly alternatives. In general, vintage pieces have less of an environmental impact than brand-new decorative items, so seek these out as often as possible. Recycled pieces are also a good bet, and some retailers offer many choices, including doormats made from old rubber flip-flops, lamps made of old circuit boards, coasters made from vintage records, and the like.

Alternatively, you can choose to bring the outdoors in by decorating with "found" natural items such as fallen pine cones, sea glass, seashells, gathered stones, arrangements of fallen branches, and pressed and framed leaves and flowers. When choosing small, decorative items, follow the standards set for the other items in this chapter—avoid plastics, heavily lacquered or painted items, and fabrics that are treated with pesticides—and remember that creativity is key in decorating your home.

ECO-ARTWORK Quality artwork can bring life to even the drabbest of spaces. While it's practically impossible to choose paintings, sculptures, and pottery for your home based solely on their environmental friendliness—you also have to like the way the items look, after all—some choices are a little less toxic than others. Like wall paints and furniture finishes, the colors used in paintings can contain solvents like turpentine and xylene, both neurotoxins, and heavy metals such as arsenic, cadmium, and lead. Modeling clays can contain PVC, which is full of phthalates.

When possible, opt for wall art created with water-based paints such as liquid tempera, gouache, and watercolor, which are likely to contain fewer toxic substances than oil paints. Once you bring a painting home, have it mounted under glass—especially if it contains high-VOC oil paints or other toxic pigments—which will help minimize any off-gassing in your home.

As for sculpture, keep an eye out for items made with PVC-free clays (such as beeswax clay), items crafted from metal, wood carvings (especially good if the wood is reclaimed), and pieces made of recycled materials. And when possible, buy from artists in your area or pick up locally made pieces on your travels; this will help eliminate the environmental costs (such as carbon emissions) of shipping and transporting items across the globe.

Scents & Candles

Candles set the scene for a romantic dinner or a cozy winter night—but how healthy is that glow? Some candles release 100 times more soot than others; chemicals released from the glow may include formaldehyde, acetaldehyde, and acrolein. Read on before striking that match.

CANDLE WAX Many mass-produced, bargain-priced candles on the market are made of paraffin wax, a petroleum-based product that releases toxic particles into the air when heated or burned. In fact, researchers have found that polycyclic aromatic hydrocarbons (PAHs)—carcinogenic by-products of combustion that have been linked to lower birth weights in babies of exposed mothers—reach inordinately high levels in churches after candles or incense is burned. Gel candles, often found in the home fragrance section of grocery stores, are also petroleum-derived and problematic.

As a result of these findings, many candle manufacturers are turning to nonpetroleum alternatives. Beeswax, used for centuries in candles, is an excellent substitute for paraffin as it has a similarly solid texture and can be used for pillar, poured, molded, or taper candles. A relatively newer entrant to the candle market is soy wax, which is created from hydrogenated soybean oil. With a texture that's slightly softer than beeswax, soy wax is most often found in poured candles, but soy-based pillars and tapers are also available. It's also usually priced lower than beeswax, which is an expensive raw material. Both options burn far cleaner than paraffin, and the candles made from these materials often last longer than their petroleum-based counterparts.

CANDLE WICKS Regardless of what type of candle wax you choose, you'll want to find out what's in the wick, too. Many candle wicks contain lead, a neurological toxin, which is released into the air when burned. Instead, choose candles with all-cotton wicks, which have no such effect. Many candles state that they're lead-free on the package, but if you're unsure, you can examine the tip of the wick. If you see a dark, stiff metal core, steer clear.

CANDLE FRAGRANCES As is the case with most home products, natural and plant-based are the healthiest choices for candle scents. The vast majority of the candles sold are made with synthetic fragrances, which may contain hormone-disrupting phthalates. Essential oils, which are made by pressing or distilling fragrant flowers, fruits and herbs such as lavender, rose, eucalyptus, and grapefruit, make for far healthier fragrances. Many people prefer essential oil candles to artificially scented ones, as they're less cloying and have aromatherapeutic benefits.

Be diligent about reading labels, though; just because a candle is lavender scented doesn't mean it's all natural. Look for phrases like "100 Percent Pure Essential Oil Fragrance" and "No Synthetic Fragrances" on the label.

Houseplants

There's something comforting and energizing about the sight of living, breathing plants that share the indoors with us. In the summer, houseplants connect us to the natural world growing and blooming outside; in the winter, they offer a much needed dose of greenery and fresh air.

In addition to producing oxygen and reducing carbon dioxide levels in the outdoor environment, some plants, studies have shown, can help purify the air inside your home.

AIR-PURIFYING PLANTS Through the natural process of photosynthesis, plants take in carbon dioxide and expel fresh oxygen. Along with that carbon dioxide, they can take in chemical pollutants that off-gas from building materials, inks, and fabrics. Studies of typical homes suggest that as few as 15 houseplants can significantly reduce indoor contaminants.

The key to harnessing plants' purifying power? Choose the right species. Boston fern (*Nephrolepi exaltata bostoniensis*), golden pothos *(Scindapsus aureus)*, nephthytis *(Syngonium podophyllum)*, and spider plants *(Chlorophytum elatum vittatum)* are known to reduce indoor levels of formaldehyde;

areca palm *(Chrysalidocarpus lutescens)*, moth orchid *(Phalenopsis)*, and the dwarf date palm *(Phoenix roebelinii)* can remove xylene and toluene; and gerbera daisy *(Gerbera jamesonii)*, chrysanthemum *(Chrysanthemum morifolium)*, spider plant, and peace lily *(Spathiphyllum)* can remove benzene. Other beneficial houseplants include bamboo palm *(Chamaedorea)*, Chinese evergreen *(Aglaonema)*, English ivy *(Hedera helix)*, indoor dracaena species *(Dracaena deremensis, D. marginata,* and *D. fragrans)*, and the snake plant, also known as mother-in-law's tongue *(Sansevieria trifasciata laurentii)*.

If you have young children or pets in your home, exercise extra caution when choosing houseplants and cut flowers. Many can be toxic if ingested, including poinsettias, delphiniums, irises, and poppies.

THE FACTS

Fern and flower workers in Costa Rica and Ecuador have been found to have a marked increase in symptoms of pesticide poisoning, according to reports from the Pesticide Action Network.

CUT FLOWERS A fresh, fragrant floral bouquet never loses its appeal, whether as a gesture of love or a colorful centerpiece. Yet many flowers sold in florists' shops and markets have a less-than-pleasant past. The floral industry uses the highest level of pesticides of all agricultural sectors, and since the majority of flowers we buy originate from other regions such as Central America, they may carry pesticides that are banned in the U.S., such as DDT. Shockingly high levels of chemicals can remain on beautiful bouquets: When the nonprofit Environmental Working Group tested a sampling of roses in 1997, it found residues of several pesticides at up to 1,000 times the amounts in comparable food products. In addition to compromising your personal health, heavy pesticide use on flower farms pollutes waterways.

Thankfully, florists are beginning to offer organic flowers. Even better, you can go to farmers markets or nearby farms to purchase organic flowers that were locally grown, not only to avoid pesticides but also to gain the satisfaction of knowing your flowers didn't travel thousands of miles on a fuel-guzzling plane or truck to get to your flower vase.

If you're having trouble finding local flowers, check out Local Harvest, an organization that connects consumers with small farms in their area. If you have a green thumb, try growing your own flowers; organic seeds, bulbs, and plants are increasingly available from garden retailers. Hydrangeas, peonies, and flowering bulbs like tulips and narcissus boast spectacular blooms in spring and summer.

Take Action

- ✓ Buy only FSC-certified wood furniture and avoid items made from pressed-wood products.
- ✓ Choose natural fabrics for upholstery. Avoid fabrics or cushion fillings that have been treated with stain protectors or fire retardants.
- ✓ Opt for vintage leather furniture instead of new items.
- ✓ Forgo vinyl wallpaper in favor of paper wall coverings, and use adhesives made from plant starch.
- ✓ When it's time to replace your carpets, avoid synthetic materials and glues. Look for natural fibers like wool.
- ✓ Purchase curtains made from natural, untreated materials like organic cotton. Vacuum and launder them often to reduce dust and other particulate matter in your home's air.
- ✓ Choose window shades made of wood or woven bamboo instead of PVC blinds, which can contain lead.
- ✓ Replace incandescent lightbulbs with compact fluorescent ones.
- ✓ Pick mattresses made using organic cotton fabric; look for padding made of natural latex or wool. Avoid polyurethane "memory foams," which can release harmful chemicals.
- ✓ Warm up under organic cotton and wool (or Pure Grow wool) blankets and comforters instead of polyester and acrylic ones.
- ✓ Rest your head on a pillow filled with wool, kapok, buckwheat, or down instead of one containing petroleum-based fibers.
- ✓ Cover your bed with organic cotton or linen sheets.
- ✓ Explore fabrics like bamboo, hemp, and linen for towels.
- ✓ Decorate with vintage and recycled picture frames, knickknacks, and artwork.
- ✓ Skip traditional paraffin candles and go for naturally scented beeswax or soybean ones instead.
- ✓ Add indoor plants to every room in your home; ones proven to remove toxins are especially beneficial.
- ✓ Let organic, locally grown flowers provide a finishing touch to your decor.

The Science of Off-gassing

The products we purchase to beautify our homes, from carpets to cleaning products, can contain substances that migrate or "off-gas" into the air around us. Put simply, chemicals want to spread evenly rather than concentrate in one place. How fast they are able to reach equilibrium with their surroundings is determined by the properties of the chemical, the size and ventilation conditions of the room or building, and interactions with other chemicals.

A fundamental property of chemicals is their "vapor pressure," which describes how readily a chemical goes from a liquid or solid state into a gaseous state. Chemicals with high vapor pressures will readily volatilize—become gas in the air. Volatile organic compounds (VOCs) can cause headaches, nausea, eye and skin irritation, and breathing difficulties. Some can even cause cancer.

Other chemicals, semivolatile organic compounds (SVOCs), migrate into the air but also stick to surfaces. As a result, they volatilize out of products and float around until they settle on some dust particles, only later to revolatilize into the air. SVOCs include several phthalates, which are endocrine-disrupting chemicals used as plasticizers in toys and as components of polyvinyl (linoleum) flooring and cushy carpet pads. Other SVOCs include flame-retarding chemicals known as polybrominated diphenyl ethers (PBDEs) that have been used to treat mattresses, drapes, and consumer electronics.

Chemicals come in forms other than gases and dust. Some substances come as fine particles that can be inhaled deeply into the lungs, where they may activate the immune system and cause respiratory illness. Improperly vented woodstoves and scented candles can emit polycyclic aromatic hydrocarbons (PAHs), which are known to cause cancer. Cigarette smoke contains PAHs, formaldehyde, and numerous other toxic and cancer-causing substances.

The substances in indoor air are also governed by the properties of the room. Chemical gases tend to expand into the entire volume of their container, so a person will be exposed to more in a small bathroom or hobby room than in a high-ceilinged living room. The amount of ventilation, or air exchange from presumably cleaner outdoor air, is another significant factor.

Temperature, humidity, and light can make some substances more hazardous by altering their chemical nature. For example, high temperatures and humidity can increase the volatilization rate of formaldehyde. Humidity can also encourage the growth of microbial contaminants such as mold, mildew, and dust mites, all of which can cause allergy-like symptoms and exacerbate asthma. Conversely, light may also help break down some contaminants that are photosensitive.

The air pressure in a house can also affect the dispersal of chemicals. A vented attic may draw warm air up from the lower floors, but it also can suck toxic gases like radon and carbon monoxide up from the basement.

Some chemicals become more harmful when they react with other substances. Most people know not to mix household bleach (sodium hypochlorite) with ammonia, but bleach also reacts with the acid in tile cleaner to make chloroform, a toxic gas. Dishwasher detergent can react with food residues to give the person who opens the dishwasher a lungful of chloroform.

Air fresheners and personal care products can also undergo reactions with other substances. Pine-smelling cleaners and lemon-scented air fresheners contain substances called terpenes that react with ozone generated by air purifiers or ozone smog from outdoors to create VOCs and ultrafine particles that can trigger allergies, asthma, and respiratory illnesses. Men's aftershave, women's foundation make-up, and other personal care products also contain terpenes. Reaction with ozone causes harmful VOCs and ultrafine particles to form directly around the face, where they can be inhaled.

Not all chemicals are toxic to human health. Consumers should read labels and continue to pressure retailers to provide household products and furnishings that beautify our homes without sacrificing our health.

OFF-GASSING Furniture, upholstery, appliances, and building materials all carry risks to the environment and to the health of those at home. Consumer choices and living habits can minimize the off-gassing potential in your household.

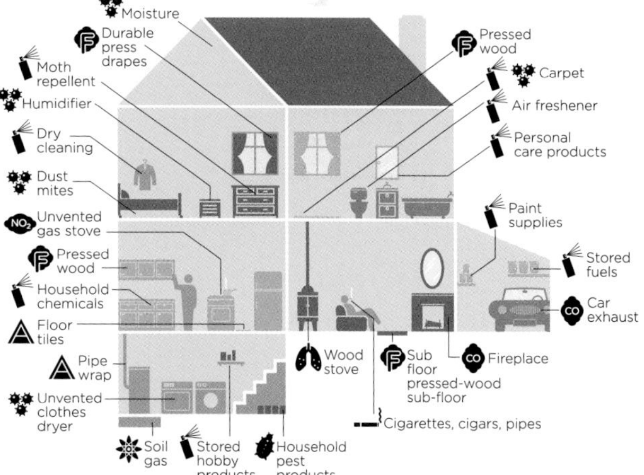

Biological pollutants
Organic pollutants
Carbon monoxide
Formaldehyde
Respirable particles
Environmental tobacco smoke
Asbestos
Nitrogen dioxide
Radon
Pesticides

5

SOAPS & CLEANSERS
MOISTURIZERS
LIP & HAIR CARE
DEODORANTS
SUN PROTECTION
FRAGRANCES
COSMETICS
NAIL CARE
DENTAL HEALTH
SHAVING PRODUCTS
FEMININE HYGIENE
INSECT REPELLENTS

Natural Personal Care

At one time, grooming was an uncomplicated endeavor: a little soap and water to wash away the day's dirt, a few strokes with a hairbrush each night. These days, taking care of oneself isn't so simple. From cracked heels to crow's feet, there's a product for almost every skin ailment and beauty woe. Drugstores' health and personal care aisles stretch for miles, filled with ever larger selections of skin creams and hair styling aids, and beauty "emporiums" have popped up in malls everywhere. As the basic remedies of centuries past have given way to chemical formulations, the ingredient lists on our products have become more complex, too.

It's no wonder that many consumers put the blinders on when it comes to the health and environmental impacts of their purchases—trying to find a decent moisturizer or shampoo from among this multitude of products is challenging enough. And yet, one of the primary routes for toxic chemicals to enter our systems is through our skin. Lotions, perfumes, sunscreens—elements of all of these products make their way into our bloodstream eventually. So why wouldn't you want them to be as pure as the foods you eat?

Sadly, few consumers realize exactly how impure their personal care products can be. Most people incorrectly assume that if these products are allowed on store shelves, they must be safe. That assumption couldn't be further from the truth, especially in the United States. The U.S. Food and Drug Administration (FDA) relies on companies to do their own safety testing and does not require that cosmetics be tested for safety before they are sold. Ingredient safety is reviewed by an industry-funded panel, the Cosmetics Ingredient Review (CIR) panel, not a government health agency. Consequently, the largely self-regulated cosmetics industry frequently fails to adhere to the CIR's advice or any safety standards set in other countries. The Environmental Working Group reports that more than 750 personal care products sold in the U.S. violate industry safety standards or cosmetic safety standards in other industrialized countries, including Canada, Japan, and the nations of the European Union.

THE FACTS

In an investigation of the ingredients in more than 23,000 products, the Environmental Working Group found that nearly 1 of every 30 products sold in the U.S. fails to meet one or more industry or governmental cosmetics safety standards. Nearly 400 products sold in the U.S. contain chemicals banned from use in cosmetics in other countries, and over 400 products contain ingredients that cosmetic industry safety panels have found unsafe when used as directed on product labels.

The reasons to green up your medicine cabinet don't stop at your health. In addition to inundating our bodies with ingredients of unknown safety, a good portion of mass-market personal care products deplete nonrenewable resources such as petroleum and can negatively impact our environment if they end up in the waste stream. Often the positive-sounding names of the ingredients belie their dire environmental impacts. Mineral oil, ubiquitous in moisturizers, baby oils, tanning oils, and lip products, is a by-product of the highly polluting oil-refining process. The active ingredient in antibacterial soaps, triclosan, has been found to harm freshwater ecosystems and may contribute to the formation of so-called superbacteria.

For products that are easier on your body and the planet, a few basic principles will set you in the right direction. First, be gentle. With cosmetics as with cleaning products, we've been conditioned to believe that stronger is better. But in many cases, manufacturers fill their soaps and shampoos with too-harsh detergents that strip the skin and pollute our waterways. Unless you're a coal miner or a zookeeper, chances are you're using more powerful cleansers than you need. Second, get back to basics. A growing trend in skin care and spas these days is hand-blended, botanical treatments such as sugar scrubs spiked with essential oils and lavender–shea butter body moisturizers. They're equal to, if not more effective than, their synthetic counterparts. Third, don't assume that a product called herbal or natural on the label will use exclusively healthy or confirmed safe ingredients. For help navigating the health and beauty aisles, let this chapter be your guide. Product by product, you'll learn how to spot safe, nontoxic, and Earth-friendly products to make you look and feel your best.

ECO-TIP: THE DIRTY DOZEN

The *Green Guide* considers these common cosmetic ingredients to be the most hazardous. The trouble is, they're everywhere. Scan the labels of products you use regularly for these problematic chemicals, and look for products that are free of all 12.

1. **Antibacterials:** Increasingly popular in hand soaps and deodorants, antibacterial agents wipe out all bacteria, good and bad. Overuse of antibacterials may reduce their effectiveness against disease-causing germs like *E. coli* and *Salmonella* in the future, as bacteria grow increasingly resistant. The overuse is also responsible for the contamination of our environment with triclosan. This common antibiotic, which has been detected in breast milk, interferes with testosterone activity in cells and produces dioxins when exposed to sunlight, making it damaging to the environment. And it's hardly necessary: Numerous studies have found that washing with regular soap and warm water is just as effective at killing germs.

2. **Coal Tar:** Coal tar, used as an active ingredient in dandruff shampoos and anti-itch creams, is a known carcinogen. Coal tar-based dyes such as FD&C Blue 1, used in toothpastes, and FD&C Green 3, used in mouthwash, have been found to be carcinogenic in animal studies when injected under skin.

3. **Diethanolamine (DEA):** DEA is widely used in shampoos to increase their lather. Its compounds and derivatives include triethanolamine (TEA) and monoethanolamine (MEA). All three can react with other ingredients in the product to create nitrosamines (compounds shown to cause cancer in laboratory animals). Contamination is more likely if the end product also contains bronopol (see #5, page 170). DEA is also a possible hormone disruptor and depletes the body of choline, an essential nutrient for cell functioning and development.

4. **1,4-Dioxane:** 1,4-Dioxane is a known animal carcinogen and a probable human carcinogen that can appear as a contaminant in such personal care items as shampoo and body wash. It is found

in products containing sodium laureth sulfate and ingredients that include the terms "PEG," "-xynol," "ceteareth," "oleth," and most other ethoxylated (chemically altered) "eth" ingredients. The FDA monitors products for the contaminant but has not yet recommended an exposure limit. Manufacturers can remove dioxane from surfactants through a process called vacuum stripping, but they don't necessarily do this for cosmetics. A 2007 survey by the Campaign for Safe Cosmetics found traces of dioxane in dozens of children's bath products and adult personal care products, and 15 percent of the shampoos tested contained amounts above the FDA's suggested maximum of ten parts per million.

5. **Formaldehyde:** Formaldehyde has a long list of adverse health effects, including immune-system toxicity, respiratory irritation, and cancer in humans. Yet it still turns up in baby bath soap, nail polish, eyelash adhesive, and hair dyes as a contaminant or breakdown product of diazolidinyl urea, imidazolidinyl urea, bronopol, and quaternium compounds.

6. **Fragrance:** The catchall term "fragrance," which permits manufacturers to keep their fragrance formulations under wraps, may mask substances called phthalates, which act as endocrine disruptors and may cause obesity and reproductive and developmental harm. Avoid phthalates by selecting products scented with essential oils such as lavender and rose instead.

7. **Lead and Mercury:** Neurotoxic lead may appear in products as a naturally occurring contaminant of hydrated silica, one of the ingredients in toothpaste, and lead acetate is found in some brands of men's hair dye. Brain-damaging mercury, found in the preservative thimerosal, is used in some mascaras.

8. **Nanoparticles:** Tiny particles of minerals and other ingredients are appearing in an increasing number of cosmetics and sunscreens in order to make them more blendable. Unfortunately, they may penetrate the skin and damage brain cells. Of most concern are nanoparticles of zinc oxide and titanium dioxide,

used in sunscreens to make them transparent. When possible, look for sunscreens containing particles of these ingredients larger than 100 nanometers. You'll most likely need to call companies to confirm sizes, but a few manufacturers have started advertising their lack of nanoparticle-size ingredients on labels. (See "Green Dictionary: Nanoparticles," page 188.)

9 **Parabens:** Parabens, which have weak estrogenic effects, are common preservatives that appear in a wide array of toiletries. They may be listed on labels as methyl-, ethyl-, propyl-, butyl-, or isobutylparaben. A study found that butyl paraben damaged testosterone production and reproductive function in mice, and a relative, sodium methylparaben, is banned in cosmetics by the European Union (EU). Parabens break down in the body into p-hydroxybenzoic acid, which has estrogenic activity in human breast cancer cell cultures.

10 **Petroleum Distillates:** Possible human carcinogens, petroleum distillates are prohibited or restricted for use in cosmetics in the EU but are found in several U.S. brands of mascara, foot-odor powder, and other products. Look out for the terms "petroleum" and "liquid paraffin."

11 **P-Phenylenediamine (PPD):** Commonly found in hair dyes, this chemical can damage the nervous system, and can cause lung irritation, severe allergic reactions, and blindness. It's also listed as 1,4-Benzenediamine, p-Aminoaniline, and 1,4-Diaminobenzene.

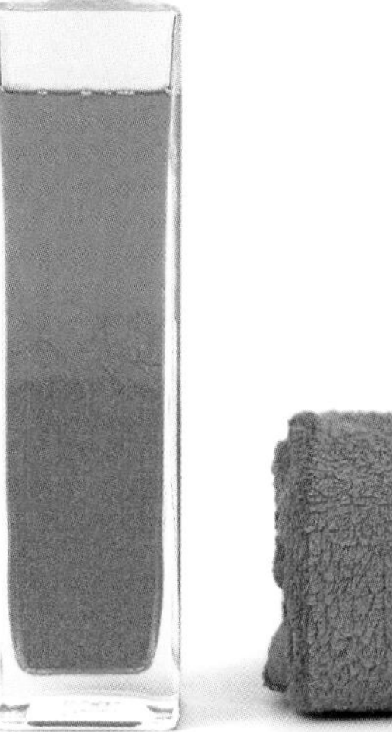

12 **Hydroquinone:** Found in skin creams and undereye treatments, hydroquinone has a bleaching effect and is used to reduce age spots and to lighten skin. It is neurotoxic and allergenic, and there's limited evidence that it may cause cancer in lab animals. It may also appear as an impurity not listed on ingredients labels.

Soaps & Cleansers

Basic soaps are created by combining fats (traditionally animal grease or plant oils) with alkaline materials (originally wood ash, but later lye). They are Earth-friendly products, but most today—filled with preservatives and foaming agents, and heavily perfumed—are a far cry from the original.

PASS THE BAR Many bar soaps are made from sodium tallowate, which is a combination of lye (sodium hydroxide) and either vegetable oil or animal fat (usually from cows or sheep). Lye, the caustic ingredient, turns the fat into soap, and it is eliminated during the soap "curing" process. So while these ingredients won't necessarily compromise your health, those concerned about animal welfare often choose to avoid animal-based soaps. Castile soap is a popular alternative. Although true Castile soap is an olive oil–based formula historically crafted in the Castile region of Spain, today the term is loosely applied to many vegetable-based bar and liquid soaps. Clear glycerin soaps are also popular, although they come with caveats. While glycerin can be a by-product of the soapmaking process and is added back in to some soaps as a humectant, or moisturizing agent, synthetic glycerin may be made from propylene alcohol—and there's no way to tell the difference from the label. Glycerin soaps may also contain fragrances and synthetic colors. In general, glycerin soaps are best avoided, as are supercheap, mass-market soaps, because they usually contain coloring agents and heavy fragrances. ▸For more on fragrance, see pages 190-92.

THE DIRT ON SULFATES Liquid cleansers are sometimes made with ingredients similar to those in bar soap—plant or animal fats combined with potassium hydroxide instead of lye. But these mostly natural products represent the minority. Most of the hand soaps, shower gels, bath bubbles, and facial cleansers on the market today are made with surfactants rather than soaps—specifically, a group of chemicals known as sulfates, along with the unhealthy trio of related chemicals diethanolamine (DEA), monoethanolamine (MEA), and triethanolamine (TEA). ▸See "The Dirty Dozen," pages 169-171. Like

soap, surfactants make washing with water more effective by causing oil and dirt to be suspended in the water so they can be carried away more easily. They also help to create a thick, foamy lather.

The most common sulfates are sodium lauryl sulfate (SLS) and sodium laureth sulfate (SLES), which is a milder, ethoxylated (chemically altered) version of SLS. Other sulfates include sodium myreth sulfate and ammonium laureth sulfate. Used in addition to or in lieu of soap, all three help to break up dirt and oil, boosting the performance of cleansers. Unfortunately, these ingredients are a little too good at their job, and they can cause dry skin, hair loss, and scalp irritation. Worse yet, the ethoxylation process that turns SLS into SLES can contaminate the product with dioxane, a human carcinogen. Both to avoid unwitting exposure to dioxane and to help keep hair and skin properly conditioned, you should look for sulfate-free shampoos, sold by a growing number of manufacturers. Read the labels closely to ensure the formulas are actually free of sulfates: "SLS-free" doesn't necessarily mean sulfate-free.

While the experience of using a surfactant-filled shampoo or cleanser is undeniably pleasant—plenty of suds, squeaky-clean skin—there are a few unpleasant side effects. First, these surfactants are overly harsh. They can cause irritation in sensitive individuals, depleting the protective layer of oil on skin and hair and making them prone to dryness and environmental damage.

GREEN DICTIONARY

SURFACTANT

Surfactants are chemicals that, when added to a liquid, enhance its ability to spread, bubble, and soak in. Surfactants are common ingredients in skin and hair cleansers.

Second, surfactants can react with other ingredients in the formula to create carcinogenic compounds. And as much as those big bubbles feel like they're cleaning the skin, a fluffy lather isn't necessary to remove dirt and oil. Though it may take some getting used to, try switching to low-sudsing formulas that are free of sulfates, DEA, TEA, and MEA. Look for gentler cleansers including those containing milder surfactants like cocamidopropyl betaine, sorbitan laurate, sorbitan palmitate and sorbitan stearate.

If you've always used supercharged mass-market cleansers, you may find that you have to use more soap or shampoo to feel clean at first. As you get used to the formula, though, you'll realize that you don't need nearly as much. For facial cleansing, you may also want to try oil- or cream-based products that actually hydrate the skin while removing dirt and makeup.

While "oil-free" was the buzzword in decades past, dermatologists and skin care experts now agree that today's lighter oil-containing formulations can provide great hydration without clogging pores. Oil-based products can also be more effective than foamy cleansers at removing makeup.

Moisturizers

Body lotions, body oils, day creams, night creams, eye creams—the basic purpose of all these products is to do one thing: soothe dry skin. In addition to a hydrating agent such as oil or water, most moisturizers contain a host of other ingredients, some safe but some with troubling downsides.

ABOUT FACE Facial moisturizers come in a mind-boggling array of formulations. All anti-aging, anti-blemish, anti-inflammatory claims aside, their main benefit is replenishing skin's natural moisture reserves, making it look smooth and firm. Several ingredients can facilitate this process.

Water simply hydrates, replacing what the body loses during daily activity and as a result of exposure to the elements. Oils, whether plant-based or synthetic, work in tandem with the skin's own sebum, the natural oil secreted by glands in the skin. Humectants, such as glycerin, glycols, and hyaluronic acid (sodium hyaluronate), draw moisture from the air into your skin, while occlusives, such as silicone and petrolatum, act as sealants and prevent moisture from escaping.

Of all these moisturizing ingredients, the occlusives draw the most criticism for their detrimental health and environmental effects. Both silicone (including dimethicone and cyclomethicone) and petrolatum (marketed as petroleum jelly) are derived from crude oil, a nonrenewable resource whose processing can be resource-intensive and can cause pollution. Critics also argue that occlusives create too solid a barrier between the skin and the air, preventing skin from breathing. While neither silicone nor petrolatum appears to be toxic to humans, petrolatum can cause allergic skin reactions in sensitive people, including babies.

The class of humectants called glycols, a kind of alcohol —including such common ingredients as propylene glycol, ethylene glycol, diethylene glycol, polyethylene glycol (PEG), and butylene glycol—also carries risks. Glycol ethers are solvents found in liquid soaps and cosmetics. Some glycols can affect the reproductive system

or cause birth defects, and overexposure to glycols may result in kidney damage and abnormalities of the liver. Glycols may also cause contact dermatitis. Choose moisturizers that contain glycerin, a safer humectant, instead. Glycerin can be synthesized or made from animal or vegetable oils; opt for vegetable when possible.

What draws the most concern from environmental health experts, however, are not the moisturizing formula bases but the many preservatives, colors, and fragrances that are usually added to extend the shelf life of these products and to increase their appeal. Since moisturizers are liberally applied and almost fully absorbed into the skin, these additives have more potential to cause allergic and other adverse reactions than products that are ordinarily rinsed off, such as soap or shampoo. While the safety of their long-term use is unclear, moisturizers and other leave-on products pose more of a threat from cumulative exposure.

While preservatives do help prevent spoilage and bacteria growth, many can have adverse effects. Most notorious are the parabens, a class of preservatives that have hormone-mimicking properties. Other preservatives release small amounts of formaldehyde, considered a human carcinogen. For this reason, avoid products containing the following ingredients: bronopol, diazolidinyl urea, DMDM hydantoin, imidazolidinyl urea, and quaternium-15. All of these contain formaldehyde, release formaldehyde, or break down into formaldehyde.

Finally, colors and fragrances are sometimes added to improve moisturizers' appearance and scent. Skip the coal-tar colors, which can be carcinogenic, and avoid products containing "fragrance" as an ingredient, as this can mask the presence of hormone-disrupting phthalates. For more on these, see "The Dirty Dozen," pages 169-71.

Seek out healthy hydrators that avoid the above ingredients. The best alternatives will include such ingredients as water, plant hydrosols, aloe, and plant oils such as those derived from the olive, sunflower, apricot, almond, and jojoba plants. All these can effectively soothe dry skin without posing health risks.

GREEN DICTIONARY

PARABENS

A group of preservatives used in many kinds of toiletries and cosmetics, parabens demonstrate weak estrogenic effects in the body and may be linked to the development of breast cancer. A 2004 study published in the Journal of Applied Toxicology found parabens in tissue samples from human breast tumors. Look for the growing number of products labeled "paraben-free," and avoid products that contain butyl-, ethyl-, isobutyl-, methyl-, or propylparaben.

ECO-TIP: HEALTHIER AGE FIGHTERS

Injections and other cosmetic procedures may be trendy, but there are many less invasive, more healthful ways to stave off wrinkles and other signs of aging. Check out what these ingredients can do to keep up that youthful glow.

✓ **Antioxidants.** Sun exposure, smog, smoke, and the stress of daily life create free radicals—negatively charged ions that can damage healthy cells and contribute to wrinkles and other signs of aging. Taken orally or applied topically, the antioxidant vitamins A,C, and E help strengthen your defenses. Also helpful are antioxidant-rich foods such as artichokes, beans, berries, russet potatoes, and nuts.

✓ **Peptides.** Some peptides (short strings of amino acids) boost skin's production of collagen when applied topically. The "plumping" effect may reduce the appearance of wrinkles and sagging skin.

✓ **Alpha-hydroxy acids (AHAs).** These acids help rid the skin of dead surface cells and make wrinkles less apparent. They are derived from fruit and milk sugars (and can also be synthesized). Glycolic acid often comes from sugarcane, malic acid from apples and pears, lactic acid from milk, citric acid from citrus fruits, and tartaric acid from grapes.

✓ **Licorice root extract.** As an alternative to potentially unsafe skin lighteners like hydroquinone, women in Asian countries have long used licorice root extract to help even out skin tone and reduce the appearance of the dark spots that can appear as skin ages.

BETTER CHOICES FOR YOUR BODY You should choose a body moisturizer with the same care that you use to select facial moisturizers: Avoid petroleum products, glycols, parabens, formaldehyde-releasing ingredients, and artificial scents and colors. But because of the amount of product applied to the skin—usually several ounces, sometimes applied more than once a day—it's even more important to be diligent about picking body products with safe ingredients.

ASK THE EDITORS

Q Are all plant oils ecofriendly?

A Sadly, not all plant-derived products are harvested and processed with nature's best interests in mind.

Palm oil is a prime example. Most palm oil comes from Southeast Asian countries such as Malaysia, Indonesia, and Thailand. While some palm oil is produced in an environmentally sensitive manner, the Center for Science in the Public Interest reports that in these regions, irreplaceable rain forest is being cleared to make room for oil palm plantations. Those rain forests provide a critically important habitat for Sumatran and Bornean orangutans, Sumatran rhinos and tigers, Asian elephants, and other endangered species. The steady loss of rain forest is pushing those species closer to extinction.

For this reason, avoid purchasing moisturizers and other body products made with palm oil unless the manufacturer specifically indicates that its raw materials are sustainably harvested.

There are several safe moisturizing ingredients you can use on your body that you won't typically find in facial products because of their thick texture. One is shea butter, a thick plant butter derived from the nut of the shea, or karite, tree. Shea trees are native to western and central Africa, and they are sustainably harvested by the local people. Traditionally, it is forbidden to take shea nuts off the tree, so all shea butter is made from nuts that have fallen to the ground, which means that the harvest does not deplete the ongoing supply—it is a sustainable product.

Shea butter, incredibly moisturizing, is used in Africa as a massage cream, to stave off stretch marks, and to provide sun protection. (Don't rely on it as a sunscreen, though.) Similarly, cocoa butter, kukui nut butter, mango butter, and coconut oil offer deep hydration and are often blended into moisturizing body care products.

Lip Care

Every time you eat a meal, sip a beverage, or lick your lips, small amounts of your lip balm or gloss make their way into your mouth. And yet many lip care products contain things you would never want to eat. Luckily, more natural, nontoxic alternatives abound.

BETTER BALMS Most lip balms, glosses, and salves are made using a base of petrolatum—petroleum jelly—which comes from a nonrenewable resource and which can cause irritation of sensitive skin. To protect and soften your lips without petrolatum, turn to products that combine beeswax with plant oils and nut butters. Shea butter, cocoa butter, and coconut oil (which is more like a paste than an oil) all coat the skin and seal in moisture as well as petrolatum, while sunflower and apricot-seed oils smooth out the balms' texture and leave lips slightly glossy. Avoid balms that are made with artificial colors, flavors, or scents; better choices rely on dark-colored fruit extracts and essential oils such as peppermint to enhance the products' appearance and flavor.

ECO-TIP: KNOW YOUR NATURAL INGREDIENTS

While mainstream cosmetics' high-tech formulations do call for a little extra caution, not all botanical ingredients are totally safe, either. Exercise caution with these plant extracts:

✓ **Balsam of Peru.** A resin extracted from a tree that is actually native to El Salvador, it's sometimes used as an antiseptic skin treatment and is frequently used as a fixative in perfumes. It's also one of the most allergenic ingredients found in cosmetics and can lead to contact dermatitis (rash). Avoid it if you have sensitive skin or are prone to skin allergies.

✓ **Citrus Oils.** Essential oils of lemon, orange, grapefruit, and lime add all-natural fragrance to bath and body products, but they may also increase sun sensitivity. Dermatologists often advise against

these products before sun exposure, and suggest using extra sun protection when going outdoors.

✓ **Chamomile.** A favorite flower for brewing herbal tea, chamomile is also used in beauty products as an anti-inflammatory ingredient. It's closely related to ragweed and may trigger allergic reactions in some people. If you're a seasonal allergy sufferer, you may want to avoid chamomile in your cosmetic formulations.

✓ **Lavender and Tea Tree Oils.** Lavender oil's sweet fragrance makes it ideal for bath and skin care products, and tea tree oil's antiseptic properties give it blemish- and infection-fighting power. However, a 2007 study published in the *New England Journal of Medicine* linked the use of these oils in topical products with prepubertal gynecomastia, or the development of breasts, in young boys. To be safe, avoid using these two ingredients on small children.

Hair Products

To get our tresses looking oh-so-shiny, we subject them to all manner of products and treatments, hair care routines that can have unseen, untold impacts, not only on our family's health, but on the health of the planet.

SAFER SHAMPOOS For the most part, the key issues with shampoos are the same as with skin cleansers, so you should follow the same guidelines and avoid the same problematic ingredients. The common lather-producing sulfates sodium lauryl sulfate (SLS) and sodium laureth sulfate (SLES) may irritate the skin. SLES and other ethoxylated ingredients may be contaminated at minute levels with the carcinogen dioxane. As with liquid soaps and body washes, shampoos may contain the formula-boosters diethanolamine (DEA), monoethanolamine (MEA), and triethanolamine (TEA), which are hormone disruptors and known irritants. Dandruff shampoos often contain coal tar as an active ingredient, which is troubling considering it's a known carcinogen.

Finally, shampoos can contain fragrances and preservatives that may affect the endocrine system. ▸See "The Dirty Dozen," on pages 169-171, for ingredients to avoid whenever possible.

Of course, all these warnings don't mean you should resort to washing your hair with biodegradable dish soap. If you're having trouble locating safer shampoos at your hair salon or drug store, head to the natural-foods store instead, and look for brands that are forthright about the safety of their ingredients.

STYLING AIDS Unlike the heavy styling products of decades past—greasy pomades, hard-as-nails hairspray, goopy green hair gels, and mounds of mousse—today's offerings are designed to help create more natural-looking 'dos. And yet, the formulas sold in most salons and drugstores today are far from natural. Most use petroleum-derived silicone compounds to smooth flyaway strands, large amounts of preservatives to extend products' shelf life for at least a year, and strong perfumes. While it's true that styling products go on your hair rather than on your scalp, some contact with your skin is inevitable. Avoid using any of the Dirty Dozen ingredients on your hair, and seek safer alternatives. Certain nongreasy plant oils like jojoba, which closely resembles the skin's natural oils, can be applied to dry hair to eliminate frizz and add shine. For adding structure to short hairstyles, look for products made with beeswax, carnauba wax, and vegetable gums.

THE FACTS

A 2008 study by the Environmental Working Group found that almost 90 percent of hair coloring and bleaching products contained coal tar—a known neurotoxin—or peroxide—known to cause skin burns.

ECO-TIP: HUNTING FOR BETTER BEAUTY PRODUCTS

Not sure which brands make the grade, or where to find them? Start by taking these steps.

✓ **Review all your favorite products by visiting the Environmental Working Group's Skin Deep Cosmetic Database of personal care products, which rates nearly 25,000 products against 50 definitive toxicity and regulatory databases. Products receive a score between 1 and 10 and a green, yellow, or red light based on the group's standards of safety. If you're using mostly yellow- and red-light products, search for better options using the categorized product listings.**

✓ **Check out the website for the Campaign for Safe Cosmetics to see who has signed the group's compact. All of the member companies' products must meet the criteria in the European Union's Cosmetics Directive 76/768/EEC.**

✓ **As you familiarize yourself with the toxic ingredients commonly found in personal care products, start reading the fine print on your products. Don't feel you have to know every ingredient on the list; just get used to thinking about what you put on your body. If you gravitate toward products whose ingredients you can understand (sunflower seed oil, cocoa butter, aloe vera, rosemary essential oil) you're likelier to end up using products that are better for you.**

✓ **Shop at drugstores, natural-foods stores, and beauty boutiques that have flexible return policies. That way, you can easily return or exchange the product if you find out that your new shampoo or lotion contains troublesome chemicals.**

HEALTHIER COLOR Anyone who has ever worked in a salon can tell you that it takes a lot of chemicals to change your hair color. First, you must prepare the hair shaft to receive color, which can require a caustic compound like ammonium hydroxide or hydrogen peroxide, which causes the hair cuticle to "swell." Then you need to apply a dye, often containing coal tar or lead acetate, and get it to stick. None of this is easy on your hair, which is why there's a huge market for products meant to restore its lost luster and texture post-dye job.

But your hair isn't the only thing that's affected by this cocktail of ingredients. Hair dye solutions can contain alkylphenyl ethoxylates, or APEs, which break down into alkylphenols, two of which are suspected hormone disruptors. Those caustic chemicals that open up the hair shaft can also irritate mucous membranes and burn skin. Even more concerning, some dyes increase the risk of certain types of cancer. Prolonged use of dark—particularly black—permanent hair dyes has been linked to an increased risk of non-Hodgkin's lymphoma and multiple myeloma, and a study published in the *International Journal of Cancer* in February 2001 found that women

THE FACTS

A May 2002 U.S. Geological Survey study found traces of triclosan, an antibacterial agent used in many soaps and deodorants, in 57 percent of streams surveyed. According to the Alliance for the Prudent Use of Antibiotics, overuse of triclosan fosters the development of antibiotic-resistant bacteria.

who use permanent hair dyes once a month are twice as likely to get bladder cancer as women who don't dye their hair at all.

There are steps you can take to mitigate the damage. First, semipermanent dyes and lighter-colored permanent dyes generally pose less of a danger than dark, permanent hair colors, so if you're choosing between shades, it's usually best to go lighter (unless you have naturally dark hair; in general, the more drastic a color change you seek, the more chemicals you'll need to use to achieve your desired shade).

Second, find a stylist who uses less toxic professional dyes, or purchase your own at-home kit. Some hair dyes contain no petrochemicals and are up to 99 percent plant-based; while not perfect, they're a better choice than other professional salon dyes. Some that fit this description are used by some stylists but are also available for home use. While they may contain some hydrogen peroxide or ammonium hydroxide, as long as they are plant-based, they will most likely contain lower concentrations of irritants than standard dyes and provide a good option for subtle hair color changes.

Third, do what you can to reduce your exposure to any kind of hair dye. This can mean choosing highlights that are painted onto sections of hair instead of applying an all-over hair color, or reducing the frequency of your salon visits. Last, and perhaps most important, avoid coloring your hair while pregnant or nursing, as any chemicals that make their way into your system can be passed along to your developing baby.

Another alternative is to choose herbal hair colorants rather than dyes. These treatments stain the hair cuticle without damaging it. The most common ingredient in these is henna, derived from the herb *Lawsonia inermis*, but there are also products made from plants like beets, indigo, rhubarb, and walnuts. (You should still use care with these dyes, as they can be allergenic.) Lemon juice can help lighten blond hair, although it has a tendency to dry it out. If you choose any of these hair coloring methods, be sure to grow hair out completely before and after using chemical colorants, as plant-based and chemical colorants can react together unpleasantly.

ECO-TIP: HOMEMADE BEAUTY REMEDIES

For truly natural personal care, try a few of these do-it-yourself beauty treatments using ingredients from your own kitchen.

- ✓ **Sugar scrub.** Blend white sugar with a plant oil such as olive, almond, or jojoba. Use just enough oil to form a thick paste, then add a few drops of your favorite essential oil for fragrance. Use this scrub to exfoliate dry, scaly patches of skin.
- ✓ **Oatmeal bath.** Soothe sunburned skin by adding a cotton sachet filled with old-fashioned oats to your bath tub.
- ✓ **Yogurt mask.** Soften skin by applying a thin layer of plain, whole-milk yogurt to a clean, dry complexion. The natural lactic acid helps speed cell turnover and increase skin's radiance.
- ✓ **Chamomile eye soother.** Steep two chamomile tea bags in warm water, then place them in the refrigerator to chill. Apply the cool, moist bags to closed eyes to relieve puffiness. But note: People who are highly allergic to ragweed should avoid chamomile.
- ✓ **Hot oil treatment.** Before hopping in the shower, apply several tablespoons of jojoba or olive oil to dry hair and comb it through. Put on a shower cap and step into the shower; the heat from the water will help the oils to penetrate the hair shaft. After a few minutes, remove the cap and shampoo as usual.

Antiperspirants & Deodorants

For better or worse, Americans have come to expect their nearby neighbors to use toiletries to prevent or obscure natural body odor. Skin irritation and asthma are common side effects of these products, but there may be worse.

SWEAT STOPPERS Antiperspirants contain astringent compounds, usually aluminum, zinc, or zirconium salts, which block pores, reduce sweat production, and keep underarms dry. These compounds are a leading cause of irritation from antiperspirants, and they can cause contact dermatitis or small, itchy bumps called granulomas on sensitive underarm skin. The compounds vary in their potential to produce irritation; aluminum chloride is the most common cause of rashes, while aluminum chlorohydrate is less likely to irritate.

While the most reliable way to avoid irritation and any other health risks is to forgo the use of antiperspirant altogether, that may not be practical. The best choice, then, is to look for so-called crystal or rock antiperspirants, which are composed of ammonium alum (ammonium aluminum sulfate) or potassium alum (potassium aluminum sulfate). These antiperspirants often look like a clear or whitish stone, moistened then rubbed on the skin. These sweat-blocking minerals can also be found as the active ingredients in more traditionally packaged antiperspirant products. Either way, these aluminum compounds are the least likely to cause dermatitis.

ODOR ELIMINATORS In addition to (or in lieu of) antiperspirant compounds, many people choose products that contain deodorizing ingredients, such as perfumes and antibacterial agents. These prevent sweat from mingling with surface bacteria and producing an odor, or they mask the odor. Both types of ingredients have downsides. Perfumes can contain allergenic compounds and phthalates. ▸For more on phthalates, see page 190. Antibacterial agents, such as triclosan, are known to contaminate groundwater once they are washed off the body, and can harm freshwater ecosystems. They're also frequently criticized for contributing to antibiotic-resistant bacteria.

ASK THE EDITORS

Q **Is it true that antiperspirants can cause Alzheimer's disease?**

A The controversy surrounding the relationship between antiperspirants and Alzheimer's stems largely from the results of a few studies conducted in the 1960s and 1970s that showed elevated aluminum levels in the brains of Alzheimer's patients. Since aluminum is an ingredient commonly used in mass-market antiperspirants, many blamed (and still blame) these products for causing the disease.

Most major medical organizations remain unconvinced of a solid connection between the two. The World Health Organization (WHO), the U.S. National Institutes of Health (NIH), the U.S. Environmental Protection Agency (EPA), and Health Canada all take similar positions. Additionally, more recent studies suggest that, rather than causing Alzheimer's, aluminum may simply accumulate because of tissue damage inflicted by the disease, or that it may have entered study samples as a contaminant.

Nevertheless, some environmental health experts do suggest minimizing exposure to aluminum as a precautionary measure, simply because we do not know the long-term effects of frequent exposure to aluminum, through the skin or by ingestion. Their advice extends to aluminum cookware, foil, and beverage cans. They also point to some common antacids that contain aluminum.

If you prefer to avoid aluminum, you're better off choosing deodorants instead of antiperspirants. While deodorants don't prevent sweat, they can help eliminate underarm odor, and they do so without the use of aluminum.

Sun Protection

Taking care of your skin means protecting it from excess sun exposure. We need some sun, but too much of it may lead to painful sunburns, unwelcome signs of aging, and even skin cancer. There are different types of skin cancer, but exposure to the sun's ultraviolet rays increases the risk of all of them.

STANDARD SUNBLOCKS Most of the sunscreens that line conventional grocery and drugstore shelves are what's known as chemical sunscreens or chemical blocks. While they allow the sun's rays to penetrate the skin, they rely on synthetic chemicals to absorb the radiation and prevent it from burning or damaging your skin. Examples of chemical sunscreen ingredients include benzophenone (also called benzophenone-3 or oxybenzone) homosalate, octyl-methoxycinnamate (octinoxate), padimate-0, avobenzone (Parsol 1789), and ecamsule.

While effective at preventing sunburn and reducing your risk of skin cancer, these ingredients are associated with some troubling effects on health. Benzophenone may cause irritation and rashes in some users, and appears to mimic the hormone estrogen in the body. In a 2001 study published in *Environmental Health Perspectives*, estrogen-sensitive breast cancer cells in test tubes multiplied when they were exposed to five out of six chemical sunscreens, among them benzophenone-3, homosalate, and octyl-methoxycinnamate, indicating that the substances were behaving like estrogen. While the medical community has not made any recommendations based on this research, the results suggest that these chemical sunscreens may disrupt users' endocrine systems. As the skin more readily absorbs benzophenone than other sunscreen ingredients, the presence of that ingredient in sunscreen products is particularly concerning.

THE FACTS

Skin cancer is the most common of all cancers in the U.S. According to the National Cancer Institute, 40 to 50 percent of all Americans who live to age 65 will face non-melanoma skin cancer at least once in their lives.

Another potentially dangerous sunscreen ingredient is padimate-O, a derivative of the ingredient para-aminobenzoic acid, known as PABA. For years PABA was a standard ingredient in sunscreens, but because it stained clothing and caused allergies in some people, most manufacturers removed it from their formulas. Some studies have indicated that padimate-O causes DNA damage,

which might, over time, lead to cancer. As these studies were not conducted on humans or living animals, it's difficult to draw solid conclusions about its safety or the hazards of using sunscreen products containing it.

GREEN DICTIONARY

SPF

A sunscreen's sun protection factor, or SPF, is based on an FDA-approved rating of how quickly exposed skin will burn while wearing the sunscreen compared with going without. For example, if your skin usually burns in 10 minutes, an SPF-15 product will buy you 10 x 15 minutes, two and half hours, in the sun.

The ingredients mentioned above are used in sunscreen formulations because they effectively protect the skin from ultraviolet-B (UVB) rays, which were known to cause sunburn and skin cancer. Now our collective attention has recently shifted to ultraviolet-A (UVA) rays, which, while less carcinogenic, are more plentiful than UVB, hence just as dangerous. Good sunscreens protect against both types of ultraviolet rays, since both can contribute to cancer and photoaging.

To be sure a product is effective against both UVA and UVB rays, look for ones labeled "broad-spectrum." You should also follow the application instructions precisely. Most people use just 25 to 50 percent of the recommended amount of sunscreen, says the Skin Cancer Foundation—a mistake that reduces the effectiveness of any product you've slathered on.

Avobenzone is one of the most common UVA-protective ingredients used these days, but it, too, has come under scrutiny. This time, the controversy doesn't revolve around safety; rather, it's because the protection the ingredient offers is unclear. Unless it has been stabilized, avobenzone has a tendency to break down under sunlight, potentially rendering it less effective. As a result, stabilized avobenzone is becoming increasingly popular and is frequently recommended by dermatologists.

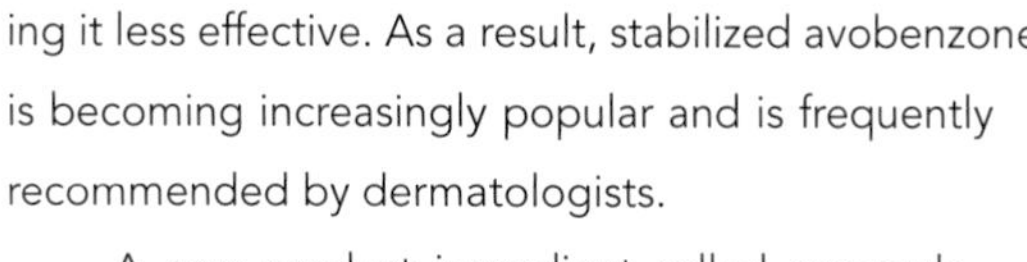

A new product ingredient called ecamsule is, like avobenzone, a UVA-protective sunscreen, making it a popular choice of dermatologists and consumers concerned with UV-related signs of aging. Though it has been available in Europe and Canada since 1993, it was approved by the FDA only in 2006. Unfortunately, products containing ecamsule also often contain ingredients on the *Green Guide's* Dirty Dozen list (pages 169-71), but it's

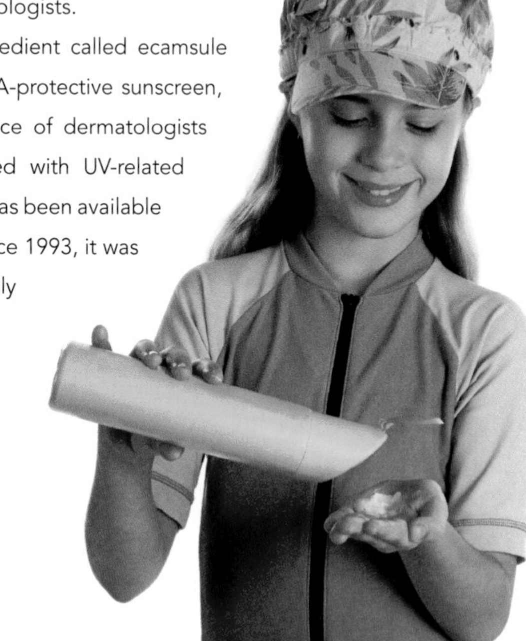

possible that new formulations including ecamsule (or a similar ingredient) will find their way into a wider variety of sunscreens in the coming years.

THE MINERAL MOVEMENT Mineral-based sunscreens form a protective physical barrier on the skin that deflects both UVA and UVB rays. Titanium dioxide and zinc oxide are the most commonly used minerals, blended into creams today through micronization, a process that reduces the size of the mineral particles. It's unclear whether these smaller particles are being absorbed by the skin, however, and, if they are, what effects they may have on human health. Some research indicates that zinc oxide and titanium dioxide, particularly if they enter the body through cuts or inhalation, can damage cell DNA. Damage may occur more readily from particles of microscopic size.

It's important to note that the term "micronized" doesn't necessarily mean "contains nanoparticles." The difference is their size: Microns are one millionth of a meter, while nanometers (nm) are one billionth of a meter. Basically, 1,000 nm = 1 micron. Yet cosmetics companies often don't differentiate, or they use the incorrect term on their labels. The FDA has not set a definition for the nano-scale ingredients in personal care products. If you're concerned about the risks, check with your products' manufacturers to find out whether they use nano-size minerals, or buy only from companies that specifically state that they do not.

GREEN DICTIONARY

NANOPARTICLES

Mineral particles that have been fragmented to sizes below 100 nanometers are known as nanoparticles; they are often used in sunscreens and mineral makeup products because they are less visible when applied to the skin.

ECO-TIP: A SAFER WAY TO TAN

No matter what the dangers, some folks will always love the look of a suntan. For them, there's an endless array of self-tanning products to give skin a glow without UV exposure. The key ingredient in most is dihydroxyacetone (DHA), an FDA-approved compound that reacts with the sugars in the top layer of skin cells, producing a sunless tan that lasts a few days. Some have speculated that self-tanners may help reduce skin cancer risk. A 2003 study published in the journal *Mutation Research* found that chemically induced pigmentation from high concentrations of DHA absorbs a small amount of UV rays, which may slow skin cancer development. For something even more temporary, look for mineral-based bronzers, which wash off.

ASK THE EDITORS

Q **I've heard that sunscreen doesn't prevent skin cancer, and can actually cause it. Is there any truth to this rumor?**

A For the most part, the American medical community—including the American Academy of Dermatology, the American Cancer Society, and the Centers for Disease Control and Prevention—believes that sunscreen use plays a beneficial role in helping to prevent skin cancer. Other groups, such as the American College of Preventive Medicine (ACPM), have questioned its value, pointing out that the evidence supporting sunscreen's cancer-preventive capability is incomplete, especially its influence on malignant melanoma (MM), the most deadly form of skin cancer.

Some critics go even further, speculating that the dramatic rise of skin cancer incidence over the past several decades is somehow related to the rise of sunscreen use. In reference to MM, the ACPM has written that "there is insufficient evidence that chemical sunscreens protect against MM and they may, in fact, increase risk." While most health practitioners tend to disagree, the ACPM does point out that sunscreen wearers tend to place too much faith in sunscreen and spend more time in the sun than those who don't wear any sun protection. Whether or not certain ingredients in the sunscreens themselves cause cancer is undetermined; to this point, there's been little research into that possibility.

Ultimately, the choice to wear (or not wear) sunscreen is yours. But there's no arguing about the fact that sunscreen prevents painful sunburns, and that it reduces the visible signs of aging. For most consumers, this is reason enough to apply a product with SPF. Whatever you do, remember that sunscreen ranks a distant second to sun avoidance, especially where skin cancer is concerned. Cover up and seek shade, especially during peak sunlight hours (between 10 a.m. and 4 p.m.).

Fragrances

As humans, our sense of smell is inextricably linked to our memories and experiences. We recognize the scent of a loved one's cologne on a sweater; before buying a new shampoo or hand cream, we take a good, long whiff.

Just because a product smells good doesn't mean it's good for you. While the earliest perfumes were innocuous extracts of real flowers, fruits, and herbs, most of today's scent additives are synthetic. Worse yet, the National Institute of Occupational Safety and Health has found one-third of the substances used in the fragrance industry—both natural and synthetic—to be toxic. Some chemicals commonly found in scented products, such as acetone (used in cologne and nail polish remover) and methylene chloride (used in shampoo and cologne), also appear on the EPA's Hazardous Waste list. Follow these guidelines to find fragrances and perfumes without health and environmental risks.

COLOGNE CHOICES The vast majority of perfumes and colognes on the market today contain a blend of natural and synthetic components, including phthalates. Since it's not likely you'll find a complete ingredient list on any of them, consumers who wish to avoid phthalates are better off skipping most of the products sold at department stores and drugstores.

Fragrances based on essential oils, though harder to find, are usually a safer bet and often provide full ingredient disclosure. They generally consist of herbal, fruit-derived, or floral plant oils blended with a neutral "carrier" oil such as almond or olive oil. They may also contain a nontoxic solvent, such as alcohol. These perfumes can often be found at natural-foods stores or specialty boutiques.

As with traditional perfumes, the fragrance may be dabbed or sprayed on; occasionally you may also see "solid" perfumes in the form of a longer-lasting balm. Whatever your preference, look for products with complete ingredient lists, and avoid anything with the generic term "fragrance" (unless you're certain that the product line is phthalate-free).

GREEN DICTIONARY

PHTHALATES

A class of chemicals commonly used as solvents and fixatives in fragrances, phthalates are hormone disruptors that have been shown to cause birth defects and lifelong reproductive system damage in lab animals.

PRODUCT SCENTS Even if you don't wear perfume, you probably still come into contact with fragrance ingredients every day. Nearly every soap, deodorant, body lotion contains them—even some that are labeled "unscented." According to the American Academy of Dermatology, fragrances are the most likely of all skin care ingredients to trigger allergic contact dermatitis.

As with perfumes and colognes, the key is to avoid any skin care products that list the word "fragrance" among the ingredients, as this term can hide allergens as well as hormone-disrupting phthalates. Look instead for products scented with essential plant extracts such as lavender, orange, or rose—listed simply on labels as "essential oil," along with the type of plant—or with no fragrance ingredients listed at all. Doing so will help reduce your chances of inadvertently coming into contact with irritating or allergenic ingredients. (Note that if you are allergic to a type of plant or flower, you should steer clear of any product that contains its essential oil.)

THE FACTS

In the Environmental Working Group's 2002 cosmetics industry review, entitled "Not Too Pretty," all 17 of the fragrances tested were found to contain phthalates.

Cosmetics

While the number of safer, more Earth-friendly makeup brands is on the rise, the choices are still limited, and many don't provide the same selection and performance as mass-market brands.

Since demand for natural cosmetics is still relatively low, fewer industry dollars are spent on developing healthier products. Pressure on the cosmetics industry to modify and improve its formulas is mounting, however. Consumer groups such as the Campaign for Safe Cosmetics aim to educate consumers about the risks of certain cosmetic ingredients; this particular campaign also encourages manufacturers to sign a pledge stating that their products meet or exceed the European Union's stricter formulation standards (which ban the use of known carcinogens and mutagens in cosmetic products). Purchasing your products from companies that have signed on with the campaign is an excellent start, but since it's likely that you'll also buy a few products from mainstream manufacturers, learning to spot the most troublesome ingredients is wise.

FACE FIRST In the quest for a flawless complexion, women employ all manner of concealing, oil-absorbing, light-reflecting products. There are liquid, cream, and powder foundations, long-wearing formulas, and ultra-sheer tinted moisturizers. Whatever your preference among these options, the first step toward healthier makeup is to choose products that are free of the Dirty Dozen chemicals (▸listed on pages 169-71). While it's always prudent to avoid these ingredients in personal care products, it's particularly important for items like foundation, which sit on your skin for extended periods of time and are likelier to be absorbed than products that are applied on top of the foundation. Common offenders in foundations, concealers, and powders include parabens and formaldehyde-based preservatives such as DMDM hydantoin, diazolidinyl urea, imidazolidinyl urea, and quaternium-15. Synthetic fragrances, often used to mask the chemical odor of some products, may contain phthalates.

One of the Dirty Dozen, nanoparticles, can be tricky to avoid given the increased popularity of the newer mineral-based foundations. While these powder foundations generally contain fewer irritants, preservatives, and oils than traditional foundations and are less likely to cause dermatitis or clog pores, they're not necessarily all-natural and do come with caveats. The primary minerals used in these products are zinc oxide and titanium dioxide (the same ingredients used in mineral-based sunscreens), along with mica and iron oxides (for pigment and iridescence). The particles are often fragmented down to mere nanometers in order to increase the products' blendability and texture, but it's unclear whether this increases their absorption, or whether there are health consequences if the particles are absorbed.

Instead, look for products that do not contain nanoparticles—many manufacturers address the issue on their websites—and read the ingredient list carefully to see what other ingredients the formulas contain. Some manufacturers coat mineral particles with silicone oils including dimethicone, which helps the foundation spread more evenly. While these materials aren't irritating, they're derived from petroleum, a nonrenewable resource. Lauryl lysine, a combination of the amino acid lysine and coconut oil-derived lauric acid, is a more sustainable alternative.

THE FACTS

Cosmetics manufacturers can submit product formulations and reports of adverse reactions to the government on a voluntary basis. According to the FDA, only about 35 percent actually do.

ECO-TIP: READING LABELS

Labels on the health and beauty products at your local drug or department store affirm the safety and effectiveness of many products. But what do the words on those labels really mean? Here are four of the most common—and most misunderstood.

✓ **Natural:** Slapped on everything from soap to hairspray, this overused term is fairly meaningless. In theory, it indicates that the ingredients are plant-based and minimally processed, but the term is unregulated by the FDA and can be used on products that contain animal-derived ingredients, petroleum products, synthetic colors and fragrances, and more. Sadly, it's not an indicator of product quality or safety, in any capacity.

✓ **Organic:** Since no separate organic standards for personal care products have been established, manufacturers may use the term "organic" any way they wish. Some use it to indicate that the ingredients are carbon-based. Use of the term—including the USDA "organic" symbol on a label—does not mean that the product was made without synthetic ingredients.

✓ **Hypoallergenic:** While intended to guide allergy-prone consumers toward less irritating products, this term isn't comprehensive or reliable, and is not based on any federal standards. Many "hypoallergenic" products leave out only the most common allergenic substances. Other undesirable ingredients, such as talc or sulfates, may still be included.

✓ **Noncomedogenic:** Theoretically this term, which indicates that animal and/or human testing shows that a product won't clog pores, is akin to a green light for acne sufferers. But since blemishes are caused by a number of factors, including skin care routine, hormones, nutrition, and genetics, it's tough to predict whether a product will trigger breakouts. Many assume that noncomedogenic products are oil-free, or that oil-free products won't clog pores, but neither is necessarily true.

COLOR HINTS Eyes and mouths are extremely sensitive—not to mention major entry points for germs and chemicals—yet few women give a second thought to what's in their makeup products, despite all the coloring agents, metals, and irritants they can contain. Certain FDA-approved coloring agents, labeled as FD&C or D&C colors, are far from safe; some contain lead acetate, a heavy metal that is toxic to the nervous system, while others are allergens, irritants, or linked with cancers. FD&C Blue 1 and Green 3 themselves and impurities in other colors—D&C Red 33, FD&C Yellow 5 and FD&C Yellow 6—have been linked with cancer.

Petroleum is also an ingredient of concern, from a safety and ecological perspective. Petroleum-derived fibers such as nylon and polyester are frequently used in mascaras to lengthen and thicken lashes, but they may also lead to contact dermatitis. Many lipsticks, balms, and glosses have a petrolatum (petroleum jelly) base, which moisturizes but can cause allergic reactions.

Some mascaras, especially those marketed as "lash-building," have been found to contain a preservative called thimerosal that contains mercury, a known neurotoxin. Thimerosal may also cause allergic reactions. Additionally, in October 2007 the Campaign for Safe Cosmetics released study results on 33 national brands of lipsticks, reporting that lead had been detected in more than half of those tested. Levels ranged from 0.03 to 0.65 part per million (ppm), and one-third of the lipsticks exceeded the 0.1 ppm FDA standard set to protect children from ingesting lead.

You needn't abandon makeup altogether, however. Many companies have signed the Compact for Safe Cosmetics, pledging to replace toxic chemicals with safer alternatives in their products. These brands are safer bets in general (though you should always read labels to see what your products contain). Read labels, or go to the Campaign for Safe Cosmetics website for an up-to-date list of the companies and products abiding by the compact's rules.

Online shopping can be a boon to consumers, as e-retailers often list the products' ingredients, which you can compare against your Dirty Dozen list before you buy. Natural-foods stores frequently stock cosmetics that contain fewer toxins, so they're a good place to see and test products in person.

And don't underestimate your local drugstore or department store. Though the vast majority of products sold at national retailers contain unhealthy ingredients, with a trained eye (and a list of Dirty Dozen ingredients in hand), you can pick out the less toxic choices among them.

ASK THE EDITORS

Q **What's the difference between "unscented" and "fragrance-free"?**

A For consumers with sensitive skin and allergies, seeking out unscented and fragrance-free products is practically second nature. But while these labels can guide you in the right direction—companies are supposed to declare fragrance on labels—they're not fail-safe.

Although these two terms both imply that a product has no fragrance, "unscented" often refers to products that contain "neutral" fragrances to cover up the smell of certain natural and synthetic ingredients, while "fragrance-free" has no added fragrance at all. This distinction isn't always reliable because the FDA has no set definition for the two terms, which leaves their usage to the manufacturer's discretion. If you're in doubt, read labels closely and look for products with short, simple, readable ingredient lists; the more complex the formula, the higher the chances of hidden fragrances slipping by the consumer unnoticed. And before slathering on that lotion or cosmetic, always do a small "patch test" on your arm to determine whether a product will trigger an allergic reaction.

HOW TO BE ANIMAL-FRIENDLY Sadly, many personal care products' ingredients have a history of animal cruelty. The FDA mandates that cosmetic ingredients be "adequately substantiated for safety" prior to sale, and products whose safety has not been determined must be labeled as such. And yet, there are no clear criteria for this testing and labeling. To reassure consumers that ingredients are safe, companies often conduct painful and sometimes deadly procedures on animals, testing for eye and skin irritation and gathering "lethal dose" data—although there is no requirement that products be tested on animals. Further complicating matters, the popular "Cruelty-free" and "No Animal Testing" labels do not guarantee that such tests have not

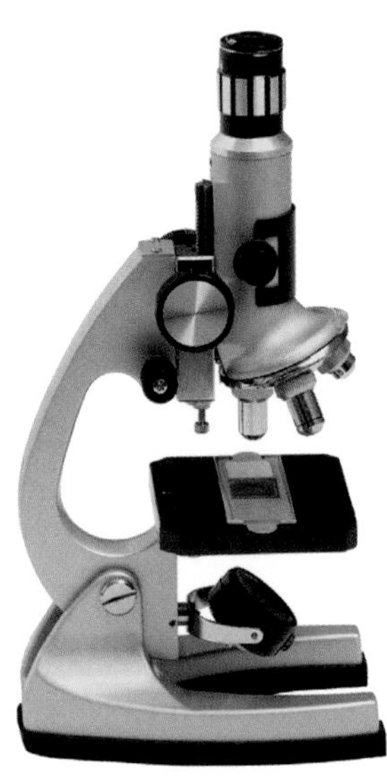

been done. Neither claim is legally defined or verified by an independent organization. In reality, manufacturers whose products bear these labels often commission outside laboratories to conduct the testing.

There's good news for animal lovers, however. On the manufacturing side, if a company wishes to use ingredients already in use in the marketplace, no new tests need to be performed. And when new products and ingredients are introduced, the vagueness of the FDA requirement permits alternatives to animal testing, such as computer modeling and laboratory tests conducted on human tissue.

The most reliable label to look for is the Leaping Bunny, which signals products made by companies that follow the Corporate Standard of Compassion for Animals. The label was developed by animal protection groups, including the Humane Society of the United States and the American Anti-Vivisection Society, which formed the Coalition for Consumer Information on Cosmetics (CCIC). Companies whose products bear the Leaping Bunny logo pledge not to conduct or commission animal testing. The CCIC also offers a list of companies certified as refraining from animal testing on its website. See "Resources."

Nail Care

A whole industry now revolves around fingernails: painting them, sculpting them, adding on to them. But while modern nail care products beautify our hands, they can also present health risks and environmental problems.

A whole industry revolves around painting, sculpting, and adding on to fingernails. But while modern nail care products beautify our hands, they can also present health risks and environmental problems. The products don't stay on the tips of our fingers; because our nails are made of keratin (a fibrous, highly porous substance capable of absorbing up to three times its weight in water), whatever chemicals are in nail products can be absorbed. And whatever is left in the bottle goes into the landfill. The next time you head to the salon for a manicure, here's what to seek out, and what to leave out.

POLISH IT OFF Lots of ingredients contribute to the high gloss and deep hues of nail enamel, and many of those ingredients come with serious consequences. The most problematic ingredients are phthalates, particularly dibutyl phthalate (DBP). ▸See "Green Dictionary: Phthalates," page 190. In nail polish, these ingredients act as plasticizers, helping the enamel to stay flexible and preventing brittleness and cracking. Unlike other personal care products, where phthalates can hide behind the term "fragrance," nail polish is required by law to list all its ingredients on bottles or boxes. DBP is particularly concerning because its health effects are potentially very serious—it may mimic, block, or disrupt hormones, is a probable carcinogen, and has been linked to reproductive birth defects.

THE FACTS

In 2008, the Environmental Working Group reported that the known hormone disruptor dibutyl phthalate (DBP) was found in 104 out of the 226 nail products they studied.

And phthalates aren't the only troublemakers. Exposure to toluene, a common nail polish solvent and neurotoxin, triggers asthma attacks and can even cause asthma in healthy people. Formaldehyde, used as a preservative in nail products, is a likely carcinogen and can cause severe respiratory symptoms, nausea, and allergic reactions. It provokes irritation at air levels as low as 0.5 ppm). Nail polish is a particularly potent source of formaldehyde exposure. In a study conducted at Battelle Memorial Institute in Columbus, Ohio, a three-inch-square coating of wet nail polishes emitted between 50 and 800 micrograms of formaldehyde—significantly more than an equal area of particleboard.

The news isn't all bad for fans of nail polish, however. In response to demonstrations and pressure from groups such as the Campaign for Safe Cosmetics, many of the major players in the nail care industry now make products without DBP, toluene, or formaldehyde. Look for information about "three-free" nail polishes online. Most nail polishes still contain hazardous ingredients, however, according to the cosmetics watchdog website Skin Deep. ▸See "Resources."

Consumers can also look for water-based formulas. Some of them can peel off, so you don't need nail polish remover.

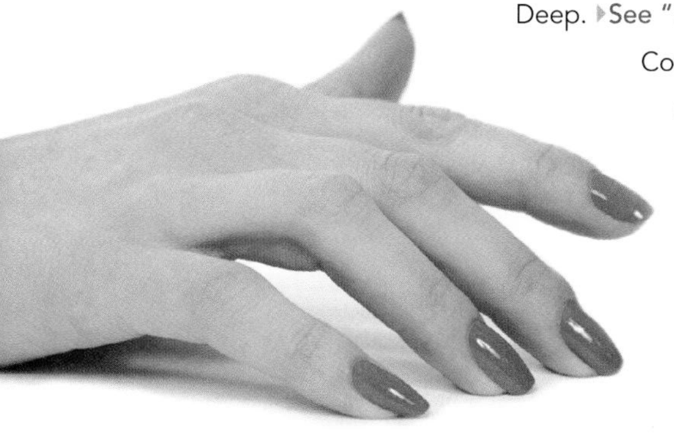

NAIL TREATMENTS In addition to traditional trim-and-polish manicures, many salons also apply artificial nails. These are typically made from acrylic resins, which can cause allergic reactions such as redness, swelling, or pain in the nail bed. Additionally, the adhesives used to secure the artificial nail to the real nail, such as methacrylic acid, can cause irritation or reaction, according to the FDA. But the biggest reason to avoid artificial nails is the solvent used to remove them: acetonitrile. If swallowed, this chemical breaks down into cyanide, with potentially fatal results. At least one child has died after ingesting a mouthful of artificial-nail remover containing acetonitrile.

Dental Health

The steps to good oral hygiene are simple: brush, floss, and see your dentist regularly. There's more to good oral health, though. Get to know what's in your oral care products, and you will be able to choose the options best for you and your family.

BRUSHING UP A toothbrush is just a toothbrush? Well, maybe—although there *are* toothbrushes made of recycled materials that don't require as many resources to produce, and there *are* toothbrushes with detachable brush heads so you can replace just the brush. And what goes on that brush is even less straightforward.

Toothpastes frequently contain a number of cleansing agents, sweeteners, and other chemicals, many of them on the list of the Dirty Dozen (see pages 169-71). These include sodium lauryl and laureth sulfates, detergents that can irritate the skin and gums; parabens preservatives, which may be linked to the development of breast cancer; and other synthetics such as artificial colors and flavors.

Buying a safer alternative isn't as easy as picking up any "natural" product on the shelf, however. While you may want to look for products that don't contain sulfates and synthetic colors and flavors, it's important to note that many alternative products do not bear the American Dental Association seal of approval, because they do not contain fluoride. See "Ask the Editors," page 201. While these fluoride-free toothpastes can still leave your mouth fresh and clean, they may not provide the same level of cavity protection as fluoride-containing varieties. Consider first whether you want to use a fluoride-containing toothpaste, then move on to the other ingredients. Some companies, aware of the challenges in selecting oral care products, offer both fluoride-free toothpastes and fluoridated toothpastes that have a less toxic base.

BETTER FLOSS On top of regular brushing, once-daily flossing is an essential step toward preventing gum disease. And your choice of floss is more important than you might imagine.

According to the Environmental Working Group, some flosses contain forms of perfluorochemicals (PFCs), which have been linked to enhanced tumor growth and cancer. Instead, head to your natural-foods store and pick up greener floss varieties, which do not contain PFCs and which support additional Earth-saving measures by using recycled packaging, vegetable waxes, and essential oils for flavoring. Though nearly all flosses are made of petroleum-derived nylon, the better choices forgo petroleum-based paraffin wax in favor of nontoxic beeswax, carnauba wax, or jojoba wax.

MOUTHWASH MAKEOVER Swish, gargle, spit. If you're not going to swallow your mouthwash, why worry about its ingredients? There are two reasons. First, your mouth is full of highly absorbent mucous membranes, which readily absorb chemicals. Second, after you spit, whatever is in your mouthwash goes directly down the drain, with the potential to contaminate wastewater and, potentially, drinking water.

Key ingredients to avoid when choosing a new mouthwash are sulfates and coal-tar colors, both found on the *Green Guide's* Dirty Dozen list. The common colorants FD&C Blue 1, Green 3, Yellow 5, and Yellow 6 are potentially harmful to human health.

So while a pretty blue mouthwash may look healthier and more appealing than a dingy yellow one, don't be swayed by color. Look instead to the ingredients, and choose mouthwashes free of artificial colors and sweeteners.

Shaving Products

There's an irony in searching for natural hair removal products, given how unnatural the process is. But a well-groomed face and smooth, hairless legs have become the norm, and nearly every grocery store stocks a vast array of products to make the shaving process go as smoothly as possible.

RAZORS' EDGE In addition to depleting a nonrenewable resource (petroleum), disposable plastic razors create a good deal of waste each year. Consumers now may choose from a wide variety of razors with replaceable heads, coming from both mainstream manufacturers and alternative companies. Some razors are made from recycled materials and are themselves recyclable. The choice may not seem significant, since you do still toss the used razor head, but keeping just one plastic razor handle per week out of the wastebasket adds up over time.

THE FACTS
Americans throw away about 2.5 billion disposable razors every year, according to the Pennsylvania Department of Environmental Protection.

Another option? Use an electric razor equipped with a rechargeable battery. If this one-time purchase saves you from years of weekly razor purchases, it can be a good option. (Just don't leave it charging overnight, which eats up excess power.) Or, consider alternative hair removal methods, such as waxing with nonparaffin wax or "sugaring," a technique in which a sticky gel is used to pull unwanted hair out by the root.

A CREAM SHAVE As with soaps and lotions, conventional shaving cream is likely to contain some of the Dirty Dozen ingredients (see pages 169-71). Shaving cream comes in cans that often contain propellants such as propane or isobutane, chemicals that are extremely flammable. A better, gentler option for your skin and the planet is to use lower-foaming but equally effective shave creams sold at natural-foods stores. Or go the old-fashioned route: Use a bar of shaving soap, which can be worked into a lather using a shaving brush.

ASK THE EDITORS

Q **Is fluoride safe?**

A According to the American Dental Association (ADA), fluoride helps protect teeth, reducing decay in baby and adult teeth. But the key is getting the proper amount. Some people, especially children, get too much fluoride, which can actually cause fluorosis, opaque white patches or permanent brown on the teeth.

But brown teeth isn't why critics rally against fluoride use in our water systems. Many believe it can actually cause cancer. Some animal and human studies have linked ingestion of fluoride in drinking water to an increased risk of osteosarcoma, a bone cancer. The ADA reviewed the issue in 2006, conceded that excessive fluoride exposure in infants could lead to fluorosis, and issued an "interim" list of reduced fluoride recommendations for infants and young children while the matter is being further investigated.

If you're a concerned parent, take these steps to ensure your children are receiving the proper amount of fluoride:

- ✓ Kids should brush at least twice daily with a fluoridated toothpaste and floss once a day under parental supervision. Non-fluoridated toothpastes should be used for children who are not yet capable of spitting it out (generally, age two and under).
- ✓ Children under six should not use fluoridated mouth rinses, because they may swallow them.
- ✓ Call your local water company or the Department of Public Health to check fluoride levels in your tap water. If it's above 1.2 parts per million, using a reverse-osmosis or water-distillation unit can help reduce the fluoride levels. If you don't have fluoridated water, talk to your dentist about whether your kids would benefit from a prescription fluoride supplement.

Feminine Hygiene

While they're needed only a few days each month, women have used sanitary products made of paper and plastic for decades. It all adds up to a great deal of waste and pollution. There are other ways of doing it.

Typically, these absorbent products consist of a mixture of rayon (from wood pulp) and cotton, bleached with chlorine to break down the fibers and produce a perfectly white, sanitary look. The process of chlorine bleaching releases dioxin, which has been associated with cancer, birth defects, and immune and endocrine problems, including lower sperm counts in men who are exposed to dioxin in the environment. Although industry practices have improved, chlorine bleaching of paper products is a leading source of dioxins in the environment, along with incineration of waste, and the consequences linger. These toxins disperse around the globe, collecting in animal tissues—and humans aren't the only ones at risk. Dioxins are believed to cause deformities and reproductive problems in fish and birds, among other animals.

THE FACTS
During her lifetime, the average woman uses as many as 11,000 tampons or sanitary pads.

Additionally, sanitary products often employ petroleum-based plastic linings, applicators, and wrappers, which only add to our collective reliance on this polluting and nonrenewable resource. And at the end of the products' life cycle, the vast majority of them get flushed down the toilet or tossed in the wastebasket, eventually ending up in our already overstuffed landfills. How can you skirt the problem? Seek out less processed, more biodegradable varieties of feminine hygiene products, and don't be afraid to explore less conventional alternatives.

BETTER PADS & TAMPONS While personal exposure to dioxins via tampons and pads isn't high—a study published in the January 2002 issue of *Environmental Health Perspectives* estimates that dioxin in tampons "does not significantly contribute to dioxin exposures in the United States"—use of chlorine-bleached products contributes to atmospheric dioxin levels. By choosing products that are unbleached or whitened with chlorine-free bleaches (such as hydrogen peroxide), we can help reduce our contribution to this problem. These days you'll find non-chlorine-bleached tampons and pads at both

natural-foods stores and conventional grocery stores; nationally available brands are helping bring chlorine-free products into the mainstream market.

If you are choosing between plastic-wrapped products and those wrapped in paper, the latter is the lesser of the two evils. Likewise, tampons with cardboard applicators are preferable to those with plastic ones; although nonrecycled cardboard isn't ideal, it's more biodegradable than nearly indestructible and petroleum-depleting plastic.

UNCONVENTIONAL ALTERNATIVES Though it's still a niche market, there's a growing interest in alternative, reusable sanitary products. Many natural-foods stores and online retailers carry washable cotton pads and undergarments similar to those used before disposable feminine hygiene products came on the market. You may also consider menstrual cups worn inside the body, designed to be washed and reused.

Insect Repellents

Whether you're an outdoor enthusiast or just want to enjoy a late-summer picnic, chances are you'll need to use some sort of bug repellent. It's a wise move: Not only are insect bites uncomfortable—they can also cause disease.

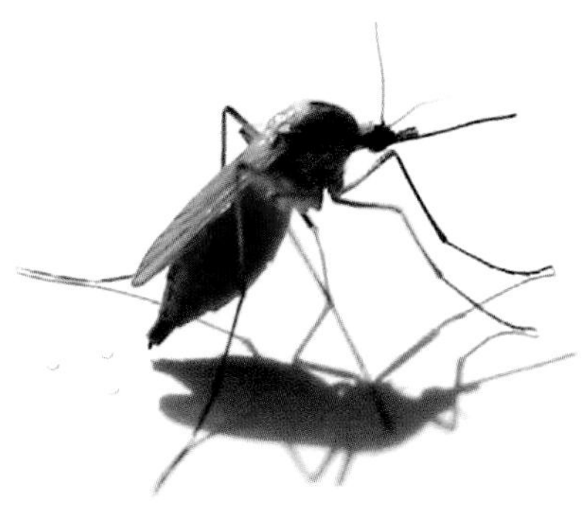

In tropical locations, mosquitoes can carry malaria or dengue fever; in temperate regions, the incidence of mosquito-borne West Nile virus and eastern equine encephalitis virus in humans is increasing. Ticks are known carriers of Lyme disease.

But most conventional insect repellents come with risks, too—eye irritation, skin reactions, and, in severe cases, seizure. When possible, it's advisable to prevent insect exposure instead of battling it with sprays and lotions. Keep arms and legs covered by light-colored clothing, wear shoes and socks, and avoid being outside when it's buggiest, generally from dusk to dawn. And when you do have to bare your skin, weigh the following options as you fend against stings and bites.

THE FACTS

From 1999 to 2000, the U.S. Geological Survey sampled 139 U.S. streams, many of which were vulnerable to pollution from industrial sites or livestock operations. DEET was detected at very low levels in 74 percent of the samples.

COMMERCIAL REPELLENTS Most standard insect repellents available at drugstores contain N,N-diethyl-m-toluamide, or DEET, an ingredient that's been widely used since the late 1950s. While offering protection against insects, especially mosquitoes, DEET is a known eye irritant and may cause skin problems such as blisters and rashes in some users. DEET has also been associated with adverse neurological symptoms: lethargy, confusion, disorientation, and mood swings. Multiple seizures have been reported in some people, and at least five people have died after dermal exposure. Improper use of DEET products may have been to blame; some of these individuals used larger amounts of DEET than recommended on the label. Children may be more vulnerable to DEET's potentially toxic effects than adults.

ECO-TIP: SPRAY SMART

Where insect-borne disease is of concern, the risks of DEET use may be outweighed by its repellent reliability. If you decide that a DEET-containing repellent is necessary, take these precautions.

- ✓ Go for lower concentrations. A formula with 10 percent DEET will keep mosquitoes at bay for two hours. The effectiveness plateaus at 30 percent.
- ✓ Skip the double-duty products. Avoid formulas that combine sunscreen with DEET. While sunscreen should be reapplied frequently throughout the day, one application of DEET could suffice, and multiple reapplications increase your chances of being exposed to unsafe levels.
- ✓ Keep it on the surface. Do not apply DEET-containing products to children's hands or faces, as it may enter eyes or be ingested. Keep it away from cuts, wounds, or sunburned skin.
- ✓ Spray sparingly. Use as little insect repellent as possible, and apply it to exposed skin only. Follow label directions regarding length of effectiveness, and be conservative about reapplying.
- ✓ Wash it off. Cleanse DEET-sprayed skin thoroughly with soap and water as soon as you come indoors.

PLANT-BASED PEST CONTROL For those who wish to avoid DEET, herbal insect repellents that rely on botanical oils—citronella, lemongrass, eucalyptus, pennyroyal, and other—can discourage insects, but they are generally less effective (and more expensive) than DEET, providing protection for less than 20 minutes. Mesh clothing can protect some parts of your body.

Take Action

- ✓ Avoid the chemicals listed as the Dirty Dozen whenever possible.
- ✓ Choose sulfate-free soaps and cleansers.
- ✓ Go for face and body moisturizers that are free of parabens.
- ✓ Choose semipermanent hair dye in lighter shades. Opt for highlights.
- ✓ Try "crystal" antiperspirants and avoid deodorants with triclosan.
- ✓ Try mineral-based sunscreens; limit your sun exposure.
- ✓ Scan ingredient labels and avoid products bearing the generic term "fragrance," which can hide hormone-disrupting phthalates.
- ✓ Look for mineral-based makeup made without nanoparticles.
- ✓ Avoid petroleum derivatives and heavy metals (such as lead and mercury) in lip and eye makeup.
- ✓ Recycle your personal care products' containers.
- ✓ Look for the Leaping Bunny logo, used by companies that pledge not to test their products on animals.
- ✓ Use nail polishes that are free of formaldehyde, toluene, and phthalates.
- ✓ Use toothpastes and mouthwashes made without artificial colors and flavors.
- ✓ Make sure your tap water's fluoride levels are not too high.
- ✓ Select razors with replaceable heads.
- ✓ Choose nonchlorine bleached feminine products packaged with less plastic.
- ✓ Limit your use of DEET-based insect repellent, and prevent bites by wearing appropriate clothing.

Beauty Products: Not Only Skin-deep

Skin is a supple suit of armor that shields the body from microbes, ultraviolet radiation, chemicals, and many other would-be invaders. It regulates body temperature, keeps moisture inside the body, sweats when needed to cool the skin, and senses the environment with its millions of nerve endings that detect pain, pressure, and temperature. But skin is not completely impervious. Many of the lotions and soaps we apply to skin contain chemicals that can weave their way through the skin and into the bloodstream. Let's take a look at how this happens.

The first line of defense is the paper-thin epidermis. Flat, dead skin cells make up the epidermis's topmost layer, the stratum corneum. At the bottom of the epidermis, skin cells continuously divide and make more cells. The cells produce a tough, coiled protein called keratin that moves much like a spring to give the skin its elasticity. It takes about one month for new skin cells to make their way up to the surface to replace the ones that are regularly sloughed off.

Getting through the epidermis is no easy feat. Fats and cholesterol molecules crammed between the cells make a waterproof wall that keeps body moisture in and many water-soluble chemicals out. So-called fat-loving (lipophilic) chemicals, however, can cross more easily than water-loving (hydrophilic) chemicals. Lipophilic chemicals are found in many cosmetics—and also in pesticides, designed so that they penetrate into the bodies of insects.

The thickness of the epidermis varies throughout the human body, with the skin on the palms and soles being the thickest and hardest to penetrate. Hairy areas may be more susceptible to chemical entry, however, because hair follicles can act like slides down which chemicals sail into the lower skin layer, the dermis.

About half an inch thick, the dermis is packed with strong fibers of elastin and collagen. Embedded in the dermis are hair follicles and glands that secrete oils, scents, and sweat. Here, tiny blood vessels course beneath the skin, and nerve endings reach up toward the skin surface. The number of blood vessels varies depending on the body part. The face, for example, has a lot of them. Chemicals that manage to make it this far can jump into the bloodstream for a quick ride around the body before exiting, usually through the urine.

The dermis harbors enzymes that break down chemicals, often converting fat-loving chemicals into water-soluble ones that the body can easily dispose of in the urine. Sometimes these metabolites are more toxic than their parent compounds. Coal tar, used in some hair dyes, is a fat-soluble polycyclic aromatic hydrocarbon (PAH) that crosses through the skin, where enzymes convert it into a metabolite that may contribute to cancer risk.

The amount of chemical absorbed depends not only on the fat- or water-loving nature of the chemical but also on the amount applied, the area of skin it is applied to, the concentration of the chemical in the lotion or oil, and the length of exposure. Skin can act as a reservoir, storing fat-loving chemicals in the stratum corneum and releasing them into the bloodstream over time.

Infants, especially those who are premature, are far more sensitive than adults to chemicals applied to the skin. Infants swabbed with alcohol-based antiseptics prior to having their umbilical cords cut were found to have elevated alcohol levels in their blood. Children's skin is sensitive, too: Shampoos containing lindane, an ingredient prescribed for the treatment of lice, have caused irreversible neurological damage in children.

Many of the substances found in sunscreens, cosmetics, and baby lotions have not been adequately tested for their ability to absorb through the skin of children. Most of these chemicals do not have the noticeable toxic effects of lindane, yet the effects of long-term exposure are not known.

Several types of phthalates used as fragrance enhancers in cosmetics—and suspected of interfering with hormone function—are known to cross the skin and are detectable in the blood and urine. So are many sunscreen chemicals. Until more is known about the long-term effects of these chemicals, wise consumers will peruse labels to make decisions before purchasing lotions and creams.

Clothing & Accessories

FOR THE AVERAGE GREEN CONSUMER, THE PROGRESSION from an unsustainable lifestyle to an Earth-friendly one goes something like this: Start recycling. Switch to organic foods. Install energy-saving lightbulbs. Buy greener cleaners. Reuse shopping bags. On we go, unplugging TVs and toasters, and switching to more fuel-efficient transportation. But as we make our way through our newer, greener daily routines, few of us ever stop to consider the impact of what we're wearing. Are our clothing items and accessories made in sweatshops, from materials of unknown origins? These fabrics that come closest to our skin—how environmentally friendly and healthful are they? Do you know what's in your denim jeans? Is your carbon footprint made by an Earth-friendly shoe?

Of all the planet-saving decisions we can make, rethinking conventional clothing is perhaps the hardest thing for many people to do. Maybe it's because the vast majority of clothing sold in the United States, from discount-store T-shirts to luxury handbags, is made with little consideration of the items' long-term consequences.

Dominating the market, conventionally grown cotton comes at a high environmental cost; according to the Pesticide Action Network North America, cotton farmers around the world use nearly $2.6 billion worth of pesticides annually. These pesticides are some of the most hazardous available and can harm farmworkers, contaminate groundwater and surface water, and kill beneficial insects and organisms in the soil.

Clothing made of petroleum-based synthetic fabrics like acrylic and nylon runs a close second, deepening our reliance on this expensive, polluting, and nonrenewable resource. Irresponsible production of fur and leather items takes a more direct toll on animals, while the treatment of workers at the sweatshops used by many manufacturers brings new meaning to the word "inhuman." Sadly, clothing made with a conscience is the exception, not the rule.

It's time to make over our wardrobes. Green fashion may be a niche, but it's one with vast potential, both aesthetically and environmentally. Green style blogs have proliferated on the web, spotlighting new eco-conscious designers as they emerge. The past few years have seen a rise in "eco-fashion" shows and "eco-boutiques" in major cities. Big names in fashion have sprouted offshoot lines made using sustainable materials. Social responsibility has become a selling point for companies like American Apparel. And respected designers pride themselves on their use of environment-friendly textiles. All signs point to an impending boom in ecologically sound clothing. The green and the mainstream, it seems, are beginning to merge.

So where do you start? Your underwear? Outerwear? Shoes? Ultimately it doesn't matter. Start where you're comfortable, perhaps swapping out your conventional cotton T-shirts for organic-cotton ones. Not so hard, right? As you begin to familiarize yourself with eco-friendly brands and materials and gradually incorporate more sustainably made items into your closet, you're likely to be impressed, both by the quality of items now available and the seamlessness of integrating them into your wardrobe.

Being green no longer entails wearing shapeless dresses, drab beige pants, and flat, clunky shoes—although, truth be told, there are plenty of those items still floating around the market for those who are so inclined. Transitioning to better choices simply means taking one more thing into account when you shop—considering the product's sustainability along with the usual criteria like color, fit, and current fashions. With a little practice, shopping for environment-friendly items will become second nature.

Clothing

If you have to choose one thing to change, start with what you wear most often. Basic clothing items like jeans, T-shirts, and light sweaters can form the foundation of your green wardrobe. Look for garments with less toxic, more planet-friendly fabrics.

COTTON TALES Before it becomes the shirt on your back, conventional cotton has a storied—and sordid—history. Cotton-industry ads might have you believe that it's the world's purest material, but unsustainable modern growing practices have sullied cotton's reputation. Because crops are highly prone to attack by insects and other pests, cotton farming accounts for about 25 percent of global insecticide use and more than 10 percent of global pesticide use (which includes the use of insecticides, herbicides, and defoliants) annually.

Stateside, the 10.5 million acres of conventional cotton grown in 2007 were sprayed with a staggering 55 million pounds of pesticides: Cotton agriculture ranks third, behind corn and soybeans, in the total amount of pesticides used, according to USDA reports. Of the top 15 pesticides used on U.S. cotton crops, 7 are considered potential or known human carcinogens. Two of the most frequently used classes of pesticides include organophosphates and carbamates, both potent nervous system toxins that may sicken workers and contaminate the soil and groundwater.

Pesticides aren't the only cause for concern. Farmers used 571,000 tons of nitrogen fertilizer on U.S. cotton in 2006, according to USDA records. Workers who are overexposed to nitrogen fertilizer can go blind. Nitrogen can also leach from the soil into groundwater, and high levels of nitrates in drinking water are known to cause methemoglobinemia, "blue baby syndrome."

Still doubtful about the risks of conventional cotton? Consider the impacts of just four of the top chemicals that are used (or were once used) on crops of cotton:

THE FACTS

According to the Sustainable Cotton Project, about one-third of a pound of chemicals is used to make just one conventional cotton T-shirt.

METHYL PARATHION. During heavy rains in 1995, this pesticide flowed from cotton fields into Big Nance Creek in Lawrence County, Alabama. More than 240,000 fish were killed.

TRIFLURALIN. This herbicide is highly toxic to aquatic organisms, which are harmed by water runoff from cotton fields. It's also an endocrine disruptor. It can harm the reproductive systems of wildlife, and the EPA lists it as a possible human carcinogen.

CYANAZINE. Found to cause breast cancer in laboratory animals, this herbicide was phased out of domestic use by the end of 1999, but it may remain in use outside of the U.S.

TRIBUFOS (ALSO KNOWN AS DEF AND FOLEX). A defoliant, tribufos causes plants to lose their leaves, which makes harvesting cotton easier. It is a potent neurotoxin and a likely human carcinogen at high doses, according to the EPA.

It all adds up to this: Buy clothing made from organic cotton. To be certified, farmers of organic cotton crops must show that they have not used synthetic pesticides or fertilizers for the past three years. They use biological pest control measures, such as insects; they rotate their crops to alleviate soil-borne pathogens and remove weeds by hand; and they improve soil health and fertility via composting and cover crops. Organic fiber does cost about twice as much as conventional cotton, carrying over to a 25 percent premium for the finished product. Organic cotton fiber represents only 0.1 percent of the world's cotton supply, although demand is rising.

WOOLEN WEAR When most people think of wool, they envision pleasant, pastoral scenes, but the actual process of shearing sheep for wool is hardly idyllic. Because lice, ticks, and mites tend to take up residence in sheep's wool, farmers must often dip their livestock in organophosphate pesticides, which create healthrisks for animals and farmworkers and can contaminate groundwater.

ECO-TIP: BLEACHED OR UNBLEACHED?

When it comes to buying better cotton, organic farming methods are only half of the equation. After the cotton is harvested, it typically undergoes a number of processes, including bleaching. The cotton is usually whitened with chlorine bleach, a process that releases dioxin, a carcinogen and hormone disruptor, into the environment. Aware of the inherent problems with chlorine bleaching, many companies and even environmental organizations sell clothes, bedding, and tote bags made from unbleached cotton. Such products are not necessarily organic, however, so while they avoid one potential health risk, they are still derived from cotton that was treated with pesticides. The fabric's off-white hue and labels touting the product's "naturalness" can prove confusing.

Of course, there are also manufacturers who take the opposite tack, using organic cotton but applying chlorine bleach and toxic heavy-metal dyes to achieve the desired colors. (For more information on fabric dyes and treatments, see pages 219-23.) In both cases, manufacturers are able to capitalize on growing consumer interest in green products, while continuing to contribute to pollution and other environmental problems.

Although it's true that both of these options—unbleached conventional cotton and bleached-and-dyed organic cotton—are an improvement over mainstream merchandise, they address only half of the problem. For the most environment-friendly wardrobe, seek out organic fabrics that are undyed or colored with low-impact pigments.

To increase their size and yield, sheep are frequently given hormones and antibiotics even when they are not sick, a practice that contributes to bacterial resistance. Once the sheep are shorn, their wool is traditionally cleaned and processed using alkaline detergents.

Fortunately, there are two solid options for consumers who love the look and warmth of wool clothing: certified organic and "Pure Grow" wool. To be certified organic in the U.S., wool production must adhere to the same strict USDA standards as certified organic meat, dairy, and other animal-fiber products. To that end, organic wool producers cannot use chemical pesticides on their sheep. Certified organic wool also helps prevent land degradation from overgrazing.

Initiated in Sonoma County, California, the Pure Grow wool program follows federal organic livestock standards but has also implemented stringent rules regarding how the wool is handled once it's shorn. Pure Grow wool producers follow organic agricultural practices. When shopping, look for sweaters, hats, and other wool items bearing either of the two labels—certified organic or Pure Grow—to support more responsible wool production and to reduce your potential exposure to pesticide residues.

LESSONS IN LINEN Few consumers realize it, but the same plant that yields heart-healthy flaxseeds and flaxseed oil is also the source of linen fabric. The fibers of the flax plant are versatile, durable, breathable, and—the best part—easily produced organically. Flax is naturally pest-resistant, eliminating the need for heavy pesticide use. It's surprising, then, that there's not much of it grown in the U.S. Though the USDA has been evaluating the possibility of developing the flax plant as a commodity, all textile-grade flax fiber in the U.S. is currently imported. So in the quest for certifiably Earth-friendly linen shirts, blouses, and skirts, it's unfortunately necessary to look for products made abroad (generally an undesirable habit, given the cost and energy use required to ship things overseas). In Europe, Quality Assurance International (QAI) and the International Federation of Organic Agriculture Movements (IFOAM) certify organic linen, slowly becoming available in the States.

SIZING UP SILK Looking at a tissue-thin, elegantly cut silk dress or blouse, it's hard to imagine that such a pretty fabric could come from as strange a source as moth larvae. But that's how silk is made, and raising silkworms is often a chemical-heavy endeavor. The pesticide methoprene and the steroid hormone phytoecdysone are frequently used to slow the worms' growth rate, to increase silk production and to synchronize readiness of the cocoons for harvest. Furthermore, in order to preserve the long silk threads, the pupae are traditionally killed—either by baking or drowning—before they can break out of their cocoons.

If this troubles you, seek out "wildcrafted" silk, which is usually produced without pesticides and hormones and without killing the pupae. Alkena Textiles, a joint venture among China, Switzerland, and Germany, claims it produces "organic" silk in accordance with the European Economic Community (EEC) organic standards. While these standards prohibit the use of methoprene, they do not address the treatment of the worms. Ahimsa Peace Silk, on the other hand, is made from the cocoons of semi-wild and wild moths in India. By allowing the pupae to emerge from their cocoons on their own, this process produces silk without chemicals or cruelty. Wildcrafted silk also helps maintain the forest habitat of moths, as it connects the livelihood of tribal spinners and weavers to the preservation of these trees. For more information on fabrics, see pages 136-137.

SEMI-SYNTHETICS Three wood-based fabrics—rayon, Tencel, and acetate—have garnered much attention of late, billed by manufacturers as more sustainable options. All three are made out of cellulose, derived from the pulp of trees including beech and eucalyptus (though tropical hardwoods and even cotton are also potential sources). While these materials begin as biomass, the end result is a synthetic too far removed from the original source to be considered a "natural" fiber akin to cotton, linen, wool, or silk.

The environmental friendliness of a finished rayon, Tencel, or acetate fabric can be tough to gauge, too. Rayon is a prime example: While some manufacturers claim that the cellulose is left over from the processing of wood products, the material could be unsustainably sourced from virgin wood. According to Co-op America's *WoodWise Consumer Guide*, "about a third of the pulp obtained from a tree will end up in finished rayon thread." The rest is discarded. Extracting the fiber also requires powerful chemicals like sodium hydroxide and carbon disulfide and no small amount of water.

Tencel (the registered trade name for lyocell), the newest of these fabrics, was developed by one of the world's largest manufacturers of rayon, and the company presents the fabric as a more environmentally friendly option. Making Tencel, compared with rayon, requires less water and does use biodegradable solvents; the material itself is biodegradable as well.

THE NEW ALTERNATIVES Recently a new crop of fabrics has emerged, made from unconventional materials such as bamboo, soy, and hemp. Of these, bamboo has garnered the most attention, not only because bamboo requires few, if any, pesticides to grow, but also because of the versatility of the product. Bamboo fabric has been likened to silk or even cashmere. It's also quick-drying, absorbent, naturally antibacterial, and suitable for athletic wear.

Less common but equally promising is soy fabric. Developed in China in 1999, soybean fiber is just beginning to appear in items like socks, sheets, and yoga clothing. The fiber is created by extracting proteins from the remainders of tofu production, fused with organic compounds into a fiber strong enough to be spun into yarn.

A more tried-and-true fabric alternative is hemp, which has been cultivated for use in clothing and other products for thousands of years. Its advantages are many: Hemp bark contains some of the strongest, longest fibers on the planet, which provide better insulation than cotton fiber, and the plant requires few, if any, insecticides or herbicides. But hemp's successful cultivation in the U.S. is hindered by its relationship to the drug marijuana. Hemp belongs to the same species as marijuana *(Cannabis sativa),* and despite the fact that hemp grown for fiber contains little THC (tetrahydrocannabinol, the psychoactive ingredient in marijuana), antidrug regulations have been a major roadblock to its cultivation and sale in the United States. The U.S. Drug Enforcement Agency (DEA) has effectively banned hemp production since the 1950s. Consequently, most hemp for cloth is grown in China and Eastern Europe, and most organic hemp seeds used in food and personal-care products—hemp oil is touted for heart- and skin-improving benefits—come from Canada.

Because of this complicated situation, you won't find any products made with "USDA Organic" hemp in stores—at least not yet. Several states have attempted to legalize the cultivation of industrial hemp; so far, only North Dakota has succeeded in legalization at the state level.

International organic standards for hemp have not yet been established, so although hemp is typically grown with fewer pesticides, consumers should not assume that hemp has been organically grown. To be sure, it's best to ask the manufacturer.

ASK THE EDITORS

Q **I'm often advised to buy "natural" fabrics like cotton or linen, both by health experts and environmental organizations. What's wrong with synthetics?**

A The definition of "natural" and "synthetic" fabric differs depending on who you talk to. Some would argue that all fibers go through some degree of processing, and therefore nothing we wear is truly natural. In general, though, the term "synthetic fabrics" usually refers to petroleum-based materials including acrylic, nylon, and polyester. The advent of these fabrics in the 1960s promised consumers futuristic miracle clothes that needed no ironing or special treatment, and soon they were being worn and tossed in washing machines across America. But such conveniences come at a price to the environment and our health. Manufacturing synthetic fibers requires a great deal of energy, and can release lung-damaging pollutants such as nitrogen and sulfur oxides, particulates, carbon monoxide, and heavy metals into the air, as well as the greenhouse gas carbon dioxide. The fabrics themselves may contain residues that off-gas into the air we breathe.

Of course, the lines between natural and synthetic do blur with some of the new fabrics, such as bamboo, soy, and recycled plastics, as well as the wood pulp-based fabrics such as rayon and Tencel. All of these require more processing and energy to produce than "natural" fibers such as organic cotton, silk, linen, hemp, or wool. Both types of materials are better for the planet than petroleum-based synthetics, however, so choose them whenever you can. Petroleum-based fabrics should be avoided as much as possible.

RECYCLED FABRICS It sounds too good to be true: recycling a Coke bottle, then buying a jacket made from the plastic. But thanks to a fabric known as EcoSpun' it's possible for consumers to reap the benefits of their diligent recycling. Though technically the material qualifies as polyester, it's made from post-consumer materials, primarily plastic soda bottles, instead of the usual petroleum. Consequently, EcoSpun fleece and other textiles have the capacity to keep billions of pounds of plastic out of our landfills each year. And they're getting easier to find: Several companies use EcoSpun fabric in jackets, hats, gloves, and other outerwear items; it's often listed on labels as "EcoSpun," "Recycled Plastic," or "Recycled Polyester."

ECO-TIPS: EARTH-FRIENDLY ATHLETES

For active types, looking for Earth-friendly clothing to wear while working out presents a conundrum. On the one hand, the typical nylon or acrylic workout clothes rely on nonrewable petroleum. On the other, natural fibers like cotton retain moisture and thus don't always cut it when you're sweating. Fitness clothes are often treated with anti-odor, antibacterial, or antimicrobial substances such as triclosan, which can react with chlorinated water to form chloroform, a probable human carcinogen, and can harm aquatic life if released into the environment.

What's a yogi, runner, or gym rat to do?

First, consider fabrics that blend cotton (preferably organic) with bamboo. Like synthetics, bamboo has moisture-wicking properties and can help you keep cool while working out. Recycled materials, such as EcoSpun, can also give you the performance of a synthetic without requiring the use of additional petroleum. And no, you don't need to head to specialty stores to find such items; mainstream companies all offer workout gear made with these more sustainable materials.

Of course, there are caveats. One fabric you'll have trouble avoiding in fitness clothing is spandex, which is added for extra stretch. A combination of polyester and polyurethane, spandex

(trademarked as Lycra) is blended into just about everything, so just look for the lowest percentage possible. One thing you can skip is antibacterial triclosan, often added to towels, socks, and other fabric items. Look for the trade names "Microban" or "Biofresh" on labels—and if you see them, steer clear.

Clothing Treatments

Most fabrics and garments are treated with dyes and finishing agents like wrinkle protectants, stain guards, and fire retardants. Most of these treatments are pollutants, with residues that can linger for a long time.

DANGEROUS DYES? Conventional textile dyes "fix" pigments to the fabric using heavy metals, many of which may be harmful to human health. The EPA has listed several dyes as hazardous waste materials. These dyes present risks to both plant workers and consumers, as they may trigger contact dermatitis and asthma symptoms. As awareness of these dangers increases, more products boast "low-impact" dyes, purportedly less polluting. A low-impact dye meets the requirements set by the Oeko-Tex Standard 100, a globally uniform testing and certification system that assigns specific tolerance levels of chemicals to clothing. There is no enforcement of the term's use, however, and some low-impact dyes contain many of the same petrochemicals and heavy metals as conventional dyes.

THE FACTS

Due to cotton's natural resistance to dyes, large quantities of wastewater are generated during the dyeing process, and roughly half the chemicals used to color the fabric end up as waste in rivers and soil.

"Color-grown" cotton is a second alternative. Long cultivated in Central and South America, ancient color-grown cotton was short-fiber cotton, poorly suited to the modern textiles industry. Then, while working on a cotton farm in the 1990s, Sally Fox started a breeding program to develop long-fiber brown cotton suitable for modern textiles. The result was two lines of color-grown cotton products: Colorganic, which is certified organic, and Foxfibre, which is mostly (but not completely) organic. Today's color-grown cotton still comes from South and Central America, Mexico, and the southeastern United States.

FABRIC FINISHES Modern fabric finishes that are applied to fabrics to simplify their care—finishes that make them "Permanent Press," "No Iron," "Water Repellent," and "Flame Retardant"—may actually cause more problems than they solve. Formaldehyde, a common indoor air pollutant found in permanent-press and some fire-retardant clothes and home textiles, is an upper respiratory irritant and a carcinogen.

Perfluorochemicals (PFCs) are a class of chemicals found in Scotchgard, Stainmaster, Gore-Tex, and Teflon fabric coatings and sprays. A 2001 study by Scotchgard maker 3M found that PFCs showed up in the blood of 96 percent of the children tested, with some children showing levels ten times as high as the average. The PFC variety found, PFOA, has been associated with testicular, prostate, and bladder cancers among workers. PFOS, another PFC compound, was removed from 3M's Scotchgard in 2000 following pressure from the EPA over the chemical's developmental and reproductive toxicity.

Also problematic are polybrominated diphenyl ethers (PBDEs), used as fire retardants in some clothing items. Animal studies indicate that PBDEs disrupt thyroid hormone levels and harm the growth of developing brains. If fire safety is a concern, a far better option is to choose garments made with wool, which is naturally flame resistant. ▸For more on PBDEs, see page 137.

DRY CLEANING DOS & DON'TS Dry cleaning commonly requires a solvent called perchloroethylene, or perc, a toxic organochlorine originally developed as a metal degreaser. In the 1980s, the EPA began studying perc and found that levels remained elevated for as long as one week after newly dry-cleaned clothes were placed in a closet. A March 1996 report by the nonprofit Consumers Union found that people who wear freshly dry-cleaned clothes once a week for 40 years could inhale enough perc to increase their cancer risk sigificantly.

The chemical also raises an environmental issue. Until the mid-1980s, it was legal for dry cleaners to pour spent perc down the drain, and it is now a major groundwater contaminant in more than one-quarter of U.S. water supplies. Leading the fight against perc use, in January 2007 the California Air Resources Board voted to phase out perc dry cleaning by 2023.

There are several good alternatives to perc dry cleaning. The method considered the greenest is known as wet cleaning. Fabrics such as wool, silk, linen, and rayon are cleaned using water and nontoxic, biodegradable detergents in computer-controlled washers and dryers (or, when necessary, by hand) and finished with ironing or steam pressing. The cost is generally comparable to that of dry cleaning.

ECO-TIP: THE FIGHT AGAINST FUR

Many believe that the fur industry contributes to animal pain and suffering. In our culture, the decision to wear fur is purely fashion-based. To learn about ways to end the animal cruelty involved in the fur trade, check out People for the Ethical Treatment of Animals and the International Anti-Fur Coalition.

The drawbacks? First, the process does require water usage. Second, the results vary depending on who handles your clothes. In a survey conducted by the Center for Neighborhood Technology, 45 out of 50 rated wet cleaning "good" or "excellent." In 2003, however, Consumer Reports noted that wet cleaning left a wool jacket severely pilled and a linen-blend skirt shrunk. If you're interested in switching to professional wet cleaning, ask friends and colleagues for recommendations, and wait until you've tried the service before handing over your best suits and sweaters.

Another perc alternative uses liquid carbon dioxide (CO_2), also used for decaffeinating coffee, which has no reported adverse health risks. In this process, developed by a private company with funding from an EPA contract in 1994, CO_2 is captured from existing industrial and agricultural emissions so it does not contribute to global warming. In 2002 Hangers Cleaners, a national chain specializing in CO_2 cleaning, won a Most Valuable Pollution Prevention Award from the National Pollution Prevention Roundtable.

There are a few downsides, however. Unlike wet cleaning, the detergents used in CO_2 cleaning do contain some volatile organic compounds (VOCs). Also, the cost of buying the CO_2 cleaning equipment is nearly double that of buying a wet cleaning system, making the process less financially feasible for small businesses. The higher price may be worth it, though. *Consumer Reports* found that CO_2 cleaners offered the best results in tests for shrinkage, discoloration, and preservation of texture—better than perc-based cleaning.

THE FACTS

Perchloroethylene is estimated to have contaminated one in ten public drinking wells in California, according to the Coalition for Clean Air. According to the EPA, it is one of the top ten most toxic air contaminants in the state.

Although other dry cleaning alternatives, including hydrocarbon solvents and siloxane, have seen an increase in popularity in recent years, environmental experts do have some reservations about them. These new techniques are recognized as less toxic than perc, but both the EPA and the Coalition for Clean Air have determined that these solvents can't be labeled safe for health or the environment until considerably more testing is done. Hydrocarbon solvents, such as DF2000 and N-propyl bromide, are

GREEN DICTIONARY

PERCHLOROETHYLENE
A commonly used dry cleaning solvent, perchloroethylene (also called tetrachloroethylene) has been named a hazardous air pollutant by the EPA; the International Agency for Research on Cancer calls it a probable human carcinogen. Perc is known to cause headaches, nausea, and dizziness, and has been linked to reproductive problems including miscarriage and male infertility, as well as disorders of the central nervous system.

petroleum-based and may be toxic or contain VOCs, and the EPA has noted concern over their high flammability. Like CO_2 systems, hydrocarbon-solvent systems are expensive to set up. Siloxane solvents, while not chlorinated themselves, are currently manufactured using chlorine, which may result in dioxin emissions. Siloxane is also extremely flammable, and the EPA notes that it may be carcinogenic.

Given all these caveats, it's important for consumers not to base their decisions on labels such as "green cleaning" or "green technology." These terms can mean a variety of things, and some self-proclaimed "Earth-friendly" cleaners even use perc. Ask your cleaning firm what specific methods and chemicals it uses before making your decision.

Accessories

Bags, shoes, wallets, and belts—small purchases, but they can have a big impact on the planet. Look at the material as well as the design. Is it leather? PVC? Was it made in a sweatshop? You may not be able to make all accessories 100 percent green, but some change is better than none.

IN THE BAG Today's fashion world is bag-obsessed. With prices edging into the thousands for a status handbag, new styles' appeal is judged on a number of factors including price, size, styling, color, celebrity endorsements, and designer label. What rarely enters the picture? The bag's environmental impact. Perhaps that's because, by and large, few of today's handbags could be considered even remotely green. For consumers who insist on carrying trendy pieces, there are few that won't do damage to the environment.

The most time-tested handbag material, leather, is conditioned—a process called tanning—using a cocktail of chemicals that includes mineral salts (chromium, aluminum, iron, and

zirconium), formaldehyde, coal-tar derivatives, and various oils and dyes, some of them cyanide-based. Many of these toxic tanning agents can seep into nearby waterways and pollute the air, especially in developing countries where enforcement of environmental standards is particularly lax. Tannery effluent also contains large amounts of other pollutants, such as protein, hair, salt, lime sludge, sulfides, and acids.

A second option, popular with bargain hunters and consumers trying to avoid the chemical usage and animal origin of leather, is polyvinyl chloride, also called vinyl or PVC. Yet vinyl has problems of its own. During manufacture and when incinerated as garbage, PVC produces dioxins, potent carcinogens that may harm immune systems. Dioxins (also produced during chlorine bleaching) accumulate in fatty tissue, have been found to contaminate breast milk, and can easily be passed up the food chain.

To increase its flexibility, vinyl also contains plasticizing chemicals called phthalates, which are known hormone disruptors and have been associated with serious reproductive health problems. One of the most common types, di-2-ethylhexyl phthalate, is also considered a probable human carcinogen.

THE FACTS

More than 95 percent of leather produced in the U.S. is chrome-tanned, as is most of the world's leather. All wastes containing chromium are considered hazardous by the EPA.

The only truly green handbags are made from environment-friendly fabrics such as organic cotton, hemp, or bamboo. But few such bags exist, and rarely do you come across a style suitable for pairing with dress clothes or business wear. What's a style-savvy shopper to do? The most viable choice may be to purchase vintage or used items. By extending the life cycle of products, be they leather or PVC, you can avoid contributing to the pollution associated with the production of new items. High-end vintage and consignment shops and auction websites like eBay hold a treasure trove of gently used (and pleasantly low-priced) bags and purses to suit current trends.

A newer, less conventional approach is to subscribe to services that allow fashion followers to "rent" stylish handbags for a monthly fee, so that subscribers can enjoy a variety of styles over the course of a year while sparing the Earth—and their wallets—the consequences of producing a new leather or PVC item every time they've got an itch for a new satchel.

ECO-TIPS: SKIP THE SWEATSHOP GEAR

Walk into almost any clothing store in the U.S., and you'll see the products of sweatshops—factories where hazardous working conditions, subminimum wages, and grueling hours are the norm. Garment workers in developing countries, usually in Asia and Latin America, often labor for just pennies an hour. Pay may be higher for those working in the U.S garment industry, but 60- to 80-hour workweeks and disregard for labor laws sometimes prevail. Some sweatshops also use child labor. Clothes don't bear labels listing their origins, so consumers have little to go on. A few pointers:

✓ Look for "Made in the USA" labels—cautiously. Manufacturing in the U.S. may be far from perfect, but clothes made domestically were probably created under better environmental and working conditions than elsewhere. There are exceptions, however. Although the Northern Mariana Islands are a U.S. commonwealth, the majority of garment workers there are women lured in from elsewhere in Asia by false promises and forced to work on meager wages for years. (Manufacturers there don't have to abide by U.S. minimum-wage laws.) Though negative publicity has led to labels saying "Made in the Northern Mariana Islands, USA," clothing made there can still bear a "Made in the USA" label.

✓ Stay up to date on the worst offenders. Over the years, many big-name manufacturers have come under scrutiny for their labor practices. Some have made commendable strides to improve worker welfare—and others have not. Check in with organizations like Sweatshop Watch, the Clean Clothes Campaign, Behind the Label, and the Fair Trade Federation to see which companies are behaving badly and which ones have cleaned up their act.

✓ Be loyal to the good guys. Certain companies have been outspoken in their opposition to sweatshop labor, including Birkenstock, Edun, and Timberland. Money talks, and consistently spending your hard-earned cash on products from companies whose ethics you admire sends a message that's loud and clear.

ON YOUR FEET As with handbags, the primary options for footwear are leather and PVC, and neither option is perfect. But there's another factor to consider when buying shoes: Footwear often contains foam padding, either made from polyurethane or EVA (ethylene vinyl acetate). Polyurethane foam can contain flame-retardant chemicals known as polybrominated diphenyl ethers, or PBDEs. Although the human health effects of PBDEs aren't crystal clear, studies have shown rising levels of the chemical in human breast milk. According to studies by Health Canada and Environment Canada, PBDE levels in breast milk in North America have increased by 100 times over the past 20 years. In animal studies, these compounds have been shown to damage the liver and brain and to interfere with thyroid hormone production. While PBDEs have been banned in Europe, U.S.-made polyurethane foam can contain as much as 30 percent PBDEs by weight. For more on PBDEs, see page 137.

Dress shoes present a more difficult challenge, but there are a few green options for casual shoes, sneakers, and sandals. Look for shoes constructed of cloth instead of leather or PVC; while many of these will be made of synthetic materials such as nylon or acrylic, the environmental impacts of these options are slightly less problematic than leather (which is tanned with toxic mineral salts) or PVC (the most polluting form of plastic). Shoes made of organic cotton, hemp, natural rubber, and recycled materials are also starting to gain popularity, so keep an eye out for these in stores and online. When you do need to buy leather shoes, buy the highest quality, best constructed pair you can find—the longer they last, the fewer pairs of shoes you'll have to buy in the long run. And never underestimate the ability of a shoe-repair shop to get a worn-out pair back into shape with new soles and stitching. The longer you can extend the lifetime of your shoes, the less impact your feet will have on the planet.

ECO-TIPS: ENDANGERED SKINS

Although U.S. manufacturers have curtailed their use of threatened and endangered animal species, leather goods remain a problem in some other countries. Consumers should be careful to avoid products made from the following animals:

- ✓ Sea turtles
- ✓ Black caiman, American crocodile, Orinoco crocodile, and Philippine crocodile
- ✓ Lizards originating in Brazil, Costa Rica, Ecuador, Peru, Venezuela, and India
- ✓ Snakes originating from Central and South American countries
- ✓ Seals

Jewelry

Jewelry symbolizes many good things—success, love, generosity. But in today's world it can also conjure up some less pleasant images. The mining of precious gemstones and metals has fueled many bloody conflicts, and the practice can inflict damage on local ecosystems.

MINED METAL Excavating gold—or any metal, for that matter—is hardly an ecologically sensitive endeavor. According to the EPA, hard-rock mining produces more toxic waste than any other industry in the United States.

Gold mining produces an estimated billion tons of waste rock and another billion tons of milled ore each year in the United States. Additionally, gold mining leads to acid mine drainage (AMD), acidic water resulting from a combination of sulfides, water, air, and bacteria. AMD seeps out of both active and inactive mines and causes poisonous heavy metals (including arsenic, lead, and mercury) to be released from ore. In addition to polluting municipal water supplies, AMD can harm birds and other wildlife that drink the tainted water. Given the often minute yields from enormous mining operations—as little as one ounce of gold from a hundred tons of material—the cost overwhelms the reward.

The process of extracting gold from raw ore isn't much gentler on the planet. The two most popular chemicals used to separate gold are cyanide and mercury, both of which leave behind toxic waste. Cyanide is used in a process called heap leaching, in which tons of earth are sprayed with cyanide, which bonds with gold particles and collects at the bottom of the heap. The combination of cyanide and milled ore is stored in underground ponds, which are disturbingly prone to collapse.

In 2000, the collapse of a Romanian mine's cyanide reservoir released toxic waste into the Danube and Tisza Rivers, killing thousands of tons of fish in Europe's worst river pollution disaster in a decade. Cyanide also contaminates water supplies near gold mining operations and kills wildlife. Mercury was used in a similar way during the California gold rush; over a century later, leftover mercury in California still seeps into nearby lakes, killing fish and other wildlife. Mercury is still used in mines in the Amazon.

A few mining corporations have taken measures to curb such environmental disasters, such as Colombia's Corporacion Oro Verde, or Green Gold Corporation, which is dedicated to reversing the harms of large-scale mining on the country's diverse ecosystems. Oro Verde forbids the use of mercury, cyanide, and any other forms of toxic pollutants and requires all areas mined to achieve ecological stability within three years after the completion of mining operations. Still, such policies are rare.

"Recycled" gold, silver, and platinum are growing in popularity; while the practice of melting down jewelry to create new pieces is nothing new, increased consumer awareness of mining's impacts has led to renewed interest. Another option is to simply buy vintage gold, silver, and platinum jewelry (often referred to as estate jewelry). There's no shortage of unique, vintage pieces available at jewelry and antiques stores and auction websites such as eBay. Not only are they easier on the Earth than newly mined metals, but they're often more affordable, too.

GENTLER GEMSTONES Mining diamonds and other gemstones is not easy on the planet, but it's the social issues surrounding the diamond industry that have garnered the most attention and uproar in the past few decades. Roughly 49 percent of the world's diamonds are mined in impoverished African nations. Because of their value, diamonds have become a currency of sorts for the continent's bloody political conflicts. Commonly referred to as blood diamonds or conflict diamonds, these gems happen to originate in areas controlled by military forces, and their trade funds civil wars. In Angola, Sierra Leone, and the Democratic Republic of the Congo, wars involving the economics of diamonds have killed or displaced millions of people.

In an attempt to combat the problem, a large group of diamond-producing and diamond-trading countries (including the United States) banded together in 2002 to create the Kimberley Process Certification Scheme (KPCS). Their intent was to set standards to prevent illegally traded conflict diamonds from entering the legitimate diamond market. Unfortunately, the KPCS has been criticized by human rights groups for its inability to uphold those standards. Kimberley Process member countries have allegedly failed to submit accurate data on their trade statistics, making it difficult to track the flow of conflict diamonds between countries.

The diamond trade has also been plagued by instances of unethical corporate behavior. De Beers, which controls 60 percent of the trade in all rough diamonds, paid the maximum ten-million-dollar fine as part of a guilty plea in a ten-year-long dispute over its role in diamond price-fixing.

If you're in the market for diamonds, a few measures will minimize your contributions to social conflict and dishonest dealings. Once you've found a jeweler you trust, ask if he or she can provide a "Certificate of Origin" stating that the diamonds for sale came from government-controlled areas where conflict diamond mining is not an issue. If a Certificate of Origin is not available, find out which company supplies the store's stones and research that particular supplier's environmental standards and policies before purchasing. Another smart move is to buy diamonds mined in Canada and Australia, which will ensure that you aren't buying conflict diamonds. If your jeweler sells African diamonds, ask for the supplier's name and if he or she can provide a KPCS (Kimberley Process Certification Scheme) Certificate of Origin. While certainly not foolproof, a KPCS certificate does help to lower the chances of inadvertently purchasing a conflict diamond.

Finally, as with gold, seeking out estate jewelry is an excellent choice. Since diamonds are the hardest material available, they don't undergo any wear and tear over the years and can easily be remounted into new settings. And

explore other, colored gemstones such as sapphires and emeralds. Although colored gems are mined and can still be traded illegally, their value is far lower than diamonds' and they generally don't have the same politically charged associations.

ALTERNATIVE MATERIALS So what can you do about daily costume jewelry? Luckily, there's no limit to the creative, sustainable materials available. As with other clothing items, the key to sustainability is buying quality pieces made to last through more than one season, and looking for materials that don't require the use of nonrenewable resources such as plastic. Handmade jewelry from found materials such as sea glass, recycled glass, seashells, various seeds and nuts, and carved reclaimed wood abounds at craft fairs and specialty boutiques. Likewise, look for fairly traded pieces when possible, as sweatshop labor has often crafted the lower priced costume jewelry.

Take Action

- ✓ Buy basics made from organic cotton and wool. Look for fabrics like hemp, linen, and bamboo, which come from naturally pest-resistant plants.
- ✓ Seek out wildcrafted silk.
- ✓ Skip the synthetics, like polyester and nylon.
- ✓ When possible, opt for unbleached clothing with truly low-impact dyes.
- ✓ Avoid fabrics treated with stain guards, water repellents, and anti-wrinkle agents.
- ✓ Take your clothes to a greener cleaner for wet cleaning or CO_2 cleaning.
- ✓ Go for vintage leather and cloth handbags.
- ✓ Choose high-quality, long-lasting leather items. Avoid leather made from the skins of endangered species. Avoid PVC accessories.
- ✓ Learn which retailers use sweatshop labor and shop elsewhere.
- ✓ Buy jewelry made from conflict-free, recycled, and sustainable materials.

Making Rayon

A 19th-century silkworm epidemic was the catalyst for the creation of the first man-made fabric, rayon.

In 1884 a French nobleman, Count Chardonnet, figured out how to convert wood pulp into fibers that could be spun into thread and woven into fabric. Dubbed Chardonnet's silk or rayonne, the newly invented material garnered international acclaim. Enthusiasm for the new fabric waned, however, when consumers discovered that it had a tendency to shrink and pucker over time. Since then, improved versions of rayon have been invented, including acetate and viscose.

The starting material of rayon comes from trees, but it is by no means a natural fiber. Multiple steps transform cellulose, the hardy material that makes up plant cell walls, into long filaments or strands. In a nutshell, a battery of machines, aided by chemicals, chop and chew the cellulose up into evenly sized, tiny bits and pieces, then other machines shape the stuff into strands and clean it of any impurities.

Viscose rayon starts as fine wood pulp of a higher grade than the pulp used for making paper. The pulp consists of long, chainlike molecules of cellulose that have been purified to remove lignin and other plant components. Flat sheets of this high-purity cellulose soak in vats of sodium hydroxide, also known as caustic soda or lye, the same substance found in household drain cleaners. During this steeping process, the cellulose chemically reacts with the soda and becomes soda cellulose. Next, giant wringers squeeze the liquid out of the fibers, and shredders chop the cellulose into fine, fluffy flakes referred to as white crumb.

Now the material is ready to be aged. Oxygen in the air engages with soda cellulose in a chemical reaction called oxidation, which breaks down the cellulose into smaller chains. Aging has to be done for just the right amount of time to create evenly sized chains of the form necessary for making the filaments that will be spun into in a weavable thread.

The aged white crumb next travels into a giant mixer, where it reacts with gaseous carbon disulfide to form cellulose xanthate. This process, called xanthation, helps the cellulose break down further into smaller, evenly shaped pieces. It also produces yellow impurities, which can be dissolved with the addition of a caustic solution. After much mixing, the result is a golden yellow mixture with the thick consistency of honey. Because of its honeylike viscosity, the raw material at this stage has been given the name "viscose." It can also be called "cellulose xanthate." Next, the viscose is left to sit and ripen, a phase during which chemical reactions continue. Cellulose xanthate is unstable, so a portion of it reverts back to cellulose and releases carbon disulfide, which can escape or react with other cellulose molecules and further break them down.

Finally the viscous liquid is ready to be transformed into fine threads or filaments. Filters remove any nondissolved materials and bubbles. Pumps push the viscose through a showerhead-like device called a spinneret. Out of each hole comes a thin ribbon of liquid viscose.

These ribbons shoot directly into a bath of chemicals that force the liquid viscose to harden into filaments. The chemical cocktail contains zinc sulfate, sulfuric acid, and sodium sulfate. Zinc clings to xanthate, pulling the cellulose chains close together. The zinc-xanthate complexes then fall away, leaving pure strands of regenerated cellulose filaments. Sulfuric acid and sodium sulfate also help solidify the strands and remove the xanthate groups.

Finally, a stretching machine lengthens and aligns the filaments. Washing machines further remove impurities. At last the viscose rayon filaments are ready for spinning into yarns that can be woven into fabrics.

Viscose rayon is far from perfect as a replacement for natural fibers. Despite improvements, it still shrinks when wet unless it has been pretreated with a protective coating. Many of the chemicals involved in viscose production are harmful to the environment if dumped in streams or allowed to escape into the air. Viscose rayon is no longer manufactured in the United States, but production continues in China, India, and many other nations. It may look good, but there's more to clothing made of viscose rayon than meets the eye.

GROWING UP GREEN

Healthy Kids & Babies

MAYBE YOU GREW UP RECYCLING YOUR JUICE BOXES AND wearing organic cotton cloth diapers. If so, you're several steps ahead of the average environmentally aware consumer. For most of us, the realization of our environmental impact doesn't set in until we're well past childhood, after our day-to-day habits like driving an hour to work and buying disposable paper towels are well established. En route to a greener life, we begin to integrate healthier choices—bamboo floors instead of hardwood, recycled toilet paper instead of conventional. Our reeducation happens gradually, and we hope that our actions, small and large, add up to positive impact.

Except, of course, when we are expecting children.

There's nothing like having a child to make a person acutely aware of the consequences of his or her daily habits, and inspire a frenzy of well-intentioned changes. For the sake of the arriving baby, a coffee-adoring mother learns to love decaf or do without; parents-to-be set about baby-proofing the kitchen. Ordinary decisions begin to take on new meaning: Is this shampoo safe for our brand-new baby? Should we move those knick-knacks to a higher shelf? A soon-to-be parent starts to wonder about the impact of chemicals in plastic toys, the safety of the paint on the nursery walls. And then comes the guilt-ridden revelation that we're handing our children a planet plagued by pollution and waste. Panic sets in.

Although there's certainly no shortage of hype in the baby-gear industry—hence the burgeoning popularity of $900 strollers and infant-education

DVDs—the current trend toward less toxic, more environmentally friendly baby goods is certainly a fashion worth following.

It's hard to dispute the fact that our ecosystem affects our children's health, both in utero and long term. A 2006 study published in *Environmental Health Perspectives* found that women who delivered very preterm babies (before 35 weeks) had higher levels of mercury in their hair, which has been associated with higher consumption of mercury-contaminated fish. Certain pesticides and carcinogenic polycyclic aromatic hydrocarbons (PAHs), byproducts of combustion, readily cross the placenta; polybrominated diphenyl ethers (PBDEs), found in fire retardants, have shown up in nursing mothers' breast milk. ▸For more on PBDEs, see page 137.

Even more troubling, newborns may not be the only ones at risk for ill effects. An animal study published in the September 2006 issue of *Endocrinology* suggests that prenatal chemical exposure may raise future generations' risk of cancer, kidney disease, and other abnormalities; when exposed to the pesticide vinclozolin at the time of sex determination during pregnancy, rats developed lasting harm to reproductive cells that was passed on to their offspring and subsequent generations. The long-term consequences of this chemical exposure are still unclear, but many parents understandably wish to avoid bringing their child into contact with hazardous substances of any kind, in any quantity.

Of course, many a new parent has been driven to the brink trying to make all the right choices, all while running on little to no sleep. In fact, frustration with the lack of options in the natural baby care industry has inspired the launch of countless companies "for parents, by parents" in recent years. Environmental consulting companies will now come in and review the toxicity of your home, and many interior designers specialize in making kids' rooms and nurseries more green.

But creating a healthy home environment for your tots doesn't have to be difficult, expensive, or require consultation with a professional. Take things one step at a time, using the information in this chapter as your guide. And keep in mind that raising happy, healthy children isn't just about buying the right goods. Don't underestimate the impact of a positive example, and sharing your own green lifestyle habits with your kids. That way, they can grow up recycling juice boxes and picking up litter, passing on the wisdom for generations to come.

Pregnancy & Nursing

Creating a healthy environment for your baby starts early, and any steps you can take to decrease your exposure to potentially harmful substances during pregnancy are well worth the effort. Healthy eating, nontoxic cleaning, and natural personal care are all the more important on the nine-month fast track.

When you're pregnant, you are not just eating for two—you are making major lifestyle decisions that could affect your child for the rest of her or his life. It's all the more important to pay attention to the sorts of guidelines offered throughout this book. Here's a checklist of important things to consider.

✓ **EAT SAFER MEAT & DAIRY PRODUCTS** Certain toxins, such as PCBs, which may cause neurological damage, and dioxin, a carcinogen, are stored in animal fat. Avoid fatty cuts of meat and high-fat dairy products; opt for lean meats and skim milk instead.

✓ **STICK TO LOW-MERCURY FISH** Mercury, a potent neurotoxin, can harm a developing fetus, increasing the child's risk of brain damage and learning issues. Skip high-mercury fish such as fresh tuna, canned albacore, wild bass, swordfish, and tilefish, choosing safer varieties like sardines, wild salmon, and farmed striped bass. Consumption of moderate-mercury fish, such as canned light tuna, should be on a limited basis. ▸See "Eco-Tip: Safer Seafood," pages 26-27.

✓ **PASS ON PESTICIDES IN FOOD, LAWN, & GARDEN** A 2004 study published in *Environmental Health Perspectives* found that higher levels of the pesticides chlorpyrifos and diazinon in umbilical cord blood corresponded to lower birth weight and lower birth length; more recent studies have linked prenatal pesticide exposure to autism, high blood pressure, and gestational diabetes (which affects the mother). It's smart, then, to choose organic foods, as they are grown without synthetic pesticides. In particular, look for organic varieties of the following fruits and vegetables, since they tend to harbor high levels of pesticides when grown conventionally: peaches, cherries, apples, pears, nectarines, strawberries, grapes, lettuce, potatoes, spinach, celery, and sweet peppers.

Also, avoid the use of lawn and garden pesticides, especially while you're pregnant, as these have similarly detrimental health effects.

✓ **AVOID TOXIN-RELEASING HOME IMPROVEMENT PROJECTS** If you live in a house built prior to 1978, chances are good that lead paint was used in the interior. Avoid any projects that involve sanding or stripping painted surfaces, as this can release lead particles into the air, where they can be inhaled. Lead can remain in the body for several months, and prenatal lead exposure can interfere with nearly every aspect of fetal development, causing brain and kidney damage, according to the Columbia Center for Children's Environmental Health. And any home improvement project involving paints, glues, lacquers, or solvents has the potential to release volatile organic compounds (VOCs) into the air you breathe; it's best to avoid these during pregnancy as well.

✓ **CHOOSE NONTOXIC CLEANING MATERIALS** Corrosive drain cleaners, corrosive scouring scrubs, and heavily perfumed floor polishes have no place near you and your developing child. Even innocuous-seeming air fresheners are best avoided; a study published in the October 2003 *Archives of Environmental Health* linked exposure to air fresheners during pregnancy and within six months of birth to both diarrhea and earache in infants and headaches and depression in mothers. ▸For more on household cleaning, see Chapter 2.

✓ **SKIP THE PERFUMES & NAIL POLISH** Both can contain ingredients called phthalates, which are known hormone disruptors. Nail polish formulas can also include formaldehyde, a known carcinogen. Instead of commercial perfumes, try ones made from plant-based essential oils; to get your nails gleaming, simply file and buff them to a shine.

✓ **FIND OUT WHAT'S IN YOUR WATER** Tap water from municipal water supplies can contain toxic chemicals, harmful bacteria, high levels of chlorine, and lead. Fortunately, it's not hard to obtain a copy of your town's drinking water report, which lists the quantities of problematic contaminants. They're

ASK THE EDITORS

Q **Is organic infant formula any better than conventional? What about soy?**

A Most experts agree that breast milk is the best option for feeding infants, both because it provides complete nutrition and because the mother's milk contains beneficial antibodies that will support babies' developing immune systems. But if you decide to transition your infant to formula, you'll find there are three types: cow's milk, soy, and elemental formula. All come in ready-to-use, concentrated, and powdered forms; the latter two are designed to be mixed with water. Cow's milk formula is the most common, and while considered safe by most doctors, it does come with the same caveats as conventional milk. Dairy cows are often given large doses of antibiotics and hormones in order to increase milk production. For this reason, many parents choose to feed their babies organic formula, which is made from hormone- and antibiotic-free cow's milk. ▸ For more on the benefits of organic dairy products, see pages 30-32.

For babies who are allergic to the proteins in regular milk formula or who can't tolerate the milk sugar lactose, pediatricians often recommend soy-based formula. Elemental formula is meant for babies who have a family history of milk allergies; it may contain milk proteins but it's processed for easier digestion and is less likely to cause allergic reactions than standard cow's milk formula. It's unclear whether these two options offer better or worse nutrition than standard formula in the long term. Whatever your choice, be sure to discuss your decision with your baby's doctor to be sure your child receives adequate nutrition.

typically mailed out to residents annually, and you can get help in reading them from the EPA's Safe Water website. See "Resources." Check for the presence of trihalomethanes, chlorination by-products which may increase the risk of miscarriage at levels above 75 micrograms per liter. If you use well water, test it annually for nitrate. All parents should test for lead, which can leach from corroded, older pipes that feed your home.

✓ **USE SAFER FOOD CONTAINERS** Polycarbonate (#7) plastic, a popular material for reusable, hard plastic water bottles, has been found to leach hormone-disrupting bisphenol-A into beverages. Storage containers made from #3 PVC can leach phthalates, and #6 polystyrene can release styrene, a carcinogen, into food. Store food and water in glass, ceramic, stainless steel, or safer reusable plastics such as #2, #4, or #5, and avoid heating any kind of plastic in the microwave, as it encourages leaching.

✓ **STEER CLEAR OF SMOKE** Automobile exhaust, industrial emissions, tobacco smoke, and soot-producing candles all release fine particulate matter into the air. In addition to irritating your respiratory tract, smoke contains polycyclic aromatic hydrocarbons (PAHs), linked to low birth weights and smaller head circumferences in newborns.

After the baby is born, keep in mind that you're not off the hook—chemicals are readily transferred to your child via breast milk, so it's just as important to keep up healthy habits if you're planning to nurse. Pediatricians recommend breast-feeding because it provides the child with the mother's healthy antibodies, increasing babies' resistance to infections. It also decreases the risks of childhood obesity, juvenile diabetes, childhood cancers, and allergies, in addition to giving babies a possible IQ boost. And yet, despite all these benefits, even women who breast-feed their babies often use formula as well. Although the World Health Organization and many medical authorities recommend breast-feeding exclusively during the first six months, only 36 percent of women worldwide and fewer than 12 percent of U.S. mothers choose to do so. If the possibility of passing contaminants to your baby via breast milk troubles you, rest assured: By and large, the benefits of breast-feeding outweigh the risks. In fact, breast-feeding may help counteract the effects of inadvertent chemical exposure during pregnancy.

Baby Bottles & Food Containers

Whether you fill it with breast milk or formula, at some point you'll probably use a baby bottle. And once your little one starts taking solid food, you'll need portable storage for toting bite-size snacks. Some choices are better than others for baby food containers.

BOTTLE BLUES As a material for baby bottles, plastic is far from the best. Breast milk stored in plastic may lose a high percentage of its antibodies for *E.coli* bacteria and much of its fat content, since fat adheres to plastic and may remain in the bottle. Plastic containers can also scratch with frequent use, which increases the chances of chemical leaching (especially with polycarbonate—#7 plastic—which releases bisphenol-A) and bacterial contamination. Freezing and warming plastic bottles may also promote leaching.

The better choice for baby bottles is tempered glass (shown at left). Not only does it not leach chemicals, but it can be sanitized by boiling or a high-heat dishwasher cycle. Examine glass often for any cracks or chips.

If you still prefer to use plastic, opt for nonleaching, easily recyclable varieties. Polyethylene (#2, #4, or #5) have not been found to leach potential hormone disruptors; many mainstream companies manufacture baby bottles made from these types of plastic.

If you plan on freezing and storing your breast milk, avoid plastic containers made of #3 PVC, as it can leach phthalates and adipates, linked to reproductive harm and liver cancer in mice. Reusable containers and bags made from #1 plastic can also leach phthalates. Wide-mouth glass canning jars are a decent choice for storage, as they won't crack when heated or chilled. (Just be sure to leave a little room in the top of the jar, as the liquid can expand and contract as it freezes and thaws.) Bags made of #2 or #4 polyethylene have not been found to leach toxic chemicals. Still, remember that all of these plastics, safe or not, are derived from petroleum, a nonrenewable resource. Only buy as many plastic bottles as you really need.

Finally, choose clear silicone bottle nipples and pacifiers; they're longer lasting and safer than the amber-colored rubber ones, which can contain low levels of contaminants known as nitrosamines. These substances, which have been found to cause cancer in lab animals, can be ingested through bottle nipples, but it's unknown whether this kind of exposure increases cancer risk in humans. The Food and Drug Administration (FDA) regulates the amount of nitrosamines allowable in rubber nipples, but low levels are still permissible. Silicone nipples, by contrast, are nitrosamine-free. Regardless, inspect all bottle nipples regularly and discard any with cracks or tears, which can encourage bacteria growth and pose a choking hazard.

DISH DECISIONS As with baby bottles, plastic is a less desirable material than glass, ceramic, or stoneware, simply because these alternatives don't leach phthalates or bisphenol-A. Certain types of fine china and ceramic do contain lead, though, so either keep kids away from the good stuff or use lead test strips (available at hardware stores) to find out whether these dishes are safe. ▸For more on safe dishware and kitchenware, see pages 50-60.

Of course, parents of babies and young children may want something less prone to breakage. Bamboo dishware is an excellent choice, as it's sturdy, lightweight, and virtually unbreakable. Disposable plates and bowls create waste, especially those made of hard-to-recycle styrene; if you must use disposables, choose either plastic plates you can recycle (#1 and #2 plastic plates are usually accepted, but check with your local authority to be sure) or buy recycled paper brands. ▸See "The Science Behind It: Plastic Picnicware," pages 406-407.

ON THE GO In today's convenience-minded culture, "kid food" has become synonymous with tiny, individually wrapped portions. Baby food, applesauce, crackers, fruit juice, and other snacks all come sized for one and packaged to last forever. The problem with these superconvenient single servings is the amount of waste they generate, most of it unnecessarily.

A six-cracker package of cheese-and-cracker snacks, for instance, comes wrapped in plastic, and then ten of those packs are placed inside a cardboard box. The cardboard box is then shrink-wrapped, and most people carry it home from the grocery store in a plastic bag. It's less wasteful (not to mention less expensive) to buy your tot's favorite foods in bulk and simply

THE FACTS

The average American child generates 67 pounds of packaging waste from school lunches every year. That means an elementary school with 250 kids takes out more than 16,000 pounds of lunchroom trash annually.

measure out single servings as you need them. For dry foods, zipper-type plastic bags can be used, rinsed, and used again; wet foods can be stored in reusable, nonleaching plastic containers. ▸For plastic types, see "Bottle Blues," page 239. Recycle glass baby food jars and any plastic containers that you can clean thoroughly.

As your child gets older and needs to tote around larger snack portions or even whole meals, enlist the help of reusable cloth bags or a sturdy lunchbox and a thermos or stainless-steel water bottle. Avoid plastic film, which can release chemicals into your foods; try wrapping sandwiches and other large items in butcher paper or a cloth napkin instead.

Baby Clothes

As you prepare to welcome a new addition to your family, you'll need to stock the nursery drawers and closet with baby clothes. It's easy to fall for the fuzzy booties, hand-knit cotton caps, and itsy-bitsy overalls that line the store racks. But good looks aren't all that count.

Be vigilant in your pursuit of knowledge about the clothing you put on your baby. Certain fabrics may come from pesticide-laden crops; others deplete dwindling natural resources. Some are treated with toxic dyes and fire retardants, while others are 100 percent natural. When you're ready to stock up on onesies, T-shirts, and socks, do all you can to ensure that the items in your cart—and on your baby-shower registry—are the healthiest ones available.

SAFER FABRICS Breathable, comfortable, easy-care cotton is by far the most common material used in baby clothing. But before it's a T-shirt or a set of pajamas, cotton is a crop heavily treated with pesticides and synthetic fertilizers, including toxic organophosphates, which can contaminate soil and groundwater. Cotton is also frequently bleached using chlorine and colored using dyes and heavy-metal fixing agents. ▸For more

ECO TIP: SEMI-ORGANIC OUTFITS

If your budget doesn't allow for an all-organic wardrobe, choose organic for the bottom layers of clothing—the onesies, T-shirts, and pants—that come closest to your baby's skin. And considering how much time babies spend sleeping, organic pajamas and sleep sacks aren't a bad idea, either.

on conventional cotton production, see pages 211-12. These factors are troubling enough for the average adult, but of even more concern when it comes to babies. Due to their small size and developing immune systems, infants and toddlers are especially sensitive to chemical exposure. For this reason, it pays to go organic, especially with the items that come closest to babies' skin.

Admittedly, organic cotton baby items are a bit more expensive and tougher to find than their conventional cotton counterparts, but that seems to be changing. Thanks to growing awareness of pesticide exposure and the booming interest in natural products, organic cotton is becoming mainstream. Small manufacturers sell organic pieces online and at various retail stores, and even mega-retailers may carry a small selection of pesticide-free cotton clothing at very manageable prices. In addition to looking for organic, check to see if the items are treated with bleaches or heavy-metal dyes.

In sweaters and other woolens, seek out certified organic or Pure Grow wool whenever possible, as it indicates that the farms did not treat their sheep with any pesticides. As with cotton, look for undyed or naturally dyed wool. Avoid any clothing items made with synthetic materials such as nylon, acrylic, or polyester, as these are petroleum-derived and may carry chemical residues. ▸For more on environment-friendly wool and other fabrics, see pages 212-18.

CLOTHING CARE Washing the mountain of burp cloths, onesies, socks, and bibs—pure drudgery. There's not much you can do to avoid it; however, there are ways you can make it less taxing on the planet and your child's skin. Use vegetable-based, phosphate-free, and fragrance-free detergents. Choose oxygen "bleaches" or natural whiteners such as baking soda and lemon juice instead of traditional chlorine bleach, which can irritate skin and pollute waterways. If items get heavily soiled or stained with dark liquids such as fruit juice, soak them in cold water immediately to reduce your need for heavy-duty stain removers. Skip the fabric softeners and static-removing dryer sheets; if you're washing natural fabrics like cotton, you're unlikely to need them anyway. And even if you choose organic cotton fabrics exclusively, be sure to wash items at least once before allowing your child to wear them. Formaldehyde and other chemical residues may have been transferred to the clothing in shipping or storage, since stores and manufacturers don't typically keep organic and nonorganic fabric items separate. For more on sound laundry practices, see pages 81-85.

Diapers

In the debate over cloth versus disposable diapers, there's no clear winner. As some environmental groups point out, "It's a wash." Consider the pros and cons of each option before making your decision.

DIRTY DISPOSABLES? After the introduction of disposable diapers in the 1960s, concern began mounting over the waste they create—an estimated 5,000 to 9,000 diapers per child, depending on when they become toilet-trained. Diaper manufacturers began studying the environmental impacts of their products in the 1980s and concluded that disposable diapers are actually less resource-intensive than cloth diapers, due to the water, energy, and detergent involved in laundering. The cloth-diaper industry countered these findings with its own research, confirming that cloth diapers used fewer resources overall and disputing the disposable-diaper supporters' prior claim that their products were compostable. Few consumers would actually compost diapers, they argued, and landfills don't provide ideal conditions for diapers to break down. The relative wastefulness of different diaper systems has been hotly debated ever since, and because resource consumption assessments are based on so many factors, it's hard to gauge exactly how disposables stack up against cloth diapers.

Most disposable diapers contain an absorbent wood-pulp product called cellulose, and it is that component that raises the most environmental concerns. In addition to depleting our natural forests, it's usually bleached with chlorine using a process that produces dioxin, a highly toxic by-product of pulp and paper bleaching. Dioxin is considered a persistent organic pollutant (POP), meaning that it accumulates in the environment and is not readily broken down. A known carcinogen, dioxin can be found in meat, fish, dairy products—and human breast milk.

To increase their absorbency and reduce their bulk, disposable diapers today also contain sodium polyacrylate crystals, a superabsorbent polymer (SAP). These crystals can absorb up to 800 times their weight in water, turning into a gel when wet. Controversy arose in the 1980s when it was believed that SAP in tampons was the cause of several cases of toxic shock syndrome; later research indicated that tampon usage habits, not SAP, were to blame. In any case, the use of SAP in diapers differs from its use in tampons, since diapers do not go inside the body. But they can break open, especially when wet, and gel can end up on a baby's sensitive skin. Because SAP so readily attracts moisture, direct contact could lead to skin irritation, and ingestion could cause gastrointestinal irritation.

As a result of these concerns, several self-proclaimed natural brands of disposable diapers have appeared on the market, all purportedly better for the planet than mainstream disposables. The main advantage to these is their non-chlorine-bleached materials; some manufacturers have also attempted to use wood pulp certified by the Forest Stewardship Council (FSC) or the Sustainable Forestry Initiative (SFI). Even these greener disposables use SAP, however, and most have a plastic outer layer that impedes their ability to biodegrade (although they're not likely to break down in the conditions of a landfill, anyway). If you're set on using disposables, though, these options do slightly less damage to the environment.

THE FACTS

Disposable diapers make up about half of the garbage by volume for an average family with one baby, according to the London-based Women's Environmental Network.

Even so, disposable diapers of all kinds draw criticism from the cloth-diaper camp. For instance, the liquid-absorbing abilities of disposable diapers—even those without absorbency boosters like SAP—are considered a drawback by some. An always-dry diaper may make it harder for your child to recognize when he or she pees, so many cloth-diaper advocates claim that babies in disposables take a year longer to potty train. Whether or not this is true, it's important to change all types of diapers frequently, as wetness can cause skin irritation.

Finally, all types of disposables pose another environmental problem, and a dirty one at that. Because diapers are usually bagged and tossed without first flushing the matter inside, millions of tons of untreated sewage go into landfills each year, an unsanitary practice that raises the potential of groundwater contamination. Modern landfills are constructed to contain leaching water, so the possibility is remote, but fecal material, if it were to escape through leaks or via insects and other pests, could potentially transmit

ASK THE EDITORS

Q **My baby is prone to diaper rash. Given that, which is better—cloth or disposable diapers?**

A While the American Academy of Pediatrics advises parents that diaper rash is less common with the use of disposable diapers, that doesn't mean cloth is the cause of those red, bumpy spots. What causes diaper rash is moisture and the subsequent chafing. Because disposables tend to contain superabsorbent crystals, the surface of the diaper stays drier and there's less chance it'll cling to the skin and chafe. Regardless of which type of diaper you use, frequent diaper changes will help reduce the incidence of rashes. In other words, don't wait for the big messes to swap out a dirty diaper. Even if Junior is just wet, it's time for a diaper change.

parasites, viruses, and bacteria into groundwater. When possible, it's a good idea to flush the contents before tossing the diaper in the waste bin.

CLOTH CONCERNS Cloth diapers, then, may seem like the perfect solution. But they come with caveats as well. First of all, they too come bleached most of the time, a process that releases dioxin into the atmosphere. Second, they're typically made of conventionally grown cotton, which contributes to global pesticide use in a way that disposable diapers do not. To avoid both of these problems, seek out unbleached, organic cotton diapers, available from a multitude of online retailers.

For many, the biggest concern with cloth diapering is the cost, perceived to be much higher than disposables. While it's true that cloth diapers require a larger initial investment—diapers, diaper covers, and laundry supplies—the cost decreases significantly over time, especially if you plan to have more than one baby. If you use cloth diapers, you'll need to purchase about three to four dozen diapers, which you can use the whole time your child is little and reuse for the next baby, or sell.

The next consideration is laundering, which can tax both your wallet and the planet if you're not careful. Laundering diapers at home incurs ongoing costs for electricity and water. You can cut these costs down by line-drying your diapers instead of using a clothes dryer. Another way to lessen the environmental impact is to wash only full loads of laundry, and to use a vegetable-based soap to reduce your use of nonrenewable resources and contamination of wastewater by phosphates and other detergent additives. ▸For more on green laundry options, see pages 81-85.

For the time-strapped, diaper-laundering services do still exist, although they're less popular now than they were before the advent of disposables. These can be an excellent option if time, rather than cost, is your main concern. Just be sure to find out what cleaning products the service uses. It may employ harsh detergents and chlorine bleach, and the larger the region it covers, the larger its carbon footprint. In the larger scheme of things, the drawbacks of a diaper service may outweigh the benefits.

DIAPER HYBRIDS Ultimately, finding the best diaper is a personal decision, and it doesn't have to be all-or-nothing. In fact, many parents use both types of diapers, switching depending on their plans for the day, their schedules, or even the child's age and size. In an effort to offer the best of both worlds, a new option has entered the diaper market: "flushable" diapers, which are a sort of hybrid of the two. Called gDiapers, they consist of a conventional cotton cloth diaper cover, a nylon liner, and a wood pulp/SAP pad insert. When changing a diaper, you rip open the flushable insert, dump its contents in the toilet, and flush. The products have been tested and approved by the National Sanitation Foundation, and the flushable pad met the Water Environment Research Foundation acceptance criteria.

Since this diaper alternative's disposable component is sent down the toilet, landfill waste is avoided. Flushing the pads does require extra water, but typically 20 percent less than is used during laundering, says the manufacturer. Since the outer cotton pants don't need to be washed after every diaper change—caregivers wash the nylon liner, or simply wipe it down—the overall amount of water and energy spent on laundering is considerably less than with cloth diapers.

The gDiapers do come with a few drawbacks, most notably that they're not available in organic cotton. Since the company couldn't find a chlorine-free wood pulp manufacturer in the United States, it opted instead for elemental chlorine-free pulp certified by the Sustainable Forestry Initiative. Elemental chlorine releases some dioxin into the environment but not as much as with the regular chlorination process. Still, in the debate between cloth and disposable diapers, these new hybrids may represent a happy medium.

Baby Care

Diapers and clothes aren't the only things to touch your baby's skin. Each day, you're likely to use a multitude of personal care products to keep your child clean, dry, comfortable, and smelling sweet. Time to start reading labels with your baby's skin and health in mind.

COMING CLEAN Babies are messy—there's no doubt about that. But before you lather up your tot in just any old soap or baby shampoo, consider what's in that cleanser. Many liquid soaps and shampoos contain sodium lauryl sulfate and/or sodium laureth sulfate (SLS and SLES), surfactants that increase cleansers' foaming action. They can strip babies' sensitive skin of moisture and possibly lead to irritation. For more on sulfates, see page 172-173.

Shampoos can also contain parabens, a class of preservatives that have estrogenic properties and have been detected in breast cancer tumors, and phthalates, a set of fragrance additives that are known hormone disruptors. Also look out for diethanolamine (DEA), a wetting agent used in shampoos to create thick lather, and the similar chemicals triethanolamine (TEA) and monoethanolamine (MEA). All of these can react with other ingredients called nitrites (often present in preservatives) to form carcinogenic nitrosamines, which can be absorbed through the skin, says the FDA. For more on DEA, TEA, and MEA, see "Eco-Tip: The Dirty Dozen," pages 169-71.

Formaldehyde, a carcinogen, can be present in the preservatives DMDM hydantoin, diazolidinyl urea, imidazolidinyl urea, quaternium-15, and bronopol. Avoid cleansers that contain these ingredients. (You may not see phthalates on the label: Choose fragrance-free products to be safe.) If you use bar soap, choose vegetable-based soaps that are color- and fragrance-free or that use essential oil fragrances exclusively, which will limit your baby's exposure to problem ingredients.

SKIN SOFTENERS After bathing and diaper changes, you'll probably want to apply some kind of moisturizer to keep your infant's skin from drying out. As with cleansers, there are several ingredients to look out for in lotions, baby oils, and diaper-rash creams.

First, and perhaps hardest to avoid, are petroleum-based moisturizers, out of concern for the environment as much as for health reasons. Listed on labels as petroleum jelly, petrolatum, and mineral oil, they're a cheap, easy solution for sealing in skin's moisture. Certain individuals with highly sensitive skin may also have allergic reactions to petroleum products. In any case, the most compelling argument against petroleum-based products is their source: crude oil, a polluting, nonrenewable resource.

Instead, look for moisturizers made with plant oils such as jojoba, apricot seed, sunflower, and almond. For very dry skin and to prevent diaper rash, plant butters such as cocoa and shea work well. As for preservatives, avoid parabens and anything with formaldehyde-releasing DMDM hydantoin, diazolidinyl urea, imidazolidinyl urea, quaternium-15, or bronopol. Look for unscented or essential oil–scented formulations.

POWDER FRESH Frequent diaper changes and a sprinkling of powder on baby's bottom are the best ways to prevent uncomfortable diaper rashes from forming. Not all baby powders are created equal, though.

Many are made with talc, a natural mineral that can be contaminated with asbestiform fibers; numerous studies of miners and millers show a link between talc and lung cancer. While talc is often used in skin care products to absorb moisture, its safety is widely debated. To avoid talc completely, turn instead to fragrance-free, cornstarch-based baby powders, which provide ample protection against diaper rash.

ECO-TIP: OLD-FASHIONED BABY CARE

Sometimes simpler is better, especially when it comes to caring for your infant. If you want to avoid putting chemicals on your baby's tender skin, head to the grocery store, not the drugstore, for your baby-care supplies. A few tried-and-true suggestions:

- ✓ **Pure cornstarch, available in the baking aisle, makes an excellent baby powder.**
- ✓ **Olive oil has long been used by mothers in the Mediterranean to keep their babies' skin soft. Look for organic, cold-pressed light olive oil, which isn't treated with chemicals and doesn't have a strong olive smell.**
- ✓ **Pure castile soap is gentle enough to be used on babies' skin and hair.**
- ✓ **Baking soda can help control diaper odors in the nursery; if you use disposable diapers, sprinkle some in the wastebasket after each changing.**

WIPING UP Disposable baby wipes can seem like the greatest invention for parents of infants and toddlers. Not only do they make diaper changes a breeze, but they come in handy for cleaning up meal messes and wiping dirty little hands. On the downside, many baby wipes contain alcohol, heavy perfumes, and preservatives like quaternium-15 and parabens. The wipes themselves, which are usually made of cotton and/or wood pulp, are also typically bleached using chlorine, which releases dioxin into the atmosphere. Instead of these, consider using non-chlorine-bleached, biodegradable wipes, which have the added benefit of being alcohol-, fragrance-, and paraben-free. Similarly, avoid using conventional, bleached cotton balls and swabs; not only does the chlorine bleach have environmental consequences, but the heavy pesticide use on cotton crops is troubling. Look for unbleached, organic cotton products.

SUN PROTECTION There's no question that sunscreen is an essential for young children, as UV rays can cause painful sunburn and inflict lasting damage to the skin. According to a study published in the April 2005 *Journal* *of the American Academy of Dermatology*, regular use of SPF 30 sunscreen during childhood helps prevent the formation of moles and may reduce the risk of developing melanoma as an adult. Unfortunately, most parents aren't always diligent about sun protection, forgetting to apply sunscreen to their children's skin regularly, neglecting to reapply it, or not using enough. The Skin Cancer Foundation points out that most people use just 25 to 50 percent of the recommended amount of sunscreen, resulting in an actual sun protection level far lower than what's indicated on the bottle.

To lower your child's risk of developing sun damage or skin cancer down the road, start early. Infants under six months should be kept out of direct sunlight as much as possible, and should be geared up with clothing and accessories that keep their delicate skin shielded from the sun's rays—long sleeves, hats, and umbrellas all offer protection. Once infants are six months or older, protect their skin using mineral-based sunscreens, which act as a physical block and deflect the sun's rays rather than allowing them to penetrate the skin.

Products that employ the minerals titanium oxide and zinc oxide as sunscreen ingredients are increasingly popular, and unlike early versions, today's formulations don't leave a whitish cast on the skin. Most natural-foods stores stock plenty of mineral-based sunscreens. Avoid using sunscreens containing chemicals such as benzophenone, homosalate, and octyl methoxycinnamate (also called octinoxate), which have been shown to interfere with the body's hormonal systems; and padimate-0 and Parsol 1789 (also known as avobenzone), which may damage cell DNA on exposure to UV rays. ▸For more on the differences between mineral and chemical sunscreens, see pages 186-89. To ensure your kids get the optimum amount of protection, follow these guidelines:

- ✓ Every day, apply a sunscreen with SPF 15 or higher on all body parts that will be exposed, including face, arms, legs, feet, and hands. This goes for cool, cloudy weather as well as hot summer days.

- ✓ Sunscreen should be applied generously to exposed skin at least 20 minutes before going outside, in the same quantity as one would use body lotion.

- ✓ Reapply every two to three hours and after swimming, sweating, and toweling off—even if the formula is waterproof.

Baby Supplies

Few manufacturers concern themselves yet with environmentally friendly baby gear. Synthetic fabrics are cheap and easy to clean; plastics are tough and affordable. Rather than drive yourself nuts searching for alternatives, consider longevity, durability, versatility, and design.

STROLLERS, SEATS, & SLINGS Few pre-baby buying decisions are as complex as the almighty stroller. There are umbrella strollers, joggers, convertible car-seat systems, and tandem strollers. There are cheap strollers and there are very, very expensive ones. Regardless of what you choose, there's a good chance that you'll have to buy one that uses materials that may not be health-promoting or environment-friendly.

Most strollers are constructed from a combination of materials, including aluminum frames, plastic and rubber wheels, plastic trays, synthetic fabric seats, and foam cushioning. To make your decision less taxing on the planet, buy the most versatile stroller you can possibly find—a midsize stroller system that combines a car seat and stroller yet folds into manageable dimensions is ideal. This will eliminate your need to buy several incompatible components such as a car seat, stroller, "snap and go" car-seat frame, and so on as your baby's needs change. Look for durable construction, sturdy wheels, and PBDE-free cushioning, which has not been treated with fire retardants. ▸For more on PBDEs, see page 137. Also consider the size capacity of the stroller, and whether it can accommodate a larger infant or toddler or if it will have to be replaced in a year or two. Then there's the issue of a jogging stroller—do you really need one? Or will a standard stroller with ultrastable wheels do the job for your evening walks? All of these considerations can help you make a more mindful choice the first time around, eliminating the chance that you'll need more strollers and accessories down the road.

Car safety seats pose a similar issue; you'd be hard-pressed to find an environment-friendly car seat, and you might not want one in any case. Safety is of the utmost concern with car seats, and you'll want a model that's been safety tested by the National Highway Traffic Safety Administration.

ECO-TIP: BUY EARLY

Baby gear can contain harmful chemicals including phthalates from plastic, PBDEs from fire-retardant foam cushioning, and VOCs from synthetic fabrics, glues, and dyes. Purchase baby items early so they can off-gas in a well-ventilated, infrequently used place. (But don't expose yourself to VOCs while you're pregnant.) By the time the baby arrives, the rate of off-gassing should be less than when you first brought the items home.

Look for a durable car seat with a PBDE-free cushion, and buy a car-seat cover, which will provide an additional layer of protection between your child and the plastic seat and can be washed as necessary.

For short shopping trips, puttering around the house, or even in place of a stroller, many parents like to wear baby backpacks or slings. Because the baby is worn close to the mother's or father's body, this option provides valuable bonding time. Unbleached organic cotton slings, which are secured with a knot or buckle, are readily available.

Then there's the ever popular BabyBjörn brand of baby carriers, first introduced in 1973 when buzz began to circulate about the importance of close contact between parents and babies. These European-made, ergonomically designed carriers meet international Oeko-Tex Class 1 standards, a designation that means that they have been tested to ensure that formaldehyde, carcinogenic colors, phthalates, pesticides, and other potentially harmful residues are absent or only minimally present.

CHANGING PADS Plush, cushioned pads make the diaper-changing process a more comfortable one for baby, but they're often made from questionable materials. The thick, contoured changing pads designed to top a changing table often contain polyurethane foam, which may release small amounts of the neurotoxin toluene. Others are covered in PVC plastic, which can contain hormone-disrupting phthalates as plasticizing, or softening, agents. Parents who wish to avoid these two materials skip a changing pad altogether, opting instead for a folded wool or organic-cotton blanket as a changing cushion.

But if you already own a changing pad or need one to fit a changing table you already own, you can purchase a cloth changing pad cover. Unbleached, undyed organic cotton is best, as it's grown without pesticides and won't introduce any new chemicals into the mix; such pads are easy to find at online retailers and even in mainstream stores.

While a layer of fabric won't contain all fumes, it may provide a bit of extra protection and, at the very least, it will keep your baby's tender skin off the pad itself and provide you with a diaper-changing surface that you can remove and launder.

Kid-Friendly Decor

Designing a nursery or a child's bedroom is fun and challenging. While it's an opportunity to create an appealing retreat for your child, it's important to create a play and sleep space that is nontoxic and environment-friendly.

FURNITURE Much of the available furniture for kids' and babies' rooms is made to last no more than a few years, constructed of cheap synthetic materials. It's hard not to be lured in by low prices, but make a point of bypassing cribs, beds, bureaus, changing tables, bookshelves, and toy boxes made with pressed-wood products that contain formaldehyde-releasing glues. ▸For more on furniture materials, see pages 131-38. If you can, select solid hardwood cribs and beds finished with low-VOC paints or lacquers; if you can't find any locally, try looking online. Or you can buy unfinished hardwood furniture and finish it yourself with an oil, a water-based polyurethane sealer, or a low-VOC or otherwise environmentally friendly paint.

Antique cribs might catch your eye, but steer clear of any that have decorative cutouts or corner posts, both potentially hazardous as your baby begins to explore. Before you commit to an antique or a used crib or bassinet, you must also be sure it's not painted with lead-based paint. The EPA's National Lead Information Center can help you identify potential lead-based paint in used furniture. ▸See "Resources."

Very few hardwood cribs and kids' beds are made from FSC- or SFI-certified wood, unfortunately. ▸For more on these standards, see pages 131-33. But one way to reduce your environmental impact overall is to choose convertible crib models, which you can adapt to fit an older child. Although many don't come from certified-sustainable forests, the reduction in furniture items you'll need in the long run makes sustainability a bit less of an issue.

THE FACTS

Federal safety standards require that slats on a baby crib be spaced $2^3/_8$ inches apart. All cribs made after 1974 conform to those dimensions, but antique cribs might not.

PAINTS & WALLPAPER Cheery colors make a child's bedroom pop. Certain paints, however, add something else, distinctly less appealing: toxic vapors that escape when the paint is applied. To avoid exposing babies and kids to large amounts of volatile organic compounds (VOCs) like benzene, methylene chloride, and formaldehyde, which are known or suspected carcinogens, choose water-based, low-VOC paints. ▸See "Green Dictionary: Low-VOC," page 134.

If you are pregnant, let someone else do the painting. After the job is done, keep the room well ventilated, and avoid spending time there for the next several weeks. And as a reminder, don't attempt to sand or strip old paint in a pre-1978 home; even if the top few coats of paint are lead-free, you still risk disturbing lead-containing layers that lie below.

Instead of paint, many parents opt to wallpaper kids' rooms. Steer clear of ever present vinyl wallpaper, which can emit phthalates and other fumes. ▸For more on wallpaper, see pages 141-42. Hang it using nontoxic, starch-based adhesives or wheat paste, which provide lasting grip but fewer VOCs than traditional wallpaper glues.

Children's Bedding

Growing kids sleep long hours, making it all the more important to provide a safe place to rest. Synthetic bedding materials off-gas; conventional cottons depend on overused pesticides. There are alternatives, but you have to think, read, and inquire as you buy.

MATTRESSES & PADS Most conventional crib (and kids') mattresses are made from layers of polyurethane foam, nylon, polyester, and vinyl—all derived from petroleum. They're frequently treated with water- and stain-proofing chemicals, and since federal law requires that crib mattresses be fire resistant, most companies also treat their products with fire retardants called polybrominated diphenyl ethers (PBDEs). What this adds up to is a whole lot of chemicals in one small mattress, many with proven health risks. Synthetic fabrics can release toluene, which has a wide range of adverse health implications; PBDES accumulate in breast milk and in fat, may harm the liver and thyroid, and have been shown to inhibit brain development in animals.

Luckily, there are alternatives. A few companies specialize in all-natural mattresses made with organic cotton, wool padding, and natural rubber, and they come in kids' and crib sizes. Since wool has natural fire resistance, these types of mattresses can be made without chemical treatments that can irritate skin or off-gas into the air, yet still meet federal safety standards. At $300 or more, these can cost significantly more than conventional crib mattresses, but for many parents, the peace of mind justifies the price tag. Completely untreated, wool-free organic-cotton mattresses are available too, but since they have no fire protection, they cannot be purchased without a doctor's prescription stating that you or your child has a chemical sensitivity.

If you do buy a conventional (and more affordable) mattress, take a few measures to minimize the impact. Let it air out as much as possible before the baby arrives, or before allowing your child to sleep on it. An untreated cotton mattress cover can provide a comfy barrier between the sleeping baby and any off-gassing chemicals, while offering added protection against accidental leaks. (Be sure to wash it regularly to keep it clean and fresh.) Of course, cotton is still cloth, so the cover won't seal out fumes and odors entirely, but it will provide a partial barrier. Avoid polyethylene, surgical rubber, and PVC mattress covers; because they don't allow the mattress to breathe, they create a breeding ground for bacteria and mold. And since the PVC covers themselves can release VOCs, they won't do anything to protect your child against chemical exposure. Instead, consider a naturally water-resistant wool pad, which can be added between the organic-cotton mattress cover and the crib sheet, providing an excellent second line of defense.

SHEETS & CRIB SETS Colorful sheets are cute and fun, but the cotton used to make them certainly doesn't grow in those bright prints and patterns. En route to your baby's bed from the cotton fields, the raw material used for most sheet sets, dust ruffles, and crib sets is treated with pesticides, chlorine bleach, dyes, and possibly fire retardants and stain treatments.

Since sheets are the last layer that comes between the bed and your child (other than clothing), make them organic, unbleached, and undyed. Crib sets, the fabric coverings that protect the baby from the sides of the crib, should be organic and undyed as well, since an active infant is likely to touch and mouth the fabric from time to time. Since so many parents consider organic sheets an essential, these are some of the easiest natural baby products to find. A quick Internet search will turn up many options, and local retailers may carry them as well. Keep in mind that "organic" sheets may be dyed with chemicals, so if you prefer colors or prints on your child's bedding, look for products that have been colored with low-impact dyes

BLANKETS & THROWS To reduce the risk of sudden infant death syndrome (SIDS), the American SIDS Institute recommends that parents put nothing (including comforters and blankets) in a crib besides the baby and the clothes he or she is wearing. But you're likely to need at least a few small receiving blankets to keep your baby cozy in your arms or in a car seat, and twin-size blankets and comforters will be necessary for older children. When shopping for these items, follow the same guidelines set for clothing: Choose organic cotton whenever possible, preferably unbleached and either undyed or colored with low-impact dyes. Look for certified-organic or Pure Grow wool, which comes from sheep not treated with pesticides. Additionally, keep an eye out for alternative fabrics such as bamboo fiber. Taken from the fast-growing, usually pesticide-free bamboo plant, the fibers are ultrasoft, durable, and perfect for use in receiving blankets and throws. Avoid synthetic textiles like acrylic and nylon in both blanket exteriors and the fluffy fill: They can emit VOCs, and they come from nonrenewable petroleum. For more details on bedding, see pages 149-56.

Kids' Clothes

Parents of newborns and infants are understandably nervous about chemical exposure through clothing, so organic baby wear is fairly easy to find. Not so for older children's clothing—and the task gets even harder as children start caring about keeping up with the latest fashion trends.

EVERYDAY OUTFITS For everyday clothing, it's hard to beat organic cotton. The health risks of wearing conventional cotton may not be exceedingly high, as many of the chemicals used on the crops are removed during the textiles' processing, but the purchase of organic products still supports more sustainable farming practices. Conventional cotton farming relies heavily on organophosphate pesticides and fertilizers, many of them carcinogenic, which can contaminate groundwater and add to the environmental burden our children are set to inherit.

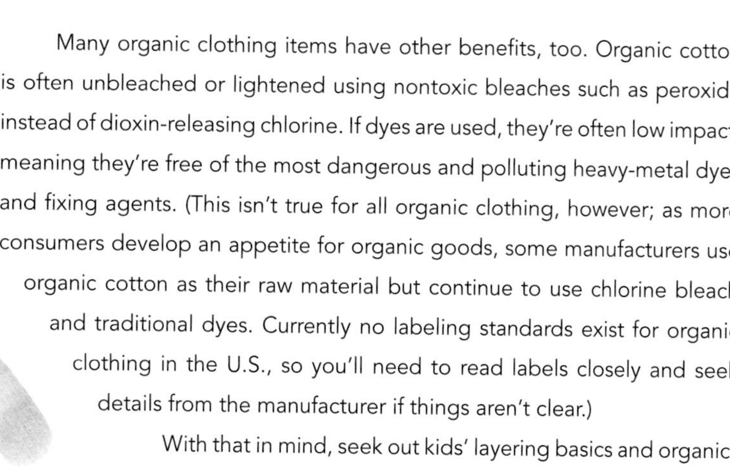

Many organic clothing items have other benefits, too. Organic cotton is often unbleached or lightened using nontoxic bleaches such as peroxide instead of dioxin-releasing chlorine. If dyes are used, they're often low impact, meaning they're free of the most dangerous and polluting heavy-metal dyes and fixing agents. (This isn't true for all organic clothing, however; as more consumers develop an appetite for organic goods, some manufacturers use organic cotton as their raw material but continue to use chlorine bleach and traditional dyes. Currently no labeling standards exist for organic clothing in the U.S., so you'll need to read labels closely and seek details from the manufacturer if things aren't clear.)

With that in mind, seek out kids' layering basics and organic-cotton underwear from environmentally conscious companies. For sweaters and dressier kids' clothing, look for items made from certified organic or other regulated fabrics such as Pure Grow wool, which is free of pesticides. For help locating manufacturers and retailers of safer, organic clothing, check out the Organic Consumers Association website, which lists member businesses by state. Likewise, the Organic Trade Association lists over 45 manufacturers and retailers of organic children's clothing in its directory.

SPORTS & PLAY When it's time for kids to get down and dirty, synthetic materials are the standard. Durable, easy-to-clean, petroleum-based polyester, acrylic, and nylon are ubiquitous in team uniforms; sweat-wicking synthetics are standard in athletic wear. If your kids play group sports, there's no getting away from these materials. But when your children are just toddling around the yard or playing a pickup game of basketball in the park, there are some better choices. While they don't "wick" as well as polyester or nylon, cotton sweats and knits do allow the skin to breathe, and they're fine for most active endeavors.

For cold-weather sports and rugged activities, explore recycled synthetics. Several outdoor clothing manufacturers sell different styles of kids' outerwear, including jackets, pullovers, and mittens, made from recycled polyester, which is manufactured from old soda bottles, worn-out garments, and secondary fabrics. For more on ecological fabrics, see pages 211-19.

Seek out environmentally friendly items, but don't drive yourself mad; from a health perspective, playing football in a nylon jersey beats watching TV in organic cotton pjs any day.

Toys

Playthings are probably the most suspect of all products for children. Millions of toys have been recalled for lead content, choking hazards, and other safety issues. Toy stores are filled with items made from unsustainable materials, many of which soon end up in the landfill. What's a parent to do?

LURKING LEAD The use of lead paint on toys made in China led to massive recalls in 2007. Lead, a potent neurotoxin, can form a dust on the surface of lead-containing products as they gradually break down; heat, sun, and frequent handling can speed up this process. Paint can also flake off and be ingested. For decades, lead paint was the standard in homes and consumer products because of its relatively low cost, but in recent years its use has been all but eliminated in products sold in the U.S.—or so most people thought.

Several popular toy lines manufactured in China were found to contain lead-based paint. In August Mattel—previously considered the gold standard in children's product safety for its diligent control of its Chinese manufacturing facilities—recalled over one million toys due to lead concerns. A European retailer detected lead in toys by Fisher-Price, a subsidiary of Mattel, leading the company to pull its stock of 83 different toys from store shelves. And these two recalls, while certainly the most wide-reaching, weren't the only recent instances of lead appearing in toys—they simply brought the problem to the attention of American parents, front and center.

If you already have painted toys in your household and wonder whether they could be toxic, review the website of the U.S. Consumer Product Safety Commission (CPSC) to see if any of the products in your home have been the subject of safety warnings. When bringing home a new toy, painted or otherwise, check the latest toy advisories on the CPSC's website to see if it's the subject of any recent warnings. And if you notice that your child's painted toys show signs of wear, such as scratches or flecking, recycle or dispose of them.

To avoid potential problems in the future, skip toys coated with any kind of paint unless labels or manufacturers' statements specifically indicate that they're lead-free.

PLASTICS GALORE All kinds of toys, from dolls to building blocks to cars, are made with plastic these days, the most common type being polyvinyl chloride, also identified as vinyl or PVC. There are many reasons to avoid this petroleum-based material, but the biggest issue for parents is the presence of phthalates, the toxic softeners used to make the plastic soft and pliable.

Phthalates have been found to affect reproduction and sexual development in laboratory experiments on animals. Research at the University of Rochester, for example, suggests that high phthalate levels in mothers during their final months of pregnancy may affect the genital development of their children. The research also points to potential effects on puberty and fertility. Furthermore, one of the most common phthalates in vinyl, DEHP, is a probable human carcinogen known to cause other serious health problems including liver and kidney abnormalities.

Since phthalates can migrate, or leach out, and since young children often put toys into their mouths, the European Union has already banned the most dangerous phthalates in toddler toys. Many companies are voluntarily removing them. Some states have initiated legislation to keep them out of kids' products. Phthalate-containing plastics may still be sold, however.

To avoid the risks of PVC and other phthalate-containing plastics, do your homework. If the product's materials are not listed on the packaging, contact the manufacturer or visit its website for more information. If you need assistance, Greenpeace has run an extensive campaign alerting people to the dangers of PVC, especially those posed to children, and their website contains lots of advice.

The simplest and most obvious solution to the continuing problem is to avoid buying toys made of plastic.

WOOD IS (MOSTLY) GOOD Solid wood is one of the safest materials you can find for kids' toys, and there's no end to the variety of wood products you'll find—blocks, train sets, toy cars, and so on. While wooden toys do contribute to the depletion of forests, they last much longer than toys made of paper or plastic, so in life cycle terms, solid wood toys benefit the environment.

The best woods are certified as sustainably produced hardwood by the Forest Stewardship Council (FSC) or the Sustainable Forestry Initiative (SFI). For more on sustainably produced lumber and its certification, see page 295. Unfortunately, certified-sustainable wooden toys aren't easy to come by, but more may come on the market if parents ask for them.

As long as the toys are made of solid wood, not pressed wood or plywood, the risks are negligible, especially when compared with the dangers of some plastics. The finishes used on solid wood products are the main concern. Be sure the toys your children play with are treated with nontoxic finishes. Finishes of natural oils or beeswax are the safest.

Be on the lookout for toys, such as puzzles, made from pressed wood—thin strips of wood or conglomerates of wood particles that have been glued together. The glues used in pressed-wood products can give off toxic fumes like formaldehyde. If you're unsure whether a product contains pressed or solid wood, take a look at the edges: If you can see layers of wood along the edges, it's most likely pressed wood and may have been made with formaldehyde. See "Green Dictionary: Formaldehyde," page 296.

GETTING CRAFTY These days, even arts-and-crafts time isn't completely risk-free. Unless your kids are master macaroni jewelrymakers, even their art supplies could harbor unsafe ingredients.

Some paints and glues can release VOCs into the air. Even crayons are not immune from problems: In 2000 the U.S. Consumer Product Safety Commission (CPSC) verified reports that major-brand crayons contained asbestos. Some polymer modeling clays—which actually contain no clay at all, but are made of polyvinyl chloride (PVC)—have been found to contain significant levels of phthalates. Even after washing, phthalate residues were found on the hands of children and adults who had worked with polymer clay. This sort of clay requires oven baking to harden, and when the clay was baked, phthalates also migrated into the air, raising the possibility of exposure by inhalation.

For the safest art projects, stick to watercolor paints, less likely than oil-based paints to contain VOCs. Encourage your children to make cards and collages using construction and scrap paper and to create papier-mâché sculptures using cornstarch or wheat flour paste. You can make your own modeling dough by mixing 1 cup flour, ½ cup salt, 1 tablespoon vegetable oil, and

1½ teaspoon cream of tartar with 1 cup water, then stirring it over low heat until it forms into a ball. Add a few drops of food coloring for color.

The bottom line for craft materials that are healthy for children and the planet? If it's edible, it's probably the safest. Always resourceful, kids will prove to you that homemade projects can be more fun than ready-made and store-bought materials.

Take Action

✓ While pregnant, limit your exposure to toxic household chemicals and foods containing pesticides and mercury.

✓ Opt for glass baby bottles with silicone nipples.

✓ Store food and drinks in reusable containers made of #2, #4, or #5 plastics.

✓ Buy babies' and kids' clothes made of organic cotton, or layer nonorganic items over organic underthings.

✓ Choose unbleached disposable diapers or organic-cotton cloth diapers.

✓ Pamper your infant with products free of preservatives, harsh detergents, perfumes, talc, and mineral oil.

✓ Keep young babies out of the sun completely, and slather the sunscreen on older kids—every single day.

✓ Since it's tough to go nontoxic with these items, buy versatile, long-lasting baby gear such as strollers, car seats, and carriers.

✓ For cribs and kids, choose natural mattresses not treated with fire retardants, or cover conventional mattresses with pads and covers made of natural wool and organic cotton.

✓ Don't fill the nursery with toxic paints and furniture finishes. Opt for low- or no-VOC products whenever possible.

✓ Purchase organic cotton bedsheets and receiving blankets, with no- or low-impact dyes.

✓ Skip the hyped-up plastic and painted toys; go for solid wood items and homemade crafts instead.

Anatomy of a Diaper

The modern disposable diaper is a feat of engineering. These leakless wonders soak up vast quantities of urine and ferry moisture away from the skin, leaving babies (and parents) with a comfortable feeling. Let's take a look at how they are engineered to do it:

The top sheet is the part that comes in contact with the baby's skin. Its job is to absorb urine into the diaper as quickly as possible. The sheet may be coated with a soaplike chemical called a surfactant that lowers the surface tension of water, reducing water's tendency to form droplets and increasing its ability to soak into the diaper.

Just beneath the top sheet lies the "acquisition and distribution layer," or ADL. Typically composed of synthetic fibers such as polyester, this layer may extend the length of the diaper or just cover the diaper's target zone—the area that absorbs the most urine. The ADL helps move liquids into the absorbent pad beneath, giving the wearer a sense of dryness. It also helps distribute urine throughout the diaper so that it can come into contact with more of the diaper's secret weapon, the superabsorbent material.

At the heart of the diaper is the superabsorbent pad composed of fluffy cellulose harvested from pine trees and an extraordinary material known as sodium polyacrylate. When dry, sodium polyacrylate is a fine saltlike powder, but it has the remarkable capacity to absorb over 500 times its own weight in pure water. (Less urine is absorbed, since it contains 0.9 percent salt, but the amount is still impressive.) The urine becomes trapped in the polyacrylate, turning the granular powder into a slushy gel that resembles wet snow.

Sodium polyacrylate is a molecule shaped something like a long bracelet with lots of charms dangling from it. These "charms," actually carboxylate groups, love to bind to water. When dry, the molecular bracelet stays tightly kinked upon itself. Adding water changes this, though. The water molecules attract the sodium away from the polyacrylate chain.

Without the sodium to keep the polyacrylate tightly coiled, the bracelet unwinds. The "charms" (now, coming loose, called carboxyl ions) are free to snap onto the water molecules. As more water molecules crowd onto the charm bracelet, the strand unwinds further, which has the effect of allowing even more binding of water molecules.

Beneath the superabsorbent pad of a disposable diaper lies a layer of stretchy tissue paper, followed by the diaper's outer layer, or back sheet. This layer, a polyethylene lining, may be given a clothlike look by overlaying a polypropylene sheet, cheerfully adorned with images of whatever cartoon characters are toddlers' favorites of the season. The polypropylene back sheet keeps liquids from exiting the diaper yet still provides breathability, so that its wearer's skin doesn't overheat.

To prevent leaks, elastic leg cuffs are now standard equipment on disposable diapers. The cuffs are usually made of polyurethane or spandex, an elastic material that can stretch to four times its original length before it breaks.

Leg cuffs are sometimes coated with a water-repelling layer of polypropylene to further prevent leakage. Waists are secured with elastic tape or, in premium diapers, stretchy hook-and-loop-tape (also known as Velcro), which can be repositioned for a better fit.

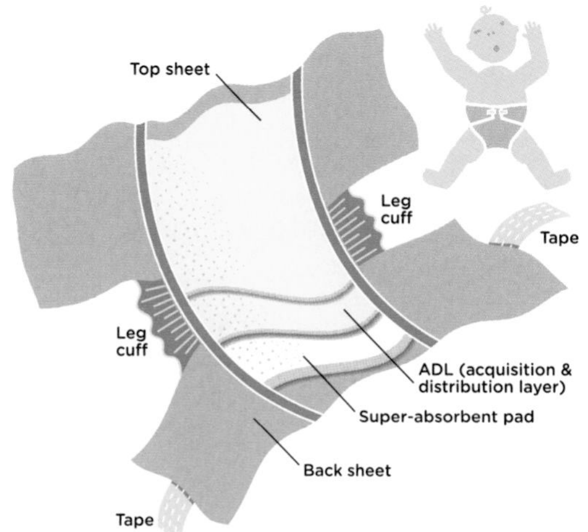

DISPOSABLE DIAPER Highly engineered, today's disposable diapers depend on several layers of synthetic materials, each designed to play a different role in the complicated process of catching and holding waste while minimizing baby's discomfort .

Once all the parts of the diaper have been assembled, this marvel of baby product engineering is ready for its first (and only) performance. After nobly collecting its cargo, the diaper is relegated to the landfill, where it takes decades to degrade.

Someday, diaper recycling and composting may reduce the flow of disposables into our landfills. One California city tried a diaper-recycling program, sanitizing the components and recycling the plastic and wood pulp, but it didn't prove cost-effective and was discontinued after six months. For now, disposables may be the better choice for some families, compared with constant laundering. Neither solution is ideal.

Transportation & Travel

As more of us sit stuck in traffic, worrying about the rising cost of gas and our effects on global warming, the question of how we travel is becoming an increasingly important concern—for our pocketbooks, and for the planet.

For most of us, hopping in the car to get us where we want to go is a mindless habit. We simply don't think twice about how we get around to run errands, take the kids to school, and commute to work. Unless you live in a large city, chances are your community is built largely around car travel, with roads and highways connecting neighborhoods and shopping malls reached best by automobile. The truth is that many of us are so used to traveling by car, we rarely stop to consider the implications of choices that we are making, let alone other options. For those in cities, a public transportation system may be an alternative. Others are starting to think twice about where they work and live, opting to live closer to the office or shopping areas. Americans might consider emulating workers elsewhere in the world, choosing to ride a bike instead of drive a car to and from work daily.

Many will decide they still need to drive, but that they should investigate the ever increasing market in greener, more fuel-efficient cars. Car shoppers will find a larger choice of cars on the market that not only emit fewer air pollutants but also cut down on greenhouse gas emissions. Car manufacturers are designing new versions of hybrid cars that run on a cleaner, more fuel-efficient mix of electricity and gasoline, while others are making cars that run on alternative fuels, such as ethanol or biodiesel. In the not-too-distant future, cars powered solely by electricity or hydrogen fuel cells promise to transform the automobile—and the world we know today—profoundly.

Longer trips, whether for business or pleasure, raise new environmental concerns as well. Vacation and travel decisions make a huge impact on the environment. How to travel, where to go, and in what ways to visit new parts of the planet—all these represent important questions to be answered with green lifestyle principles in mind.

Carbon Footprint

The amount of carbon dioxide, the gas contributing most heavily to global warming, has increased 30 percent in Earth's atmosphere since preindustrial times. It's essential for individuals and families, as well as nations, to pay attention to their carbon footprints.

Your carbon footprint is essentially the effect your personal actions have on the climate: the greenhouse gases you produce, measured in units of carbon dioxide. Many of your actions generate carbon emissions, from driving to lighting and heating your home, air travel, and the solid waste you produce. By measuring your carbon footprint, you can get a sense of your own contributions to climate change and—more important—learn where you can make changes to help cool the planet.

For example, consider your driving habits. Our transportation choices have a profound impact on how much we contribute to emissions of carbon dioxide, and ultimately to global warming. When you drive your car, each gallon of gasoline you burn produces carbon in the form of carbon dioxide. Depending on its fuel efficiency, your car can easily generate its own weight in carbon dioxide each year. In fact, between our driving, energy consumption, and other sources of carbon dioxide emissions, the average American is responsible for about 20 tons of carbon dioxide emissions annually, a far greater amount than any other industrialized country in the world.

So how can you reduce your carbon footprint? A helpful first step is to determine how big your carbon footprint is now. You can calculate the carbon footprint from your transportation choices and other activities by using one of many online calculators. The Environmental Protection Agency (EPA) offers one, but there are others as well, easily found through an Internet search for "carbon footprint calculator."

As you use one of these calculators, you may be surprised to see how large your footprint is. You can also explore how small changes in your travel habits can make a big difference for the planet. Consider how you can shrink your footprint by driving a more fuel-efficient car or by switching to a car that uses alternative fuel sources. Better yet, drive less by riding your bicycle, walking, taking public transportation, or carpooling.

Cars

Automotive vehicles represent one of the largest sources of carbon dioxide emissions in the United States, second only to energy generation for light and heat. Passenger vehicles make up almost one-third of smog-forming emissions nationally. While we drive, our planet suffers.

In 2005, there were nearly 250 million registered passenger vehicles in the United States—nearly one for every man, woman, and child in the country. In fact, the number of passenger vehicles in the U.S. has been outnumbering the number of licensed drivers since 1972. Contrast China and India, where in 2002 there were only an estimated 16 to 17 cars for every 1,000 people.

With so many cars in our garages and on our roads, Americans do a lot of driving. About 90 percent of us drive to work, and national figures from 2001 show that daily travel in the United States totaled about four *trillion* miles. So much driving has taken its toll on the planet. In 2000, 210 million motor vehicles in the United States were responsible for emitting over 302 million tons of carbon dioxide. It's a figure that exceeded the total carbon emissions of every nation in the world in 2005 except for three: China, Russia, and Japan. Consider that if you own even a midsize car and drive it 12,000 miles a year, your vehicle produces about five tons of carbon a year.

But the fact is, many Americans don't drive small or midsize cars, instead opting for larger sport-utility vehicles (SUVs). During the 1990s we became enamored with these gas-guzzling vehicles, and for a while, SUVs were the fastest growing segment of the auto industry. In 1999, SUV sales reached almost 19 percent of the total light-vehicle market. SUV sales were up in 2007 over those in 2006, but in 2008 they turned the corner. GM reported that sales dropped 27 percent on 2008 SUV models, and industry-wide SUV sales dropped 32.8 percent in the first quarter of 2008.

Larger and heavier than typical automobiles, SUVs require more fuel per mile to operate and produce greater amounts of pollutants and 40 percent more greenhouse gases than the average car. As more and more people have switched from cars to less fuel-efficient SUVs, the United States as a whole has only increased its oil demand to fuel these vehicles. And in a time of improving technology, SUV fuel efficiency has remained nearly unchanged over the past decade.

These sobering figures highlight that the choices you make—not only in what kind of car you drive but also how much you drive—profoundly affect the quality of the air we breathe and our ability to confront the challenges of global warming. Even with continued improvements in air quality, almost 100 million people in the United States—including children and the elderly, both at higher health risks from pollution—still live in areas with unhealthy levels of air pollution, much of which can be attributed to the increased use of passenger cars and trucks.

Riding a bike instead of driving would save most American car owners, who drive on average 40 miles per day, approximately two gallons of gas each day. Compare those numbers with driving your car and its carbon dioxide emissions, and you'll have even more reason to swap your car keys for your bike helmet.

GOING HYBRID Not too long ago, hybrid cars, which run on a combination of electricity and gasoline, seemed little more than a science experiment. But now, hybrid cars are big business, and thousands of them, coming in all shapes and sizes, are appearing on our roads in increasing numbers across the country. No longer limited to one or two choices, car shoppers will find a wide range of hybrid car models appealing to different consumer tastes, including options from carmakers such as Ford, Toyota, Honda, Nissan, Lexus, and Mazda, with other manufacturers poised to soon follow. And with gas prices continuing to rise, you can feel even more motivated to choose a hybrid as your next car. Compare the fuel costs for the most efficient hybrids, which get up to 60 miles per gallon, with a conventional gas-guzzler, and the savings quickly add up.

ELECTRIC CARS Another enticing option is an electric vehicle. Propelled by an electric motor powered by rechargeable battery packs, electricity-powered cars have several advantages over gasoline-powered cars. Although the source of the electricity to charge the car, such as a coal- or gas-fired power plant, may contribute to pollution, electric cars themselves emit no tailpipe exhaust. Electricity-powered cars also provide quiet, smooth operation and stronger acceleration, and they typically require less maintenance than gasoline-powered cars.

Unfortunately, there are downsides to electric vehicle technology too. Electric cars available today can go only about 150 miles or less before needing recharging, making them far less convenient, particularly for Americans accustomed to driving frequently and over long distances. What's more, fully recharging the battery pack can take four to eight hours, and packs are typically heavy, bulky, and expensive. Until researchers can improve battery technology to increase driving range, weight, and cost, you're unlikely to see many electric vehicles on the highway or any major auto manufacturers offering them. But if you're looking for an Earth-friendly way to take short trips around town, some companies offer neighborhood electric vehicles.

FUEL CELLS Many big automakers are working on vehicles powered by fuel cells that use a chemical reaction between hydrogen and oxygen to generate electricity. Fuel cell cars are virtually pollution-free, since the chemical reaction gives off only water as a by-product. Fuel cell cars can be fueled with pure hydrogen gas stored in high-pressure tanks or with hydrogen-rich fuels such as methanol, natural gas, or even gasoline. Even better, fuel cell vehicles can be twice as efficient as similar-size gas-powered cars and can also incorporate other advanced technologies to increase efficiency.

Like electric cars, you won't find fuel cell cars on the road just yet. High costs, lack of infrastructure to fuel the cars with hydrogen, and onboard hydrogen storage safety issues mean that fuel cell cars are several years away from practical use. General Motors predicts fuel cell vehicles in showrooms by 2012. While fuel cell vehicles may not be available for your next car purchase, they may someday revolutionize how we get around.

CLEAR THE AIR According to the EPA, driving a car is the single most polluting thing that most of us do. Cars release pollutants from the tailpipe as a result of the fuel combustion process, but they also release pollutants from under the hood and throughout the fuel system whenever heat causes fuel evaporation. In fact, motor vehicles across the U.S. emit millions of tons of pollutants into the air each year. In many urban areas, motor vehicles are the single largest contributor to ground-level ozone, a major component of smog and the most serious air pollution problem in northeastern and mid-Atlantic states. Cars can emit several pollutants classified as toxic, including benzene, formaldehyde, and lead. Auto emissions also contribute to the environmental problems of acid rain and global warming.

Motor vehicles generate three types of pollutants: hydrocarbons, nitrogen oxides, and carbon monoxide. Hydrocarbons react with nitrogen oxides in the presence of sunlight and elevated temperatures to form ground-level ozone, which can cause eye irritation, coughing, wheezing, and shortness of breath and can lead to permanent lung damage. Nitrogen oxides also contribute to the formation of ozone and acid rain and to water quality problems. Carbon monoxide is a colorless, odorless, deadly gas that, when inhaled, reduces the flow of oxygen in the bloodstream and can impair mental functions and visual perception. In urban areas, motor vehicles are responsible for as much as 90 percent of carbon monoxide in the air.

All these pollution problems come as a result of the combustion of gasoline or diesel, which powers the vast majority of cars on roads around the world today. The search for fuel alternatives is a search for methods of locomotion that do not require the same chemical reactions inside an engine, and hence do not involve the same detrimental effects to health and the environment.

GREEN DICTIONARY

ETHANOL

Ethanol (ethyl alcohol), the same type of alcohol found in alcoholic beverages, can be used as a fuel. It can be mass-produced through the fermentation of sugar or the hydration of ethylene from petroleum and other sources. Bioethanol is the term for ethanol produced from the starch or sugar from a wide variety of crops. Cellulosic ethanol, made from whole plants, may provide a planet-friendly fuel alternative.

ASK THE EDITORS

Q **I want to make my next car purchase, but I'm concerned about cost. How do I make the best choice for my family and the planet?**

A No car today can truly be called "green." Even experimental zero-emission cars still contribute to environmental problems. Particulate matter that rubs off of tires may be worse for public health than what is found in exhaust pipes. Brake linings deposit pollutants into the environment. Popular hybrid cars still use gasoline along with electricity that in most cases still comes from coal, oil, or nuclear power. Sprawl, which paves over land and begets greater use of cars, is still an automotive by-product of cars. In short, walking, biking, using mass transit, tele-commuting, carpooling and minimizing your auto trips are the best alternatives.

Some of us have no choice but to drive. A good place to start looking for more environmentally friendly cars is the U.S. Environmental Protection Agency's online Green Vehicle Guide. This website identifies the greenest car choices with its SmartWay and SmartWay Elite labels, highlighting cars with the best environmental performance when it comes to both air pollution and greenhouse gas emissions. It includes both hybrid cars and fuel-efficient conventional cars. To help you select a more fuel-efficient vehicle, the EPA and the Department of Energy also publish an annual online Fuel Economy Guide.

Once you've found greener car options, estimate the number of miles you'll drive it every year, then factor in the cost of gas to find how long it will take to earn back the higher cost of a green alternative. If you're a daily commuter or frequent weekend driver, you may be surprised how fast a fuel-efficient car pays for itself.

Meanwhile, the search is on with equal urgency for gasoline- and diesel-fueled cars that operate more efficiently and pollute less. While overall the fuel efficiency of cars on the road in the U.S. hasn't changed significantly over the past 30 years—due primarily to the popularity of SUVs—automakers have stepped up to offer consumers more fuel-efficient cars of all types. The better gas mileage a vehicle gets, the less fuel it burns, meaning fewer natural resources are used and less pollution is created at every step, from the extraction and processing of the fuel to its burning.

Several companies make cars that significantly cut down on air pollution. Although the federal EPA sets minimum standards for car tailpipe emissions, state clean air regulations such as those in California have taken limits on tailpipe emissions a step further, prompting carmakers to produce vehicles designated "Super Low Emission" (SULEV) or "Partial Zero Emission" (PZEV). These models operate with up to 90 percent fewer emissions than conventional fuel- powered cars. Standards for these types of cars have been set by the California Air Resources Board. Other states, including New York and Massachusetts, have adopted California's tougher emission standards.

GREEN DICTIONARY

BIODIESEL

Biodiesel is a fuel made from biological sources and equivalent to diesel that can be used in unmodified diesel engine vehicles. Biodiesel has been manufactured from algae, vegetable oils, animal fats, and recycled restaurant grease. As a fuel, biodiesel is safe and biodegradable, and it reduces air pollutants, such as particulates, carbon monoxide, and hydrocarbons. It typically produces about 60 percent fewer carbon dioxide emissions than petroleum-based fuel.

CAR CARE Your maintenance decisions and habits affect your car's fuel economy—hence both your pocketbook and your pollution quotient. Even small actions can add up to big savings in both realms. Simply keeping your tires properly inflated, for example, can improve your gas mileage by more than 3 percent, by reducing the drag on your car's engine.

Replacing a clogged air filter can improve your car's gas mileage by as much as 10 percent, and protect your engine as well. You can even improve your gas mileage by 1 to 2 percent by using the manufacturer's recommended grade of motor oil. Not bad returns for things that take a few minutes and not much money.

Keeping your engine properly tuned will also save on gas mileage and cut down on your car's pollution emissions. Fixing a car that is noticeably out of tune or has failed an emissions test can improve its gas mileage by an average of 4 percent, although results vary based on the kind of repair and how well it's done. Fixing a serious maintenance problem, such as a faulty oxygen sensor, can improve your mileage by as much as 40 percent.

FUELING UP Considering our planet's dwindling, nonrenewable oil reserves and climbing gas costs at the pump, alternatives to gasoline are attracting some serious attention from drivers across the country. Innovators have gotten creative in tapping new fuel sources.

An increasing number of pioneering drivers are turning to biodiesel, produced by removing glycerin from vegetable oils, to fuel diesel car engines. And while biodiesel fueling stations are still few and far between, retail biodiesel stations are popping up across the country, offering drivers both pure biodiesel and biodiesel/petroleum blends. Country singer Willie Nelson has even branded his own biodiesel, called BioWillie, which can be found in Texas and surrounding states, with plans to expand nationwide. And while it takes some work to retrofit engines, a handful of diesel car owners are actually navigating the roads on waste vegetable oil from restaurants, turning the oil used to make last night's french fries into a very cheap—and greener—fuel alternative.

Another growing fuel alternative is ethanol, made from feedstock with a high sugar content, like sugarcane or corn. Nearly one-third of U.S. gasoline already contains ethanol in a low-level blend to reduce air pollution. Most gasoline car engines will already operate well with mixtures of 10 percent ethanol. But now fuel innovators have created a fuel blend that's mostly clean-burning ethanol for use in cars that are designed to use flexible fuels. Ford, DaimlerChrysler, and GM are among the automobile companies that sell "flexible-fuel" cars, trucks, and minivans that can use gasoline and ethanol blends ranging from pure gasoline to as much as 85 percent ethanol (also called E85). By 2007 there were at least six million E85-compatible vehicles on U.S. roads. Switching to ethanol can substantially reduce petroleum use in automobiles.

ECO-TIP: CHECK YOUR TIRES

Keeping your tires properly inflated can save you gallons in car fuel purchases and avoid hundreds of pounds of carbon dioxide greenhouse gas emissions every year.

THE FACTS

Using 100 percent biodiesel instead of petroleum diesel as an automobile fuel reduces CO_2 emissions by more than 75 percent.

ECO-TIP: EXPLORE E85

There are now over 1,300 service stations across the country offering drivers "E85," a blend of 85 percent ethanol and 15 percent gasoline. To find stations near you, consult the U.S. Department of Energy's online station locator. Pull on up to the alternative pumps to fill up on biodiesel, E85, compressed natural gas, and other futuristic fuels.

CUT BACK ON COMMUTING The most straightforward way to reduce automotive carbon emissions is simply to drive less. Instead of jumping into the car for short errands, walk or bike instead. Organize a carpool. Talk to your employer about telecommuting one or two days a week, another way to cut back on your travel impacts. Go to work via public transportation.

Bicycles

There is no cleaner, healthier, or more efficient way of getting around than on a bicycle. From China to Holland, traveling by bike is a way of life for billions of people around the world.

Every day, residents in cities across Asia swarm the streets with bicycles, riding to work or school, while in Europe, miles of bicycle paths and lanes, along with bicycle parking and showers in workplaces, entice citizens to take to the streets on two wheels. Europe is the world leader in bicycle use. In Amsterdam or Copenhagen, one-third of trips to work or for errands are made by bicycle. In Holland, Denmark, Germany, Sweden, and the United Kingdom, bikes and pedestrians share the road with cars. In Melbourne, Australia, biking to work has increased fivefold within a generation, with 4,100 trips made each day in 2001.

In the United States, more than 100 million Americans own bicycles, but we lag far behind our European counterparts and have yet to wholeheartedly catch on to the many benefits of bicycling. The infrastructure for bicycles—such as roads and parking facilities—is less expensive to build and less land-intensive than that for cars. Moreover, bicycles don't contribute to air or noise pollution, and they reduce traffic congestion. They also offer a chance for people to improve their physical fitness at a time when obesity is at record levels.

Granted, U.S. companies and communities are slowly doing more to encourage two-wheeled travel, by building more bike lanes on roads, promoting bike-to-work days, and providing

ASK THE EDITORS

Q **Are biodiesel and ethanol good choices as alternative fuels?**

A While both biodiesel and ethanol hold promise, neither fuel is a perfectly green choice. Biodiesel emits higher levels of smog-forming nitrous oxide than conventional diesel, a problem which biodiesel manufacturers are working to correct. And both biodiesel and ethanol are often blended with petroleum diesel or gasoline, resulting in continuing greenhouse gas emission worries. Critics, however, point out that ethanol made from plants requires more energy and fossil fuels to produce—29 percent more when made from corn—than the energy it generates. But supporters say useful byproducts that can be made from ethanol production, such as feed for livestock, can help save energy and partly offset the energy used to make it. Of course, crops like corn feed people too, and others worry that increased demand of corn for ethanol production will cause corn prices to rise, hurting the world's food supply. The takeaway message? While alternative fuels have received a lot of hype, no car or fuel choice on the market today offers a perfectly green solution.

bike lockers and showers at work. The League of American Bicyclists has designated 52 cities and towns as Bicycle Friendly Communities. Among these is Davis, California, which recently became the first community to achieve Platinum recognition and boasts a bicycle commuting trip rate of 17 percent. Since 1990 Portland, Oregon, has increased its bikeway length fourfold, and its bicycle riders have tripled in number, while Chicago has built nearly 100 miles of bicycle lanes and 10,000 bike racks. Bicycle advocacy groups, now active in 47 states, are helping by increasing bicycle awareness, making bikes more available, and providing bicycle maintenance support and education.

BETTER ON A BIKE Invest up front in a bike that withstands the demands of your life, whether they include commuting around town or recreational off-roading on the weekends. Aluminum bicycle frames, the most common and affordable, are less durable than steel frames, which are more expensive and harder to find. Carbon-fiber and titanium bikes have a long life span but can carry a hefty price tag. Folding bikes are great for space-challenged city apartment dwellers, but if space isn't an issue, buy a full-size bike, which will be cheaper to maintain in the long run. If you're looking to cut down on costs or are just starting to bike, buying a used bicycle is a good place to start.

Cars dominate our crowded streets, so take care to be safe as you share the road. Stick to bike paths and roads with bike lanes, and make sure that car drivers can see you. Many cities now publish handy bike maps, either in print or online, to help you safely navigate traffic. Keep your tires properly inflated and check your brakes before every ride. Wear a helmet and brightly colored clothing, use lights, and obey traffic laws.

BREATHE DEEPLY As a bicycle rider, you will find that you become more aware than ever of the air quality where you live and ride. Globally, millions of people suffer from poor air quality. The World Health Organization has found that three million people, mostly in developing countries, are killed worldwide by outdoor air pollution annually from vehicles and industrial emissions, and 1.6 million indoors through using solid fuel. While air quality conditions in the U.S. may not be as dire, many people here at home suffer the effects of air pollution too. Avoid routes heavily trafficked by big, diesel-powered trucks and buses, which spew particulate matter that not only triggers respiratory problems like asthma and lung disease but also increases the risk of heart attacks and strokes.

Before heading out for a ride, check you local Air Quality Index (AQI), a way that the federal government tracks and reports daily air quality. It tells you how clean or polluted your air is and what associated health effects might be a concern for you. The AQI focuses on health effects you may experience within a few hours or days after breathing polluted air, tracking five major air pollutants: ground-level ozone, particle pollution, carbon monoxide, sulfur dioxide, and nitrogen dioxide. Ground-level ozone and airborne particles are the two pollutants that pose the greatest threat to human health, by irritating the respiratory system and causing coughing, throat discomfort, and

ECO-TIPS: BIKING YOUR WAY

For local information on biking, look up your city or town in the League of American Bicyclists' online directory to find everything from regional advocacy groups and event listings to repair shops and safety courses.

infections. On days with particularly bad air quality, your best bet may be to avoid long exposure to the air outside your home or workplace.

Buses & Trains

Around the world, communities support extensive systems of buses, trains, and subways, which run regularly to convenient destinations for just a few dollars per fare, an environment-friendly and sociable way to travel.

THE FACTS

Using public transportation to commute to work at least four days a week, eight miles round trip, can save 54 gallons of gas and 1,140 pounds of CO_2 emissions a year.

TAKE THE BUS Riding the bus to work or shopping is not only a convenient option; it's also by far a greener choice. Motor vehicles are the largest source of urban air pollution, generating more than two-thirds of the carbon monoxide in the atmosphere, a third of the nitrogen oxides, and a quarter of the hydrocarbons. According to the American Public Transportation Association, however, motorized public transportation uses about one-half of the fuel consumed by cars, sport-utility vehicles, and light trucks. Public transportation is also dramatically safer than car travel. According to the National Safety Council, riding a transit bus is 79 times safer than car travel. Many employers now offer to subsidize bus passes for employees, and many communities subsidize buses as well, making bus travel an even more economical option.

A new generation of bus service, incorporating some of the benefits of rail, is also taking off. It's called Bus Rapid Transit (BRT), offering faster, smoother rides because buses travel in their own lane separate from roadways. Such systems overseas in places like Brazil, Colombia, and China have all significantly reduced costs, commute time, and environmental impacts. BRT lines are also running or are planned closer to home in Los Angeles, Cleveland, Boston, Pittsburgh, Honolulu, Ottawa, Seattle, and other cities.

RIDE THE TRAIN When you travel in Europe, you come to recognize the possibilities of train travel. There, grand train stations buzz with activity, as dozens of trains come and go, carrying commuters, families, and travelers. Few Americans, however, take full advantage of the train possibilities right here at home. While not offering train travel options as extensive as those in Europe, cities and regions around the United States offer several ways to enjoy the benefits of train travel.

THE FACTS

The average car in the U.S. releases about 1 pound of carbon dioxide for every mile driven. Avoiding 20 miles of driving per week by taking the bus would eliminate about 1,000 pounds of personal greenhouse gas emissions per year.

Many communities are building "light rail"—systems that generally uses single or paired rail cars or trams, powered by electricity drawn from overhead cables, moving along tracks laid down on private rights-of-way or streets: the trolley of the 21st century. From Boston and Baltimore to Takoma and San Diego, with many cities in between, light rail is offering convenient, publicly supported in-town travel. Other communities offer the more familiar alternative, heavy rail transportation systems, whether it's subway systems that tunnel underground or elevated systems on tracks above, or—in many cities—a combination of the two. Light or heavy rail, subway or elevated—any mode of public transportation represents a choice for the sake of the planet.

THE FACTS

A train can use up to 70 percent less energy and cause up to 85 percent less air pollution than a commercial jet aircraft.

More and more people are making that choice, too. According to the American Public Transportation Association, ridership increased 30 percent in the decade starting in 1995, reaching a total of 10.1 billion rides in the U.S. in 2006. In 2006, the average weekday ridership on New York's subways was a whopping 4.9 million, the highest daily number since 1953. Other cities like Denver and San Diego are quickly catching up, building their own commuter rail and light rail systems to get people out of their cars and moving around the region in a more environment-friendly way. Denver's FasTracks project includes over 115 miles of new light rail and commuter rail trains. In San Diego, the city's trolley currently runs on 51.1 miles of track, achieving a ridership of 107,000, with 11 more miles of tracks in the works.

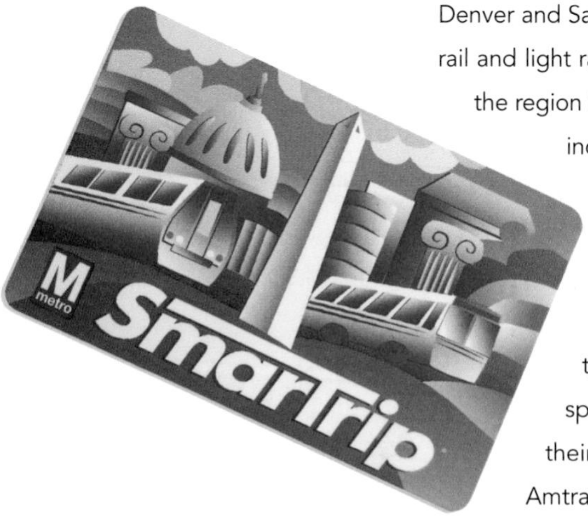

For long-distance travel, surface heavy rail systems—typically higher-capacity, higher-speed systems including high-speed and commuter or regional trains—are typically built on their own dedicated rights-of-way, separate from road traffic. Acela, Amtrak's high-speed train service operating between Washington, D.C., and Boston via Baltimore, Philadelphia, and New York, has brought the benefits of high-speed train travel to the United States.

Travel Gently

Travel and tourism is the number one industry on Earth, with 750 million people spending two trillion to three trillion dollars on trips annually. Only 25 million traveled internationally in 1950, but today tourism is big business—with big implications for the planet that we all explore.

For many of us, traveling is a time to leave our worries behind and to let ourselves be pampered. But consider that even while on vacation, our choices and actions affect the environment, from the energy we use in hotels to the food we eat and the activities in which we engage. We can choose more responsible ways to travel.

Such is the premise of "ecotourism," which The International Ecotourism Society (TIES) defines as "responsible travel to natural areas that conserves the environment and improves the well-being of local people." According to this new ethic of tourism, responsible travelers not only minimize their impact on the natural world but also contribute to conservation efforts and benefit the local economies and indigenous communities where they are traveling. Ecotourism is a relatively new concept, but it has already become a powerful force in the travel industry, promoting greener resort destinations; seeking activities that depend on renewable energy; supporting the harvest and serving of organic and local food; sponsoring the conservation and protection of plants and animals; and in all ways expressing and acting out of respect for local communities. TIES suggests:

- ✓ Minimize your impact;
- ✓ Build environmental and cultural awareness and respect;
- ✓ Provide positive experiences both for visitors and hosts;
- ✓ Provide direct financial benefits for conservation;
- ✓ Provide financial benefits and empowerment for local people; and
- ✓ Raise sensitivity to a host country's political, environmental, and social climate.

THE FACTS

A Boeing 777 uses 6 gallons of fuel per passenger per hour and emits 0.06 ton of carbon dioxide per passenger per hour.

ECO-TIP: HOW TO TRAVEL RESPONSIBLY

Here's a "Traveler's Code for Traveling Responsibly," offered by Partners in Responsible Tourism, a network of travel agents, tour operators, and nonprofits concerned about the environmental and cultural effects of their industry.

NURTURE CULTURAL UNDERSTANDING

- ✓ Travel with an open mind: Cultivate the habit of listening and observing; discover the enrichment that comes from experiencing another way of life.
- ✓ Reflect daily on your experiences and keep a journal.
- ✓ Prepare for your travels: Learn the geography, culture, history, beliefs, some local language; know how to be a good guest in the country or culture.

BE AWARE OF SOCIAL IMPACTS

- ✓ Support the local economy by using locally owned restaurants and hotels and by buying authentic local products made from renewable resources.
- ✓ Interact with local residents in a culturally appropriate manner.
- ✓ Make no promises that you cannot keep (sending photos, helping with a school).
- ✓ Don't make an extravagant display of wealth; don't encourage children who beg.
- ✓ Get permission before photographing people, homes, and other sites of local importance.

MINIMIZE ENVIRONMENTAL IMPACTS

- ✓ Travel in small, low-impact groups.
- ✓ Stay on walking trails.
- ✓ Pack it in, pack it out; assure proper disposal of human waste.
- ✓ Don't buy products made from endangered animals or plants.
- ✓ Become aware of and contribute to projects benefiting local environments and communities.

The practice of sustainable tourism requires that tour operators, resorts, guides, and travelers all make sure that their presence has no negative effect on their host locales. We travelers can do our part by favoring businesses that minimize pollution, waste, energy consumption, water usage, landscaping chemicals, and excessive nighttime lighting, making sure that we leave no tourist footprints behind and that we do not leave behind an environment diminished by our visit.

The National Geographic's Center for Sustainable Destinations has further defined the concept of ecologically and socially responsible travel, introducing the term "geotourism." Simply put, geotourism respects, sustains, and enhances not only the natural but also the cultural character of a place—history, culture, heritage—and actively seeks to contribute to the well-being of its residents. Geotourism incorporates the concepts of sustainable ecotourism and goes one step further, on the principle that tourism dollars can not only protect a destination's environment but can actually help its culture thrive and express itself.

Tourism has a huge impact on many parts of the world, and tourism management, according to the Center for Sustainable Destinations, can have a tremendous impact on protecting or degrading the environment, culture, and character of many parts of the world. The center has developed a charter, a statement of principles, which they invite governments and tourism agencies to follow. As of 2008, a number of locales and nations have signed the charter, including Guatemala, Honduras, Romania, Norway, and Peru. The Center also partners with *National Geographic Traveler* magazine to post periodic "destination scorecards" that highlight the places doing best at following the principles of environmentally and culturally respectful tourism.

Geotourism creates travel experiences that are richer than the sum of the individual parts of a vacation, appealing to visitors with diverse interests. Good examples of geotourism involve local communities, businesses, and citizen groups in providing locally distinctive and authentic travel experiences. In turn, visitors can interact and learn directly from local residents and at the same time know that they are investing their travel dollars directly in locally owned businesses. The result is a rich and rewarding travel experience full of unique stories to pass on to friends and relatives at home.

GREEN DICTIONARY

CARBON OFFSETS

Carbon offsetting means mitigating the greenhouse gas emissions you produce during your daily activities through payment of a fee to fund projects that reduce overall greenhouse gas emissions. Opportunities now exist that allow you to offset the carbon impacts of your air travel, driving, home energy use, and other activities. As the nonprofit group Carbonfund.org suggests, "Reduce what you can, and offset what you can't."

GET GOING Many a travel adventurer begins by boarding a commercial jet and flying hundreds or thousands of miles away to a new and exciting location. From this very first step, the environmentally responsible traveler needs to be aware.

Aircraft designers may be working on lighter, more fuel-efficient planes, but currently commercial air travel produces a staggering amount of pollution: an average of almost 0.4 ton of carbon dioxide per passenger per flight, a staggering number when multiplied by the number of passengers that are in the air on a given day worldwide. Planes are comparable to cars in their fuel consumption per passenger mile, but emissions at higher altitudes have 2.7 times the environmental impact of those on the ground.

Fortunately, creative minds have found temporary fixes for a situation that, in the long run, is going to demand revolutionary new ideas. Several organizations, as well as some airlines and online booking services, offer you options to lower your trip's environmental impacts by purchasing "carbon offsets" that contribute money to renewable energy or tree planting projects that help to minimize your carbon footprint. By spending just a few extra dollars—even as little as five dollars, depending on your trip—you can help make your air travel a little greener. Look for the option on airline websites, or ask the agent when you make reservations.

ECO-TIP: THE COST OF CRUISING

One megacruise ship generates an astonishing amount of pollution every day:

- ✓ **25,000 gallons of sewage from toilets**
- ✓ **143,000 gallons of sewage from sinks, galleys, and showers**
- ✓ **7 tons of garbage and solid waste**
- ✓ **15 gallons of toxic chemicals**
- ✓ **7,000 gallons of oily bilgewater**

GREEN DESTINATIONS You can do your part to support good geotourism by choosing destinations that thoughtfully manage tourism's impacts and support local communities. But choosing places to go—not to mention

ASK THE EDITORS

Q **I've been researching hotels and tour operators for an overseas trip I'm planning with my family, and I've come across some choices touting that their green claims have been "certified." What are ecotravel certification programs, and how do they work?**

A If you aspire to travel green while overseas and are looking for choices, it can admittedly be a daunting task to research and pick out from the crowd the greenest hotels and tour operators. That's where a growing number of organizations are stepping in to do the homework for you by offering to independently investigate and certify hotels, services, and operators.

There are dozens of certification organizations around the world, many certifying businesses in a particular region or country. The certification label Green Globe is perhaps the best known for international sustainable travel and tourism. The nonprofit conservation group Rainforest Alliance has also built partnerships with tour operators in 25 Western Hemisphere countries including the U.S., Mexico, and Brazil. Its Sustainable Tourism Certification Network of the Americas sets baseline standards that include environmental impact assessments, staff training, environmental monitoring, biodiversity conservation, and benefits to local communities.

specific lodging and activities once you get there—is no small task. Guidebooks, websites, and travel agencies offer seemingly countless choices, but you need some guidance in choosing the most green and sustainable options.

The National Geographic Society's Center for Sustainable Destinations continues to assess the environmental and cultural health of prime destinations, including the world's islands, natural and cultural heritage sites, and the U.S. national parks. The center's website lists these findings, along with many other links to helpful traveler resources. See "Resources." While there is no international third-party certification as yet for tour operators, many other organizations also monitor and report on travel and tourism practices, including TIES, Sustainable Travel International, the United Nations Environment Programme, and Conservation International. Look for a tour operator that minimizes impact on plants and animals, builds environmental awareness through education, invests in conservation efforts, provides direct financial benefits for conservation to local communities, and respects local culture, among other considerations.

Hotels and resorts are increasingly aware of the rewards of improving their practices, catering to increasingly green-minded customers. Websites are beginning to offer the growing list of hotels, resorts, and lodges that have committed to reducing their energy and water use, supporting local communities, and offering guests eco-friendly activities. The International Ecotourism Society's Travel Choice directory lets you search for ecofriendly travel agents, tour operators, lodges, or hotels. As you do your research, keep the principles of ecotourism and geotourism in mind. Do they employ local citizens and support projects to benefit the local community and ecosystems? Are they certified by eco-travel organizations or have they won any ecotourism awards? What sorts of policies have they implemented to reduce water consumption, conserve energy, or recycle waste? How do they educate visitors about local natural areas, wildlife, energy conservation, and local culture?

ECO-TIP: DITCH THE JET-SET LIFESTYLE

Take longer trips to fewer locations—join the new Slow Travel movement. Such trips are especially rewarding if you can stay with friends or family or in family-run hotels, stock up on local food, and rent a bike to fully explore the area. You get to experience the local culture on a deeper level and with less of an environmental impact. What's more, you'll get an arguably richer experience if you stay in one place for a whole week rather than trying to take in all of a country—let alone the high points of a continent—during a single whirlwind vacation.

VOLUNTEER VACATIONS If you're looking for a richer travel experience, consider philanthropic opportunities combined with travel, allowing you to help local communities with environmental projects, educational materials, construction, or other goods and services. A good place to jump-start your research is Travelers' Philanthropy, which includes links to a wide range of philanthropic opportunities, from tree planting to health and education projects.

Volunteering your time to environmental projects can be a particularly rewarding experience. Organizations around the world offer opportunities to participate in scientific studies, tree planting and restoration projects, wildlife rehabilitation, and many other projects. The nonprofit Earthwatch Institute links volunteers directly with scientists in conservation field research, ranging from studying climate change patterns in Canada's Arctic regions to tracking the habits of rare animals in Madagascar to ensure their survival. Another nonprofit, Globe Aware, develops locally identified, one- to two-week "mini–Peace Corps" projects around the world aimed at promoting cultural awareness and environmental sustainability.

Take Action

- ✓ Commit to biking to work at least a few days a week.
- ✓ Explore alternative automobile designs and fuels for greener driving.
- ✓ Take the bus or train more often.
- ✓ Consider buying a hybrid or greener car for your next car purchase.
- ✓ Keep your car well maintained to maximize your fuel efficiency.
- ✓ Cut down on driving by carpooling, telecommuting, and combining errands.
- ✓ Support eco-friendly destinations on your next trip.
- ✓ Consider walking, taking public transit, or renting a hybrid or greener car on your next trip.
- ✓ Offset your carbon emissions on your next flight.
- ✓ Consider a volunteer vacation for your next trip.

Hybrid Electric Vehicles

The traditional gasoline internal combustion engine is a relatively wasteful device. Only 15 percent of gasoline's chemical energy goes into operating the vehicle: The rest is lost to heat, friction, and idling. Electric motors, in contrast, are 90 percent efficient at converting electrical energy into motion. They are limited in speed, however, and they run out of juice relatively quickly.

Hybrid electric vehicles combine a gasoline-powered engine with a battery-powered electric motor to supply power to the wheels. Since they use less gas, hybrids have the potential to substantially reduce tailpipe emissions while saving consumers money at the pump.

Today's hybrids come in several gradations, depending on how and when the vehicle uses its electric motor. The classic or "full" hybrid vehicle is one that can use either the gasoline engine or the electric motor or both. A hybrid usually has a slightly smaller gasoline engine than a similar-size conventional car, which it typically uses for fast highway driving and climbing hills. The electric motor handles acceleration from a stop and low-speed urban driving, and it provides "power assists" for hills and passing.

The brain of the hybrid car is the electronic controller, which governs the two power sources. It is sometimes compared to a stagecoach driver whose wagon is hitched to a horse and a donkey. Each animal has its own, gait, speed, and endurance level, and managing the two requires precision.

The controller starts working from the moment the driver starts the car. When the driver steps on the gas, a computer analyzes how quickly and how far he or she has pushed the pedal, and figures out how much power to draw from the two supplies to attain the desired speed.

The controller sends instructions to a power-split device, which is a gearbox connecting the two power sources. The gas engine and electric motor each have long rods, or shafts, that lead into the gearbox. Inside the gearbox, gears connect the shafts to the driveshaft, which transfers rotation motion to the wheels. In full hybrids, the power split device connects to a third shaft that can send power to an electrical generator.

The electrical generator is where electricity is made to recharge the battery. Fully electric cars need to be plugged into the grid for recharging, but hybrids get their batteries rejuiced during driving and braking. When the car is moving along at steady speeds, the gasoline engine is busy converting gasoline's chemical energy into driveshaft rotation. This rotation can turn not only the car's wheels but also a shaft inside the electrical generator, where the rotational movement is transformed into electricity using a basic concept in physics: that a rotating magnet inside a conducting wire coil will generate electrical current. The electrical energy can be pumped into the battery.

Another way that hybrids recharge the battery is during "regenerative braking." With conventional brakes, a pad presses against the wheel, using friction to slow the wheel's rotation and wasting a lot of energy as heat. A regenerative brake slows the car by converting some of the energy of movement into electrical energy. During regenerative braking, the electric motor works backward. Instead of using electricity to power the motor to turn the wheels, the wheels turn the motor and create electricity. The motor places a drag on the driveshaft, and the car slows down.

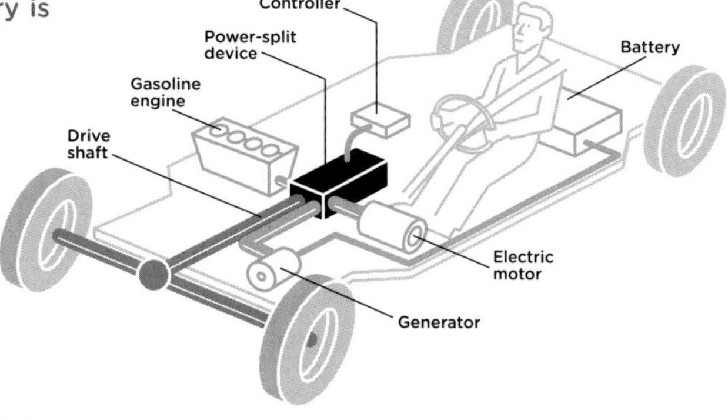

HYBRID CAR In a hybrid electric vehicle, power comes from two sources: a gasoline engine for starting and accelerating and an electric motor for maintaining speed. Batteries store unused energy for later use.

Despite their efficiency, electric motors require large battery packs to store and supply all the electricity they need. In many models, this battery pack is stored at the back of the vehicle. Unlike a conventional lead battery used to start a gasoline engine, these nickel metal hydride (NiMH) batteries can store large amounts of electricity.

The plug-in hybrid is an optional modification that allows the driver to plug the car into the electrical grid at home. By charging the battery with a source other than the gasoline engine, the car has even more stored electricity to use for local driving. Plug-in hybrids could be the wave of the future, allowing drivers to use even fewer gallons of polluting—and pricey—gasoline.

9

FRAMING & WALLS
SIDING & ROOFING
BATHROOMS
FLOORING
HEATING & COOLING
INSULATION
KITCHENS
WATER HEATERS

BUILDING THE FUTURE

Green Home Improvement

NOT SO LONG AGO, THE MENTION OF A "GREEN HOME" conjured up images of some futuristic social experiment or perhaps the eclectic design of a geodesic dome. But in the last few years, that's all radically changed. Green building has become a nearly mainstream concept, with environmentally minded architects, contractors, and building supply stores popping up in every major city. In fact, green building is surging across the country, from corporate headquarters to city halls and homes.

Green building is revolutionizing the traditional American dream home. In truth, conventionally built homes aren't so dreamy when it comes to your health and the planet. A century and a half since Henry David Thoreau built his little cabin on Walden Pond, the poetic ethic of simplicity and harmony with nature has been displaced by the typical multithousand-square-foot suburban palace with a three-car garage. If we took Thoreau on a tour, he'd be surprised to learn that today's building products and furnishings emit dangerous volatile organic compounds (VOCs), such as formaldehyde and benzene, and can trigger respiratory, allergic, and neurological reactions.

Such chemicals, which are nearly ubiquitous in the typical American home, may include neurotoxic toluene from polyurethane foam insulation; VOCs—which irritate the respiratory tract and are potential carcinogens—from paints, glues, finishes, and carpets; formaldehyde in pressed wood products and wood finishes; and phthalates, which have been linked to reproductive problems, obesity, and asthma, from polyvinyl chloride (PVC) pipes, siding, and floor tiles. Imagine Thoreau's shock at the sight of bulldozers mowing down trees to make room for a house built with scarce hardwoods from far-flung places and construction crews filling dumpsters with enough scrap wood to build another Walden cottage—or entire Walden subdivisions.

Counter Thoreau's worst nightmare with the vision of a greener home, built in harmony with the Earth, with attention to the health and well-being of those who produce the building materials, those who build the home, and those who live in it. For more and more people, the new dream home is a green home, and many neighborhoods boast examples of home projects built in creative ways to save on energy, water, materials—and medical expenses.

Taking inspiration from traditional "sustainable" dwellings, such as pueblos and yurts, the green homes of today seek to repair the link between their occupants and the rest of nature. And it's not just an isolated fad, as tens of thousands of green homes have already been built across the country. The trend is attracting a broader economic spectrum of homeowners too, thanks to public awareness, new technologies, and a growing market in environmentally friendly building materials and methods.

So what exactly defines a green home? The U.S. Green Building Council has developed Leadership in Energy and Environmental Design (LEED) standards including many vectors in the environmental impact of a building: site location, use of energy and water, healthier materials, recycling, use of renewable energy, and protection of natural resources. Beyond LEED, there are also many regional and local programs that have developed their own standards for green homes. From roofing to framing materials, and from paint to plumbing, opportunities abound to make both new and existing homes healthier and more ecological.

Why consider green building in your new home or renovation project, when it may cost more than conventional building? It's simple: Green building not only makes sense for many reasons having to do with your health and the health of the planet, but a look at the longer-term costs reveals significant savings as well. Building your house to use energy and water more efficiently, for example, allows you to cut back on your electricity, home heating and cooling, and water bills. According to the U.S. Energy Information Administration, the

country's residential sector is responsible for about 22 percent of our national energy use—no small sum—and the average American house costs about $1,500 in energy every year. But with some basic steps, you can make your household energy use as much as 30 to 50 percent more efficient, according to the Green Building Council. And that benefit comes from simply installing Energy Star–certified appliances or even from such easy upgrades as utilizing proper insulation and programmable thermostats to automatically control your heat and air conditioning. Imagine the benefits that even bolder moves could reap, such as capturing the energy of the sun to meet your hot water and electricity needs.

Green building is also a hands-down winner when it comes to your health. Realtors are seeing more and more interest from potential home buyers in green and health-conscious designs due not only to rising alarm about global warming, but also to concerns about "sick building syndrome," a condition promoted by poor indoor air quality that can lead to serious illness. According to the U.S. Environmental Protection Agency (EPA), levels of air pollutants—including allergenic dust mites, lung-clogging particles of soot and grime, and toxic VOCs that evaporate from many household materials—can be from two to one thousand times higher indoors than outdoors. In addition to having healthier air, green-built homes also expose their owners to far less mold and other allergy triggers.

Of course, you don't have to start from scratch to be green. Consider the many ways you can reduce toxins and energy consumption in your home, from buying more efficient appliances to choosing more environmentally friendly paint for your next painting project. Building green is equal parts science and ethics, but mostly it's just common sense. You can keep what you love about your house while adding green features over time.

So where do you start your building project? Whether you're plan-

ning to build from scratch or simply wanting to incorporate more green features into a home you already own, it pays to map out a vision—and make a plan. You'll need to think about both your goals and your budget. Are you looking to cut back on energy bills, or is your main concern environmental health hazards? Evaluate which measures make the most sense for where you live and for what you plan to do with your home over the long run.

If you're a current homeowner planning an addition or renovation, one place to start is to identify any environmental hot spots in your house right now. Is the air quality in your house affected by emissions from improperly vented gas or oil appliances, or from mildew and mold? Your home also may be emitting VOCs from plywood, adhesives, wallboard, cabinetry, carpeting, flooring, foam, and upholstery; while some materials may have completed any off-gassing after a few years, others may become more toxic over time. Finally, consider testing your home for asbestos, radon, and lead from old wall paint. Knowing your current challenges may give you food for thought as you plan your project.

THE FACTS

For a glimpse at trends in green home building, just look at the numbers. A 2007 survey by the National Association of Home Builders found that more than 97,000 homes across the country had been certified by voluntary, builder-supported green building programs. That represents an increase by more than 50 percent since the last such survey, conducted in 2004, which counted 61,000 such homes.

As you map out your green building plans, consider that it's not just building materials that you'll want to incorporate, but a "whole house" mentality, too. For instance, you can build a healthy, aesthetically pleasing environment by arranging interior walls and openings to enhance circulation of air and light and by avoiding the kind of lot-filling house that disregards adjacent buildings and ignores openness, natural asymmetry, or connection to the environment outdoors.

Think about the site of your new home or addition. First off, you can orient the house to take advantage of the climate, the sun, and the views. By situating windows to face south, you'll maximize light and warmth from the sun in winter. Design for the most appropriate amount of natural light and ventilation, using elements such as windows near the roof of the house that can suck out the hot air in summer. And consider using local, environmentally sustainable materials whenever possible.

Unless you're an experienced do-it-yourselfer, you'll probably need the services of an architect, building contractor, or both. Picking the right professionals can make all the difference in getting the green home that you want instead of experiencing a homeowner's worst building or remodeling nightmare. You can look for environmentally knowledgeable builders in local green building organizations, such as the U.S. Green Building Council's member

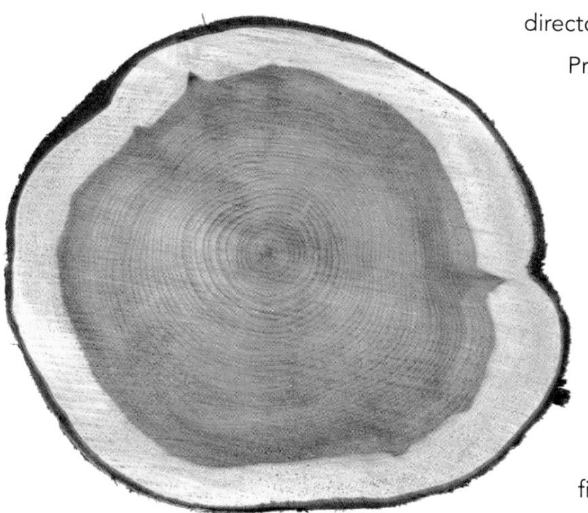

directory. The state of California has a Certified Green Building Professionals program, and similar regional programs are starting up. If you can't find any green building professionals listed for your area, stop by your local building salvage store and ask for names of contractors specializing in green design and building.

As you interview architects and builders, be clear about your green objectives. Ask to see examples of green building projects they've completed, and solicit ideas for how they'd get your project done. Don't hesitate to be specific and hold firm to your dream.

AVOIDING ASBESTOS If you're starting on a renovation, be on the lookout for asbestos, which may be found in homes built before the 1970s. A mineral fiber long valued for its strengthening and insulating abilities, asbestos became suspect when studies of those who worked around it constantly, in factories and shipyards, revealed higher than normal levels of lung cancer, mesothelioma (a cancer of the lining of the chest and abdomen), and asbestiosis (a disease involving the scarring of lung tissue). The harm occurs from breathing airborne asbestos fibers. Beginning in 1989, the U.S. government has issued a series of warnings, culminating in a ban of certain asbestos-containing materials At the same time, many municipalities have voluntarily removed asbestos-containing materials from public buildings, and manufacturers have voluntarily discontinued product lines containing the fiber. Today, the threat lurks in existing homes and not in building materials on sale for new construction.

Asbestos may be found in insulation around steam pipes, boilers, and furnace ducts; in vinyl floor tile and the adhesives or felt underlayment of old linoleum; in roofing, shingles, and siding; and in drywall joint compound. In many circumstances, however, asbestos-containing products are better left untouched. If you suspect asbestos in your home, consult your local health department or environmental safety board, where you can get help in identifying contractors professionally trained to remove asbestos. They will know what special precautions to take and how to dispose of the hazardous materials.

GREEN DICTIONARY

LEED

LEED stands for Leadership in Energy and Environmental Design. Developed by the U.S. Green Building Council, it is a rating system for green buildings and represents the nationally accepted benchmark for their design, construction, and operation. LEED ratings reflect sustainable site development, water savings, energy efficiency, materials selection, and indoor environmental quality.

Framing & Walls

So you've decided to go ahead with that long-planned addition to your home, and you want to make it a green one from the get-go. There's hardly a better place to start than with the bones of your house—the framing and walls.

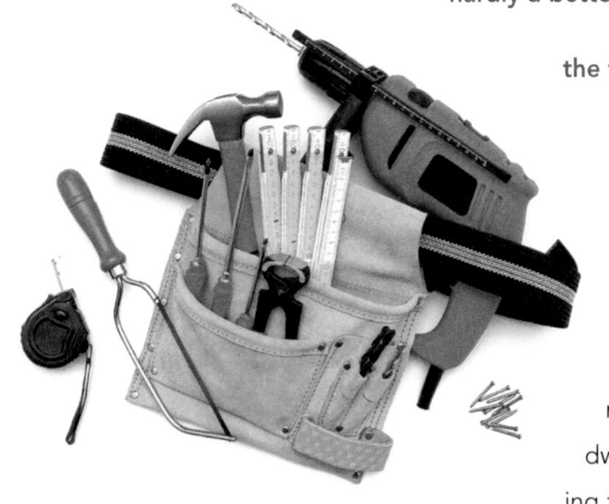

While it might be tempting to source your lumber from the nearest home improvement store, think first of your many options for making your framing choice a greener one. Consider that one of the largest uses for wood is for home building: Americans break ground on around 1.5 million new homes every year, and the average single-family dwelling requires about 15,000 board feet of lumber, according to the National Association of Home Builders. The U.S. Forest Service has estimated that in an average home this figure equates to 88 trees, or 3.2 acres of forest.

New ideas are edging out old stick-framing techniques. Advanced framing, also called optimal value engineering (OVE), represents a coordinated effort to reduce the amount of lumber used in framing a building by clever planning, redesign of certain elements, and use of alternative materials such as foam sheets and metal hangers to minimize the linear feet in two-by-fours that your construction requires. Some techniques are as simple as creating smaller living spaces than what Middle America has become accustomed to and designing so as to make the most of pre-cut, pre-assembled, or modular building systems.

If you're hiring a designer or a builder, mention OVE and see if it might be a viable alternative. If you are designing or building yourself, there are resources available to help you make the right decisions. The National Association of Home Builders publishes free Model Green Home Building Guidelines, for example, available for download on its website. The National Institute of Standards and Technology offers free software called BEES (Building for Environmental and Economic Sustainability) that helps a homeowner

ECO-TIP: HOUSE OF STRAW?

Straw-bale buildings made of bales of straw from wheat, oats, barley, and other grains boast super-insulated walls. Properly constructed and maintained, straw-bale walls covered with stucco exterior and plaster interior prove waterproof, fire-resistant, and pestfree.

or builder perform an entire life cycle assessment of building materials, from procurement to waste disposal.

You can find creative and sustainable framing materials, such as engineered wood made from recycled materials or salvaged wood. Or you can ensure that any new wood you use comes from forests managed to maintain their long-term health—a practice ignored by many timber companies, which routinely use herbicides and clear-cutting procedures.

THE FACTS

According to a 2003 study by the National Association of Home Builders, building the average American single-family home (2,320 square feet) generated between 6,960 and 12,064 pounds of construction waste.

There are also innovative non-wood options for exterior walls and framing. Consider ICFs—insulating concrete forms—which represent a framing system that combines sheets of foam insulating material used as frames for poured concrete, providing structure and insulation in one non-wood material. Rammed earth construction methods use plywood sheets as forms into which a mixture of soil and cement is poured and then compacted mechanically. A futuristic version of the ancient adobe building technique, this alternative seems most popular in the southwestern United States, but with careful preparation it has potential for other regions of the continent and the world.

FOREST-FRIENDLY FRAMING For new lumber, look for wood certified by the Forest Stewardship Council (FSC). This international organization, backed by many of the world's leading conservation groups, has made it a bit easier for home builders to use wood from trees grown and harvested responsibly. Since 1993, the FSC has certified more than 120 million acres of forest worldwide—about one percent of all forests. While that's a small number, the availability of certified lumber continues to increase. The growing breadth of FSC-certified and reclaimed products means that their prices are becoming more competitive with conventional lumber.

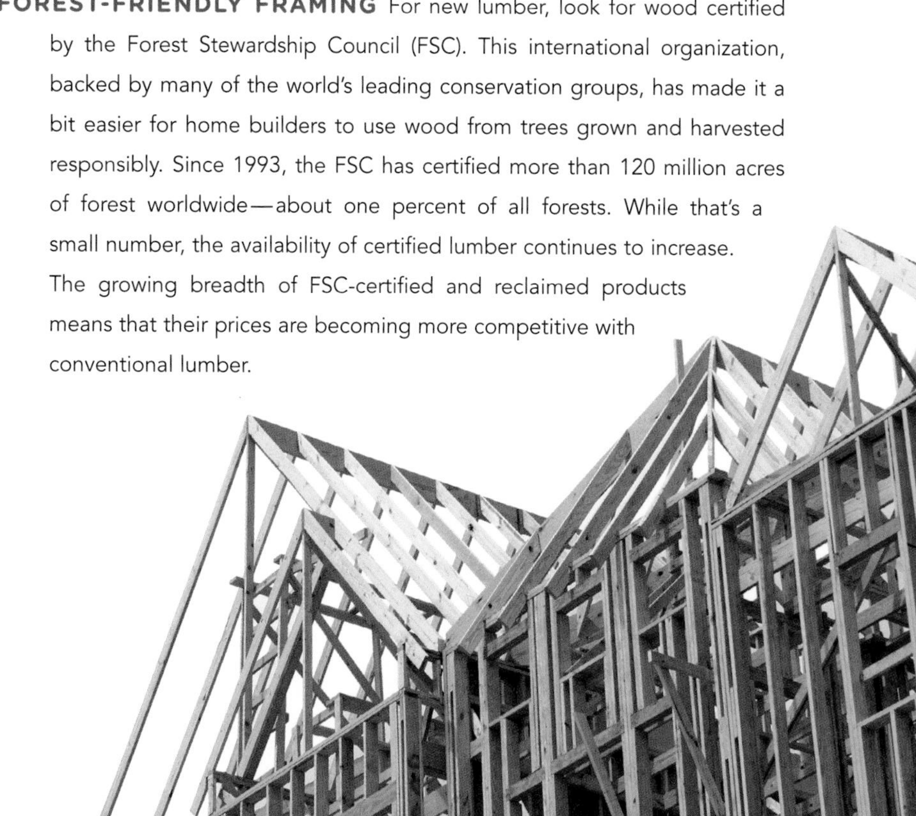

LIKEABLE LUMBER With the dwindling number of old-growth forests from which to source large-diameter wood products, engineered lumber products are your best bet for larger framing needs, such as beams and columns. Not only do they spare larger trees, they also offer the additional advantage of being both stronger and less prone to warping than conventional lumber. You can find laminated veneer lumber (LVL), manufactured by gluing thin layers of fast-growth wood together, which is then sawed into dimensional lumber. LVLs will work for studs, headers, joists, beams, and roof rafters, among other purposes. Engineered I-beams, with the central stock of plywood and flanges of LVL or solid wood, can be used as floor joists or roof rafters.

The great advantage of such engineered wood products is that the manufacturer can use misshapen trees—much more than can be used in the creation of solid-wood lumber products that require a long, straight grain. The trouble lies in the fact that conventionally engineered composite materials made with wood chips and other wood waste have typically been held together by adhesives containing formaldehyde. Manufacturers are slowly turning to greener glue methods, however, so look for engineered lumber products held together with soy-based adhesives.

GREEN DICTIONARY

FORMALDEHYDE

Formaldehyde is an industrial chemical used to make other chemicals, building materials, and household products. A volatile organic compound, it vaporizes at normal room temperatures. According to the Consumer Product Safety Commission, formaldehyde can cause watery eyes, nausea, coughing, chest tightness, wheezing, skin rashes, allergic reactions, and burning sensations in the eyes, nose, and throat. It's been observed to cause cancer in scientific studies using laboratory animals and may cause cancer in humans. The people who are most at risk are young children, the elderly, those who are already ill, and pregnant women.

PANELS & PLASTER For wood paneling and other non-weight-bearing lumber needs, you can take your green ambitions a step further. Drywall—also called gypsum board, plasterboard, or Sheetrock—is a common manufactured building material used for the finish construction of interior walls and ceilings. It is made by pressing gypsum—calcium sulfate dihydrate, a naturally occurring mineral—between paper board. Drywall is fairly benign to work with and live around, but mountains of waste are generated from the disposal of excess drywall around the country. Measure carefully and take advantage of the variably sized sheets of drywall when you buy for your building project. Hold onto partial pieces, for they will come in handy when you need to patch and fill in. Full to half sheets of drywall can be donated to charitable causes such as Habitat for Humanity. Joint compound comes in reusable plastic buckets, easy to wash out and use for carrying tools or other materials. Some states have programs to recycle the mineral content of discarded drywall. Large-scale builders should investigate recycling their drywall scrap.

For home paneling projects, plywood may come to mind. Conventional plywood is made of fast-growing, lightweight wood, usually southern

THE FACTS

About 12 percent of new construction drywall is wasted during installation. Considering that the U.S. produces about 15 million tons of drywall annually, an estimated 1.8 million tons are wasted every year.

pine. In recent years Asian tropical rain forest trees, commonly called lauan, have been used for plywood as well. Protests against American retailers have reduced the amount of lauan on the U.S. market, but it still may be sold and should be avoided, because of the pressures such logging exerts on the terrain and the people who live where these forests grow.

Plywood is a standard-sized construction material made by joining thin slices of wood, their grains often at right angles for strength, and gluing them together into a solid sheet. Most hardwood plywood—used indoors for cabinetry and paneling—is composed of a core layer, often lauan, and faced with higher-quality woods like pine. Manufacturers have traditionally used urea-formaldehyde glue, which has been classified as a human carcinogen and which can off-gas for years. New plywood products are coming onto the market every year, so homeowners can ask for greener alternatives.

Softwood plywood is used for exterior and structural applications (such as walls, floors, roofs), and its adhesive consists of phenol formaldehyde resin, a more water-resistant glue that off-gasses at a relatively slower rate than urea-formaldehyde glues. Ironically, we tend to use the worst products indoors, where they can do the most harm, according to the Healthy House Institute, a consortium of health and building experts.

ECO-TIP: FINDING SALVAGED WOOD

The Rainforest Alliance's SmartWood program certifies salvaged, reclaimed timber under its Rediscovered Wood label. SmartWood verifies claims about sources, makes sure the wood is collected responsibly, and tracks it through production, providing assurance for consumers. You can also look for reclaimed wood in your area by calling salvage, renovation, and demolition companies.

Oriented strand board (OSB) is an engineered panel product made from strands, flakes, and wafers of wood gathered into mats, processed with heat and pressure, and treated with an exterior binder. Particleboard (PB) and medium-density fiberboard (MDF) are also products using heat, pressure, and glue to bind together wood fibers and even sawdust, making fuller use of harvested wood than ever before. The effects on our forests are good, but the glues still can present a problem. By and large, PB and MDF are still manufactured with formaldehyde-based glue, considered a human carcinogen. As consumers keep up the demand, manufacturers are finding better glue alternatives. Ask for non-formaldehyde glues when you shop for particle- and fiberboard. But beware: One of the most common glue alternatives, methylene-diphenyl diisocyanate (MDI), while nontoxic in the home, has the potential to cause grave health problems to workers in PB and MDF plants. Better to look for boards made with vegetable-based resins and adhesives.

Greener paneling options are being developed. Straw, the fibrous chaff left over in grain farming, is now being collected and sold instead of burned in the fields. Strawboard and agrifiber boards present green alternatives to particleboard and reduce carbon emissions significantly. Bagasse, the fibrous left-overs from sugarcane, is also being turned into a new alternative sort of particleboard. Kirei is an innovative Japanese product made from the waste fiber of sorghum, one option for paneling materials that are friendlier to the planet. Kirei is relatively expensive, however, and builders must factor in the transportation costs—both to the pocketbook and to the environment—that get it from Japan to other destinations. Fiberboard products made with post-consumer newsprint waste and recycled wood fiber are also available.

If your project includes replastering walls, be aware that premixed plasters contain preservatives or other ingredients containing VOCs, so it's a good idea to put paint primer over them as soon as possible to seal and prevent off-gassing. Look for zero-VOC primer paint, which will be clearly labeled as such in the hardware store. Or search your community and hire a plasterer who mixes traditional plaster, which is made of gypsum, rock, and sand—a combination that largely avoids VOCs.

A NEW HOME FOR OLD MATERIALS One of the best options for your building project is to reuse wood that's been salvaged from old barns, torn-down houses, old factories, and even the hulls of ships. Although recycled wood tends to be more expensive, it can prove to be a good choice when its benefits are factored in. Supplies of virgin wood are dwindling, which means that conventional lumber prices are rising; add to that the fact that recycled wood may last three to four times longer than standard lumber. Why? Much of the reclaimed lumber on the market comes from old-growth trees, which means that the wood is of finer grain and higher quality than what's commonly available as new lumber today. Reclaimed lumber has dried fully, and so it tends to warp and shrink less than new boards.

In addition to finding reclaimed wood to meet your lumber needs, ambitious homeowners can also reuse old doors and windows, often available at little cost from secondhand stores, construction salvage stores, or auctions—or even for nothing, if you happen to be at the right place at the right time during a large renovation job in your area. Building to fit existing hardware, which may be nonstandard or warped over time, can be a challenge, so don't take this on if you're an amateur. The glass in old windows is often single-pane—not an environmentally sound alternative—but you

might be able to refit the frame with specially cut insulated glass, if you're up for the project. Salvaging windows and doors can cost more and require special attention, but you are saving materials and getting the benefit of beauty, quality, and history in your home.

Siding

Vinyl, wood, stucco—these are the most common exterior siding choices these days. While siding doesn't off-gas into your living space, you still want to make choices that look out for the health of the planet.

ECO-TIP: SIDE WITH CEMENT

One exterior siding that's low-maintenance, durable, good-looking, flame-resistant, and safe is fiber cement siding: a mixture of wood fibers and cement. The one downside is the high embodied energy in the cement itself.

Vinyl siding is inexpensive, easy to clean, and lasts a long time—but it can have a detrimental impact on the Earth and on your health. The manufacturing process of vinyl siding, made of polyvinylchloride (PVC), creates dioxins, damaging to both human health and the environment. Dioxins released into the environment are consumed by fish and animals, which are in turn eaten by human beings. Research on dioxins has linked them to hormonal interference, neurodevelopmental problems in children, and cancer.

Some wood siding, while natural in look, actually requires large boards sawed from mature trees. By choosing FSC-certified wood or engineered wood-composite siding, you will ensure that you are not pressuring the planet's forest reserves. Choose species native to your area when possible, avoid exotic woods from endangered forests, and use plant-based wood stains.

In many ways, old-fashioned stucco siding presents the least complicated environmental solution. A finishing plaster made with portland cement and additives for consistency and color, it is applied wet and dries to a hard, strong, fire-resistant finish. Nonvolatile, it does require occasional painting.

Anyone considering cement in his or her building plans needs to consider the embodied energy of the material: the accumulated amount of energy it has taken to acquire, process, and transport a material to the place where it will remain as part of a house or other building, plus all secondary manufacturing or transportation activities required to support that building task. Cement has a relatively high embodied energy.

These days, stucco exteriors are rarely made the traditional way, with concrete, but are more often made of synthetic materials. By this technique, a polymer base in which a thin mesh of fiberglass is embedded, over which a finish or color coat is applied. The base often contains acrylic or butyl resins, which off-gas VOCs.

New composite products coming on the market—combinations of cement and wood fibers, for example—represent an interesting stucco alternative. Also consider exterior siding made from recycled materials. Sidings made of steel or aluminum, for example, often contain a high recycled content, with the added advantage of being recyclable themselves at the end of their useful life.

Roofing

There's good reason to be picky about what sits atop your house. The right roof can mean planet-friendly benefits and long-term cost savings, not to mention increased comfort for you and your family.

DITCH THE ASPHALT Most shingles begin with a mat, often fiberglass but sometimes recycled wood or paper, which is coated with asphalt, a thick hydrocarbon that is a by-product of the oil refining process. Asphalt shingles are relatively cheap, but they can be short-lived as well, and when replacement and environmental costs are figured in, they're far from the best choice. Organic asphalt shingles are not much better, because manufacturing requires more asphalt. Asphalt can fume unpleasantly on hot days. Worst of all, asphalt shingles soon end up in the landfill.

Clay tiles are a better choice, because they are abundant and durable, though if you live in a cold climate, you should make sure you buy freeze-resistant tiles—look for the lowest percentage of water-absorption possible. Slate tiles can also be a good choice. They last a long time, but they are hard

to install, and the energy spent getting them to your house site may add up unless you happen to live near a quarry. Used slate tiles are sometimes available. Metal roofs can be a good solution, as can rubber tile, which is often designed to look like slate. Roofs made from recycled rubber, natural clay, and stone compare well with traditional asphalt. And if you're really willing to buck tradition, there's the option of "green roofs" that consist of living plants—grasses, flowers, and other vegetation—which can capture and filter water runoff, create habitat for wildlife, and provide better insulation than traditional roofing: a neat twist of combining form and function.

Admittedly, roofing can be a challenge, but there are exciting, environmentally advanced roofing possibilities to choose. Some materials are better than others, however. It's best to make the correct choice from the beginning, rather than paying later in leaks, not to mention dollars, due to a flimsy roof that's not environment friendly either.

LIVE ROOFS A green roof is a layer of living plant material built on top of the roof. It incorporates waterproofing, filter cloths, systems for drainage and root management, and a lightweight growing medium and plantings. The number and configuration of layers can vary from system to system. In Germany, one in every ten flat roofs has gone green, with living plants on top.

Green roofs trap and filter storm water and provide habitats for birds and insects. They provide insulation, keeping the house warmer in winter and cooler in summer. They tend to last longer than traditional roofs, because they protect the framing from ultraviolet light and extreme temperature changes.

A green roof retrofit starts with a waterproof membrane. A drainage layer spreads over that, to funnel water off the roof. On top of that, a filter fabric holds in the soil medium, about three inches deep, in which your chosen roof plants will grow.

Green roof designs can vary tremendously. They are generally classified as either extensive, with relatively shallow growing beds and one or two easy-to-grow plant species, or intensive, with more elaborate, even multilayered

THE FACTS

Striving for 200 or more citywide, Chicago offers grants to build green roofs. A garden blooming with more than 100 species of plants covers the rooftop of Chicago's City Hall, symbol of the project.

systems. In the United States, the cost of establishing a green roof is estimated at $15 to $20 per square foot. In Germany, where the industry is more highly developed, the cost goes down to about $8 per square foot. U.S. citizens may be eligible for utility rebates and state- or city-government incentives for establishing a green roof on their home.

ECO-TIP: COOL ROOFS

Help your roof reflect the sunlight, and it will cool the house below. Some sheet or coating products can cut peak cooling demand by 10 to 15 percent. Visit the Energy Star website for more on cool roofing products.

If you're considering adding a green roof, you must first be sure that your existing roof can support it. The weight of green roofs varies tremendously with their design. Trusses may need to be able to support between 20 and 200 pounds per square foot, depending on the system used. A slight pitch to the roof, up to about 20 percent, or 4:12, works best, although plants can be made to grow on just about any roof surface.

Flat roofs need special provisions for drainage. The good news is that modular systems are becoming more widely available, giving regular homeowners more opportunities to retrofit their roofs. The Green Roofs web portal is a great place to learn more about green roofs and research your options.

ROOFTOP POWER PLANT If you live in a part of the country with ample sunshine, consider turning your roof into an energy-generating resource. Roofs can be the mounting platform for either solar collectors or photovoltaics, both of which can turn a patch of roof into a little household power plant.

Solar collectors absorb the heat from sunlight and store it in water or antifreeze, which is piped from the roof through other parts of the house. The heat from solar collectors can provide all a household needs for domestic hot water or a swimming pool. It can also go part or all of the way, depending on weather and other circumstances, to meeting a house's heating needs when diffused through a system such as a radiant floor.

Photovoltaic (PV) systems capture sunlight in electronic cells and turn it directly into electricity. Photovoltaics come in various forms, the most common being modular panels, but flexible photovoltaic films are gaining in popularity and new products are coming on the market all the time. ▸See "The Science Behind It: Photovoltaics," pages 320-21.

And while you're at it, why not consider combining PVs or solar collectors with a green roof? According to the Scandinavian Green Roof Institute, the shade provided by PV cells or collectors can encourage even more biodiversity on your green roof. You and the environment just may find yourselves in a win-win situation.

Bathrooms

Roughly 60 percent of a home's inside water consumption takes place in the bathroom, according to the California Urban Water Conservation Council. As such, it's an important place to conserve our planet's precious resource.

CUT THE FLUSHING Sending nearly 20 percent of your annual household water down the drain, the toilet is by far your home's largest water user. Standard toilets use seven gallons per flush, and environmentally savvy toilet designers began by figuring out how to bring that number down. Low-flow toilet models that surpass even minimum federal standards—currently 1.6 gallons per flush (gpf)—are easy to identify, thanks to the EPA's WaterSense label, which signals toilets independently tested and found to use 1.28 gpf at most to flush 350 grams of solid material.

There are ways of achieving even greater toilet water efficiencies, however. Dual-flush toilets, long common in Europe, are now being introduced on the American market. With them, one method of flushing creates the standard 1.6-gallon flow, while another, reserved for liquid waste, allows half that amount, 0.8 gallons of water, to flow through. Pressure-assisted toilets use water pressure to compensate for the smaller amount of water going through. Flush water surges forcefully through the bowl, 1.6 gallons or 1 gallon at a time. Some of these enhancements, which ensure a satisfactory flush despite less water, cannot be retrofitted onto standard toilets, so ask plenty of questions as you're shopping for parts.

No one has to buy a new toilet to economize on water, however. The simplest way to do so with an older, high-volume toilet is simply to place bricks or other heavy objects inside the toilet bowl or, for a slightly higher-tech solution, to purchase one of various toilet water dams that attach inside the bowl and reduce the space to be filled up with water after a flush.

As for cost, bathroom renovators on a budget will be happy to know that a fair number of WaterSense toilets fall in the low-to-middle price range. Also, keep in mind that some water-strapped municipalities will provide rebates for water-efficient appliances, dropping that price still lower.

Some toilets can even allow you to go waterless. Consider the composting toilet, a highly engineered technology that uses microbes and, in some cases, heat or electricity to break down human waste into a nutrient-rich material that can eventually be used as safe fertilizer for trees and non-edible plants. A number of composting toilet models, representing nearly a dozen manufacturers, are on the market today, all of them designed to reduce any health risks or answer any aesthetic concerns. Some composting toilets require several years of treatment before the waste can be removed and used as compost. Standard national and international testing organizations have verified the safety of these toilets, but health departments in some cities still ban their use. They use no water but may use some electricity. For some, they represent an ideal solution to dwindling water supplies and the need to replenish the earth with nutrients.

SAVE IN THE SHOWER Showers use a tremendous amount of bathroom water, too, but you don't have to sacrifice comfort or cleanliness to reap big water savings. As with toilets, so with showerheads: New products on the market have been designed for ample flow with minimal water usage. We used to take showers that rained down more than two, maybe even three gallons of water per minute. But not any more.

THE FACTS

Water World: The average American uses 100 gallons of water a day.

The current federal standard calls for showerheads to be gauged at 2.5 gallons per minute (gpm). Many new showerheads on the market today use a frugal 1.6 gpm. They are designed so that the water droplets are larger, holding on to heat and offering the feel of a more abundant shower. Low-flow showerheads not only cut your water use by an impressive 20,000 gallons per year, but also save you 10 to 16 percent of the cost of heating that water.

FRUGAL FAUCETS While federal plumbing standards require that faucets in new homes use no more than 2.5 gpm of water, faucets in older homes may have flow rates of 3 to 5 gallons per minute, according to the U.S. Department of Energy—hardly a water-saving situation. There is a solution, short of replacing the faucets: Install aerators. Aerators are simple discs that restrict the flow from your tap. They can reduce the flow to 1.5 gpm, or even less. Aerators, which are available at any local hardware store, are easy to install and cost-effective, too. In just a few minutes, you can turn your old guzzler into a water-friendly faucet.

Some new faucet systems include a tank mounted under the sink that captures water coming down the drain and then feeds it into the toilet tank. Toilets still require more water than goes down your bathroom drain, and so such systems typically won't supply all of your toilet's water needs. But they can cut toilet water consumption by a significant amount—about 40 percent. You can also find foot-valve-operated faucets—common on boats and slowly finding their way into houses—that can make it easier to stick to the "turn off the water while brushing your teeth" rule. While these systems haven't been widely reviewed or tested, manufacturers claim that they can save you up to 50 percent of your faucet's water use.

You can also follow the example provided by more and more public restrooms, and install household versions of motion sensors, which turn on and turn off in response to a hand waiting to be washed. They are somewhat more expensive than standard handle-operated faucets, but between your water bills and the reduced draw on our planet's precious water resources, you will be saving more than you spend.

GOING GRAY Another way to spare the planet's water is to consider installing a graywater system for your home's outdoor irrigation needs. Graywater systems reuse the water from your clothes washer, bathtub, showers, and sinks—a whopping 50 to 80 percent of total wastewater from your household—for other purposes. You can devise simple systems—reroute your laundry water to the shrubs in your backyard—or you can invest in more complex, engineered systems, new twists on an ancient idea, which use sand, gravel, or mechanical or biological filters to clean water and prevent the growth of anaerobic bacteria.

BATHROOM DETAILING Finally, finish off your planet-friendly bathroom with a PVC-free shower curtain. Your cheapest alternative to conventional PVC curtains are polyethylene vinyl acetate (PEVA) liners, as durable as PVC but without the hormone-disrupting, asthma-inducing phthalates contained in PVC. Or why not splurge on the ecological gold standard, hemp, which also resists mildew? Choosing a glass door rather than a shower curtain can be an effective solution as well. And, for your bathroom lighting needs, make wise choices. Consider compact fluorescent (CFL) or linear fluorescent vanity bulbs.

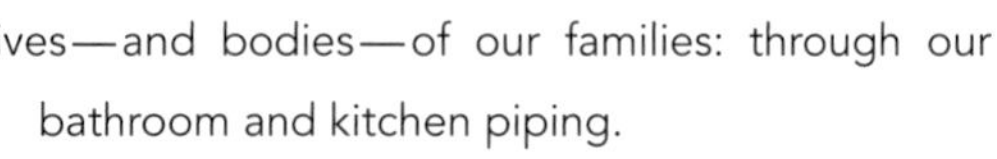

PIPES & THEIR PROBLEMS Lead has been in the news recently, primarily because of lead-based paint used in children's toys. But there is an even more invisible and insidious way that lead may be entering the lives—and bodies—of our families: through our bathroom and kitchen piping.

If you live in a house or apartment apartment building constructed before 1930, it's essential that you determine whether any of your plumbing pipes are leaching lead into your drinking water. Drinking water is responsible for about one in five cases of human exposure to lead in the United States, according to the EPA.

How to find out? Contact your local health department, or go online to the EPA website, which lists state-certified water testing laboratories. From them you will receive a simple water testing kit. For the clearest result, follow the instructions that come with the kit, which will probably ask you to take samples both from pipes in which water has been standing for a few hours and from pipes through which water has been flowing for a few minutes. (Lead leaches into the water as it stands in the pipes.)

Let's hope that the results of the test will reveal that the lead levels in your water aren't problematic. Nevertheless, if your water comes through old plumbing, you may want to install a water filter on your kitchen faucet or get into the habit of running drinking water through a pitcher filter. For more on drinking water, see pages 37-43.

Flooring

From laminates to tile and from hardwoods to cork—including new flooring options made from recycled materials—the floor you choose can be kind not only to your family's feet but to the Earth as well.

A CONCRETE CHOICE Whenever possible, avoid using vinyl tile, which can off-gas phthalates, toxic plasticizing chemicals. Instead, look for natural linoleum, cork, or ceramic tile, installed with no-VOC grout and glue.

Or, if you're building a new home or addition, consider concrete flooring. Concrete provides a low-maintenance, smooth surface that won't off-gas unhealthy VOCs or collect allergens. And with the help of low-VOC sealants and polishes, concrete floors will remain water-resistant and keep an attractive shine.

You can get creative with concrete too—it can be tinted, patterned, or even stamped to look like natural stone or tile. Under direct sunlight, concrete also acts as a "thermal mass," absorbing heat and radiating it later, moderating indoor temperatures while the mercury rises and falls outdoors. It also holds warmth well from radiant heating systems installed beneath or within the concrete.

LAY DOWN THE BAMBOO While you might associate bamboo with exotic tropical destinations, home builders and renovators are increasingly using this wood for flooring. Over the last decade or so, bamboo has emerged as an attractive alternative to conventional wood flooring. It does have the advantage of being a rapidly renewable resource: Bamboo, actually a grass, grows very fast, and many species reach maturity in three to six years, compared to the hardwoods used in traditional flooring, like maple and oak, which may take half a century to mature.

There are several disadvantages to bamboo flooring, however. First of all, it does tend to originate in tropical destinations, and transporting it to your home requires an outlay of petroleum. Second, the bamboo fibers are joined together into woodlike panels through a lamination process that requires resins, many of them containing formaldehyde. New formaldehyde-free bamboo flooring products are under development now, although even the products called solid bamboo floors do require binders or resins in their manufacture. Just to be sure, ask plenty of questions as you shop for bamboo flooring, looking for products that are designated low in VOCs.

LAMINATED & ENGINEERED WOOD FLOORING Laminated flooring offers the look of a hardwood floor without the cost—because its surface is not made of wood at all. Laminated flooring is made by attaching a paper coating, printed to look like wood, on top of a cheap and less attractive wood core. Engineered wood flooring goes one better, by attaching a real wood veneer to the cheaper wood core. Since first coming on the market in the 1990s, engineered wood flooring has become popular in the United States and Europe. It is less expensive and easier to install than hardwood flooring.

The processes and materials used to join the layers of laminated or engineered wood flooring represent the area of environmental concern. Look for laminate products assembled with alternatives to formaldehyde or urea-formaldehyde binders—this will help ensure low emissions of formaldehyde into the air. Also, look for low-VOC adhesives to adhere products to the floor, or choose floating options that snap together without the use of glue. For the best of all worlds, look for laminate or engineered products made with FSC-certified wood; the growing interest in healthy forests bodes well for growing the list of Earth-friendly flooring manufacturers.

SEAL THE DEAL Many floor finishing products, especially those derived from fossil fuels, off-gas chemical fumes, some of which have been found to be endocrine disruptors, skin and eye irritants, and asthma agitators. Although VOC concentrations diminish after application, they can continue to off-gas for weeks or can be absorbed into other surfaces such as upholstery or drapes, only to be released at a later time when the fabric is disturbed. Also avoid products containing ammonia, a respiratory irritant, and zinc, which may seep into groundwater during processing, according to the EPA. You can avoid such headaches by looking for low- or no-VOC alternatives, such as wood stains made from plant-based pigments and formaldehyde-free wood sealers. Natural finishes made from linseed oil or tree-sap resin produce a dry, bright finish. For polish and upkeep, try hard-wax and natural-oil polishes such as those made from citrus or nut oils, provided you are not allergic to those ingredients.

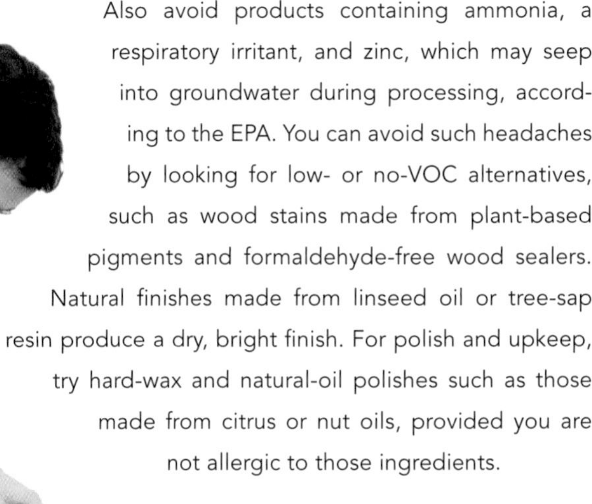

Heating & Cooling

With plans for your new home or remodel well underway, you'll need to consider how to keep warm in the winter and cool in the summer. Conventional builders may think furnace or central air, but you know there are ways far better for your wallet and for planet Earth.

GREEN DICTIONARY

DAYLIGHTING

Daylighting is an architectural term to describe the site, orientation, design, and detailing of a building to make best use of daylight for the purpose of heat and light. By wisely allowing sunlight into living spaces, you reduce your carbon footprint—less electricity used for lighting and heating—and you improve the quality of life indoors.

DESIGN RIGHT It's not just how you heat or cool your house from the inside that counts. In fact, how you orient your home to seasonal sun angles, how you shade your home, how you create natural ventilation patterns inside it, and how you insulate it can all make a big difference in heating and cooling needs. Consider, for example, that by planting trees and other landscaping around your home—or by siting a new home in relation to existing trees and greenery—you can shade it from the summer sun, cutting back on your air conditioning bills. Think through the entire seasonal cycle of the trees you're considering, however. Evergreens provide plenty of summer shade, but they block precious winter sun as well. That's important, because a significant percentage of a building's heat gain comes from the direct action of solar rays striking its surfaces.

Radiant heating systems use interior surfaces, usually the floor, of homes as a heat sink and heat distribution method. It is possible, but not easy, to retrofit a home with a radiant floor, but more likely this is an option to be considered for a new home or an addition. Most radiant floors work by pumping heated fluid through piping embedded in concrete or snaked through a subfloor. The heat source can be a furnace, a boiler, solar collectors, or some combination, and electronic controls coordinate the entire system by thermostat. Good insulation and overall system design are important, and a homeowner would do well to hire a contractor knowledgeable in radiant heating to help plan and build the system. The reward that comes from a radiant floor is warm feet all winter, accomplished without blowing heated air—and dust or other allergens—throughout the house.

Proper ventilation of your house can add up to big energy savings, too. Hot air rises, and savvy home design takes advantage of this so-called stack effect, providing pathways for hot air to travel up and out and cool air to enter during summer. High vented attics, clerestories, operable skylights, and cooling towers can all be incorporated in new design or as part of a renovation. Consider installing a whole-house fan in the attic or elsewhere in the home to boost air flow. Smart home design ensures that air conditioners run as little as possible.

Forced-air systems raise the question of the quality of all that air being moved around in your house—and they offer the opportunity to clean it, using filters at crucial locations in the ductwork. There are actually whole-house air filters available, so that whenever your HVAC system is operating, pollutants, allergens, and other troublesome particles are being removed from the air. Air filters are rated by a minimum efficiency rating value (MERV), a number from 1 to 16, which reflects the filter's ability to remove particles from the air. The higher the MERV number, the better the filter. Standard polyester or fiberglass filters rate up to MERV 5, but for fuller protection from pollutants, you should ask for a MERV 6 or higher.

HEARTH & HOME Nothing symbolizes a happy home more than the traditional fireplace, with logs burning warm and bright. But how environmentally sound is that household feature? And does burning wood represent a wise alternative to burning oil, gas, or propane?

A well-designed woodburning system can be an economical way of heating your home. As always, wise choices must be made, from the origin of the wood to the final release of gas and smoke up the chimney. Burning wood can cut fuel costs, but it can also pollute the air, inside and out. Even well-built wood stoves emit more particulate matter than furnaces.

For wood to burn most efficiently, it must be seasoned for several months at least. Unseasoned wood not only provides less heat but also gives off excess amounts of creosote, a black, tarry substance that coats the inside of chimneys and presents a fire hazard.

Since the 1980s, woodstove and fireplace designs have improved. New models use less wood, create less smoke, and make the most

ECO-TIP: SAVE AS YOU COOL

Install an Energy Star–rated programmable thermostat and set it to 78° F during air-conditioning season. You'll even find "smart" thermostats that only cool the room you're using, cutting back on energy use.

heat out of the energy available. Some advanced combustion-burning models actually reburn the smoke, which produces more heat and eliminates the build-up of creosote. Gas- and pellet-burning woodstoves are good alternatives.

Fireplaces are beautiful, but they can cause tremendous heat loss. Consider a fireplace insert, which fits inside an existing fireplace and uses vents and, in some cases, fans to distribute the heat of a fire back into the living space. Add a glass door to your fireplace and close it when you go to sleep at night. Without it, the heated air in your house will travel right up the chimney as the fire cools down. When you are not using your fireplace, keep the damper closed. You can save up to 8 percent of your home's heated or cooled air by following this one simple rule.

Never burn garbage in the fireplace, as this can produce toxic fumes, including dioxins. Studies have shown that home garbage-burning is the fifth largest source of dioxins in Canada. Compost that garbage instead.

WISER WINDOWS The types of windows you choose and how well you seal them are both important parts of any environment-friendly and energy-efficient home design or renovation. Older, poorly sealed single-pane windows let energy literally leak right out of your home. The solution? Switch to double-pane windows. They keep more heat (or cool) inside your home so you use less energy.

If you are installing double-pane windows, there are certain features to look for. In some products, the space between the panes has been filled with argon gas or other gases, which improves the windows' insulation ability. Others are tinted with special coatings (called Low-E coatings for "low emissivity") that actually reflect the sun's heat in the summer and trap heat inside in the winter. For help in choosing the right window technology for your home and climate, visit the Efficient Windows Collaborative website.

While choosing double-pane windows will get you a long way toward a more energy-efficient home, sealing them tightly is also important. Seal all holes, cracks, and gaps where escaping air can raise your heating and air-conditioning costs. In fact, most experts agree that the simple practice of caulking and weatherstripping around your home's doors and windows will reap significant energy savings in one year. Be sure to choose low- and no-VOC caulks for the project.

COOL IT Install-and-go central air-conditioning systems have been the standard in conventional homes for years, but they're nothing short of energy hogs. Central air conditioners can also contain fluorocarbon-based refrigerants, which damage the ozone layer and contribute to global warming. If you must have central air, look for an Energy Star–rated model, with a Seasonal Energy Efficiency Ratio (SEER) above 14. Ask for a unit suited to your local humidity levels. To improve indoor air quality, add a reusable electrostatic filter and wash it monthly. ▸For more on air conditioners, see pages 95-100.

Evaporative coolers, which use fans to draw air over wet pads, are great energy-saving alternatives to central air-conditioning. They can reduce indoor temperature by as much as 20 degrees, but they only work well only in dry climates, since they raise the humidity level indoors as they cool. ▸For more on evaporative cooling, see page 99.

PUMP IT UP Geothermal heat pumps are an efficient way to heat and cool with one machine, by taking advantage of the temperature differential above ground and below. Temperatures may swing from season to season, but underground they remain relatively constant throughout the entire year. Using a system of underground or underwater pipes filled with a refrigerant, like antifreeze, geothermal heat pumps exchange heat above and below ground, operating on the same principle as your refrigerator. While this process requires electricity, it uses far less than an electric heating system.

Most households will stick with the familiar heating technologies of furnaces and boilers, however. Furnaces heat air and boilers heat water; either can use electricity, natural gas, propane, or heating oil as the fuel. The heat generated in the furnace or boiler gets distributed by fans or pumps. Every step of the way, the question is: How efficiently is heat being generated, and how much of the energy becomes heat for your family?

The answer to this question is the annuel fuel utilization efficiency, or AFUE, measure. An AFUE of 89 means that 89 percent of the fuel's energy turned into heat, and the other 11 percent was wasted and did not become heat in the home. New equipment must display AFUE numbers, so look for those as you are considering a new furnace or boiler. To receive an Energy Star rating, an oil furnace must measure 83 percent AFUE or higher, whereas a gas furnace must measure 90 percent or higher. Remember: The higher the AFUE, the better.

ECO-TIP: THE PILOT LIGHT KNOWS

Consider the pilot light for efficiency in your furnace or boiler. Does it have a continuous or electric-ignition pilot light? A continuous one burns fuel no matter whether you are heating or not and often indicates an older furnace or boiler with other built-in inefficiencies.

Insulation

Home insulation reduces home energy waste. No matter what type of insulation you choose, the environmental benefits will be abundant, as long as the insulating material is used appropriately and installed effectively.

FIBERGLASS BLUES While insulating your home is an environmentally responsible thing to do, a sloppy or incomplete insulation job can result in disastrous heat loss and wasteful carbon emissions for the planet. The smart first step is simply to be sure that your home has been insulated properly.

How can you tell? Here's a simple test suggested by the U.S. Department of Energy (DOE). Find a windy day and stand in different places in your house with a lit stick of incense. Watch the trail of smoke. Does it rise up gently, or does it get blown sidelong by drafts coming in through poor seals around doors and windows, electrical outlets, and light fixtures? Take note of those places and seal them up with low-VOC caulking compound. A good insulating installation wraps your house like a blanket.

Insulation is rated according to how well it resists heat flow, or thermal resistance, abbreviated R-value. The higher the R-value, the better the product stops the flow of heat across it. The recommended R-value of insulation correlates to the climate in which you live. To determine what R-value is appropriate for your home insulation, see the DOE's calculator on the Oak Ridge National Laboratory's website.

Standard insulating materials come as rolls or batts, loose fill, damp spray, and rigid sheets. Fiberglass, the most common material of rolls, batts, and loose fill, presents environmental concerns. Formaldehyde is most often used as a binder in its production, although formaldehyde-free fiberglass products can be found. Furthermore, the tiny fibers of glass that are spun together to create those puffy spans of pink insulation can disperse into the air, inhaled by anyone installing or adjusting insulation. A number of organic materials are coming onto the insulation market, including recycled newsprint (sometimes labeled "cellulose"), denim cotton, and hemp fiber.

BLOWN FOAM Some contractors and homeowners may choose sprayed-on foam insulation, thorough and convenient. Spray foam is injected between interior and exterior walls, filling in hard-to-reach locations. While in years past these products raised significant health concerns, new formulations promise to be gentler on your family's health—and on the planet.

Soy-based foams are now available, and blowing technologies eliminate the ozone-depleting by-products of old installation methods. Today's bio-based foams have very low amounts of VOCs, are extremely fire-retardant, and, if properly installed, present no health risks. They release no loose fibers or dust and are not susceptible to mold.

THE FACTS

Often as much as 30 to 40 percent of fiberglass insulation made today comes from recycled glass bottles and other post-consumer glass

Kitchens

Kitchens typically use up to 40 percent of a home's total energy—cooking, washing, lighting, keeping food cold. From floor to ceiling lights, here are some tips for creating a more environmentally friendly kitchen.

COUNTER CULTURE Stone, ceramic tile, butcher block, stainless steel—every countertop possibility has its pluses and minuses. Laminate and plastic-derived countertops, often the least expensive, can be good choices, as long as they do not off-gas VOCs or require adhesives containing VOCs.

For a green alternative, consider composite paper countertops made from recycled paper. At least one brand of composite paper countertops is manufactured by impregnating paper with a water-based resin and then pressing and heating it into slabs that easily stand up to the demands of the kitchen. Such composite paper products can be made from up to 100 percent post-consumer recycled paper and bound with a 100 percent water-based phenolic resin, avoiding any formaldehyde in the process.

CLEVER CABINETRY Virtually all kitchen cabinets sold for homes today are made with at least some engineered wood products, a good choice as long as they haven't been processed with urea formaldehyde. Investigate before you purchase. Cabinets may have solid wood doors and drawer fronts, but the

ASK THE EDITORS

Q **As I plan my green home project, I'd like to use recycled and salvaged materials as much as possible. I've found some options for other parts of my home, but is there such a thing as "recycled" insulation?**

A Ever thought about stuffing your old jeans in your house's walls? Don't laugh. Some insulation manufacturers reuse the scraps left over from making blue jeans. Cotton insulation made from preconsumer recycled denim and other cotton-textile scrap makes good insulation—with no added formaldehyde. The cotton is treated with borate-based flame retardants.

Another option is cellulose insulation, made of recycled post-consumer paper that's shredded and treated with fire-retardants. One type, cellulose wall cavity spray, is mixed with water-activated binders and sprayed in between studs. The other, loose-fill cellulose, is typically poured or blown into attics. Loose-fill cellulose can also be blown into wall cavities through holes drilled in wallboard or exterior siding.

THE FACTS

In 2007 California's Air Resources Board initiated restrictions on formaldehyde emissions from pressed-wood products like plywood, fiberboard, and particleboard. The regulation is being phased in and won't fully go into effect until 2012. Advocates hope it will mean healthier cabinets nationwide.

less visible parts are still likely made of plywood, particleboard, or medium-density fiberboard (MDF), sometimes hidden beneath a wood or melamine veneer. The biggest concerns are the glues: Formaldehyde-based adhesives can off-gas for years.

You can find low-VOC options to conventional cabinetry, although they may have a slightly higher price tag. Another option is to coat any exposed composite wood in new cabinets with a low-VOC sealant before installing them, which should limit off-gassing somewhat. Solid wood cabinets, constructed of FSC-certified wood, may still be the best choice—if you can afford them. Salvaged shelves and cabinets, discovered in secondhand stores or building salvage yards, may provide the best value.

ENERGY-WISE APPLIANCES At the heart of every kitchen is the cooking machine: the oven and stovetop. The choice between gas and electric looms in many consumer's minds, and there is no simple answer as to which is preferable. For stovetop cooking, many cooks prefer gas, because it's more responsive. For baking, there are reasons to choose electric, since it heats an oven more evenly.

From an environmental perspective, gas is generally more energy-efficient, but electric is better for indoor air quality because it doesn't produce combustion by-products like carbon monoxide or nitrogen dioxide. It's a good idea to use smaller cooking appliances when possible, too: CrockPots, electric kettles, and toaster ovens use less energy.

While microwave ovens do cook food faster, using less energy, than oven ranges, they raise health questions to which we do not have the final answers. Microwaves use extremely high-frequency radio waves to agitate the water molecules in food, thus raising its temperature and cooking it. Since they could have that same effect on human tissue, they have been designed with important safety features, to minimize leakage of those waves. More important microwave concerns, however, involve leaching from plastic wrap and plastic containers. For more on plastics in the kitchen, see pages 56-59.

Water Heaters

Heating water for the bathroom, kitchen, and laundry can represent more than 10 percent of the energy used in a U.S. home. Much of that energy is used to keep a tank of water hot, ready when someone turns on the tap.

IN THE TANK Storage water heaters, the most common type in the U.S. today, use energy at every stage. As water sits in the tank, it has to be constantly reheated. Then, depending on piping and insulation, the water cools as it travels to the faucet. Households waste about six gallons of water per day transporting water from the heater to the tap, according to one study. For all

these reasons, some Americans are considering the technology that people elsewere in the world have used for a long time: on-demand water heaters.

GOING TANKLESS Tankless systems heat water only when you need it, making for much more efficient energy use. Common in places like Japan and Europe, tankless water heaters first began appearing in the United States about 25 years ago, but only recently have they become popular. With a tankless water heater, when you turn the faucet handle, water flows past a gas burner or electric element, which heats it on the way to the tap. This method uses less energy and wastes less water but may mean a slower and smaller flow. Gas tankless systems usually cost less than electric to operate; they also tend to have higher flow rates than electric.

ECO-TIPS: BETTER WATER HEATING

For those using conventional water heaters, the Department of Energy makes the following recommendations:

- ✓ **Insulate your heater and hot water pipes with kits available at hardware and building supply stores. Your local utility company may provide these at a discounted cost. Follow the manufacturer's instructions and don't cover the thermostat when insulating your heater.**
- ✓ **Consider replacing your electric water heater with a gas-fired one, which will generally be more efficient.**
- ✓ **Lower the thermostat on your water heater to 120°F.**
- ✓ **Install a timer on an electric water heater that can automatically turn the hot water off at night and on in the morning. The DOE says a simple timer can pay for itself in less than a year.**
- ✓ **Install a heat trap above the water heater; this is a simple piping arrangement that minimizes standby losses by preventing hot water from rising up the pipes.**
- ✓ **Drain a quart of water from your hot water tank every three months to remove sediment that prevents heat transfer and lowers the unit's efficiency.**

To find the most efficient tankless water heater models, ask about their Energy Factor (EF). This number expresses how efficiently the heat from the energy source is transferred to the water. The higher the number, the more efficient the heater. The Builders Websource provides handy comparison charts of major tankless heater brands. ▸See "Resources."

While manufacturers will claim that tankless heaters never run out of hot water, it's important to recognize the volume limits of a tankless heater. Multiple-tank systems may be necessary for a big household to be able to run hot water through a dishwasher, a washing machine, and a kitchen faucet all at the same time. Each model has a flow rate, measured in gallons per minute, and you can get plenty of continuous hot water—as long as your water needs stay within the system's flow rate. Each manufacturer bases flow rates on set temperature rises, so you will need to know your average groundwater temperature to assess the usefulness of a tankless water heater model. A local plumber or extension service agent can help with that.

You should also calculate your peak hot water demand—not the total amount of hot water your family uses in a day, but the highest amount of hot water demand your family reaches during the course of the day and night. Here is a chart of common daily uses of hot water, giving an average number of gallons for each:

Taking a shower	**20**
Taking a bath	**20**
Washing hands and face	**4**
Shaving, shampooing	**4**
Washing dishes in dishwasher	**14**
Preparing food	**5**
Washing clothes in washing machine	**32**

Using this list, calculate the number of gallons of hot water your family uses at the time of day you estimate you use the most—probably in the early morning or in the evening after dinner. This number will come in handy as you consider the best water heater technology for your household.

You may decide that a storage water heater, which can provide many gallons of hot water at once, is the better product for you. You also might consider how much money and energy you would save by installing a solar water heater, one of the easiest and most immediately cost-saving applications of solar technology.

Take Action

✓ Think ahead, and plan out your green dream home or renovation from the start and from the ground up.

✓ Consult a knowledgeable architect or contractor who is experienced with green building techniques.

✓ Look for recycled, salvaged, or FSC-certified wood for framing and other building projects.

✓ Investigate alternatives to asphalt roofs; look into the possibility of using vegetation for a green roof.

✓ Look for planet-friendly floor options, like salvaged wood, FSC-certified wood, cork, or natural-fiber carpets and rugs.

✓ Consider installing solar collectors or photovoltaic panels on your roof to tap into renewable energy savings.

✓ Use water-wise toilets, showers, and faucets in your bathroom.

✓ Look for alternative ways to cool and heat your home, including ventilation, high-performance windows, and geothermal heat pumps.

✓ Seal your house tightly and improve its insulation, investigating healthier and more environmentally friendly insulating materials, such as soy-based foams or recycled paper and denim.

✓ Use low-VOC paints and natural finishes for your floors, cabinets, and walls.

✓ Go tankless with your water heater to save on energy.

✓ Finish off your kitchen with cabinets made without formaldeyhyde and with efficient, Energy Star appliances.

Photovoltaics

Forty minutes of sunlight contain enough energy to power global energy consumption for a year. With such awesome potential, the sun easily should be able to supply our energy needs. And yet we continue to dig fuels out of the ground instead of harnessing the sun.

Solar power has yet to be embraced on a large scale due to the expense and difficulty of using it to make electricity. The photovoltaic (PV) cell is a device capable of doing exactly that.

A photovoltaic cell traps light particles called photons and converts them into electrical current. It contains a two-layered block of silicon semiconducting material, the same sort found in your computer's microprocessor. The top layer contains an excess of electrons, which are negatively charged, so it is called the N-type ("N" for negative) layer. The bottom layer is missing some electrons, which gives it a positive charge, so it is called the P-type ("P" for positive) layer. The missing electrons are called "holes."

When an incoming photon strikes the solar cell, it dislodges an electron, allowing it to travel freely. Since opposites attract, the negatively charged electrons want to travel to the positively charged P-type layer (to fill the holes). If we provide an external path for these electrons, they will flow along the path back to the P-type layer. This flow of electrons forms an electric current that can be used to power everday appliances such as lightbulbs (as in the diagram on the next page).

When PV cells were first invented in the 1950s, the efficiency of converting photons to electricity hovered around 6 percent. This poor efficiency was due to the mismatch between the energy of the photons coming in and the properties of the semiconducting material. Each photon varies in how much energy it carries: Some are weak, and some are strong. The weak photons pass right through the semiconducting material, too weak to dislodge an electron, while the strongly energetic photons displace the electrons. The extra energy is lost as heat.

This inefficiency, coupled with the high cost of manufacturing photovoltaic cells,

has led to slow adoption of the technology. Recent improvements have bumped the efficiency of PV cells to about 10 percent, however, and increased demand may have the effect of increasing supply, hence lowering cost to the consumer.

One way to improve efficiency further is by using materials other than crystalline silicon. A cadmium telluride PV cell in development has an efficiency of about 16 percent.

Another way to improve efficiency is to use a lens to amplify the light coming into the PV cell. Such a lens can concentrate light by up to 500 times. This development would mean that fewer PV cells made with stronger lenses would be needed to collect the same amount of electricity, thus reducing costs.

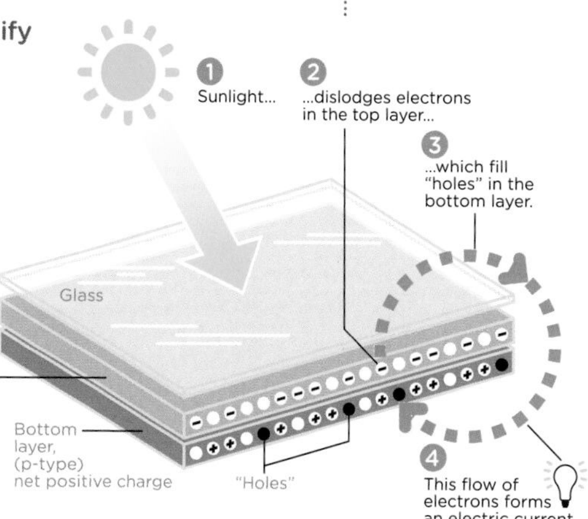

PHOTOVOLTAIC CELL Photovoltaic cells transform incoming light from the sun into electric current, which can be used to power road signals in public works or lightbulbs in private homes.

Another trick is to use a device to track the position of the sun and shift the solar panels to capture the maximum amount of light throughout the day.

Even higher efficiencies—up to 42 percent—have been obtained in laboratory studies. One design involves a layered cell that includes a small mirror. When photons enter the cell, the high-energy photons are converted to electricity in the first layer. Lower-energy photons pass through the layer and hit a specially designed mirror that sends medium-energy photons in one direction, onto one converter, while letting low-energy photons pass through to another converter.

Other ideas for increasing efficiency involve using nanosized particles called quantum dots to convert photons to electricity.

Combining PV cells with other means of harnessing the sun—such as giant mirrors in the desert to concentrate the sun's heat to boil liquids that can drive turbines—may mean that someday we can turn our gaze away from subterranean fuels and toward a bright new future.

GROW NATURAL

Plant & Garden Care

FOR SOME OF US, WORKING IN THE YARD IS A PASSION. FOR others, it's a chore. We all have a different relationship with our lawns and gardens. But no matter what your perspective is, you know the importance of keeping your property aesthetically pleasing. In addition to being a place to relax and play, the land surrounding your house is always on show for passers-by and visitors, so you want a landscape that is both comfortable to be in and also worthy of admiration. And if you're like many of the people tending lawns and gardens in the United States today, you've achieved these standards with a plan that depends on chemicals and energy to a large extent.

This resource dependency, although producing a landscape that's easy on the eyes, is taking its toll on the environment and your health. Gas-powered lawn equipment is responsible for clouding our air with pollution (accounting for about 5 percent of urban air pollution). And the chemical fertilizers and pesticides that many of us generously apply to our yards are running off into waterways, harming aquatic life, and contaminating our water sources. Not just the environment is at risk; lawn and garden chemicals are affecting human health as well. Exposure to these toxins is linked to cancer, childhood death from poisoning, and neurological and developmental problems. From the type of seeds in your garden to the type of materials in your lawn chair, there are green solutions to detoxify your backyard.

As you make lawn and garden care decisions, let these three words guide the way: reduce, reuse, recycle. Reducing the amount of waste you send to a landfill and chemicals you release into the air and ground can benefit your health and the environment. Reusing resources, such as water, will lessen your impact. Recycling waste from your yard will limit the amount of garbage you contribute to the waste stream; purchasing used but functioning products (a form of recycling) or products made from recycled materials will lessen waste as well.

Transforming your property to be more environmentally friendly can be fun and easy—and it can be a productive way to enjoy the outdoors. Your county's cooperative extension can offer resources that will help you implement your new lawn and garden care plan. The extension office, probably located at a local land-grant university, can research information to help answer questions that come up along the way. Agents at the service are also available to offer assistance with gardening and pest control. Use the map on the U.S. Department of Agriculture (USDA) website to locate the office closest to you.

If you opt instead for the help of a professional landscaping team, you can still go green. A number of companies use organic or less toxic gardening methods. To find a service in your area, you can do a quick search on the web or in the yellow pages. Before hiring a team, ask questions to be sure their practices are aligned with your green goals.

Knowing your landscape is key: By becoming familiar with your ecosystem, you can take a holistic approach to designing, implementing, and maintaining an outdoor living space. Caring for your yard will also be easier and more environmentally friendly when you treat it like a mini-ecosystem. Fostering a space that allows the soil, flowers, birds, insects, climate, and other factors to all work together will allow you to enjoy the terrain instead of battling it to maintain its health. An understanding of the interrelationships will inform your decisions and lead to a flourishing yard. Your plants won't need as much fertilizer or food, your lawn will grow greener with less water, and pest infestation will be put at bay.

By following the guides in this chapter you can find ways to enjoy a greener, self-sustaining, organic atmosphere. Not only will the growth on your property be stronger, but your connection to the land will naturally evolve along the way.

Garden-Ready

To get started on a green landscaping regimen, stock your shed (or other storage space) with useful materials. Avoid machines that emit greenhouse gases, tools that are made from harmful materials, and inefficient products.

PROTECTING YOUR SKIN If you will be working outside during the season and times of day when the sun is strongest, don't forget to protect yourself from the sun's UV rays. When you're gearing up to spend some time beautifying your yard, guard yourself with sunscreen, a hat, and sunglasses. ▸For detailed tips on sun protection, see pages 186-89.

Plan ahead for the bugs that can attack when you're working outside. We all know how annoying—and itchy—mosquito bites can be. Instead of suffering through your time outdoors, slather on a natural bug repellent. Many essential oils serve as bases for effective and nontoxic sprays and lotions, and they are safer than DEET (N-diethyl-3-methylbenzamide or N-diethyl-metatoluamide), the most common ingredient in commercial bug repellents. DEET repels a broad range of insects, but humans are likely to suffer side effects from it, including skin and eye irritations and even neurological disorders.

You can avoid these risks with less threatening alternatives. Eucalyptus oils are the most effective natural repellents, just as powerful as DEET. Catnip and citronella oils have also been shown to be effective. Soybean oils, also effective, are likely the safest insect repellent. ▸For more on insect repellents, see pages 203-205.

BALANCING YOUR SOIL The majority of growth around your home relies on soil. And you can't have a green plot without the right type of soil. A soil test kit will help you determine the level and type of nutrients present—or lacking—in your soil. These kits come with instructions and suggestions on how to alter your soil for the best balance of nutrients to grow your garden or lawn.

To start your soil testing, take a small sample of soil from your yard. If you have a larger piece of land, you may have to dig several samples since the soil's components can vary in different locations. Next, the kit will lead you through tests for nitrogen (N), phosphorus (P), potassium (K), and acidity (pH). They will help you figure out the level of each component in your soil, so that you can modify it as needed for the plants you choose to cultivate.

Most grasses grow best in soil with a pH level between 6.5 and 7, while other plants' pH preference will vary. The kit will provide guidance on ways to modify the soil by adding lime (to "sweeten" the soil) or sulfur (to make it more acidic) and will also help determine the NPK ratios that your soil's fertilizer should have, if it needs any. For more on fertilizers, see pages 335-39. By referring to your seed packets or a growing guide, you can easily determine you garden's nutrient needs.

WATER WAYS So you're noticing that your lawn is losing its green glow, and when you press down on the grass the blades are slow to spring back up. These are signs that your turf is thirsty. Be conscious of how much water you pour on, though. A good rule of thumb: Water deeply and less often. Plants grow stronger when they slowly soak in water at the roots, without flooding. Most landscapes only need water once a week, including any rain that falls. The sprinkler and watering schedule you have now may be wasting water and causing damage. Choose a hose made from recycled materials that will let water seep slowly into the roots. For gardens, an irrigation system that drips water low to the ground is best. Many traditional hoses and sprinklers distribute water too high, quenching the tops of plants but not the soil where roots can absorb the moisture. A soaker hose, which lies on the ground, lets water trickle out through pores without excess runoff. If you're having trouble keeping the moisture in or you're worried that the sun's heat will damage the hose, cover the tube with two to three inches of mulch.

Drip irrigation and trickle irrigation systems are also water-efficient choices. These systems offer a few different options for delivering water to your plants, but each allows the water to seep slowly into the ground and quench the roots. You can choose from hoses that sit next to plant stems, micro-sprinklers that project from the ground to spray water, or drip systems that are inserted into the ground to directly water roots.

No matter what style you choose, be sure to monitor how long you are letting the water run. Too much water can flood your yard and lead to diseased plants, but too little will leave your greens malnourished. You want

just enough water to moisten the soil without causing puddles. Too busy to sit around and wait for the garden to soak in enough water? Invest in a timer that connects to the hose and set it to your desired length of watering time. Perform a test run in the beginning by closely monitoring the time it takes to adequately water your garden.

ECO-TIP: WATER WISE

To make water cans, reuse empty plastic bottles that held Earth-friendly laundry detergent. Thoroughly clean out the container and poke holes in the top lid. Just fill with water, screw on the lid, and pour as you would with a commercial watering can.

Lawns are better off receiving water from a sprinkler that hits a larger surface area. Don't leave the sprinkler running for too long (15 to 30 minutes is usually plenty), and make sure you're not watering parts of your property that don't need it, such as the driveway or deck. You can also water by hand using a hose equipped with a trigger nozzle to control water flow. To test the sufficient amount of time for lawn irrigation, scatter small containers—such as tin cans or cake pans—around your yard. Time how long it takes for about one inch of water to fill the containers, and use this length of time as your standard.

Watering in the early morning or early evening is best. This will allow the soil to absorb the water before the sun beats down and causes it to evaporate quickly. It also protects tender leaves, which can be burned when bright sunlight hits beads of water sitting on them.

RAIN CATCHING With water shortages becoming an increasingly common threat across the globe, it would be wise to find every way possible to reduce water usage. Set up a rain barrel at the gutter spout on your house. You can then reuse this water for yard care. Look for barrels made from recycled or sustainable materials, or simply make your own. A lidded container holding 55 to 60 gallons can work. Cut a hole in the lid only big enough for the spout to drain into and cover openings with a screen; otherwise you invite mosquitoes to lay eggs and thirsty animals to take a swim in your rain barrel.

Rainwater washing down roofs and eaves can pick up algae, mold, bacteria, or other impurities. These contaminants will not threaten your yard or garden, but for drinking or cooking, you must filter and disinfect the water. you bring in from the barrel.

PICKING POTS Many plants grow successfully in containers and can be a gardening godsend for people who don't have a yard. Plenty of resources are dedicated to container gardens, so with enough research and creativity, you will be on your way to beautiful indoor or outdoor growth.

Of the numerous pots to choose from when designing your garden, the most popular are made of terra cotta and plastic. Wooden window boxes are also widely used and add a colorful accent to your home's exterior. Be sure to choose rot-resistant wood such as cedar, and don't forget about proper drainage. Plant roots need air, and there's only so much water that they can use—you do not want them suffocating or drowning. Be sure that the soil mix you give potted plants has an aerating component, like vermiculite or perlite, and line the bottom of a pot with pebbles to induce water flow out the bottom. If your pots do not already have drainage holes, cut or tap some through. It's essential that water run through and not puddle, a condition that can lead to rotting roots and the death of your greenery. Place a dish underneath to help catch the excess water.

The pots that you empty by transplanting their contents into your garden need not be thrown away. They can easily be reused for another planting, or even for other household uses. Terra-cotta pots work well as a home for craft projects, and plastic containers can become storage bins.

GREEN DICTIONARY

THATCH

Thatch is a layer of living and dead materials that builds up between the soil and green grass. It can keep grass roots from getting water and kill beneficial organisms.

OTHER HELPFUL TOOLS No shed is complete without a rake or two. There are basic styles that you will find useful. The first is a flexible leaf rake, made of metal or plastic and used for raking surface debris. The other is a steel rake, with tines that are not flexible, used for shaping and leveling the soil or other media, such as gravel. Search online or at your local garden store for a rake that will be suitable to your needs. There are sets available with one interchangeable handle and various tool heads. If you have need to rake a small area, use a garden fork, particularly when you want to break up thatch or aerate the soil without disturbing your plants.

Thatch, a layer of living and dead materials that develops on top of the soil, results from excessive fertilization and watering and can cause problems. Once the layer of thatch builds to half an inch thick, it reduces the amount of water that reaches the grass roots and beneficial soil-dwelling organisms. Next, your lawn turns brown. To keep thatch from suffocating your lawn, get out the rake and loosen the entanglement.

Another way to fight—or even prevent—thatch is to keep your soil balanced with enough air and water. An aerator will do the job, loosening the soil and poking holes to open a path for water and air to reach the roots. With a strong root system, your plants will be healthier. Breaking up the ground can be as easy as walking: just strap on a pair of spike-bottomed aerating shoes and walk around your yard. You can also use a digging fork to poke holes in the soil to loosen it up.

Some hand tools these days are made with recycled materials or come in sets with one handle and various tool heads. One such tool is a trowel, a small hand shovel that has many purposes in the garden. Perfect for digging, trowels help make holes for planting. A trowel is also useful for extracting weeds, transplanting bulbs or shrubs, and digging in areas that a larger shovel can't reach. If you tend to have an overwhelming weed problem, consider a weeding tool, which has serrated edges, scooped blade faces, and back wings for pulling out a complete weed, root and all. Choosing ergonomic tools will prevent aches and pains during and after working.

For cutting and harvesting plants, popular choices include pruners, loppers, and shears. The double-handled tools let you open the two sharp blades and easily slice vegetation. These cutting tools can be as small as a pair of scissors or they can be attached to a longer handle.

If you have a larger space to tend, a wheelbarrow will prove to be very helpful for transporting materials. Wheelbarrows can carry yard waste and material to and from your compost bin, and they are also useful for lugging work tools from the storage area to the parts of your property where you'll be working.

ECO-TIP: CREATIVE CONTAINERS

Get creative with your container garden and find objects that are on their way to the trash to use as pots. Old wheelbarrows, wooden crates, baskets, and clay pitchers are great choices. You can also reuse yogurt cups to sprout seeds or grow smaller plants such as herbs.

What to Grow

As you decide what you can practically grow on your own, begin by thinking about the design of your property and how you will be cultivating plants. In containers or in the ground? Different plants are suited for each.

Many seeds can be started in containers during months of frost and then transferred to the ground later in the year. Use this information to guide your thinking on seed selection. There are many varieties available, which may bring more questions and a tougher decision-making process. Once you learn about your soil and what grows best in your region, selecting your seeds can be the fun part. Your local extension agent can give you more information about certain seeds and which ones will do well in your yard. Visit the U.S. Department of Agriculture website to find an office near you.

ORGANIC & HEIRLOOM You can buy seeds online or at a local garden, hardware, or grocery store. To be sure your seeds did not come from a chemically treated area or that they were not chemically sprayed prior to sale, look for packages that are labeled "organic." "Heirloom" seeds are likely to have been grown organically as well, for they depend on reproducing generation after generation and have built up natural resistance to pests and disease.

When you choose organic seeds, you can be sure that they come from parent plants grown without synthetic fertilizer; you can also be sure that no chemicals (such as captan and thiram) were used to treat the seeds. Seeds that are not labeled organic could be harboring traces of chemical pesticides, fungicides, or dyes. Organic gardening starts with the seed, so try to choose varieties that will grow vigorously in your soil and climate.

Heirloom seeds have been passed down from the crops of previous seasons, and the species could be as old as 150 years. These are unique, open-pollinated, non-hybrid plants that have not been genetically modified. Each heirloom variety preserves biodiversity—something that mass-produced seed varieties, not to mention the commercial practice of monoculture, do not. In addition, heirlooms produce an incredible taste and

a colorful variety (tomatoes can be red, orange, yellow, or green) compared with their conventional counterparts. Tomatoes are the most common heirloom plants, but you can also find heirloom squashes, beans, cucumbers, and corn, among many others.

ECO-TIP: MOW HIGH

Never cut more than one-third of the grass height each time you mow your turf. Keeping your blades at a higher height will help your lawn absorb more nutrients and sunlight while shading out harmful weeds. Also, chopping your grass too low could put unnecessary strain on the growing plants, making them weaker and vulnerable to disease.

MINDFUL MOWING The typical suburban yard might be the greenest thing on the block, but there are environmental drawbacks to keeping a perfect lawn. Lawns represent one of the most energy-, water-, and fertilizer-consuming features in any landscape. If you have the option, give some critical thought to even having a grassy lawn. Grass does not provide a natural habitat for most wildlife, and rapid runoff, soil erosion, and flooding can sometimes come as results of grassy expanses. Grass can also be difficult to maintain, so it's important to seed a lawn with a type that's suitable to your climate. Grass that is accustomed to your local conditions will require less care—which benefits your wallet and lightens your work load.

Growing lawns means mowing lawns, and there are decisions to be made as to the machinery you use to keep them trim. Gas-powered mowers contribute to air and noise pollution and are a factor in human health complications such as asthma. To cut your grass and limit your environmental impact, consider pushing around a reel mower. If your property is a manageable size, a human-powered mower could be a great way to cut greenhouse gas emissions, sneak in an extra workout, and let your neighbors enjoy the peace and quiet.

Manual mowers cost less than most other types of mowers and are easier to maintain. However, push mowers are more susceptible to rusting and have more blades to sharpen than a motorized mower. And if you have a sloping, bumpy, or thick landscape, reel mowers might have trouble giving your turf a clean cut. Taller grass can also be harder to trim with a reel mower because the blades on some models cannot be adjusted to a high enough height. But for a yard that is on the flat side and not too large, a human-powered mower is your Earth-friendly solution.

If the thought of manually manicuring your lawn is daunting, an electric mower is another fuel-efficient choice. They produce less than one percent of the carbon monoxide discharged by their gas-powered counterparts, according to the U.S. Environmental Protection Agency (EPA). Electric mowers are available in corded and cordless varieties. Shop around for one that best suits your mowing needs.

THE FACTS

The EPA estimates that gas-powered mowers can emit as much fossil fuels in an hour as a car would during a 20-mile drive.

Don't forget to sharpen the blades on your mower as part of your maintenance routine. While experts differ, you should sharpen the blades—or have them sharpened—once every six months at a minimum and maybe even every two months if you have a lot of lawn to mow. A dull cut will leave the grass open to disease. And because the heat puts stress on your turf, mow in the early evening when the temperatures are a bit cooler and you still have enough light to navigate.

Flowers

Flowers enhance your garden and attract beneficial insects as well. Besides looking spectacular, they provide distinctively organic gifts for your friends. Be sure to choose and cultivate seeds and bulbs carefully.

KNOW WHAT'S NATIVE Planting native species in your yard can save you time, money, and resources. Since natives are already adapted to the local conditions, they require less care. They have usually developed qualities that repel pests and, being accustomed to the prevailing soil types, don't need a fertilizer to grow heartily. Along with being low-maintenance, natives also attract beneficial organisms such as bats, butterflies, and hummingbirds. Choosing a variety of natives that work well together can help balance your backyard ecosystem. The Audubon Society's website offers regional resources to learn more about natives in your area.

Native species (especially large-growing shrubs) can take up to three years to bloom. Buying a transplant will show faster results but will be more expensive. Be alert to invasive, or nonnative, species that creep into your greenery. The U.S. National Arboretum offers information on invasive species as well as state-specific resources to help identify unwanted plants.

PICKING PERENNIALS Flowers that can spring up year after year without replanting are considered perennials. Their regular reappearance means you can count on a blooming garden without having to purchase new bulbs, seeds, or transplants every year.

ASK THE EDITORS

Q I live in the city, so I can't grow my own flowers. Are the bouquets at the florist's shop safe to bring into my home?

A The sad answer is that many of the flowers that come to U.S. markets are grown in Latin America, with massive amounts of dangerous pesticides. Overfumigating is common and protective equipment is scarce, leading to serious health issues for the people working the fields to send those beautiful flowers our way.

A study performed by the Harvard School of Public Health evaluated children whose mothers worked for flower companies before giving birth. It found that nearly half of those children, 35 out of 72 tested, had been exposed to pesticides and showed higher blood pressure and poorer spatial learning abilities than those who were not exposed.

Flowers grown in such circumstances could very well be covered with pesticides even when they reach your florist's shop. Touch the blossoms as little as possible; wash your hands after handling.

Or, better yet, find a source for organic cut flowers online, in natural foods stores, or directly from local gardeners you trust.

Native perennials are the most Earth-friendly choices. Adapted to local conditions, they require far less care and human intervention. This cuts back on resources used and chemicals required. Contact your local cooperative extension or visit a local nursery to find which perennials will grow best in your region. Also consider your landscape's layout and where you will be planting the perennials. Some flowers grow best with partial shade while others do well in full sun, with no tree canopy. The world of flowers is colorful and vast, so you shouldn't have any trouble finding a variety of species that fits into your ecosystem.

ADDING ANNUALS Annuals complete their life cycle within the span of one growing season. Since annuals must be replanted year after year, starting from seed rather than buying a flat of seedlings at the nursery is an easy way to reduce the environmental impact of your garden. Many seedlings have been shipped in from overseas, are heavily sprayed with pesticides, and require energy to transport to your local garden center. Since the growers are often located in other countries, it can be tough for retailers to guarantee that organic methods were used to start your seedlings' growth.

When choosing seeds, look for the organic certification logo to be sure no chemicals or dyes were used in growing or preparation of the seeds. If you like to switch the design of your yard from year to year, annuals can be a beneficial choice. To enliven your landscape, mix up the annuals and perennials when you plant them. This will offer a carpet of different colors and a unique design each growing season. Planting different flowers together lowers the probability of a pest infestation, because each variety attracts or repels differently, and preserves the biodiversity of your backyard ecosystem.

NATURALIZING BULBS Many flowers start from a bulb that holds almost everything a flower needs to grow—bud, leaves, food, and roots, all in a protective skin. If you decide you want to plant a bulb that has already sprouted, do so in the spring, after the last frost, when the soil is warmer.

Certain flower bulbs will spread and bloom year after year without replanting. Some varieties grow well in the grass, but gardens, woodland edges, and other sunny well-drained areas are the best places to plant your flowers. Flowers that are easily naturalized include tulips, daffodils, crocuses, and alliums. These are also great selections for gardeners with allergies; since these flowers are insect-pollinated, the amount of pollen that reaches the air—and your airways—is minimal.

Smaller and low-growing bulbs that bloom earlier in the spring tend to be better for naturalizing on your lawn. This is a great way to disperse color on your turf, and you can mow over these flowers without cutting them, assuming your mower blades are

set high enough. You can plant larger bulbs that sprout higher flowers in areas that don't require frequent or any mowing, like the edge of woodlands, along the bottom of fences, or in gardens. Flower bulbs need adequate sunshine and drainage, so be sure to plant them in parts of your garden that will not puddle or get too moist (sloping sites are a good spot). Many bulbs do well under deciduous trees, as long as they receive enough sunlight during the early stages of growth.

As winter approaches, apply two to three inches of mulch on your bulb bed to keep the ground insulated. To keep bulbs blooming year after year, make sure they are properly nourished. Each autumn, apply compost to plants to help them through winter and into the next growing season.

Fertilizer & Compost

You may be anxious to get your grass growing and plants blooming with a supercharge after a dormant off-season. But before reaching for the chemical fertilizers, consider the effects: They can do more harm than good.

After spreading the toxic fertilizer on your lawn, the grass may grow faster, but that pressures you to mow more often. And after prolonged exposure to these toxins, the helpful organisms in the soil will eventually die, affecting the natural cycle of nutrition for your lawn. See "Beneficial Insects," pages 345-46. The chemicals can stick to the bottoms of your bare feet or shoes, or to the paws and coats of your pets, and residue may be carried indoors. But the chemicals don't just linger in and around your home. When the rain pours down, or you water your vegetation, the runoff carries the fertilizer's nitrates and phosphates into the water cycle, which can harm aquatic life and taint our drinking water. Why risk all that when there's a natural cure? Try one of these greener methods to spruce up your outdoor space.

COMMERCIAL FERTILIZER A soil test, which you should undertake at the start of any yard or garden project, will measure which nutrients—nitrogen, phosphate, potassium—are present in your soil, so you can determine which ones you need to add more of with a fertilizer. Many grass varieties seem to have the most success with applications of fertilizer with an NPK ratio of 3-1-2 (noted on the bag). You can easily find organic and slow-release fertilizers at local stores or online. Slow-release options will help your plants get their nutrients over time, so that growth will be gradual and stronger roots will form.

There are also simple steps to take at home to nourish your land without emptying your wallet. For one, you can leave your grass clippings where they fall after mowing. Afraid this will cause thatch? As long as you're only cutting the recommended one-third of the grass height when needed, the cut blades will add nitrogen back to the soil without causing buildup. By not gathering the clippings at the end of your mowing session (known as grasscycling), you can also shave some time off your lawn duty. And when you leave your grass at a higher height, the blades can absorb more sun and shade out weeds, making your grass greener and healthier. Another easy method of fertilizing is with compost, either prepackaged or homemade.

OUTDOOR COMPOST Composting, or the creation of natural soil enrichment from yard and kitchen scraps, is a great way to nourish your garden and cut back the amount of waste sent to landfills. Mixing compost into your soil will add nutrients, aid in the absorption of air and water, deter weed growth, and prevent soil erosion. Set up a compost system that matches your needs by either purchasing already-made organic soil conditioner or concocting your own from scratch.

If you have access to an outdoor space, you can start a compost pile (or bin). To save time and energy, prepare the pile close to the area where you will be applying the soil conditioner. Following a basic recipe can help you get started, but mixtures and care plans will vary from household to household. You may have to experiment before getting your plan right, but a general understanding of the compost process can inform your decisions.

How long will you have to wait to have usable compost? Again, this will vary; some piles may take just a few weeks to break down, while others may take a couple of years. The general timeframe is six to eight months before you see results. Once the contents of your bin have a crumbly soil-like texture, you are ready to apply the conditioner to your land. If you're

adding it to new beds in the fall or spring, apply about one-quarter of an inch to the top and rake or till the compost into the soil, about six to twelve inches deep. If you are going to be conditioning soil that already has plant growth, you only need to mix it into the top few inches of soil around the plants. See "The Science Behind It: How Compost Happens," pages 354-55.

WORM COMPOST If you don't have access to an outdoor compost pile or municipal compost collection bins, vermiculture is your best choice. Vermiculture—another name for worm composting—is suited for indoor or outdoor cultivation. To begin your worm compost, you will need a clean container with a lid. The best container materials are untreated wood, plastic, or metal. Be sure the bin has enough ventilation to reduce odor and keep the compost oxygenated. Poke small holes in the bottom for drainage. Your container should be shallow, no more than 18 inches deep, and big enough to hold a week's worth of food scraps.

THE FACTS

Yard trimmings and food scraps make up about 23 percent of the municipal solid waste in the United States.

You'll need worms, of course, and redworms are the best choice. The common "nightcrawlers" found in your yard are not suitable for shallow containers and will not be productive in your bin. Redworms, or red wigglers, are the most efficient for vermiculture. Your worms will want to start off with some bedding in the container. Tear strips of cardboard or black-and-white print newspaper and fill the bin about three-quarters of an inch high. Add enough water to slightly moisten the bedding, and then introduce the worms to their new home. When you add kitchen scraps to feed the worms, be sure to bury them beneath the bedding. The worms will eat the food and deposit their castings, which is what you will use as a soil conditioner. Just scoop the compost out of the bucket and apply it to your yard. Worm castings are an excellent source of nutrients for soil, and they can be purchased online or at garden shops if home vermiculture does not appeal to you.

If you would like to make a liquid fertilizer, or "compost tea," soak worm castings in water. There are different methods of brewing this tea, and you can even buy a commercial kit with all necessary materials. To easily make the tea at home, simply add castings to a bucket and fill it with water, one part

ECO-TIP: WHAT TO COMPOST

Most organic kitchen and yard trimmings are safe to toss into your compost bin. However, some scraps may be harmful for your soil conditioner. Although many people personalize their pile, here is a general list of what you can toss in and what you should keep out of your compost.

SAFE FOR COMPOSTING	UNSAFE FOR COMPOSTING
Cardboard	Domesticated pet waste
Paper and newspaper shreds	Citrus rinds
Fruits and vegetables	Fats, oils, grease
Eggshells	Dairy products
Animal manure	Animal bones and meat
Sawdust	Glass
Leaves	Plastic
Nutshells	Diseased plants
Coffee grounds	

castings to three parts water. Stir it everyday; after about a week of soaking in the water, the castings will become usable liquid fertilizer. This tea is high in nitrogen, so further dilute it before applying it to your plants. Put it in a spray or squeeze bottle and apply it directly at the roots.

By recycling your organic waste, you're lightening the landfill load. The more you keep out of the waste cycle, the better.

COMPOST CONTAINERS If you decide to make compost for your soil, a container will help keep your pile corralled and free from marauding beasts. Many different styles and sizes are available, so choose the one that will fit your needs. Some commercial bins are made with recycled materials or built with a rotating handle to easily turn the compost without extra tools. You can also build your own composter with scraps of untreated wood or plastic. Be sure the materials you use are not infected with a disease that could potentially harm your compost. You may prefer to compost without any outdoor container at all: Just pile the ingredients neatly in a designated spot. Or you can build a cage with woven wire or chicken wire. Be sure to cover the pile with a tarp to keep out pests and protect from too much sun or rainwater.

Plant Food

A well-balanced backyard ecosystem will provide enough nutrition for your land to grow lush without the need for human intervention. If you do need to give your plants an extra boost, however, find a natural supplement.

GO NATIVE As long as your soil contains a healthy balance of nutrients and you provide a habitat for a variety of organisms, your plants will not need a supplemental food. Planting natives is an excellent choice, as vegetation that is acclimated to the area will require less maintenance; there's no need to intervene with commercial plant food.

BOOST YOUR SOIL At some point your soil may become imbalanced, and that's when you can and should get involved. There are natural ways to add organic nutrients that promote healthier growth. First determine where the problem lies, and then take the most effective and least toxic action.

If you discover from a soil test that your pH level is too acidic and you need to add lime, one option is to crush up some eggshells and mix them into the soil. You can also add wood ash, which naturally lowers the acidity of the soil. If, on the other hand, your soil is too alkaline, one way to increase its acidity is to add coffee grounds. Some coffee shops actually make arrangements to give away their grounds, knowing what benefit they can provide to local gardens.

You can also opt for commercial plant food, as long as it's organic—no need to harmful substances to your land and end luting an area you are trying to nurture. Read the labels on plant-food containers carefully. If you see a warning code, most likely the ingredients are not safe for animals and humans. As with fertilizers, seek out slow-release products that will gradually feed your plants without stressing them.

Outdoor Pests

No matter what, there will be critters in your yard. Some are good, and some are not. Once you've identified what is doing more harm than good, you will be able to target the problem, instead of unnecessarily treating a wider area.

In the United States in a typical year, about 4.5 billion pounds of chemical pesticides are sold. People blanket their yards with pesticides, causing a cascade of problems. Haphazard pesticide use kills beneficial organisms, contaminates water sources through run-off, and puts home-dwellers at risk of chemical overexposure. Many of the chemicals found in synthetic pesticides—including methoxychlor, vinclozolin, and organophosphates—have been linked to certain cancers, fertility complications, respiratory disease, and neurological malfunctions.

The more environment-friendly methods for pest management involve long-range and coordinated efforts. By building the soil, using totally nontoxic ingredients to discourage pests, and introducing friendly creatures into your terrain, you create a growing environment with its own organic strength and resistance to damaging intruders.

PESTPROOF PLANTS Think bigger picture. To control the pests in your yard, consider your design and plant choices. You can prevent an infestation by growing pest-resistant plants that work well in your region. Choose plants that grow well together, and place them close to each other. If you're having a recurring pest problem, rotate the plants and their positions season by season, so that plants of the same family don't occupy the same portion of the garden time after time. For instance, tomatoes, potatoes, and eggplants are all related: They are members of the nightshade plant family, and their plant chemistry tends to attract similar insect marauders. With that in mind, make sure that when you plant next year's garden, you put the tomatoes, potatoes, and eggplants somewhere different from where they grew this year.

The biggest of all garden pests may just be the white-tailed deer. If you live in an area where deer can move in on your garden, you already know their tendency to nosh—or, worse, when they find something particularly

tasty, to eat a plant down to the nub! You can discourage deer invasions by planting things that seem not to appeal to their palates: daffodils and narcissus, iris, marigold, and holly, for example. But the only true way of keeping deer from a garden, especially one in which you want to plant the flowers, fruits, and vegetables that both you and the deer enjoy, is by fencing them out. ▸For more on fencing, see pages 351-52.

TRYING BIOPESTICIDES Biological control of pests, or "biopesticide," works by naturally limiting destructive organisms. Biopesticides come in many forms and allow you to be creative with your care program.

To target chewing pests, such as beetles, make a soap spray. The basic recipe calls for two tablespoons of natural liquid soap and a gallon of water. You can modify this recipe to suit your pesticide needs. Adding one tablespoon of cooking oil and two tablespoons of water to one cup of natural dish soap will make a spray to combat whiteflies, aphids, and spider mites, among other insects. You can also mask the smell or taste of plants that attract pests. Mix two tablespoons of vanilla in a quart of water for a deterrent spray, or sprinkle on garlic, onion, or hot pepper.

THE FACTS

By attracting just one bat, you can rid your yard of 3,000-7,000 insects each night. Buy or build a bat box and set it up outside for nighttime pest control.

Squirrels can be major pests on your property. Take preventive measures to protect your planted flower bulbs, bird feeders, vegetables, and other areas where squirrels may roam. Spraying one cup castor oil mixed with two gallons of water on your vegetable garden will deter squirrels from chomping without harming the soil. Or sprinkle the area with cayenne pepper, whose taste should turn them away.

A particularly clever solution is to plant flowers and build shelters designed to attract your pests' natural predators. For example, daisies bring in wasps that can control beetle populations. Tempting birds and bats with their own houses could lower insect and small rodent infestations. Or you can introduce an insect that is known to feast on your pests: Ladybugs target aphids and a praying mantis will capture any bug of a reasonable size.

If you notice an unwanted plant (that is, a weed) in your landscape, the least invasive means of control is to extract it by the roots. You can do this by hand or with a specialized weeding tool. Remember, identifying which pests are damaging your plants will let you target your research to learn of management techniques specific to that creature.

Weed Control

Just because your garden does not look clean-cut, don't assume that those uninvited plants are harmful. Some weeds can actually add to your landscape, either with color or with nutrition, for your soil or your family.

A weed is just a plant you didn't put there, and it could actually be helping your cultivars to grow. For example, clover converts nitrogen to a form that other plants can use, which lowers the amount of nitrogen you need in a fertilizer. Clover is drought-tolerant and will stay green all winter. Other weeds are edible. Chickweed, a common cold-weather garden weed, is a delicious green to add into salads. Instead of cursing the weeds, it's best to learn to identify them and value them for what they offer.

Sometimes weeds in your garden indicate an imbalance in your soil. Dandelions springing up on your lawn mean that the soil is too high in potassium, low in calcium, and too acidic. Wood-sorrel or sheep sorrel indicates high acidity. Thank these weeds for providing an on-the-spot soil test, then balance your soil, and you will likely find that they disappear organically. ▸For more on balancing your soil, see pages 325-26.

CUT OUT CHEMICALS Synthetic herbicides contain chemicals that can lead to health complications for humans and wildlife. Common offenders are 2, 4-D; dicambra; and glyphosate.

The most commonly found is 2, 4-D. This compound and its salts can be toxic for birds and bees, and it is a possible human carcinogen. Many cases of non-Hodgkin's lymphoma have been linked to 2, 4-D exposure.

Dicambra is the second most common ingredient found in herbicides. Many studies have shown a link between dicambra and depression, muscle soreness, nausea, skin and eye irritation, and loss of appetite.

Glyphosate, also known by the brand names Roundup and Rodeo, is a nonselective herbicide. This means the product will be effective on all plants, not just weeds. Glyphosate deprives the plant from absorbing nutrients, and eventually the plant dies from malnutrition. Some plants, however, have developed immunity to glyphosate, and some crops are genetically modified to resist the harmful substance. More than just attacking innocent plants, glyphosate interferes with the surrounding ecology. Wildlife habitats have been destroyed, beneficial insects and aquatic life have been depleted, and endangered species cannot put up a fight against the herbicide's strength. Humans may also suffer painful skin and eye irritations from exposure to glyphosate. This herbicide may be a great deal more toxic than its proponents claim and is of particular concern because its use is widespread and growing—unlike the plants it comes into contact with. Seems like a high risk to take for stifling an unwanted plant.

ALTERNATIVE CONTROLS Mulching is an effective method of preventing weeds—as well as conditioning the soil and conserving water. Mulch acts as an insulator and keeps the soil warmer in winter and cooler in summer. The type of materials used to mulch depends on where you are applying it. Common ingredients include bark chips, leaves, newspaper, and compost. Leaving grass clippings and chopped leaves on the lawn after mowing enriches your lawn. If you're trying to control weeds in your garden, a layer of organic mulch can help, although it should be fully composted—broken down oganically—because otherwise, the active chemical process of rotting will draw from the soil the nutrients that surrounding plants need for growing. If you're applying mulch to an already established garden, do not push it up against the plant stems—the humidity could cause disease. The U.S. Department of Agriculture's Natural Resource Conservation Service offers more information and specific guidelines for mulching on your land, such as how thick your application should be based on the material you're using. Thick mulch in humid climates can encourage pests such as slugs or snails, so be wary of counterproductive results when you are mulching.

The most important weed reduction strategy is carefully timed cultivations, using a hoe or your hands to turn the soil just after weed seeds have germinated and when the tender weed sprouts are easy to uproot. If you don't get around to squelching

the weeds that early, the next best method is to pull them up as they grow. Be sure to remove the root as well, or the weed will keep growing back. Pulling the whole weed out when the soil is moist will make your job easier. You can add weeds to your compost, where the seeds will be destroyed by the heat that the pile produces.

You can treat weeds with less toxic herbicides. When you note the beginning stages of an invasion of crabgrass, say, or ground ivy, spray the young weeds with vinegar containing at least 5 percent acetic acid. For older weeds, more concentrated vinegar works better. You can also pour on boiling water. Don't drench your plants; hold the water a few inches above them and let it drip out until the problem area is damp. Spreading black plastic over largely weeded areas is another way to discourage unwanted green growth.

Garden Helpers

Many of the organisms in your lawn and garden are actually helping your landscape. By identifying the creatures, you can better assess whether they are helpers or hurters. You may even decide to introduce more of the beneficial insects as a way to control the pest population.

If you're having trouble identifying the organisms in your yard, take a trip to the local library or garden shop and pick up a book on local wildlife. You can also search online or contact your cooperative extension. You will be able not only to identify what's crawling in your yard, but also to figure out the best organic care plan to keep your outdoor space thriving.

One solution is introducing (or keeping) beneficial insects and birds. This natural pesticide will help keep your backyard ecosystem in balance. Attacking the pests when the infestation is low to medium will grant the best results.

BENEFICIAL INSECTS Not all the buzzing, flying, crawling insects in your garden are bad news. Ladybugs may be the best example. Some people believe ladybugs are a sign of good luck, and when it comes to pest control, it's true. Ladybugs (also called lady beetles, because they belong to the order Coleoptera) are the most common beneficial insect in both the larval and adult stages. They naturally prey on aphids, the Colorado potato beetle, spider mites, leafhopper larvae and eggs, and many other soft-bodied insects. In its lifetime, a single ladybug may eat as many as 5,000 aphids. You can attract ladybugs by planting certain flowers, especially those in the family Umbelliferae, which includes fennel, dill, cilantro, tansy, and a few common weeds, including Queen Anne's lace (or wild carrot). You can also buy ladybugs online or at a garden shop and introduce the insect to your backyard ecosystem.

A common problem with ladybug release is that the predators tend to disperse and leave your yard before controlling pests. There are many tricks to encourage your ladybugs to settle in rather than fly away: releasing them in the dark, exposing them to cold conditions before releasing to slow activity, or setting the bugs free on a wet surface.

Green lacewings also feed on soft-bodied pests such as aphids, leafhopper and Colorado beetle eggs, and spider mites. Lacewings tend to work better in humid regions and on a variety of plants. They have trouble fighting pests on sticky or hairy leaves and do not do well in cramped areas (since they will just end up eating each other). Lacewings are effective both as larvae and adults, so releasing them sporadically throughout the season will ensure constant pest control. Some experts recommend introducing about 1,000 lacewings to a smaller garden or greenhouse and releasing them every two weeks during the growing season.

THE FACTS
Only about 5 to 15 percent of bugs in your yard are pests.

If you have a problem with underground pests—or pests that spend part of their life underground—consider introducing beneficial nematodes. There are more than 20,000 different kinds of nematodes, not all of them beneficial, that live in high concentrations below the surface of your soil. Release a few different kinds of beneficial nematodes and they can attack over 250 species of pests including fleas, Japanese beetles, and weevils. Nematodes thrive in moist grounds and should be released by the millions since they are so small in size. The most effective way to introduce these beneficial insects is to mix them with water and rake them into the soil.

If you live in a temperate climate, keep the praying mantis around. These beneficial insects feed on just about anything they can capture. From flies and moths to beetles and spiders, the praying mantis is one of the most effective means of pest control for a wide variety of backyard intruders. Attacking over 21 species of insects, the praying mantis will prove a nice addition to a suffering backyard ecosystem.

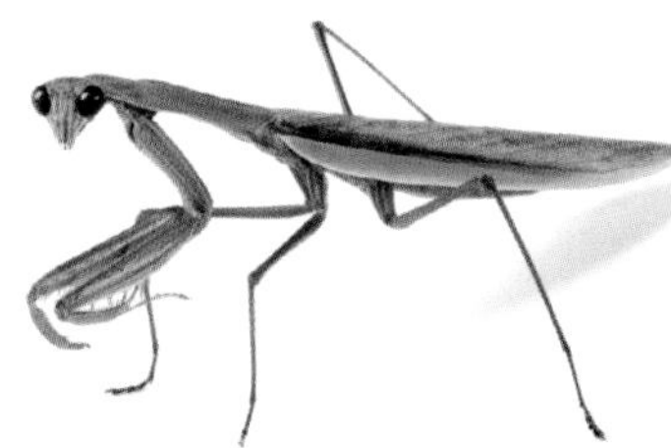

You can actually introduce praying mantises into your garden deliberately. If you purchase egg cases, you will usually receive between 100 and 400 eggs in each case. Scientists recommend applying about three cases every 5,000 square feet. The praying mantis eggs can be placed outside in the spring or fall but do better hatching in warmer weather since they will start devouring insects upon release.

FOR THE BIRDS Whether you bring in a bluebird, a chickadee, or any other bird species, you are acting in favor of biological pest control. Birds naturally prey on insects and can be responsible for lowering insect problems, such as mosquitoes. But there are other advantages as well: In addition to helping control your bug problem, attracting birds to your yard can actually make you an environmental steward.

When natural bird habitats are destroyed by activities such as urban sprawl and logging, bird species begin to dwindle. Such is the case with the bluebird—between habitat loss and nesting competition, bluebirds are facing a tragic decline in population. By installing a birdhouse or bird box in your yard, you can attract these avian species and offer them a safe place to nest, all while preserving the biodiversity of your backyard ecosystem.

When building or choosing the birdhouse for your yard, think about the construction materials, and consider an alternative material to illegally logged and chemically treated woods. Steer clear of plastics as well, though. Not only do they harm human health, but plastics have a negative impact on the environment when sent to the landfill or incinerator. Woods that are naturally rot-resistant and repel insects, such as redwood and cedar, are good alternatives, as long as they are certified by the Forest Stewardship Council (FSC), which guarantees the material is from sustainable forests. Bamboo is another great choice for birdhouses. Most bamboo is harvested sustainably and its quick growth makes it an excellent choice in areas where deforestation is a problem.

ECO-TIP: BETTER BIRDBATHS

If you're also installing a birdbath in your yard as another method of attracting birds, be sure you frequently change the water. Stagnant water left outside has a tendency to attract mosquitoes and become a breeding ground.

Outdoor Furniture

Once your yard work is over and done with, sit back and enjoy the scenery. What kind of furniture are you sitting on? The most environment-friendly options are items made from sustainable wood or recycled materials.

Unfortunately, the most common outdoor furniture choices—plastic or chemically treated wood—release harful chemicals both when they are being manufactured and when they are trashed. But now there are more choices: recycled plastic or aluminum and sustainable wood. Next time you're in the market for a patio set, keep these wiser options in mind.

RELAX WITH RECYCLED Keeping waste out of landfills is a big step toward going green, and buying recycled products contributes to those efforts. Outdoor furniture with 76 percent to as much as 100 percent post-consumer content is now widely available. Choosing recycled plastic and aluminum outdoor furniture also relieves the pressure on the wood industry, saving trees from being cut down with unsustainable methods.

But it's not only the resource savings that make recycled-content furniture a wise investment. The initial cost may be higher for these products (although a growing market is bringing prices down), but plastic and aluminum require less maintenance than wood and are resistant to rot and weather-related damage. Cleaning plastic and aluminum is easy, too. Just spray or wipe with water to remove visible dirt and pollen.

Recycled plastic lumber is becoming more and more popular. Resembling wood, it has no need of chemical finishes or paint. Plastic lumber is made from recycled plastics, including milk jugs and detergent bottles. It weighs much less than traditional wood and can be cut like wood, using standard tools. Search online or at a local garden store to find a style that works with your backyard, deck, or patio.

Recycled aluminum is another great lightweight choice. Most transportable outdoor furniture is made with aluminum, so purchasing a recycled alternative will save room in the landfills. Choose a rust-free model that will withstand various weather conditions. If you purchase recycled aluminum chairs you might also have the freedom of choosing seat covers. This can add some fun colors and designs to your outdoor décor, but be sure to seek out eco-friendly materials for the seats as well.

WOOD FURNISHINGS Sustainable wood can also be used for your furniture. Many people prefer the look of wood, and there are several varieties to choose from. To be sure your choice is environment-friendly, look for woods certified by the Forest Stewardship Council.

Also consider revamping older wood furniture before purchasing new pieces. Creative reuse will keep materials out of the waste stream and lower the demand to produce products from raw materials. If you're buying used furniture, remember that wood is more durable and, if properly cared for, should last longer than plastic or aluminum. Many wood varieties are prone to rot and insect deterioration, though, so choose carefully.

Playground Equipment

When the sun is shining and the air is warm, your children will want to spend hours climbing, sliding, swinging, and running on a playground. But how safe is the equipment on which your children are romping?

WOOD WATCH Pressure treatment forces preservatives into wood to protect it from rot and decay. Since the 1970s, chromated copper arsenate (CCA) has been used in this procedure. CCA contains chromium, copper, and arsenic, which have toxic effects on humans and the environment. Recognizing the highly dangerous properties of liquid CCA, the U.S. Environmental Protection Agency (EPA) has limited its use for residential purposes. Some states and countries around the world have banned CCA-treated wood products altogether. Many decks and outdoor structures built between 1970 and 2004 are made of CCA-treated lumber. The highest threat in CCA is the arsenic, which has been shown to increase the risk of lung, bladder, and skin cancers,

among others. Lower levels of exposure to arsenic can cause nausea or vomiting, disturb normal heart rhythms, and decrease the production of white and red blood cells.

Children, more sensitive to poisons, are also more likely to touch decks or playground equipment with their mouths or with their fingers, which they then put into their mouths. Children therefore have a higher risk of suffering the consequences of CCA exposure. Arsenic lingers in the soil under and around pressure-treated lumber structures as well as in the wood itself. If you have any reason to believe that your children have been playing on or around pressure-treated lumber decks or equipment, be sure that they wash thoroughly after playtime.

The pressure-treated wood industry reached an agreement with the EPA to stop the use of CCA-treated wood for most purposes by the end of 2003. Many alternatives are replacing CCA in newer play sets, but old equipment still contains the preservative. Use caution when visiting playgrounds, and seek out equipment for your children that is made from healthier and safer alternatives.

PLAYING IT SAFE Manufacturers of outdoor furniture and play sets are introducing alternatives to CCA in their products. But even though these chemical alternatives are less toxic, they can still potentially pose a threat to human and environmental health. Treatment replacements to look for are ACQ (alkaline copper quaternary, a water-based pesticide and fungicide), borates, copper azole, cyproconazole, or propiconazole.

But playground equipment made with nontoxic materials is a much better choice. Products made from recycled plastic and rubber or wood approved by the Forest Stewardship Council (FSC) are increasingly available. Although these models tend to be more expensive, you'll be saving your family and the environment from serious damage that could require expensive treatment to control. Materials such as composites, virgin vinyl, redwood, exotic hardwood, rubber lumber, and sustainably harvested wood are all on the market and have many benefits over chemical-laden playsets. The EPA lists these nonchemical alternatives to pressure-treated wood, noting their advantages and disadvantages, on their website.

Decks, Fences & Pools

Concerned about worldwide deforestation and chemical wood treatments, consumers have been asking for alternative materials for decks and fences—and the market is beginning to respond.

WOOD WORRIES Decks have been constructed with CCA-treated wood for years. Look for wood being treated with safer alternatives, such as ACQ, borates, and copper azole. Although not completely nontoxic, these chemical treatments are less dangerous than CCA.

Wood products are often sealed with finishes as well, substances that protect the wood from weather, water, and damage and keep it looking clean and shiny. But these finishes contain chemicals that can be harmful to humans and the environment. The two main ingredients are solvents, which keep the finish in a liquid state before use, and binders, which harden the finish once applied. Solvents are usually made from petroleum and binders often come in the form of polyurethane. Most of these volatile organic compounds (VOCs) are toxic and can linger in the air even after the finish has dried.

Besides the petroleum distillates that can cause nervous system problems and respiratory irritation, VOCs such as formaldehyde are often present. Drying agents in wood finishes can also be carcinogens—for instance, cadmium and acetate (which is also a neurotoxin). And when VOCs are used on outdoor equipment, the compounds react with sunlight to create low-lying ozone that contributes to smog. Luckily there's a way to protect not just your wood but also the environment around your yard.

Natural finishes may contain ingredients such as beeswax, minerals, and tree resins. Be cautious of those that contain d-limonene, a derivative of orange peel oil that may cause skin and eye irritations. Low- or no-VOC options are water-based, and while they still contain a small amount of petrochemicals, they emit lower levels of air pollution.

You will most likely have the best luck searching for a safer alternative online or in specialty stores that are committed to environmentally friendly products. Be sure to read labels carefully and be wary of those that include signal words such as "Warning" or "Caution."

ASK THE EDITORS

Q **I would like to line the bottom of my fence with plants. Will fencing material affect the health of those plants?**

A It is highly possible that over time, the chemicals in wooden fencing material can leach into the soil and contaminate your plants. A common offender is chromated copper arsenate (CCA), found in many outdoor wood products. This ingredient is beneficial for the wood's longevity but not for the environment or plants around the fence. To prevent harmful substances—especially arsenic—from rubbing off the fence, apply a nontoxic sealant. Try not to position edible plants near treated fences or other possibly poisonous structures. Better yet, opt for a wood that hasn't been pressure-treated but instead has been finished with nontoxic sealants. And don't forget to have your soil tested for elevated arsenic levels, just in case.

FENCING IN There are many purposes for fences in your yard—enhancing aesthetics, keeping out pests, supporting climbing plants—and options to make the barrier more conducive to an Earth-friendly property.

Seek out recycled materials and sustainable wood for fences, as you would for furniture and other structures in your yard. Be careful not to treat fencing wood with chemical preservatives, since these can leach into the soil and harm nearby growth.

A safe wood alternative for fences is bamboo. This rapidly renewable resource resists both termites and rot. Bamboo forests can produce up to 30 percent more oxygen than hardwood forests of equivalent size, and they help reduce runoff and soil erosion. Bamboo fences come in a variety of styles, and most are tightly woven to offer privacy. These fences can be found both online and at local retailers.

Many people are using recycled plastic lumber for fences as well. These structures are naturally pest-resistant and won't deteriorate like wood. Plastic lumber is generally stain resistant and can easily be cleaned with just water. You will not have to worry about chemical leaching, and plastic fences don't require sealants or paints.

NATURAL WONDERS Keeping a backyard swimming pool clean is essential for hygiene as well as appearances, but if you are using chemicals (such as sodium bicarbonate, calcium hypochlorite, and potassium monopersulfate) to maintain your pool, you may not be providing the safest place to swim. When wet or mixed with other substances, chlorine and its derivatives can cause eye and respiratory irritation. There are alternatives.

Natural pools are mini-ecosystems that work with moving water, fish, and plants to clean the water and provide natural disinfectants. In some regions, natural pools will freeze over during colder months, making them suitable for ice skating as well. Natural pool systems resemble ecosystems you would find in nature but offer clearer water (without the mud bottoms) and a safer swimming environment, since they have processes that will fight against harmful bacteria, human fluids, oils, and algae.

SALTWATER POOLS Another alternative is a saltwater pool. Saltwater is softer on your skin and advanced saline systems will automatically monitor and clean themselves. And the salt will naturally deter algae from forming. Although saltwater pools are more expensive than other pool types, many swimmers find them to be the most comfortable.

There are, however, downsides to the saltwater pool. Salt residue will be left behind on areas that the water splashes, and the pH of the water will constantly need to be monitored to keep it low. With diligent care, however, a saltwater pool can provide a healthy and environmentally friendly place to find respite from the heat.

Take Action

✓ Protect yourself from UV rays with sunscreen, a hat, and sunglasses.

✓ Make compost to use as an organic fertilizer.

✓ Trade in your gas-powered mower for a manual push or electric mower.

✓ Plant organic or heirloom seeds.

✓ Install a birdhouse to attract birds as a natural insecticide.

✓ Let grass clippings sit on the lawn; use mulch to control weed growth.

✓ Set up a rain barrel in the yard; use a drip irrigation system.

✓ Water only about once a week, including any rain showers.

✓ Choose naturalizing flower bulbs so you don't have to buy new ones each year.

✓ Make compost tea for an effective liquid fertilizer.

✓ Use eggshells in soil to add lime or coffee grounds to make soil more acidic.

✓ Plant native species.

✓ Introduce ladybugs to control aphid populations.

✓ Mow in the early evening and use high blade settings.

✓ Reuse empty containers for planting seeds.

✓ Pull weeds (including their roots) out by hand when soil is still moist.

✓ Buy outdoor furniture made from recycled plastic.

✓ Build a deck with sustainably grown wood.

✓ Choose redwood or cedar (naturally rot resistant) for outdoor equipment.

✓ Opt for playground equipment of nontoxic materials.

✓ Start annuals from seed instead of buying flats at the nursery.

✓ Don't plant edibles near chemically treated structures.

✓ Beware of pressure-treated wood in decks and play equipment.

✓ Choose natural wood finishes or those with low or no VOCs.

✓ Treat pools with minimum chlorine; explore saltwater and natural pools.

How Compost Happens

Nature is the original composter. The forest floor, littered with leaves in fall, becomes a rich, dark soil over time. All living matter decomposes. Modern composting is simply the speeding up of the natural process of decomposition.

The process typically involves tossing yard clippings, food scraps, manure, and other biodegradable debris into a large pile or bin, stirring the pile regularly, and letting nature take its course. In a few months, the heap of cast-offs becomes a dark brown, earthy-smelling soil chock-full of nutrients perfect for growing flowers and vegetables.

The superstars of the compost pile are the bacteria and fungi. These tiny organisms feast on carbon found in leaves, vegetable trimmings, and other living matter. They use carbon for energy just as humans use carbohydrates. These microscopic beasts also need lots of nitrogen, which is found in manure and fresh lawn clippings. Nitrogen-rich proteins help microorganisms break down the carbon. At microbial meals, the entree is carbon with a side dish of nitrogen to ease digestion.

Another side dish that these miniature munchers need is oxygen. Oxygen-loving, or aerobic, bacteria are some of the best decomposers of living matter. They break down carbon compounds into carbon dioxide and water, which growing plants need. At the same time, they excrete plant nutrients such as phosphorous, nitrogen, and magnesium.

Moisture rounds out the microorganisms' balanced meal. The optimal moisture level in a compost pile is about 45 to 50 percent. Too much water crowds out the oxygen that the bacteria need, while too little dries out the creatures.

Luckily, these organisms are not picky eaters, and it is generally hard to go wrong with compost as one provides a ratio of 30 parts carbon to 1 part nitrogen. A pile with too much carbon will take a long time to decompose, which explains why a pile of wood chips can sit for years without decomposing. A compost pile with too much nitrogen will have a putrid smell as it releases the excess.

In a well-managed compost pile, the first bacteria to show up are called the psychrophiles, which thrive in a cool-temperature (55°F) pile. As they start munching

on carbon, they generate not only nutrients but also heat. Millions of munching bacteria cause the pile to become warm, inviting mesophilic bacteria that flourish in warmer (70°F to 90°F) environments. The warmer climate attracts thermophilic bacteria, which prefer temperatures above 100°F and can drive the temperature of the pile to 160°F or more. The heat helps kill harmful bacteria and weed seeds.

Fungi also come in low-temperature and high-temperature versions. Fungi are like the sidekicks that consume foods that the bacteria have left behind. They break down starches, proteins, and the tough cellulose and lignin molecules found in leaves and wood that humans find so hard to digest.

Earthworms, mites, nematodes, and insects chew up larger pieces of living matter and excrete wastes that bacteria find delightful. Earthworms are especially important. They consume vast amounts of organic matter that they excrete as dark, fertile castings. These castings are rich in plant nutrients. Earthworms love to eat bacteria, too, grinding them up and returning their nutrients to the soil.

Composting is about speeding up natural decomposition. To jump-start an active community of microorganisms, gardeners often add an "activator." Activators are high in nitrogen and include items like blood meal, bone meal, fish meal, manure, and finished compost from another pile. Of these, manure is perhaps the most common. Manure from cows, horses, chickens, and other farm animals is high in nitrogen and also contains beneficial bacteria and essential plant nutrients such as phosphorous and potassium. Manure is typically about 80 percent water, so it must be dried before being added to the compost pile.

Luckily, nature is forgiving, and even when carbon-nitrogen ratios are off, oxygen is too low, or moisture is too high, decomposition still happens, although it may take longer and generate smells. Regular mixing with a pitchfork can supply oxygen; spraying the pile with water may be necessary in dry climates. Soon those once-discarded kitchen scraps and yard clippings will find a rich new life ahead of them.

11

PET FOOD
FLEA CONTROL
CATS
DOGS
OTHER CREATURES

ANIMAL INSTINCT

Natural Pet Care

IF YOU'RE READING THIS CHAPTER, IT'S LIKELY THAT YOU'RE an animal lover. And you aren't alone: According to the American Pet Products Manufacturers Association 2007/2008 National Pet Owners Survey, pet ownership is at its highest recorded level. An estimated 71.1 million U.S. households now own at least one pet. That's 63 percent of American households and a lot of pets: The survey counted 74.8 million dogs, 88.3 million cats, 142 million freshwater fish, 9.6 million saltwater fish, 16 million birds, 24.3 million small animals, 13.4 million reptiles, and 13.8 million horses kept as pets in this country. That's more pets than humans!

With numbers like these, it's no wonder that a huge industry has grown up around pets. Pets need food and water, shelter, bedding, toys, hygiene, and veterinary attention. And caring for your pet should involve more than a quick trip to your local pet store or supermarket.

In recent years, growing concerns about everything from toxins in flea-control products to the ecological effects of cat litter have made a little pre-shopping research more important than ever. The need for informed pet ownership hit home for many Americans in the spring of 2007, when reports of illness and death in cats and dogs was linked to contaminants in pet food, prompting a recall of many common brands.

Fortunately, there's much you can do to keep your companion animal healthy and happy while paying attention to the environmental implications of your choices at the same time.

Pet Food

The food you give your pet is as important as the food you eat yourself: It provides nutrients and a foundation for overall health. And just as you exercise vigilance when shopping for your own meals, you should also take care when it comes to feeding Fido.

This fact became even clearer in March 2007, when reports of pet illnesses and deaths attributed to pet food first surfaced. Recalls involved 18 firms and more than 5,300 product lines; within a month, the U.S. Food and Drug Administration (FDA) received more than 17,000 consumer complaints. Cats and dogs both were experiencing kidney failure, among other problems. Hundreds, if not thousands, of pets died.

Tests conducted by the FDA and Cornell University uncovered the chemical melamine in samples of both recalled pet food and the kidney tissue and urine of dead cats. High levels of melamine were also found in wheat gluten used as a protein source and thickener in pet food and dog biscuits. The wheat gluten had been imported from China.

Melamine is a chemical used in a variety of products, including glue, flame retardants, plastic kitchenware, fabrics, and fertilizers; it is also a by-product of several pesticides. It has no place in wheat gluten. The U.S. Environmental Protection Agency (EPA) and the United Nations Environment Programme both consider melamine of low potential risk, and the little research that has been done shows limited poisonous effects and no kidney damage. Pets who may have eaten tainted food may show loss of appetite, lethargy, vomiting, diarrhea, or changes in water consumption or in urination. For updates, check the Pet Food Recall Resource Center of the American Society for the Prevention of Cruelty to Animals. A regularly updated list of recalled pet food is available on the FDA's website.

ASK THE EDITORS

Q **I've heard of pet owners making their own dog and cat food. Is this any safer or more nutritious?**

A After the 2007 pet food scare, some pet lovers began bypassing commercial brands altogether in favor of home-cooked meals. But veterinarians advise that store-bought food has its benefits, including a scientifically formulated blend of the vitamins and other nutrients that dogs and cats need, in the right ratios.

Cats and dogs need different diets. Dietary needs also depend on the age and lifestyle of your pet. Pets with diseases and other health problems also have particular nutritional requirements.

Feeding your pets a home-cooked meal shouldn't mean just offering them table scraps. Although some human foods are fine for pets, others are a problem. Grapes, raisins, chocolate, mushrooms, garlic, and onions can be toxic to dogs and cats.

If you'd like to make your own pet food, you might start by consulting a vet or pet nutritionist (the American College of Veterinary Nutrition may be able to help you locate a certified pet-nutrition expert in your area). You can also find nutritionally balanced recipes at www.BalanceIT.com.

Be sure that the meals you prepare are cooked: Because of the risk of *Salmonella* poisoning and other pathogens, a raw-food diet is not recommended for either cats or dogs.

HEALTHIER PET FOOD CHOICES Dogs and cats are carnivores, so almost all commercial pet foods are meat-based. Since dogs and especially cats have very different nutritional needs than ours, it's best to feed them food that's formulated to meet those needs. As with meat-processing practices for human food, the pet food industry has come under fire for safety, animal welfare, and health concerns. See "The Science Behind It: Pet Food

Manufacturing," on pages 372-73. With a little knowledge, you can make smart choices when feeding your cat or dog.

The first step is to read labels. Protein pet foods (those made with meat) should list a protein source as the first ingredient, not fillers like soy, corn, or wheat. And look for pet food brands that include canola oil or olive oil rather than animal fat. Avoid brands that list "by-product," "by-product meal," and "meat and bone meal" in their ingredients, particularly if you see them at the top of the list. By-products are essentially leftover meats, like animal organs and other body parts, that aren't desired or allowed for human consumption. "Meal" is a by-product that has been rendered, or heat-processed, to remove fat and water, and it has questionable nutritional value. If you do purchase pet foods made with meal, buy only those that list a specific type of meat before it, such as "chicken meal," and avoid "meat meal" or "bone meal."

ECO-TIP: DON'T FEED THE ANIMALS

Cat and dog digestive systems aren't the same as ours. Here are some foods that you shouldn't share with your pets:

DOGS & CATS: Tomatoes, potatoes, chocolate, onions, grapes, raisins, raw meat, raw eggs, milk.

DOGS: Avocados, salty meats, raw or cooked bones.

CATS: Onions, scallions, chicken bones, canned and dry dog food.

You'll also want to pass on pet food that lists unnecessary additives, such as artificial colors and flavors, which have no nutritional value. Chemical preservatives, like butylated hydroxyanisole (BHA), butylated hydroxytoluene (BHT), and ethoxyquin, should also be avoided. Ethoxyquin is a possible carcinogen that has been linked to liver damage and other health problems in dogs.

As with food for people, pet food can be irradiated; the process, which kills bacteria like *Salmonella* by treating food with electron beams or radioactive substances, has been approved for dog and cat foods since April 2001. However, critics point out that irradiation changes the molecular structure of food and damages its nutritional profile. If you don't buy irradiated food for yourself, you may not want to buy it for your pet, either.

Instead, you can ensure that your cat or dog receives complete and balanced nutrition by choosing pet foods that are labeled as meeting the standards of the Association of American Feed Control Officials (AAFCO), an advisory organization of those state and federal bodies responsible for enforcing the laws regulating the production, labeling, distribution, and sale of animal feed. If no animal testing was performed, the label will read "(Name of product) is formulated to meet the nutritional levels established by the AAFCO (dog/cat) Food Nutrient Profiles." Foods that have undergone animal testing should bear the label "Animal feeding tests using AAFCO procedures substantiate that (name of product) provides complete and balanced nutrition." According to the Animal Protection Institute, chemical analysis of pet food is incomplete because it doesn't address how the food tastes, how well

ASK THE EDITORS

Q **I follow a dedicated vegan diet. It feels wrong to keep feeding my pet meat-based products. Can my pet go vegan too?**

A You're not alone. Some vegetarians prefer that their pets also abstain from eating meat. But this is a controversial choice, since dogs and cats do naturally eat meat. Fed a vegetarian diet, your pet may not receive all the nutrients it needs. If you choose to make your dog or cat a vegetarian or vegan, then you must educate yourself about the best, most healthful way to do so. After all, it wouldn't make sense to risk your pet's health in order to avoid the suffering of other animals. The website of People for the Ethical Treatment of Animals (PETA) has a list of vegan pet food brands, but talk to your veterinarian for specific advice. And when you're adopting a new pet, consider choosing one that's a natural vegetarian: Birds, iguanas, or rabbits might suit your lifestyle better than carnivorous dogs and cats.

it digests, and how biologically available the nutrients are. If you feel strongly about animal testing of any kind, you can choose foods with the first label.

If the melamine pet food scare has made you wary of wheat gluten in pet food altogether, you do have options. The foods affected were mainly wet foods, so you could consider switching your pet to dry food, with your vet's approval. You may be able to tempt finicky eaters by drizzling dry food with chicken broth or the water from canned tuna, taste enhancers that won't raise the caloric content significantly and are often well received by both cats and dogs. Or try a wheat gluten–free product. A wide range of by-product–free and organic pet foods are available, although not all are problem-free.

Flea Control

Fleas aren't just nuisances. They can carry disease organisms; cause allergies in you or your pet; and leave red, itchy bites in their wake. But flea-control chemicals can actually be more harmful than the pests they're meant to kill.

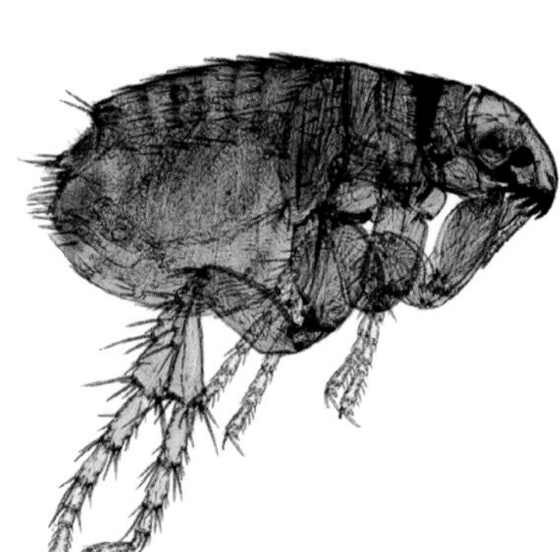

PREVENTION OVER TREATMENT To begin with, know what you should avoid. Read labels carefully, and if you can't find out what's in your flea-control product from the label, call the manufacturer to request a Material Safety Data Sheet (MSDS). Reject any product that contains any one of the following six organophosphate chemicals, usually listed as the active ingredient: dichlorvos, phosmet, naled, tetrachlorvinphos, chlorpyrifos, and malathion. Check your cupboards for older products containing diazinon or chlorpyrifos (trade names Dursban and Lorsban), which were banned in 2005. If you find any, contact your local sanitation department or hazardous waste disposal program to dispose of it properly.

Understanding a flea's life cycle will help you target the most appropriate control methods. There are four stages to a flea's life: egg, larva, pupa, and adult. At the larva and pupa stages, fleas can remain dormant for months, waiting for the right temperature and humidity conditions to emerge. (Another argument against pesticide use is that some only kill adults, leaving intact flea eggs, larvae, and pupae.)

Because fleas accumulate where your pet sleeps, you should wash your pet's bedding in hot water about once a week. This kills fleas at all stages. (Be sure to pick up bedding by the corners so eggs and larvae don't scatter.) Frequent vacuuming is also crucial, since the majority of flea eggs collect on the floor, in dust, and on furniture. Vacuum at least every two to three days, and more often during an outbreak. Be thorough: Get those cracks and crevices in floors and upholstery, too. Remember to dispose of the vacuum bag immediately or flea eggs will hatch inside it and re-infest your house. If you really want to kill those eggs, you can place the vacuum bag, carefully sealed within a black plastic bag, in the freezer for several hours.

Your best bet for keeping fleas out of hard-to-clean areas is to keep your pet out of those areas as well. And because pets can bring fleas in from

outdoors, you may want to decide to have an all-indoor or all-outdoor pet, not one that goes between the two.

You can keep fleas to a minimum outside by cutting the grass short in areas of the yard where your pet spends a lot of time. Keeping your lawn either very wet or very dry will also help, since fleas don't tolerate extreme conditions. And try spraying your lawn with beneficial nematodes. These microscopic worms prey on flea larvae and pupae, among other pests. You can find them at garden supply stores or online retailers. For more on beneficial insects, see pages 345-46.

Good grooming techniques can go a long way toward keeping your pet flea-free. During flea season, comb your pet regularly using a flea comb, which has closely spaced tines that pull fleas off animals. Dip or flick the comb into a dish of soapy water (dish soap is fine) after each stroke to drown adult fleas. Combing allows you to keep track of the flea population and take additional steps when necessary—and it makes your pet feel great.

Baths are also useful. Plain soap or shampoo and water will kill adult fleas, so you don't need toxic flea shampoos. Start with a ring of lather around your pet's neck so fleas can't jump onto the face. A healthy animal with healthy skin and fur will be better able to withstand or repel flea attacks. Dry, itchy, or irritated skin is especially attractive to fleas, so use a different soap or shampoo product if these conditions occur.

GREEN DICTIONARY

ORGANOPHOSPHATES

Organophosphate insecticides are chemicals that disrupt the nervous system of insects, thus killing them. They're also toxic to pets and humans.

And don't forget about the importance of diet. In addition to a nutritional, whole foods–based diet free of meat by-products, preservatives, and artificial colors, you may want to give your pets a few supplements, with your vet's approval. First, try vitamin B1 in the form of nutritional yeast. Doses range from half a teaspoon for small cats to two to three teaspoons for large dogs. Don't feed pets larger amounts, which can result in gas and cramps. Garlic is another good choice for flea control: Base your dose on the average of one large chopped garlic clove for a large dog each day.

PET OWNERS, TAKE HEED Flea-control products tend to be made from pesticides—poisons that are designed to kill living things. Two of the most dangerous classes of insecticides are called organophosphate and carbomate chemicals, which disrupt the nervous system of insects, leading to death. Unfortunately, these nerve-damaging, or neurotoxic, chemicals can have similar effects on mammals, including pets and humans.

According to the Northwest Coalition for Alternatives to Pesticides, over two-thirds of the 20 ingredients found in flea-control products are neurotoxic. Their studies found that almost two-thirds of the chemicals also caused reproductive problems in laboratory tests. Half of the chemicals have either been classified as carcinogens by the EPA or associated with increased cancer risks. A quarter of the chemicals were known to cause genetic damage in at least one test.

There are also reports of pets being poisoned by flea-control products. A November 2000 report by the Natural Resources Defense Council (NRDC), *Poisons on Pets*, estimated that hundreds, possibly thousands, of pets have been poisoned by these products. Since then, several of the most dangerous ingredients have been removed from the marketplace. The flea deterrents applied as spots on your pets' skin are generally safe to use.

Pet care workers, young children, and developing fetuses face increased risks of poisoning and long-term effects on the nervous system from exposure to flea-control products as well. When kids hug the family dog and then put their hands in their mouth, for example, they can ingest pesticide products used on pets. They also frequently inhabit the same space as the animal does, playing on the floor and carpeting (which traps pesticide residues), breathing in pesticide-polluted air. According to the EPA, a child's exposure to individual organophosphates in pet products on the day of treatment alone "can exceed safe levels by up to 500 times, or 50,000 percent."

Organophosphates and carbomates aren't the only worrisome ingredients in flea-control products. Foggers and bombs are flammable, and poison the atmosphere so pervasively that they should be completely avoided. According to the Washington Toxics Coalition, an environmental organization working to reduce reliance on toxic chemicals, other active ingredients in anti-flea products include dichlorvos (or DDVP), propoxur, and carbaryl—nerve poisons that may cause adverse, long-term health effects in both pets and humans.

The toxic chemicals used in flea-control products don't just disappear once you use them. Instead, they're released into the environment. Pesticides that wash down the drain after a flea bath, for instance, can contaminate

groundwater. Several organophosphate pesticides are highly toxic to fish, and some bird species and bees are also vulnerable to organophosphates, carbomates, and other pesticides.

KINDER CHEMICALS There are environmentally sound chemical flea-control agents. They carry their own risks, but they are still safer.

Desiccating dust, which includes diatomaceous earth (DE) and silica aerogel, can dry out fleas. DE can irritate the lungs if inhaled, so wear a dust mask during application, and vacuum afterward to pick up extra dust. Also make sure you are using a DE product intended for pest control and not glassified DE (used in swimming pool filters), which can cause lung disease.

Made of crushed chrysanthemum blossoms, pyrethrum- or pyrethrins-based products are toxic to humans, pets, and beneficial insects. However, a product with a small amount of pyrethrum, also called pyrethrins, can be used safely. Cats are extra sensitive to pyrethrum, so use care if cats live with you. (Note that synthetic versions of the chemical, called pyrethroids, are neurotoxins and suspected hormone disruptors, and should be avoided.)

A set of chemicals called insect growth regulators (IGRs) eliminate pests by interrupting their life cycle and preventing their reproduction. IGRs are fed to pets orally. Adult fleas will not be killed, but they won't be able to lay eggs that develop successfully. While there are some concerns about IGRs' toxicity, they are currently believed to be safer for humans than organophosphate and carbomate chemicals. Ask your veterinarian for more information.

ECO-TIP: ADOPT A PET, NEAR OR FAR

No room at home? Adopt—or support—a wild or zoo animal through programs such as these: Defenders of Wildlife; Dian Fossey Gorilla Fund International; Caribbean Conservation Corporation & Sea Turtle Survival League; Smithsonian National Zoological Park. See "Resources" for more information.

ALTERNATIVES TO PESTICIDES To cope with a flea infestation, try gentler measures before turning to chemicals. Use citrus oil, which repels and kills fleas. For dogs, slice up a lemon (skin and all) and pour one pint of nearly boiling water over it. Let it sit overnight. Strain the liquid and pour into a spray bottle. Spritz your dog generously and rub it in. You can use this solution on pet bedding, too. Be careful not to apply it to your pet's skin before he spends time in the sun, as this may cause an allergic reaction.

Cats don't like the smell of citrus, and they don't like the experience of being sprayed, so for them, make them a different remedy: Mix one ounce of pennyroyal oil with 18 ounces of water and sponge it onto your cat, massaging it in. You can use this mixture on dogs as well. Be careful in your use of pennyroyal, a fragrant but potent herb. Pennyroyal can be toxic to animals in high concentrations, so always dilute it or start with pennyroyal tea rather than oil. Pregnant women should never use or handle pennyroyal, since it is a natural abortifacient.

Keep your pet's bedding—and yours—flea-free with cedar. Beds and pillows made from this fragrant wood naturally repel fleas, but the scent eventually fades. Refresh the aroma by washing bedding, then adding a few drops of cedar oil. Cedar blocks can be placed under and between couch cushions and other furniture to repel fleas, which also dislike the scent of lavender, mint, rosemary, and sweet woodruff. You can find many herbal pet collars based on essential oils on the market. Some contain citronella, which has a very strong odor. Experiment with a few to find which works best for you and your animal.

When you're away from home, try a flea trap. You can make your own by hanging a lightbulb 6 to 12 inches above a pan of soapy water or a sticky trap. The heat from the bulb will attract fleas. Traps can also be effective in rooms where the flea population is consistently high. Ready-made electronic flea traps are available commercially for under 20 dollars.

Cats

Much of the advice regarding environmentally sound care practices for dogs will apply to cats as well, but there are certain things that cat owners need to consider that never need to enter the minds or shopping lists of dog owners.

CLEANER CAT LITTER Cat waste and litter can cause health and environmental problems. A potentially serious disease, toxoplasmosis, is transmitted through contact with cat feces. Pregnant women should take particular care, since toxoplasmosis can cause birth defects or miscarriage. Toxoplasmosis is easily avoided by limiting exposure to cat waste. Also, pregnant women who garden in areas with outdoor cats should do so with gloves on.

**ECO-TIP:
DON'T LITTER**

Getting your pet spayed or neutered helps keep the population of unwanted animals under control. According to estimates from the Humane Society of the United States, between six million and eight million dogs and cats enter shelters each year. Roughly half end up euthanized. For more information on the health and behavioral benefits to sterilization, visit the Humane Society's website.

Cat litter itself raises some health issues. Introduced in 1947, clay litter quickly became the substance of choice for those with indoor cats. But all clay litters contain crystalline silica—a known human carcinogen, according to the International Agency for Research on Cancer—and the silica dust that can result from litter may irritate lungs. Furthermore, most clay for litter is strip-mined, devastating the environment. Thankfully, Earth- and pet-friendly litters are available, made from recycled newspapers, cedar or other wood, wheat, alfalfa, oat hulls, peanut hulls, and corncobs.

Clumping litter is often made from sodium bentonite, a clay that can absorb many times its weight in liquid. While this makes clumping kitty litter convenient for absorbing and disposing of urine, if cats or dogs ingest it, it does the same things in their gastrointestinal systems, possibly even causing death. Cats spend a great deal of time grooming, which increases their chances of ingesting some of these unnatural substances. For the same reason, avoid litter with perfumes, artificial deodorizers, or colors.

Keep in mind that cat and dog waste should not go into your compost. Parasites from the pet waste may contaminate the material, which in turn contaminates your vegetable garden.

SAFER SURROUNDINGS If your carpets, furniture, mattresses, and electronic appliances contain polybrominated diphenyl ethers (PBDEs), they could pose a risk to your cat's health. Used as flame retardants in some home furnishings, PBDEs can create dust that is toxic to animals, especially cats, which may ingest large quantities of the dust during grooming. ▸For more on PBDEs, see page 137.

Researchers recently tested blood samples from 23 cats, 11 of which had hyperthyroidism, an often deadly disease most common in older cats. The cats with hyperthyroidism had higher levels of PBDEs in their blood than cats without the condition. Canned cat food may also have high levels of PBDEs, up to 12 times as much as dry food.

Dogs

Dogs have been called man's best friend, and for that reason, dog owners become nearly as faithful as the pets they raise. Healthy food and toys are one way to treat the animal that is always so happy to see you. But dogs—as well as cats—produce waste that can cause health problems.

TOYS & TREATS, COLLARS & BEDS For a tasty snack, indulge your canine in treats that use no preservatives, chemicals, hormones, antibiotics, dyes, sugar, and salt. Some manufacturers offer organic dog biscuits made from peanut butter and oatmeal. Keep your dog's tail wagging with Earth-friendly toys, such as squeaky fleece chew toys made from recycled plastic. Look for dog collars and leashes made from dye-free organic hemp, which is grown without pesticides and is stronger (and perhaps more comfortable) than cotton and other materials.

Just as your own furniture and bedding may be releasing toxic chemicals into the air, your pet's sleeping quarters are also a concern. Reduce your cat or dog's exposure to pesticides, herbicides, chemical dyes, and plastics by choosing beds made from organic cotton and other dye-free materials such as fleece, available from several manufacturers. Pet beds are now available with eco-friendly filling made from recycled plastic bottles.

GROOMING With most commercial dog and cat shampoos, soaps, and sprays virtually swimming in chemicals, you may feel tempted to forgo baths for your pet altogether. Pets have a tendency to lick their own fur, which increases their chances of accidentally ingesting grooming chemicals. Before you pass on bathing your pet, try a natural alternative. The products blend plant essences and oils for an environmentally friendly bath. They're also 100 percent biodegradable. Whatever you choose, look for fragrance- and dye-free formulas.

WASTE HANDLING AND DISPOSAL Two intestinal parasites, ascarids (*Toxocara canis, T. cati*) and hookworms (*Ancylostoma* spp.) are common in puppies (as well as kittens). Infective eggs or larvae can appear in dogs' excrement, which can then contaminate soil. Dogs' penchant for eating dirt is a primary risk factor for their contracting these parasites.

Children—who sometimes eat dirt, or put their hands in their mouth after playing in dirt—are vulnerable to them as well. Humans contract the parasite by touching the feces or an object contaminated with feces and then touching the face or mouth. Since hookworms penetrate the skin, handling or walking barefoot over contaminated soil can also result in infection.

Other Creatures

There's something about the human urge to interact with other species that spreads the range of animals that we call pets far and wide. Some choices are wise; others threaten Earth's balance. All deserve balanced care.

FEATHERED FRIENDS Although birds are now the third most common companion animals in this country, keeping them comes with its own responsibilities. If you're adopting a bird, consider its origin: Tropical birds like parrots and macaws were once imported to the United States. When legislation curbed that practice, large retail pet stores obtained their birds from "parrot mills" and other breed-to-purchase outlets—places where these birds were made to breed in large numbers. Birds raised this way have far shorter life spans than their wild counterparts.

If you want to adopt a bird, do so through a reputable sanctuary or bird referral adoption program, rather than purchasing one from a pet shop. Let your bird fly free for long periods of time each day, ideally inside a screened porch, and remove hazards like ceiling fans, open toilet bowls, electrical wires, and mirrors. Remember that fumes from nonstick cookware and self-cleaning ovens are toxic to birds. Avoid using other strong volatile chemical cleaners, insecticides, and artificial air fresheners near your bird's cage. If your bird flies freely in the house, be sure to avoid houseplants that would be poisonous, such as English ivy, philodendron, azaleas, and holly.

FISH, THE QUIET COMPANIONS Adopting a fish may seem like the simplest way to own a pet, but it still comes with responsibility and choices. The multimillion-dollar aquarium-fish trade threatens not only clown fish like Hollywood's Nemo and 1,500 other species of exported fish, but also the increasingly fragile coral reef ecosystems in which they live. Fish that end up in U.S. pet stores are often captured in Southeast Asian reefs with a debilitating dose of sodium cyanide, dumped in plastic bags, and then left for hours in the sun. The result is lethargic—or even dead-on-arrival—pet shop fish.

Choose only fish bearing the "Marine Aquarium Council (MAC) Certified" label. MAC has drafted standards to ensure ecologically sound marine-life gathering practices internationally. If you can't locate MAC-certified clown fish, try these MAC-certified alternatives: snowflake eel *(Echidna nebulosa),* yellow tang *(Zebrasoma flavescens),* and royal gramma *(Gramma loreto).* Ensure that your marine ornamentals are safe and environmentally friendly by purchasing only aquarium accessories bearing the "MAC Certified" label. And never purchase living coral material to put into your aquarium.

POCKET PETS Animals like gerbils, hamsters, guinea pigs, and bunnies might seem to require lower maintenance than their larger peers, but these so-called pocket pets have special needs.

Hamsters, gerbils, and guinea pigs should be given a two-foot-square cage at the least; provide them with a water bottle, non-wood-based bedding like straw or shredded white paper, and plenty of toys, such as empty toilet paper rolls, wooden ladders, and an exercise wheel. Gerbils can easily become depressed if kept in a solitary environment, so consider adopting two males or females from the same family for company.

Bunnies prefer to be indoors and can't tolerate extreme temperatures, but you'll need to bunny-proof your home first: Cover or redirect electrical and phone wires, which bunnies like to chew. Offer safer alternatives: a basket of shredded paper, straw, untreated wood, or empty paper towel rolls.

Remember that these animals can chew and bite and do not make good starter pets for children, despite their small size. If you do choose to adopt, do so through a shelter or rescue agency, rather than a pet store, to be sure you get a pet with a loving history.

REPTILIANS Their exoticness has made them popular pets, but reptiles like snakes, iguanas, geckos, and turtles can be difficult to care for. Snakes, for instance, require at least a 30-gallon tank, frequent checkups, carefully controlled temperatures, and application of anti-mite pesticides. Iguanas can grow up to six feet long, so they need enclosures at least 18 feet long that are properly humidified and temperature- and light-controlled. Geckos and turtles also require strict temperature control, which means investing in a source of backup power in case you lose electricity.

Captive-bred reptiles often suffer in cramped, unsanitary conditions that can create delayed health problems, and pet store employees may be poorly trained in caring for them. Because most states have banned or restricted the sale of turtles, those sold at pet stores are likely to have been removed illegally from their natural habitats or bred inhumanely. If you do choose a reptile pet, adopt one from a shelter or rescue agency.

Take Action

- ✓ Read labels on pet food: Choose those that list meat or another protein first.
- ✓ Avoid melamine and other contaminants in pet food by choosing dry and/or wheat gluten–free brands.
- ✓ Prevent fleas with frequent vacuuming, pet grooming, and bathing.
- ✓ Don't use toxic flea products; instead, choose natural alternatives.
- ✓ Bathe your pet with natural, biodegradable shampoo.
- ✓ Use Earth-friendlier alternatives to clay cat litter.
- ✓ Dispose of dog waste in biodegradable plastic bags.
- ✓ Feed your bird all-natural seed and feed.
- ✓ Choose only pet fish bearing the "Marine Aquarium Council Certified" label.

Pet Food Manufacturing

The nutritional needs of dogs and cats are not all that different from our own. Proteins, fats, carbohydrates, vitamins, minerals, and water are the basic requirements of their diets and ours. Pets need more of some things and less of others than we do, however. Cats are meat-eaters by nature, and they require animal sources of protein. A cat cannot survive as a vegetarian because plant proteins from wheat, corn, and soy lack essential amino acids such as taurine, required by cats for vision, hearing, and heart function, among other things. Dogs, on the other hand, can eat vegetarian diets because their digestive system is more adept at using proteins from plants.

Proteins help build muscles and internal organs as well as enzymes and other substances that keep the body running. Proteins are composed of chains of amino acids, ten of which are deemed essential because animals cannot make them and must get them from their diet.

Carbohydrates serve as a source of energy for the body. Cats don't need carbs for energy the way humans do, however. Cats can turn amino acids into energy-rich glucose, which humans usually get from carbohydrates. Dogs use carbs as an energy source along with proteins and fats. Carbohydrate-rich foods often are good sources of fiber, needed by dogs for a healthy gut. Beet pulp is a common source of fiber in cat and dog food. Fiber is often added as filler in weight-loss formulas so that pets can eat large portions without getting as many calories. Too much fiber, however, is not good for puppies and kittens, since young animals need high levels of proteins and fats to fuel growth.

Fats are also essential. Fats provide twice as much energy as proteins or carbs do. From dietary fats come fatty acids used for building cell walls, producing some hormones, and acting as carriers for fat-soluble vitamins. Fats also provide needed insulation, protect internal organs, and keep the skin and coat healthy. Essential fatty acids are ones that the body does not make and include linoleic acid, needed by both dogs and cats, and arachidonic acid, needed by cats.

Dogs and cats need vitamins and minerals, such as calcium and phosphorus for strong bones and teeth. And of course dogs and cats need water. Canned food

has about 75 percent water, compared with 6 to 10 percent in dry food. Canned food usually has more fat and protein, and fewer carbohydrates, than dry food, and tends to contain much higher levels of animal products.

Manufactured pet food, while by and large healthier than table scraps for pets, still reflects a compromise between adequate nutrition and the cheapest ingredients possible. High-quality pet foods list animal parts (chicken, fish, or beef, for example) as the first ingredient. Most mass-market brands, however, start with animal by-products—the animal parts that the human palate finds unappetizing or inedible (50 percent of a cow, 30 percent of a chicken), such as necks, feet, feathers, and intestines. While humans may recoil, feral cats and dogs routinely eat these parts, which can be rich sources of proteins, minerals, and vitamins.

Mass-market pet foods are also likely to contain "by-product meal," rendered by chopping carcasses and other animal parts into one-inch cubes and subjecting them to high heat to allow the fat to melt away. The solids left behind are ground into meat meal or bone meal (if bone is present). "Poultry by-product meal" is typically made up of about 60 percent protein, 15 percent fat, and 20 percent ash.

Rendered products are only as good as their sources. Hormones fed to cows, pesticides in chicken feed, and bits of polyethylene plastic from wrapped meat packages can make their way into rendering plants, although the plants do test for these contaminants. Some rendering plants accept "deadstock," which includes cattle that have died from disease. Although the high heat kills bacteria and other organisms, some pet owners have trouble with the idea of feeding diseased animals to their pets.

Another concern with by-product meal is that some rendering plants add synthetic antioxidants, which have been linked to cancer, to reduce spoilage. To the by-product protein supply, manufacturers add vegetable sources of proteins and fiber such as brown or white rice, corn, wheat, and other cereals. They also add animal or plant fat and vitamin and mineral supplements.

It all comes in a colorfully labeled can or a bag, but what's really inside is not always evident.

GREEN AT WORK

Sustainable School & Office Supplies

WHEN MOST CONSUMERS THINK ABOUT WAYS TO GO GREEN, they start at home. But how many people consider making changes in their school or office? While spending many hours each week at school and work, students and employees are consuming piles of stuff—paper, pens, coffee cups, toner cartridges, notepads. Some of these products may be processed, used, or negligently discarded. Many facilities are laden with toxic fumes and materials that complicate the health of workers and occupants. And once supplies become waste, harmful materials in them may pollute our groundwater and air. Greener products are widely accessible, and large retailers carry at least some recycled goods.

Many schools and employers are taking advantage of national education and outreach programs, such as the U.S. Environmental Protection Agency's Waste Wise initiative, a voluntary program that helps businesses reduce the amount of waste they send to the landfill. The EPA's Comprehensive Procurement Guidelines program helps companies and educational institutions choose products with a high percentage of recycled content. Meeting standards established by state and federal agencies is a great start, but it takes the efforts of individuals—employers and employees, educators and students—to enact lasting change.

Copy & Notebook Paper

Though an increasing amount of today's business is conducted electronically, we still consume a ghastly amount of paper—an average of 27 pounds of paper per year per office worker. And we rely on trees to produce it.

More than 30 million forested acres are lost each year, nearly 4 million of them in the U.S. But trees aren't the only loss. Once the forest has been clear-cut, wildlife disperses. Erosion and sedimentation in nearby waterways increase.

The process of turning wood pulp into bright white sheets of paper for copy machines and notebooks has other detrimental effects on our environment, and our health as well. To achieve the bright color of paper, the pulp is bleached using chlorine or its derivatives, creating air- and water-polluting organochlorine chemicals. The paper process can produce over 1,000 different organochlorines, the most notorious of which are dioxins. Dioxins are known endocrine disruptors which can interfere with natural hormone signals. The compounds latch onto plants and settle in water that animals often ingest, which allows them to continue up the food chain. The majority of human exposure to dioxins comes from eating animal fats in meat, dairy, and eggs. Eventually these chemicals can cause reproductive and child development problems and may compromise our immunity. The EPA estimates that one out of a thousand Americans has an elevated risk of developing dioxin-related cancers. Although many pulp mills are making the switch to a safer chlorine bleaching system, dioxins are highly present in wastewater.

THE FACTS

It's no coincidence that paper mills are located on rivers or lakes: Paper production requires a staggering amount of water, up to 70 million gallons a day. Once used, this water must be treated before it can safely reenter the system.

And, as if things weren't bad enough already, the entire process is an energy-intensive one, requiring the use of power and fossil fuels, which translates into greenhouse gas emissions. In fact, the paper industry emits

around 10 percent of all carbon emissions in the U.S. Makes you think twice about printing up extra copies, doesn't it? In addition to cutting back on your paper usage, reduce your impact by heeding the following advice.

RECYCLING REWARDS Creating paper from recycled material isn't a cutting-edge idea. In fact, before the 1880s, paper was made from old linens and rags. But all too few people recognize the benefits of recycling their wastepaper—or the consequences of tossing it. Americans use up to 40 percent of landfill space for paper waste. And once the chemical-laden paper starts to decompose, the dioxins and heavy metals leach into the ground and carbon drifts into the air.

The first step, then, is to keep as much paper out of the wastebasket as possible. Recycle every last piece of paper you can, from copy paper to magazines to the paper used to wrap new reams of paper. If your school or office doesn't have a recycling program, encourage your administrators to initiate one; the website Earth911 offers guidelines for successful workplace recycling programs.

ECO-TIP: REDUCE YOUR USE

Reusing or avoiding paper as much as you can is the best method to prevent excessive waste. Email documents instead of printing them out and, if you need hard copies, print on both sides of the paper. Use the second side of scrap paper to take notes, make lists, jot down phone messages, or post signs. If you have a notebook that has empty pages at the end of the year, pull them out and create a new book with your unused pages.

There are many ways to prolong the life of a piece of paper, so be sure to reconsider before sending yours to the trash.

BUY BETTER PAPER The second part of the equation? Be a more responsible paper consumer. By choosing a recycled variety of paper, you help support more sustainable methods of paper production, keep forests intact, save energy, and reduce the mass sent to our landfills. Recycled paper saves 60 percent of the energy that virgin paper requires to process, and using a ton of recycled paper opens 3.3 cubic yards in the landfill. Although recycled paper may be more expensive than virgin paper, the costs may be offset by buying in bulk, and the environmental rewards merit the extra few cents. And by helping to increase the demand for recycled paper, you will also be helping to lower the cost. Choosing paper made with post-consumer waste (PCW) and recycled content helps reduce the stress on forests, keeps chemicals out of the environment, and prevents waste from sitting in landfills. Look for the highest amount of PCW you can find, which represents the most efficient reuse of paper.

Slightly different from PCW, recycled content indicates the amount of material other than virgin wood—mill wastes and scraps, as well as post-consumer waste—that is used to make the paper.

Recycled paper, once considered to be of poorer quality than virgin paper, is now up to par. When searching for recycled paper, look for the PCW or the percentage of recycled content indicated on the label. Although recycled paper may not be as brightly colored as virgin paper, it holds up just as well and has many more global benefits.

If you want to avoid paper made from trees, you can choose one of the many fibers that are more sustainable, although these may be more difficult to find. Materials such as hemp, kenaf, cotton, flax, and linen are all made into paper products—commonly known as tree-free varieties—which have less of an impact on the environment.

GREEN DICTIONARY

POST-CONSUMER WASTE

PCW is paper that consumers have recycled after using it. Therefore, PCW becomes a measure of how much recycled paper content goes into a new paper product. Labels on sustainable paper products indicate percentage of PCW and also reflect that a certain amount of paper has been kept out of landfills and put back into use.

Writing Paper & Stationery

When it comes to writing a thank-you note or picking out a birthday card, the best way to show you care is to send your wishes on sustainable paper. According to the Greeting Card Association, about seven billion greeting cards are purchased each year. That's a lot of paper.

CARDS An increasing number of stationery companies now produce greeting cards with recycled and post-consumer waste content, and a quick online search will turn up plenty of retailers. That said, another way to reduce the waste created by cards is to extend their life cycle by reusing them. The colorful front covers of holiday cards can be cut and pasted onto a sheet of recycled paper to create a "new" greeting card, or they can easily be cut into smaller pieces and turned into gift tags.

LETTERHEAD & ENVELOPES If your business sends out letters on paper printed with a company logo, consider switching to an eco-friendly letterhead stock. Choose paper made from post-consumer waste or recycled materials. And choose a printer that uses vegetable-based inks or those low in volatile organic compounds (VOCs) for your logo. Think about the amount of paper your office uses and how much you could be sparing the environment.

Another big concern with paper is the added chlorine that goes into its manufacture. From processing to disposal, chlorine is harmful to the environment and is likely to pose health issues to humans who are repeatedly exposed to it. According to the Chlorine Free Products Association, producing a chlorine-free paper alternative can consume less than one-tenth the water needed to produce its counterpart. To keep the process cleaner and safer, choose paper that is totally chlorine-free, processed chlorine-free, or elemental chlorine-free.

Totally chlorine-free (TCF) is a term used for paper that is made from virgin pulp but is unbleached or processed without the use of chemical bleaches. An even better choice is paper processed chlorine-free (PCF)—recycled paper that has not been treated with chlorine or any of its

ECO-TIP: FREE STATIONERY

The next time you receive a piece of junk mail, save the return envelope inside and reuse it for your own mailing purposes.

derivatives. The third choice, elemental chlorine-free (ECF) paper, should be your last resort. This is paper that has been bleached with a chlorine derivative that reduces emissions but still produces harmful by-products such as dioxins.

Paper processed without harsh chemicals or dark-colored dyes is also easier to recycle.

ECO-TIP: LESS WASTEFUL LUNCHES

After reheating many frozen lunches in the office or ordering late-night takeout, you may begin to wonder how Earth-friendly these eating habits are. Frozen meals and takeout foods are convenient, quick, and (sometimes) delicious. But they also leave a mark on the environment. Disposable containers, bags, cups, straws, and napkins are typically used once and then dumped into the trash. To eat well at school or work without creating extra waste, consider the following:

- ✓ **Get your takeout from restaurants that use biodegradable take-out containers, and ask that they not include extra napkins, sauce packets, and utensils you don't need.**
- ✓ **Combine orders with friends or coworkers instead of buying individually packaged meals.**
- ✓ **After you've eaten, recycle any nonsoiled boxes and bags. If plastic trays bear a recycling code, rinse and then recycle them, too.**
- ✓ **Keep your own set of utensils and glassware at your desk, so you can do without disposables.**
- ✓ **Prepare your own lunch at home, store it in a reusable container, and carry it in a reusable bag. If you carry snacks in baggies, wash the baggies for reuse. And use cloth or recycled paper napkins.**
- ✓ **Drink responsibly.** Instead of using disposable cups, bring a mug, thermos, or glass cup to work. If you stir cream or sugar into your coffee, bring a spoon.

Inks

Chances are you know the smell of ink—it's that sweet, sometimes overwhelming scent that wafts up every time you open a morning newspaper or a brand-new book. Bookworms may love it, but the inks that turn blank paper into newspapers, books, magazines, and documents are far from healthy.

Many paper products are designed with petroleum-based inks fixed with heavy metals that come from nonrenewable resources, pollute waters, and are not biodegradable. And during the printing process, workers can suffer side effects from exposure to the toxins in the air. Printing chemicals (many of which are VOCs) such as toluene, xylene, methanol, and hexane can cause serious harm to humans, including developmental problems, skin and eye irritations, and neurological damage. And the consequences aren't limited to the printing done at commercial print shops. Even at home, print cartridges contain toxic pigments and generate a whole lot of bulky, toxic waste. While it's not realistic to avoid printing, you can ease your strain on the planet by shopping smart and disposing of printing supplies responsibly.

PROFESSIONAL PRINTING If your business or school relies on the services of commercial printers, it's wise to do some research on the chemicals used by different companies. Commercial printing operations are notoriously big on chemical use, but more printers are beginning to phase in alternatives such as inks that are vegetable-based or low in volatile organic compounds (VOCs), which lessen their impact on our environment and health. ▸For more on VOCs, see pages 133-34.

One popular alternative is soy-based inks, which require less ink to be used in the printing process thanks to their vibrant color. And don't worry about exposing the inks to high heat (such as those in a laser printer) because soy inks have a higher tolerance of heat than conventional inks. Although soy ink is not suitable for smaller desktop printers, you can look for a printing company that uses alternative inks (such as soy) to publish your business's documents or your school newspaper. As a consumer, you can support the print industry's environmental efforts by buying magazines and books printed using soy- and vegetable-based inks and by encouraging publishers to make the switch.

Once you're done with the papers colored with vegetable-based inks, send them to be recycled. The recycling process goes smoother because vegetable-based inks are easier to remove.

ECO-TIP: LOOK FOR TAKE-BACK CARTRIDGE PROGRAMS

Keep an eye out and buy only office equipment and supplies from the manufacturers with take-back programs, whereby they receive used parts (printer ink cartridges, for example) and take the responsibility for reusing them or recycling their materials.

CARTRIDGE CONCERNS Many companies are encouraging consumers to recycle their toner and inkjet cartridges. Toner and inkjet cartridges contain harmful chemicals and are encased with plastics and metals. When carelessly disposed of, these materials can leach into the ground or pollute our air. In a "take-back" program, cartridges are returned to the manufacturer rather than sent to the landfill. The cartridge is repaired, cleaned, and refilled with ink for resale. If your cartridge cannot be returned, make sure you dispose of it properly. Contact your municipality's solid waste department or search the Earth911 website to learn how you can recycle your unwanted cartridges. Diverting cartridges from the landfill will reduce waste and also prevent chemical leaching. A standard laser cartridge contains 2.5 pounds of plastic and requires three quarts of oil to manufacture. Saving these resources can be as simple as returning the cartridge when the ink runs out.

To extend the life of your cartridge, print only when necessary. Use the settings

ASK THE EDITORS

Q **I've been hearing much talk about "sick building syndrome" in offices. What is this and is there a remedy?**

A "Sick building syndrome" (SBS) is a broad term encompassing the symptoms that people suffer while inside a building for extended periods (e.g., in school or in the office). These are usually mild effects—headaches, nose and throat irritation, fatigue, nausea—and usually dissipate once people are out of the building.

SBS has been attributed to many factors related to a building's design and construction. If the heating and cooling systems in the building do not distribute air evenly or if outdoor air circulation is limited, the improper ventilation could cause respiratory problems. SBS symptoms may also be a result of the toxic VOCs in paints and particleboard furniture, such as benzene and formaldehyde, and an accumulation of biological particles, such as mold and pollen.

If you experience any of these symptoms and suffer a notable increase in their severity when in a specific room or building, let both your doctor and your school or office administrators know. The solution could be as simple as improving the ventilation but could also require switching to low-VOC products and paints or replacing off-gassing furnishings. And since many employers and schools are unaware of the issue, don't be afraid to present them with your own research; the EPA offers more information about SBS, its causes, and potential solutions on its website.

on your computer to control print quality. Reserve the highest quality for final copies, and use a more efficient mode for drafts or less important documents. Avoid printing fax and printer confirmation sheets and read as much as you can onscreen.

Small Office Supplies

Greening your office and school goes beyond choosing which paper to use. Smaller supplies such as pens, pencils, staplers, rulers, and push pins can be environmentally friendly as well. Simplify, reuse, consume less, recycle—those are the watchwords of an office or school committed to consuming wisely.

THE WRITE CHOICES Every desk is equipped with a selection of pens and pencils. And what happens when your pens run out of ink and your pencils are worn down to stubs? To the trash they go. But why create waste when there are many alternatives available? From recycled-content pencils to refillable pens, you can make better choices.

With over 14 billion pencils produced each year, plus billions of other pens and markers, eco-conscious choices could make a difference. Most traditional wood pencils are made from resources that have been harvested unsustainably and then finished with chemical paints and lacquers. Look for pencils made with recycled materials, from the lead to the eraser. By searching online, you can also find creative options like pencils made from recycled newspapers or even denim.

For pens, choose biodegradable or, better yet, refillable pens. Both options minimize the amount of solid matter sent to the landfill. Though not as easy to find, pens made from recycled materials are becoming more widely available and make a great alternative.

DESK ACCESSORIES Punching a small metal staple in your papers (and later pulling it out) can be wasteful. "Staple-free" staplers, sold online, punch small neat holes and fold the remaining flaps of paper together for a strong hold. This also saves energy in the recycling process, eliminating the need for the facility to remove the staples before processing the paper. You can also find staplers made from recycled materials, such as plastic. Browse the Recycled Products Cooperative website for these staplers and many other environmentally responsible supplies.

Rulers are another small item in your desk drawer or pencil case. Once made from new sources of plastic, metal, and wood, rulers are now being manufactured of recycled materials. An online search could yield a stylish ruler made from plastic bags or biodegradable corn-based plastic. Even push pins and paperclips are being made with recycled plastics and steel; they'll help you feel eco-friendly as well as organized the next time you hang a note on your corkboard or temporarily attach papers together.

Take Action

- ✓ Choose paper made with the highest percentage of post-consumer waste.
- ✓ Use both sides of copy and notebook paper.
- ✓ Make your own notebooks with scrap paper.
- ✓ Reuse the envelopes in unsolicited mailings for your letters.
- ✓ Don't use disposable cups from the break room or cafeteria—bring your own mug, glass, or thermos.
- ✓ Buy toner and inkjet cartridges from companies with take-back programs.
- ✓ Recycle your empty ink cartridges from printers, fax machines, and copiers.
- ✓ Set up a recycling program in your school or office.
- ✓ Reuse the front of greeting cards to create your own cards and gift tags.
- ✓ Choose desk accessories made from recycled materials.
- ✓ Use cloth napkins or recycled paper napkins for meals on-the-go.
- ✓ Print business or school publications with vegetable-based inks.
- ✓ Use small accessories (staplers, paperclips, etc.) made from recycled materials.
- ✓ Bring your own lunch in reusable containers.
- ✓ Act against "sick building syndrome" by encouraging a clean, properly ventilated indoor space.
- ✓ Choose light-colored paper, which can be recycled more easily.

Recycling Paper

Curbside collection has made recycling of everything from newspapers to office memos practically effortless, from a consumer's point of view. More than half of all paper used in the United States is now sent to recycling centers. But what happens once that big truck scoops up our wastepaper and drives out of sight?

At the paper mill, the bales are loaded onto a conveyor belt that dumps them into a large vat called a pulper. Inside, water and chemicals break the stuff down into small strands of cellulose, the plant fibers that make up paper. The resulting pulp flows along to the screening stage, where the watery mix courses through a series of screens designed to remove bits of glue and other contaminants. Next the pulp gets a thorough cleaning in large cone-shaped spinning tubs, causing heavier items like staples to be thrown to the sides and drain out while lighter contaminants collect in the center and get scooped away.

The pulp then gushes into a de-inking center. Paper mills often use a two-step process. In the first, the pulp undergoes washing with soap to remove small bits of ink. The second process, called flotation de-inking, removes "stickies" like glue and stickers.

The process takes place in a large vat called a flotation cell. Inside the pulp mixes with bubbles and soap-like chemicals called surfactants. The surfactants lift the stickies off the paper and the air bubbles carry them to the top of the frothy liquid where large nets skim away the waste. And there is a lot of waste: Ink, stickies, and fibers too small to be reused again make up nearly a third of the paper sent for recycling.

The next stage, called refining, beats the pulpy mix into the starting material for paper. Large beaters break down the cellulose into fine, single strands. The beating causes fibers to swell, making them ideal for papermaking. Chemicals strip dyes from the pulp, and if desired, hydrogen peroxide and bleach can bleach the pulp white. The clean and bleached pulp is now ready to be made into paper.

The pulp, which may be blended with new cellulose fibers (called virgin fiber) or used on its own, is mixed with water so that it is 99.5% water and injected into

the papermaking machinery. The first stop is the headbox, a giant metal box housing a sprayer that showers the slurry onto a large wire screen on a moving conveyor belt.

Water drips through the screen as the pulp dries and the cellulose fibers start to bond together to form a sheet. Felt-covered rollers squeeze water from the sheet, now called web, as it travels.

This web then travels through heated metal rollers that dry it. The sheet may also travel through additional coating steps for making glossy paper. The finished paper is wound onto a giant role 30 feet wide and weighing close to 25 tons. The role can be sliced with a slitter into smaller roles for shipping to printing plants.

Today, although many publishers still prefer to rely on virgin fiber, recycled paper finds its ways into more and more books and newspapers every day. According to paper industry statistics, from 1993 to 2006, the recovery rate—the proportion of all paper used that was recovered for recycling—increased from 38.7 percent to 53.4 percent in the United States.

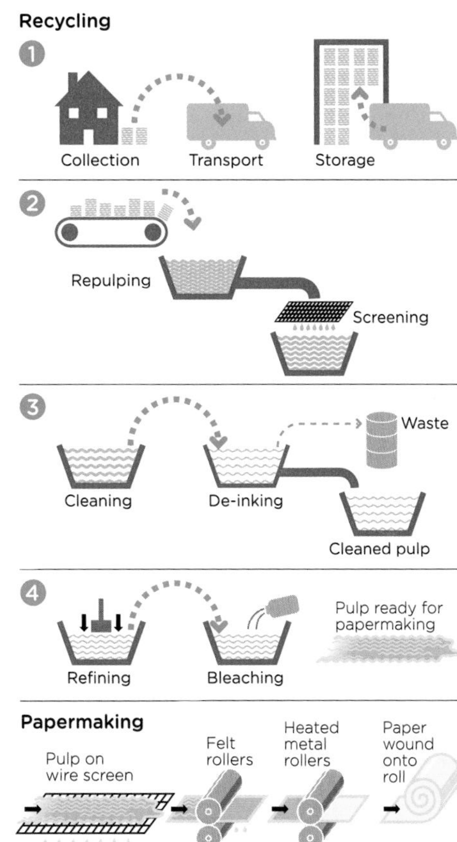

Recycling paper does result in a product that is of equal or lower quality than the original. The recycled fiber can also be used in products like wall insulation and cat litter. Up to a limit, paper can be recycled over and over: Cellulose fibers can be processed up to seven times before they wear out completely. That's not ultimate sustainability, but it's getting closer.

RECYCLING PAPER The process of recycling paper begins with its collection and storage. Then the material goes through three more chemical and physical treatment steps before it is ready as pulp to be made back into paper.

PLANET-FRIENDLY FUN

Holidays & Recreation

When it comes to special times of the year, being green is usually not something we think of first. Preoccupied about getting the right gift for that special someone, we may not stop to think about where the gift was made, what it's made of, or how long it will last. Then there's the challenge of boxing and wrapping it. An estimated 38,000 miles—yes, *miles*—of ribbon alone are thrown away in this country every year. Add to that the four million tons of gift wrap and shopping bags we toss away every year, and it's clear: Holidays are no gift to planet Earth.

We also accumulate piles of decorations, lights, costumes, and other accessories to celebrate holidays throughout the year, and, sadly, many of those accoutrements aren't so jolly either. Frequently made from cheap materials that we quickly throw away, they may also contain harmful and toxic plastics like polyvinyl chloride (PVC). But with some creative, green-minded thinking, you can avoid such hazards and throwaway options.

The holidays aren't the only times for fun. A look at the numbers tells us that Americans take our playtime seriously. According to the National Sporting Goods Association, we spent over $90 billion on sporting goods alone in 2006—a figure that doesn't take into account the many other ways we recreate. No matter what your pleasure is, you can make it even more fulfilling and friendly to the planet, whether that means the computer games you play, the art supplies you buy, or the music you support and purchase. Read on for some inspiration on having fun with eco-consciousness in mind.

Winter Holidays

Along with the giving, there's a lot of throwing away that happens through the holidays. It's estimated that between Thanksgiving and New Year's Day, Americans generate an extreme one million tons of waste a week. Make some green resolutions ahead of time this year.

GREEN GIFTING In the scramble to take care of last-minute shopping, many of us lose sight of the fact that our holiday giving doesn't have to sacrifice the environment. With a little forethought, green giving can be simple, fun, and creative.

According to a 2004 survey by the Center for a New American Dream, 81 percent of Americans say the country is overly focused on spending and shopping, 87 percent of us say our consumer culture makes it hard to teach our children proper values, and 91 percent agree that the way we live produces too much waste. What better time to address those issues than during the season of giving? Something simple and thoughtful may be appreciated much more than a pile of shrink-wrapped, mass-produced gifts.

Every holiday season, companies send out a barrage of advertisements hoping to lure shoppers and create a buzz to buy the latest gadget or the last-minute sale item. But what if this year you put shopping green at the top of your holiday to-do list? Instead of flimsy plastic toys powered by disposable batteries, why not give kids books, craft kits, or toys and games made from natural materials that will create memories and last a lifetime?

You can even take your green gifting one step further, choosing gifts that spread the word about conservation—gifts like a basket of energy-saving goodies such as compact fluorescent lightbulbs and rechargeable batteries. Even something as simple as a favorite photo in a well-crafted frame made from salvaged or recycled wood will create much more meaning than a last-minute, mass-produced gift.

If you're looking for a way to satisfy your social conscience as well as your generous heart, consider buying fair trade–certified gifts. For handcrafted gifts, look for the Fair Trade Federation endorsement. By buying

certified fair-trade gifts this holiday season, you give someone a beautiful, one-of-a-kind gift and also ensure that its creators are being rewarded for their time and effort with a decent wage and safe working conditions. Companies are accepted into the Fair Trade Federation based on their commitment to, among other things, paying at least the local minimum wage and protecting natural resources.

GREEN DICTIONARY

FAIR TRADE

According to the Fair Trade Federation, fair trade is "a system of exchange that seeks to create greater equity and partnership in the international trading system" through practices including equitable pay, healthy workplaces, and environmental sustainability.

Green-minded gift baskets brimming with healthy, local, and organic goodies also make a welcome treat, especially for those who are housebound, or swamped by houseguests, during the holidays. Check your greengrocer, natural-foods store, or farmers market for gift baskets made with local, organic produce, cheeses, meats, and spreads. If you can't find what you're looking for, several mail-order companies will create gift baskets for you full of seasonal organic produce, baking mixes, ornaments, and goodies.

Why not bring out your creative side, support local farmers, and assemble your own gift baskets? Instead of heading to the shopping mall, shop your local farmers market for apples, pears, preserves, and artisanal cheeses. By shopping locally, you can support your own community and family-run, homegrown stores. And since winter celebrations are a time of sugary indulgence, consider creating sweet homemade memories by adding some delectable treats like organic and fair-trade chocolates.

HEALTHY HOLIDAY MEALS Holiday celebrations are not just about gifts, but also about sharing hearty, comforting meals with loved ones. No gift is more sustaining than food, and there's no better way to honor family traditions with health in mind than by using organic, homegrown, and pesticide-free ingredients.

In many families, the holiday roast is a hallmark of festive meals. This year, shop for a beef roast or turkey that is certified organic. Organic beef and turkey, along with other meats such as pork and chicken, are raised without antibiotics or growth hormones and given feed free from pesticides or animal parts. For roasts, beef from cows fed grass their whole lives is leaner and tastier, as well as full of heart-healthy omega-3 fatty acids.

As the popularity of organic, grass-fed, and other environment-friendly meats has grown, so too have the options to choose more Earth-friendly alternatives. If you can't find organic roast brands in your neighborhood, shop online or look to regional meat producers, found through organizations such as Eatwild, whose Directory of Farms lists more than 800 pasture-based farms in the U.S., Canada, and abroad. You can also look for humanely raised holiday meats certified by Humane Farm Animal Care or by Food Alliance. These meats are produced by ranchers who provide safe and fair working conditions; raise animals humanely and without hormones and antibiotics; conserve soil, water, and wildlife habitat; and commit to continuous improvement of practices. Food Alliance also has a Handler Certification Program, overseeing packers, manufacturers, processors, distributors, and wholesalers.

To accompany your organic meal or enhance holiday parties, serve a bottle of organic wine or vodka, or a six-pack of refreshing organic beer; these also make great hostess gifts. After the meal, coffee lovers will enjoy a cup of certified-organic, fair-trade coffee. For dessert, bake up delightful goodies using certified-organic, fair-trade chocolate and organic fruit jams or serve succulent cakes and cookies. For more on eco-friendly foods for your table, see Chapter 1.

ECO-TIP: GIFTS THAT GIVE BACK

One way to give to others is to make a donation in their name to those truly in need. Most nonprofit organizations can be supported through gift memberships, adoptions, or purchases in the name of your family member or friend. Organizations such as Alternative Gifts International provide a list of several global humanitarian causes that will gladly accept your holiday donation in the name of a loved one.

GREENER TREES The smell of a freshly cut Christmas tree is a treat to have around the house during the holidays—but give up that romantic image of vibrant forests mantled in fresh snow. Nearly all cut Christmas trees in American homes, about 33 million a year, are farmed on only 500,000 acres of land, according to the National Christmas Tree Association. And many of those trees are raised using pesticides at the expense of native plants and wildlife.

In your search for Earth-friendly live Christmas trees and wreaths, don't trust every tree stand that calls its goods "organic." The government's organic certification doesn't apply to Christmas trees or wreaths. Christmas tree plantations typically concentrate a single species, often nonnative and fast-growing, onto a large plot of land. While many tree farms have been planted on previously clear-cut land, some farmers cut existing native forest to establish plantations. Herbicides such as Roundup (glyphosate) are used to eliminate competitive weeds, while insecticides control bugs that damage green growth. And while many of the pesticides used to grow Christmas trees will have washed off by the time you get your tree home, think of their effects on the plants, wildlife, and groundwater left behind.

ECO-TIP: SHOPPING LIST

If you're wondering where to find your nearest local farmers market for your holiday meal or gift shopping, visit the U.S. Department of Agriculture's website, which lists farmers markets in each state.

While you won't find a verifiable label for ecological trees and wreaths, that doesn't mean you can't look for vendors or tree farms that use little or no pesticide and that care for wildlife; it just means you need to ask the right questions: Where were these trees grown? What pesticides were used? How long have the trees been sitting on the lot? Groups like Local Harvest can help you find an Earth-friendly grower. Or, if you're lucky enough to live near a national or state forest, look into permits that allow you to cut your own tree or holiday boughs in areas that won't harm wildlife or lead to overharvesting.

Buying an artificial Christmas tree may seem like a good option. They don't dry out and pose a fire risk the way real trees can, and they can be used for years. On average, though, they're discarded at the tender age of six, according to the National Christmas Tree Association. And there's another big catch with artificial trees: They're made of polyvinyl chloride (PVC), which produces cancer-causing dioxins during manufacture and incineration.

If you're looking for a better all-around choice this year, consider buying a live potted Christmas tree, available at farmers markets, garden centers, and tree farms in some areas. After you've enjoyed it, you can celebrate the New Year and Earth's renewal by planting it outdoors. Some local parks departments will accept donated trees. In San Francisco or Portland, Oregon, you can even rent a tree from an innovative firm called the Original Living Christmas Tree Company. It will be delivered to you before Christmas, picked up after New Year's Day, and then planted.

Once the holidays are over, there are many better options to tossing your tree or wreath in the trash. The majority of cut Christmas trees are dumped in landfills every year, a sad fact considering the many other beneficial uses for discarded trees. In many towns and cities, you can drop off your tree at a central location, and a growing number provide curbside tree collection, picking up your tree to chip and turn it into mulch for next year's gardens, parks, hiking trails, playground areas, animal stalls, and landscaping. Some communities use whole Christmas trees for river shoreline stabilization, beach erosion prevention, or fishing reefs. You can even reuse your Christmas tree in your winter garden as decoration or as a bird feeder.

ECO-TIP: RECYCLE YOUR TREE

To find a Christmas tree recycling program, contact your local parks and recreation, public works, or sanitation (recycling) department, or the mayor's office. You can also search by zip code on the National Christmas Tree Association website or contact the organization Earth911.

DECK THE HALLS IN GREEN This year, explore the light-emitting diode (LED) holiday light options—they run on about one-tenth the energy of conventional lights and since they produce no heat, they present no fire hazard. After you've chosen a planet-friendly tree and energy-wise string of lights, top your tree off with greener ornament choices. To steer clear of ornaments that may contain lead paint and to support artisans, choose lead-free Fair Trade Federation–certified ornaments made from materials such as silk, wood, or gourds. Pull the family together to make your own decorations from gingerbread cookies, cards, origami patterns, ribbons, or those oldtime favorites—the paper chain and the popcorn-and-cranberry garland.

Halloween

Halloween inspires creativity in both adults and kids. Who doesn't like to unleash their inner witch, warlock, or masked bandit? Our accumulated boxes full of masks, capes, and makeup from years past aren't so kind to the Earth or our health, however.

BETTER GETUPS Many store-bought, mass-produced Halloween costumes are made from a scary substance: polyvinyl chloride (PVC), also known as vinyl. Because it's so cheap to produce, you'll find vinyl all over costume shops during October—not only in masks and outfits, but in Halloween accessories such as wigs, shiny leatherlike belts, and boots. To top it off, costumes often come wrapped in PVC packaging, which can leave phthalate residues on its contents.

GREEN DICTIONARY

LEDS

Tiny lightbulbs that fit into an electrical circuit, light-emitting diodes (LEDs) have several advantages over incandescent bulbs. For one thing, a higher proportion of electricity goes to generating light. Holiday lights with LEDs save up to 90 percent in energy use and last 100 times longer. They are also safer to handle and reduce the risk of fire.

But the production of PVC, a nonrecyclable plastic, releases cancer-causing dioxins into the atmosphere. Vinyl products are also likely to contain phthalates, hormone-disrupting chemicals that have been linked to reproductive abnormalities and liver cancer.

If nothing else, avoid choosing a PVC mask that covers the face, as it may release fumes you (or your child) can't help but inhale. Choose masks made of natural latex instead. Distinguish them by their odors: Vinyl smells like a shower curtain; latex rubber masks smell like balloons.

Fabric costumes, while safer than PVC ones, aren't perfect, either. Concerns over quick-burning natural fibers, such as cotton, linen, and silk, have prompted many costume manufacturers to switch to synthetics, which take longer to ignite. But synthetic fibers melt once ignited, and the melted fibers can cause severe localized burns. For more on the health effects of wearing synthetics, see page 217. Whether you choose natural or synthetic, opt for costumes with a close fit that are free of external elements (like capes, ribbons, bows, and fringe trims) that can come in contact with a flame.

To avoid these problems, why not raid your closet? Old jackets, coats, shoes, shirts, socks, and jewelry can be crafted into a limitless number of costumes with some creativity. If you can't find what you want at home, visit your local thrift store, where you'll find shelves of clothes and outfit ideas.

THE GREEN PUMPKIN For a Halloween that is truly green, search for organic or pesticide-free pumpkins grown in your area. In doing so, you'll avoid exposing yourself and your family to the pesticides that can be found on conventionally grown pumpkins, such as diazinon, a nervous-system toxin, and malathion, a nervous-system toxin and possible human carcinogen. Or grow your own organic pumpkin patch in this year's garden. Your kids can plant their own seeds, watch them grow, and pick them with their own hands.

SAFE TRICK-OR-TREATING You'll want to make sure that your kids can both see and be seen when making the rounds this Halloween. Fluorescent light sticks are popular accessories that provide visibility to kids walking in the dark and, when used correctly, don't pose a health risk. However, if the exterior plastic is punctured, the materials inside glow sticks—a mixture of hydrogen peroxide, oxalic phthalate, and fluorescent dye—can leak, causing skin irritation and severe eye pain if the chemical comes in contact with kids' eyes.

Beyond their potential health effects, glow sticks are single-use, non-recyclable plastic products that can easily be replaced with longer-lasting, more planet-friendly lights. A far greener option, for example, is to give your kids a reusable flashlight powered with mercury-free, rechargeable alkaline batteries. A few companies have also made LED flashlights or upgrades for existing flashlights, which allow you to replace standard incandescent bulbs with a cluster of longer-lasting LED bulbs.

Avoid masks, hats, and hoods that obscure vision, and forgo the eye patch as part of your child's pirate costume. Small children should wear light-colored clothing to increase visibility. If your older child is wearing a dark costume (think Darth Vader), be sure he or she also carries a bright flashlight (or a light saber).

ECO-TIP: HOMEMADE MASKS

Rather than buy masks, help your children design their own creations using paper. Or, for a more involved project, design new masks from papier-mâché. Old masks or a few layers of aluminum foil pressed to the face can act as molds. When painting masks, be sure to use water-based or latex paint.

SWEET TEMPTATIONS Nothing kills a parent's festive Halloween mood more than realizing what a nutritional nightmare the holiday can be. Your kids are left with a pile of artificially sweetened candy that wreaks havoc on their health. High-fructose corn syrup (HFCS), the most pervasive ghoul found in conventional Halloween candy, is a leading contributor to childhood obesity and is frequently made from genetically modified corn and refined with genetically modified enzymes. And it seems to appear everywhere, whether in the candy your kids are collecting or the store-bought cider you're serving at home. See "Green Dictionary: HFCS," page 31.

Luckily, there are plenty of healthier trick-or-treat choices for your child's health—and for the environment. Try shopping for organic, fair trade–certified and individually wrapped treats that you can hand out to the neighborhood kids, inspiring them to care for the

ASK THE EDITORS

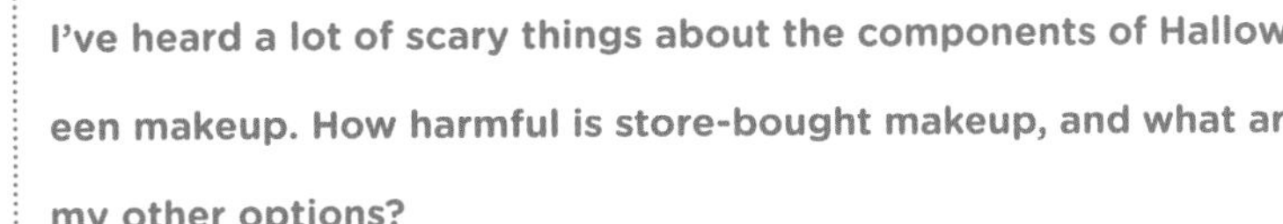

Q **I've heard a lot of scary things about the components of Halloween makeup. How harmful is store-bought makeup, and what are my other options?**

A As with regular makeup and personal care products, the Halloween makeup found in conventional drugstores—white, green, and black cream makeup, multicolored makeup crayons, and fake blood—contain a number of suspect ingredients. While they may be labeled "nontoxic," "safe," and "allergenic," many Halloween makeup products can contain ingredients that are somewhat scary, potentially contributing to long-term health issues such as cancer or endocrine disruption.

Fortunately, more safety-minded companies produce makeup products that can make you or your child look terrifying without risking your health. You may be surprised at the products you'll find at natural foods stores and health food stores, or online—products such as lines of phthalate-free nail polishes. (For specific advice on makeup products, see pages 191-98.)

The Internet and craft magazines offer many homemade Halloween makeup recipes, ranging from blood to bruises and face makeup, that use simple kitchen and bathroom staples such as ketchup, corn starch, syrup, shortening, cold cream, and food coloring.

environment, too. (It's worth a try, anyway.) Though these still contain sugar, they usually contain less refined versions of it, and are often free of artificial colors and flavorings. You'll find plenty of organic goodies in natural-foods stores; a nice assortment might include organic milk chocolate, nut brittle, and hard candies wrapped in biodegradable cornstarch packaging.

Chocolate is a Halloween favorite, coming in many forms. Yet adding to the nutritional headache of Halloween are the environmental and social impacts chocolate can have. Cacao beans grown in full sun are comparably more susceptible to disease than their shade-grown counterparts and require heavy doses of toxic pesticides and synthetic fertilizers. The cocoa crop's social ills include child slavery, which UNICEF has found in abundance on cacao plantations, and low wages paid to farmers because of market deregulation.

If you'd rather buy planet- and people-friendly chocolate, look for the "Fair Trade Certified" label, which ensures that chocolate farmers are paid a fair price for their crop. ▸For more on organic and fair-trade chocolate, see pages 35-37.

You can even sneak something fruity into trick-or-treat bags, like organic fruit snacks. And there are trans fat–free cookies, or gluten-free and wheat-free snacks. Natural-foods stores offer a wide variety of individually wrapped snack and cereal bars that work perfectly as Halloween handouts. If you can think beyond orange-and-black packaging, you can get pretty creative with your treats. You can now buy organic pretzels, chips, and popcorn through most conventional and natural-foods stores.

And for that Halloween party, why not serve corn syrup–free, organic apple cider from your local farmers market?

ECO-TIP: BETTER BAGS

For this year's goody bag, make an Earth-friendly statement by reusing a supermarket shopping bag instead of buying a throwaway plastic bag or tub. You can also decorate a plain organic cotton or recycled cotton tote or an organic cotton pillowcase using washable markers and reuse it year after year.

ECO-TIP: TRICK-OR-TREAT FOR A CAUSE

Notions of ghosts and goblins aside, Halloween can be a great time to teach your kids about helping other kids. The United Nations Children's Fund sponsors a Trick-Or-Treat for UNICEF program, encouraging young trick-or-treaters to collect change in addition to candy while they're out making their rounds. The money they raise goes to UNICEF's worldwide aid programs. You can get collection boxes at some local stores or through UNICEF's website.

UNICEF isn't the only organization for which you can trick-or-treat for donations. Look for companies that allow kids to contribute to a nonprofit through Halloween donations, among them the World Wildlife Fund and the American Red Cross. With just a little effort, you can turn fright night into smiles for good deeds done.

Boxes, Gift Wrap & Cards

Picture the perfect holiday, birthday, baby shower, or wedding scene: crisp, colorfully wrapped boxes decked with shiny ribbons and taped well enough to keep prying fingers at bay.

THE FACTS

According to the Greeting Card Association, Americans spend $7.5 billion to send some 2.6 billion cards to each other every year—many of which end up in landfills soon after they've been opened.

Now, picture the day after your party: piles of tissue paper, envelopes, cards, and wrapping paper are stuffed into trash bags and tossed to the curb, waiting to be carted off to your nearest landfill. Holidays and other special occasions create mountains of excitement, but also mountains of waste. Holiday and special-occasion gift wrap, bags, and greeting cards consume a large amount of virgin paper, but with a little foresight and careful planning you can personalize your packages and cards with less of an environmental impact. For this year's holidays and parties, consider using tree-free alternatives, creativity, and community spirit to give forests a break.

GIVE TREES A BREAK To help preserve forests, choose recycled-paper cards and stationery made from a high percentage of post-consumer waste paper—that is, cards that have been recycled from paper we've used before. When shopping at your local card store, look for cards with the recycled paper symbol printed on the back. Once you find recycled-paper cards, look for cards that have high percentages of post-consumer waste, and those with a "PCF" logo, meaning that they're made without chlorine bleaching of the paper.

If you can't find greener card options at home, the Internet offers a wide variety of choices when it comes to recycled greetings. Look not only for 100 percent post-consumer recycled content, but also for soy- or vegetable-based inks, natural alternatives to synthetic inks. You can even support conservation groups like the National Wildlife Federation or Sierra Club, which sell recycled holiday gift cards to support their conservation efforts.

Consider sparing trees this year by purchasing cards made of tree-free paper. Hemp is an excellent choice:

Hemp requires fewer resources and pesticides than trees, and its fibers can be recycled more often than paper made from wood. You can also find cards made from kenaf, which grows rapidly and renewably without needing large amounts of fertilizers and pesticides, or banana stalk, bamboo, recycled blue jeans, dollar bills, green tea leaves, even recycled junk mail. You'll even find cards with wildflower seeds in the paper; after the holidays, just plant the whole card in the ground and the paper will recycle naturally into the soil as the seedlings grow. To reach your computer-savvy family, friends, and colleagues with few material and energy resources, you can send Earth-friendly, paperless holiday greetings by using e-cards. For more on greeting cards, see page 379.

THE FACTS

In 2001 Americans threw away 73.5 million tons of packaging, making up 28 percent of all solid waste disposed in landfills.

GREENER GIFT WRAP A vast array of colors, textures, and sheens await you as you search for the ideal way to wrap presents. You found the perfect wrapping paper, made the creases just right, and topped it with a shiny ribbon. And if you're lucky, your child will delight in the silver shimmering bow for a moment before tearing hungrily through the glossy paper to the toy below. Minutes later, that once shiny paper ends up crumpled in the trash. When we watch our lovely gifts turn into a heap of gift wrap and plastic packaging after holidays and other celebrations, it's easy to see how much gift wrap contributes to our mounting piles of waste.

There are many fun, creative alternatives to traditional gift wrapping that will not only cut down on waste, but save you money and bring smiles to your friends and family. From recycled paper wrap and raffia ribbon, made from palm trees native to Africa, to thrift-store finds and creative minds, you can choose ways to lessen your environmental impact when you give gifts.

ECO-TIP: PRACTICAL PACKAGING

Instead of wasting time, energy, and paper on disposable gift wrap, place gifts in a reusable container, like a picnic basket or reusable gift tin, so that the packaging becomes part of the gift. Patterned dish towels, bandannas, and cotton T-shirts make excellent, colorful wrappers. Check out your local thrift store not only for gift ideas, but fun wrapping options too.

Try using old calendar pages, Sunday comics, or even old maps. Follow a Japanese tradition: Use a square of cloth, called *furoshiki*, to wrap your presents; try reclaimed cloth like old scarves, bandanas, shirts, or pillowcases.

If you're set on buying gift wrap, there are many alternatives to traditional wrapping paper, including materials like hemp, flax, and organic cotton. You can find 100 percent recycled brown packaging paper that you and your child can personalize by drawing or rubber-stamping on it. Sumptuous papyrus-like sheets of wrapping paper made of 100 percent kozo, the bark of fast-growing Thai mulberry trees, is also a good wrapping option, as is tree-free paper made from flax, hemp, and recovered cotton.

Concerned that your gift just won't look the same without a bow on top? Local craft stores offer hemp and raffia, and thrift stores offer an array of reusable bows. Renewable raffia and hemp twine come in bright colors and make for festive knots. Try using scarves, fabric scraps, or vintage doilies, or accent gifts with reusable festive items, like seasonal cookie cutters, a handmade ornament, or a silk flower. Keep packages secure with tape that's free of PVC (vinyl), which releases carcinogenic dioxins when produced. Instead, opt for clear cellulose tape or recycled, gummed paper tape.

ECO-TIP: DIY PHOTO CARDS

Love sending cards with family photos? Look for 100 percent post-consumer content, processed chlorine-free (PCF) greeting cards with photo-grade paper on the front, the recycled arrow logo on the back, and writing paper in the middle. Add your own photos and the stamps.

BETTER BAGS & BOXES Buying new boxes and bags may be tempting, but why not extend the life cycle of the boxes you already have? Rather than recycling the shoe boxes, shipping boxes, and gift boxes that accumulate throughout the year, stow them away for reuse the next time a holiday or birthday rolls around.

Buy from companies that use recycled and/or recyclable materials in their packaging. If you shop online, look at the various shipping options available, and consider shopping for many people at one online store so that all your items can be packaged together. If some items are out of stock, have the rest of the order held so that everything can be shipped together when it becomes available. Avoid companies that ship different types of items separately—for example, those that ship books and DVDs separately—and look for companies that ship large objects in their original packaging.

From a packaging perspective, clothing is great because it requires no additional wrapping outside of being placed in a box for shipment. If a company does place clothing in plastic bags, reuse them for as long as they last. Some online retailers also offer green shipping options and will even donate money to plant trees to absorb the greenhouse gas carbon dioxide.

If you're committed to buying new gift bags, try ones made of natural fibers or recycled content. Put this year's gifts in a recycled paper gift bag, or in a plastic gift bag made from post-consumer recycled plastic, tied with a raffia ribbon and accompanied by a recycled rice paper greeting card. And since no gift bag is complete without flowing tufts of paper to disguise its contents, look for tissue paper made from 100 percent recycled paper and processed without chlorine or heavy-metal dyes.

Games

A good 60 percent of Americans enjoy playing video and computer games. Their sales now eclipse movie box office receipts. But too many encourage sedentary activities combined with violent and unsavory fantasies. There are alternatives—many that go back to fun as defined in generations past.

ECO-TIP: DOWNLOAD IT

If you purchase computer games, consider downloading them directly from the Internet instead of purchasing them from stores or having the CDs shipped from an online retailer. It saves resources needed for packaging, printing, and shipping.

Gaming can be a great way to practice problem-solving skills, and plenty of computer games today provide a unique way to explore issues and inspire leadership. In the United Nations' popular online game Food Force, players act as aid workers on a mission to feed a fictitious war-torn island. You'll even find games that let children and adults participate in worldwide adventures with real explorers, combating global warming, deforestation, and other environmental challenges. Likewise, the Serious Games Initiative, a project of the Woodrow Wilson International Center for Scholars in Washington, D.C., is working to create and encourage computer games addressing thought-provoking topics such as education, training, health, and public policy.

Even with healthier computer game options, consider limiting your kids' time in front of the TV or computer—the American Academy of Pediatrics recommends that kids spend no more than two hours a day in front of a TV or computer screen. Instead, encourage them to apply lessons learned in educational games in their outdoor activities and daily lives. Traditional games bring the family together in real-life social interactions to learn how to strategize and negotiate. Consider old-time favorites such as charades, chess, checkers, Scrabble, or dominoes.

Music

Musicians have long been catalysts for social change and activism. Now bands are partnering with environmental nonprofits to make concerts eco-friendly affairs, both onstage and off.

GREENER GIGS Why should they bother? For one thing, theirs is an industry that uses lots of energy and generates mountains of waste. As a whole, the industry contributes 150,000 tons of carbon dioxide emissions annually through tour buses alone. And then there's the garbage. A typical midsize concert venue can go through 470,000 plastic cups, 200,000 napkins, and 600 lightbulbs each year, not to mention the 24,000 plastic bags that will hold all the garbage. Turning the tide is, thankfully, the focus of a new generation of musicians and promoters who hope to lead the music industry in social and environmental change.

Bands are looking for better ways to more responsibly coexist with our planet. Faced with massive captive audiences of young people at concerts, bands are banking on the hope that fans will pay attention to what their favorite groups are doing to reduce their own environmental footprint, take action for themselves, and spread the word about environmental concerns.

An increasing number of rock bands are serving organic food backstage, offering fans organic cotton T-shirts, printing posters and flyers on recycled paper with soy ink, and working with venues to increase recycling. They're fueling their tour buses with clean-burning biodiesel and reducing idling of buses at venues to cut back on air pollution and fuel use.

With all of this positive change in the music industry, how can you be an eco-friendly fan? There are plenty of ways to help. Ask venues to recycle, offer reusable utensils, and begin recycling programs. Carpool, ride a bike, or take public transportation to concerts. Choose organic cotton or hemp T-shirts from concert vendors if they're available. And, most important, carry your favorite band's green message home with you and do all you can to pass it on to your friends.

THE FACTS

A single concert stadium show can contribute up to 1,000 tons of CO_2 greenhouse gas emissions—not even including the emissions from tens of thousands of fans driving to and from the show.

TUNE UP YOUR INSTRUMENTS When it comes to instruments, the good thing about the music business is that old or vintage instruments are always cooler than new ones. Recycling instruments by selling them or passing them along to beginners is standard practice, and artists—along with their supporters—are constantly looking for new ways to make their instruments even more eco-friendly. Groups like Reverb—a nonprofit organization that provides environmental information at concert venues—have helped step up efforts to "green up" the music industry by promoting even small green-minded steps, like collecting used guitar strings to be made into jewelry, and by promoting bands and concerts that do their part for the planet.

Instrument manufacturers are getting into the game, too, as the tropical hardwoods prized for making instruments disappear and the supply of certified woods may not always meet demand. If you're a green-minded musician, you'll find instruments on the market made from Rainforest Alliance–certified wood, from sustainably managed forests certified by the Forest Stewardship Council (FSC), even from reclaimed wood. If you're trying to source greener wood for new instruments, the nonprofit group Greenpeace advocates responsible wood management through its Music Wood Campaign, which encourages the use of "good wood," certified as responsibly harvested by the FSC. ▸For more on FSC certification, see page 295.

Of course, renting or buying instruments used are still the most environmentally responsible—and economical—choices. That can be good news, especially when a child is just testing the waters of musicianship. Most music shops supply rentals, and music teachers and local musicians can provide names of reliable used-instrument dealers.

Take Action

- ✓ Choose durable, Earth-friendly gifts for friends and family.
- ✓ Buy recycled paper or tree-free cards and wrapping to accompany your gifts.
- ✓ Reuse boxes, gift containers, gift wrap, and ribbons.
- ✓ Serve a hearty holiday meal with organic, locally grown food.
- ✓ Enjoy a live, potted holiday tree and decorate it with energy-efficient lights and homemade ornaments.

ASK THE EDITORS

Q **I'm seeing many bands and concert tours giving me the opportunity to "offset" my carbon emissions when I buy a concert ticket. Where does this money really go, and how do I know it's going for good things?**

A Carbon offsets enable individuals and businesses—including you and your favorite performer or band—to reduce the carbon dioxide they're responsible for emitting by paying to fund projects targeted at capturing it or reducing its continued production in other places.

Concerts require large amounts of energy for lighting, sound, and transporting band members and crew—not to mention the consumption and travel impacts of thousands of fans. As more and more people are concerned about global warming and seeking to reduce their environmental footprint, carbon offsets—along with personal carbon reductions like carpooling or using mass transit to attend your next concert—provide solutions to help combat global warming.

There are a variety of carbon offset providers in the United States, sponsoring and funding projects ranging from tree plantings and increases in energy efficiency to renewable energy projects. Most rely on third parties to verify the validity of their projects. Some offset providers you may come across include Carbonfund.org, NativeEnergy, and TerraPass.

✓ Avoid plastic and synthetic costumes and makeup by making your own.

✓ Choose games that inspire, challenge, and educate both kids and adults.

✓ Choose instruments that are used or made from sustainable wood.

✓ Be a green music fan; support Earth-friendly bands and concerts.

Plastic Picnicware

Disposable cups, plates, and utensils make for easy cleanup, but what impact do they have on the environment? To find out, let's look at the life cycle of common plastic picnic items.

Disposable cutlery and clear plastic cups are made of #6 polystyrene, as are the familiar white, foamlike cups and plates, often incorrectly called Styrofoam (a registered trade name for polystyrene foam used in building). Crude oil and natural gas are the starting materials of polystyrene, and fossil fuels provide 90 percent of the energy that goes into making this plastic.

The manufacturing process begins as fossil fuels are refined to make benzene or xylene, either of which is then chemically converted to ethylbenzene, which is then transformed into styrene. All of these chemicals have toxic effects. Long-term exposure to benzene is known to cause cancer in humans; xylene is toxic to the nervous system; ethylbenzene causes kidney and testicular tumors in laboratory animals; and styrene is suspected of causing reproductive harm. Extreme care must be taken during the manufacturing process to keep these chemicals from escaping into the environment.

Styrene can be knitted into long chains called polymers to make polystyrene. Typically, manufacturers combine styrene in a large vat with mineral oil, which acts as a lubricant and plasticizer, plus antioxidants and other additives. This chemical mixture then flows through reactors under high heat, which forces the styrene monomers to join chemically with each other and form polystyrene. Molten polystyrene then pulses into an extruder, like a pasta maker, which forms it into strands. These strands shoot into a coldwater bath and harden into pellets.

The foamlike polystyrene used in coffee cups is known in the industry as expandable polystyrene (EPS), a material made by mixing the styrene monomers with a blowing agent, typically a gas such as pentane or carbon dioxide. The industry no longer uses the ozone hole-forming chemicals called chlorofluorocarbons (CFCs). The styrene monomer and blowing agent, mixed with water, are subjected to heat and high pressure. In the end, 5 to 7 percent of the blowing agent becomes trapped in the EPS polymer. Tiny lightweight beads result.

Picnicware manufacturing plants begin with either the pellets or beads of polystyrene. They heat them back to liquid form and then pour the liquid through injection molding equipment to produce cups, plates, or utensils. The newly minted items are packaged and shipped to stores, where they sit until a consumer plucks them from the shelf and takes them home.

Typically, picnicware items are used for one hour or less. Then, soiled with food, they get dumped into the trash bin.

Now the polystyrene products enter the final and longest stage of their lives, in the landfill. The items may be crushed and crumbled into smaller pieces, but the polystyrene of which they are made remains intact for decades. Ironically, the inert quality of the polystyrene material actually protects human health, because it binds the toxic ingredients that went into making it and keeps them from entering the environment chemically.

Technology exists to recycle polystyrene, but it is uneconomical, and it rarely happens. Scraps of food must first be washed off, using water sanitized with chlorine. Foam polystyrene is lightweight, but it takes up a lot of space, so collecting it requires many trips with a truck powered by fossil fuels. All in all, recycling polystyrene may cause more waste and pollution than putting it into a landfill.

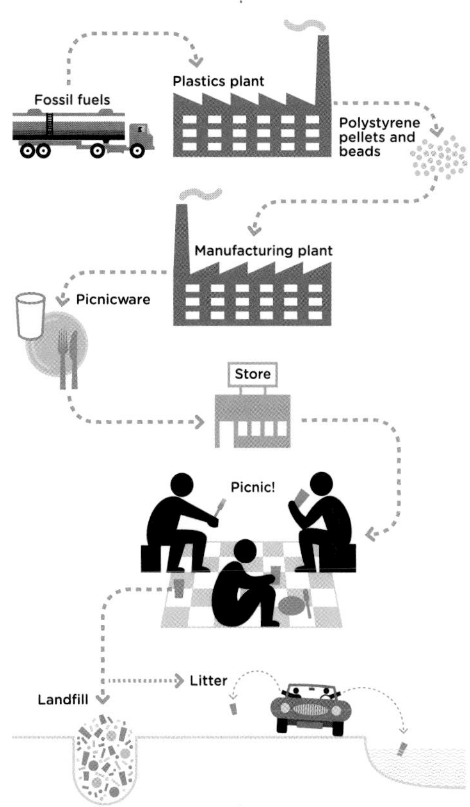

Perhaps the greatest impact of polystyrene picnicware arises when the items are discarded carelessly and become litter. This is a particular problem at sea, where white-foam coffee cups and take-out containers float on the surface and can be ingested by marine animals. Several coastal communities have banned polystyrene-foam take-out containers, and more may in years to come, if the aesthetics of the landscape and the survival of wildlife take precedence over the convenience of occasional picnickers.

PLASTIC PICNICWARE Plastic picnicware undergoes a four-part life cycle. Petroleum products are made into polystyrene beads or pellets, which are extruded as plastic items. Used briefly by consumers, the picnicware spends most of its lifetime in the landfill—or as litter.

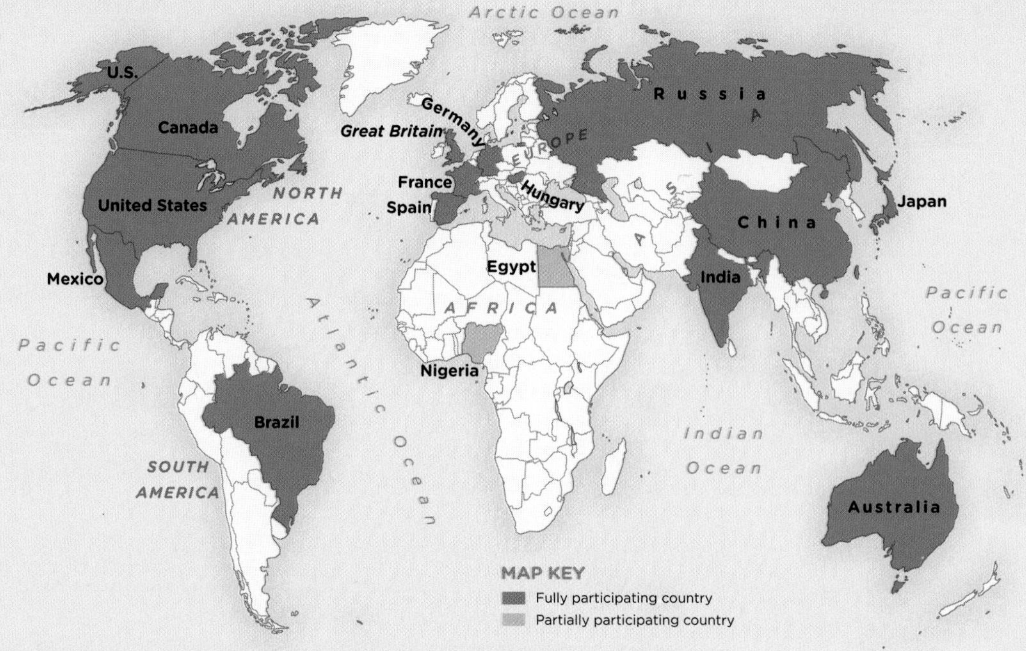

GREENDEX 2008: CONSUMER CHOICE AROUND THE WORLD

Canada
Canadians' overall Greendex ranking was next to last, the result, in part, of large household footprints and low use of public transportation.

United States
Consumers in the U.S. ranked last of all the 14 countries surveyed, in part because of how they heat and cool their comparatively large houses.

Mexico
Mexicans ranked near the top of the Greendex, yet one-third surveyed admitted to driving alone "a lot more" often than they did just one year before.

Brazil
Brazil's consumers tied with India's as the highest ranked of the entire 14-country index of sustainable behavior.

Great Britain
Consumers in England, Scotland, and Wales ranked among the lowest in water conservation but scored well on consumption of local foods.

France
A majority of French consumers—62 percent—said they drive alone most days or every day; by contrast, 70 percent of Chinese respondents said they never drive alone.

Spain
Spanish consumers scored near the middle of the Greendex, with positive marks for use of public transportation but lower ones for consumption of seafood and bottled water.

Germany
Among Westerners, German respondents scored highest for household sustainability, in part because they most likely renovated for energy efficiency recently.

Hungary
Hungarians reported a relatively small household footprint but less likelihood to follow practices such as recycling and choosing environmentally friendly products.

Russia
Seventy-one percent of Russians reported using public transportation at least once a week; 53 percent said almost every day.

China
Fifty-two percent of the Chinese consumers surveyed strongly agreed that "environmental problems are having a negative effect on my health," the highest in the report.

India
Seventy-two percent of Indian consumers polled reported never eating beef, which contributes to that country's number one ranking for food sustainability.

Japan
Japanese consumers eat fish and seafood at more than twice the rate of the average consumer in the Greendex survey.

Australia
Without any prompting, Australians listed the environment and climate change issues as the most important national problem.

Consumers in Egypt and Nigeria were interviewed face to face for this study, but these results are not included in the core reporting, since data acquired through Internet surveys and in-person interviews are not technically comparable. Future studies will include African consumers as online research becomes feasible in those regions.

Consumer Choice & the Environment—A Worldwide Tracking Survey

The Bigger Picture

Very few of us grew up fully appreciating the myriad ways in which the people who share the planet—now numbered at 6.7 billion—are connected to one another. But the 21st century has a way of driving the point home on a regular basis: Children learn the importance of animal and plant diversity in equatorial rain forests before they leave elementary school. Octogenarians receive e-mails from grandchildren working at medical clinics in developing countries. Appliances, clothing, and cars have become international products, made from natural resources that originate in one country, shipped for assembly to another, and then distributed worldwide, creating jobs—and profits—in yet dozens of other locations. The cardboard boxes stacked behind our local grocery store for recycling travel to China and back, to reemerge as packaging for our neighbor's new television a year later. The world we live in today clearly extends beyond our backyards.

What we are frequently still slow to realize, however, is the impact on all of us of what happens in someone's backyard, or goes down another person's drain, or is purchased in our grocery stores. The trick is measuring that impact so that patterns of behavior—hidden when viewed simply as one purchase, one decision, or one action—become visible. When we reveal the effect of a single choice, multiplied by thousands of residents—perhaps Japanese families ordering seafood or Brazilian families using on-demand water heaters—it's also possible to influence a man in Mexico or a woman from the United States to make a more educated choice about whether to wash a load of jeans in cold or warm water, buy a third television set, or encourage city officials to build a safer bicycle path.

To gauge these global influences and monitor progress toward sustainable goals, the National Geographic Society paired with the international polling firm GlobeScan and initiated a study to measure consumer behavior internationally. Greendex™, an annual survey, examines consumer behavior around the world, measuring factors that include energy use, the size of houses, transportation habits, and use of green products. Greendex 2008 was the resulting baseline report, which tracked first-year responses from survey participants in 14 countries. Future survey results, when compared with the 2008 findings, will allow analysts to observe and anticipate trends in consumer behavior at a global level.

The countries chosen for the initial Greendex survey represent 55 percent of the world's population in regions using 75 percent of the energy humans consumed in 2007. Greendex findings placed consumers in the United States in last place overall, with last-place finishes in three of the four areas of consumer behavior surveyed. U.S. consumers are sort of an elephant in the room, making few of the best green lifestyle choices despite several years of media attention to environmental concerns. Consumers in Canada placed second to last overall, while those in Brazil and India took the top spots, reflecting consumer behaviors that have the least negative impact on the world's environment.

To ensure that no demographic groups were overrepresented in this quantitative study of 14,000 consumers, quota caps were set for education, age, and gender. First, respondents were asked a series of questions about their daily lives and habits, and then questions broadened to opinions and knowledge about the environment and sustainable lifestyles. Respondents used Internet access to complete surveys, either in their homes or in public access points.

The data for each country were then weighted according to the latest census data to reflect the demographic profile of each country. Given the quotas and the weighting factors, the populations surveyed can be described as representative cross-sections of consumers in each country who have access to the Internet. Because of the methodology and the focus of research, survey respondents are referred to as "consumers," not to be equated with "citizens" or "individuals."

The Greendex distinguishes between behavior that consumers can change (for example, what they eat) and conditions that they cannot change (the need for heating in temperate climates). Greendex results arise from a complex calculation of 65 different variables; of all the variables involved, 60 percent are choice-driven.

Greendex 2008 represents the first of an annual survey. By providing individuals with a way to compare their own consumption patterns with a set of global reference points, the National Geographic Society hopes to increase awareness and encourage environmentally sustainable choices around the world.

Who Cares?

Consumers reported they are both increasingly affected and motivated by environmental problems, especially in large developing countries. Though their lifestyle options may be limited, this sense of responsibility often fosters a desire to take action for environmentally friendly options whenever possible.

When presented with the statement "I am very concerned about environmental problems," more than half of the consumers questioned in all 14 countries—57 percent—said they either "Agree" or "Strongly agree." Brazilians are the most unified in this regard, with 74 percent echoing their accord in this way. Even in Germany and the United Kingdom, where respondents were least likely to agree with the statement, the numbers run close to half, with survey responses indicating that 43 percent and 45 percent, respectively, of respondents "Agree" or "Strongly agree" that environmental problems present a concern.

To those who suspect that "going green" is simply a passing phase, the Greendex report suggests otherwise. When surveyors asked respondents to rate the assertion: "The environmental movement is a passing fad," the average response indicates 62 percent of the respondents either "Disagree" or "Strongly disagree," and in both Brazil and Mexico people repudiated the idea that the movement is a "fad" at rates of 75 percent. As few as 6 percent of consumers in Japan think of environmental concerns as a temporary issue.

Not surprisingly, it follows that a majority of those who took the Greendex survey agree that as individual members of a society, consumers can, and should, take an active role. Close to half of Mexican consumers surveyed "Strongly agreed" that to improve the environment for future generations, "we will need to consume a lot less." Across the board, 55 percent of those queried said they either "Agreed" or "Strongly agreed" with that statement. Only 13 percent marked "Disagree" or "Strongly disagree."

TAKING OWNERSHIP A number of factors other than consumer choices come into play, now and in the future, regarding consumption behaviors and their impact on the planet—climate, culture, regulatory frameworks, economic development—but the focus of Greendex research is strictly on consumer behavior. Few people across the countries surveyed said they believe that either their governments or companies are performing well on the environment; differences on this measure are often a reflection of the realities of institutional and governmental commitment to environmental protection and improvement. Around the globe, however, consumers are assuming some ownership of environmental problems. They feel empowered as individuals and are willing to make changes in their habits of consumption.

CONSUMER RESPONSE TO THIS STATEMENT:

"As a society, we will need to consume a lot less to improve the environment for future generations."

% of consumers in country

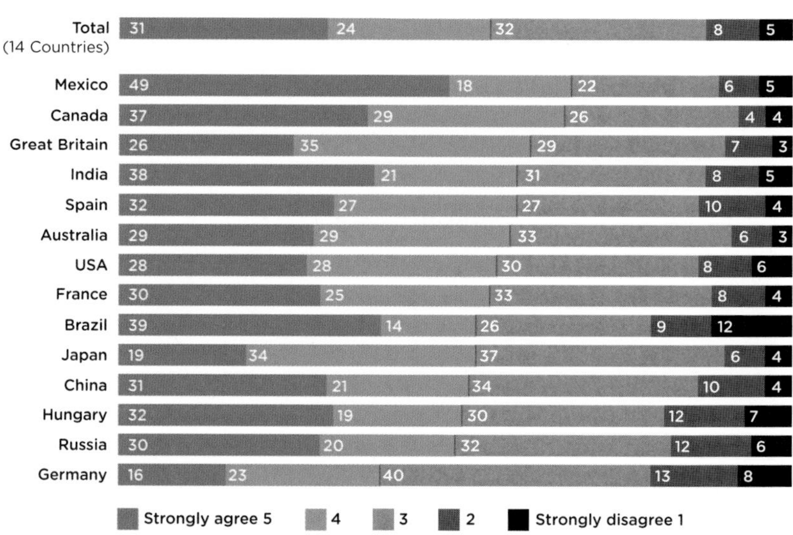

Findings from the first Greendex report have already revealed a significant difference between developing countries and the countries whose residents have already established a higher material standard of life. In Brazil, India, China, Mexico, and Hungary, consumers feel more responsible for environmental problems than those in developed countries and are more likely to agree to take action and believe it will make a difference. For example, Chinese and Indian respondents were more likely than others surveyed to say they have installed solar panels at their residence to heat water, and Indian respondents were more likely than others to say they have installed solar panels to generate electricity—choices that aid the environment. Consumers in all five countries at the top of the Greendex chart were also more likely to say they plan to make energy-saving changes, such as installing insulation and thermal windows.

WILL THOSE HABITS LAST? But Greendex researchers are also quick to point out that low consumption patterns now do not guarantee an environmentally sustainable way of life in the future in some of the same places. The strength and growth rate of emerging markets challenge residents of those regions to maintain good environmental choices even while their material desires climb with increasing rates of economic development. Smart development is essential, as is change on the part of developed nations.

For example, survey results show the transportation gap between rich and poor countries is beginning to narrow: Compared with the year before, more consumers in Brazil, China, India, Mexico, and Russia are driving alone in a vehicle. Chinese and Indian residents surveyed said they are flying more frequently and bicycling less, and more than a third of respondents in these countries said owning a big house is a very important goal in their life, reflecting a thirst for increased consumption. Survey results suggest a growing belief that people in all countries should have the same standard of living as that of the wealthiest countries—and that more are adopting sustainable consumer practices.

Housing

Of the four major components the Greendex survey used—housing, transportation, food, and goods—the greatest opportunity for improving sustainability rankings lies within housing options.

An old English saying suggests that "a man's home is his castle," but in a world of soaring energy costs, castles typically require king-size fortunes—and not just because of furnaces and air conditioners. Using 24 variables, Greendex 2008 calculated a respondent's sustainability rating for housing. The questions examined:

- ✓ The fuel sources used for heating and cooling purposes
- ✓ The size of the residence and the ratio of that size to the number of people living in the house
- ✓ The way in which water was heated and the variations in the type of equipment being used
- ✓ The type of construction and upgrades used to trap and maintain that hot or cold air (or water)
- ✓ The energy efficiency ratings of major appliances used in the home
- ✓ The amount of water usage

It's not likely that residents of the United Kingdom, the United States, Australia, and Canada—the four countries surveyed with the highest number of rooms in their primary residences—would be inclined to remove any of their rooms when remodeling just to become more environmentally healthy consumers. But efficiency upgrades to windows, thermostats, water heaters, and insulation all make important contributions toward reducing the amount of energy in a family home. Changing the proportion between the number of people living in a house and the size of the house is another way to gain a better Greendex score in this category.

If you fall into the highest category—nine or more rooms per household—you are part of the smallest percentage reporting globally: Only 8 percent of respondents fell in this category for 2008. Some choices can temper the negative impact of a large house footprint; you can plan to reduce energy usage in other ways. People around the globe often are doing just that—sometimes because of cultural and geographical considerations.

SOME LIKE IT HOT Japanese residences received low ratings in the survey, partly due to the use of oil for home heating; Chinese homes are frequently heated with coal, which taken alone, would give them a low rating, too. Other energy-saving factors however, including their relatively small per capita home size, helped Chinese consumers gain a fourth highest ranking for housing sustainability. Consumers in Brazil also earned some of the highest marks for housing. Some of that result can be attributed to small residence size, a widespread use of on-demand water heaters rather than tank heaters, and a willingness of high numbers of users to avail themselves of renewable electricity resources. Brazilian homes typically (83 percent) offer fewer than four rooms, and 80 percent of Hungarian homes fall in the same category. But whereas 69 percent of Brazilian respondents reported always washing laundry in cold water to save energy, only 27 percent of Hungarians reported always using cold water. A majority of Australians have homes of seven or more rooms—an environmentally costly choice that must be factored in with more positive choices, like doing laundry in cold water 62 percent of the time.

TRANSPORTATION People are on the move, whether by automobile in Australia, bicycle in Brazil, or jet from Japan to the United States. Self-powered options like walking or cycling are the kindest to the environment, but other choices—decreasing the distance from home to work or driving a smaller vehicle—can reduce the impact of a daily commute.

When Greendex 2008 surveyors examined the transportation habits of their internationally diverse travelers, they used 17 different variables to create a scaled ranking. Those variables measured different aspects of the factors listed below. Look the items over and consider how your own choices for getting from point A to point B are affecting the environment:

- ✓ Driving
- ✓ Driving alone
- ✓ Owning motorized vehicles
- ✓ Size of vehicle driven
- ✓ Distance vehicle driven
- ✓ Owning an ultra-low-emissions vehicle (ULEV) or hybrid
- ✓ Traveling by air
- ✓ Using public transit
- ✓ Taking trains
- ✓ Riding a bicycle
- ✓ Walking
- ✓ Location of residence relative to primary destination

THE LEADERS AND THE LOSERS Consumers in China—a large and heavily populated country—came out with the most sustainable score overall for transportation choices, a result reflecting patterns of sharing the drive, using public transportation more frequently, or choosing the two-legged and two-wheeled means of getting around: walking and bicycling.

More than half the Russian consumers polled for Greendex—53 percent—declared they used public transportation "every day or most days." Fully 41 percent of Chinese respondents report using public transportation every day or most days, a figure in stark contrast to the 5 percent of U.S. residents who claim they do. The disparity between consumers in the three North American countries sampled—the United States, Mexico, and Canada—illustrates that transportation patterns are influenced by more than just large open spaces, a geographic feature common to all three. More than a third of Mexicans surveyed report walking or bicycling "all of the time," compared with a quarter of Canadians and only 14 percent of U.S. consumers. More than four in ten, or 43 percent, of Mexicans say they use public transportation, compared with their neighbors to the north: Only 16 percent of Canadians and a mere 5 percent of Americans regularly use some form of public transportation.

MY FRIENDS ALL DRIVE PORSCHES The Greendex survey is well positioned to begin evaluating changing habits by tracking the answers to many of these same questions in 2009, 2010, and beyond. Already the answers from some respondents in emerging economies where the standards of a higher quality lifestyle are constantly changing suggest that owning a luxury car or a larger home is an increasingly important goal for families whose fortunes are on the rise.

Food Consumption

When we are young children, our food choices are largely limited to what our parents feed us. As adults in charge of shopping and cooking and feeding ourselves, we can make conscious decisions to prepare meals that help sustain not only our health but that of the planet, too. But habits and convenience are often more likely to guide our grocery carts.

Though bananas are a delightfully recognizable, easy-to-eat, and commonplace piece of produce in most American fruit bowls, it's safe to say they are rarely grown locally in the lower 48—or the upper 49th, for that matter. The same principle applies to lots of things we love to pile on our plates: Florida oranges, northern blueberries, seafood, fresh tomatoes year-round. So the call to buy and eat locally produced foods is a tough one to heed for many who take pride in enjoying menus from all around the world, and seasonal fruits and vegetables no matter what month. But two of the consumer populations in the Greendex survey that ranked high—Indian and Chinese consumers, who ranked first and fourth, respectively—did so in part because of their tendency to eat locally grown foods. Almost 50 percent of consumers queried in those populous nations reported eating local foods daily. The ratio jumps to the three-quarters mark when the category of "several times per week" is included.

PURCHASING POWER The same purchasing patterns show up in eating habits as in transportation. Consumer demand for locally produced foods is strong globally, but in those countries where purchasing power is strong, it will be harder to produce sustainable consumption without behavioral changes. Japanese and American food profiles show their residents have the least sustainable eating habits in the Greendex survey. Americans are the least likely of respondents to report consuming organic, natural, or locally grown foods. Also, U.S. residents report frequent meals that include beef, which ranks poorly in the sustainability category.

The British, French, Japanese, and U.S. consumers end up in the bottom of the barrel in this category, with only 5 percent eating locally grown items on a daily basis. In the United States, 49 percent of the respondents reported eating locally grown foods as infrequently as two or fewer times in a month. This will be a score to watch in future Greendex surveys, as farmers markets grow in popularity and supermarkets begin to stock more products from their immediate neighbors instead of—or at least in addition to—more far-flung suppliers.

Other variables that helped Greendex 2008 rank the sustainability of diets from around the world include:

- ✓ How often foods were grown or raised at home (i.e., not just locally produced)
- ✓ How often fruits and vegetables were part of a meal
- ✓ The frequency of including beef in diets
- ✓ The frequency of including seafood or fish in diets
- ✓ The frequency of including chicken in diets
- ✓ How often bottled water was consumed

WHERE'S THE BEEF? Brazil is one of the world's primary exporters of beef, so it should come as no surprise that the highest percentage of consumers eat beef on a daily basis—16 percent. This is more than three times the percentage of daily meat eating of the Chinese, the next highest consumers at 5 percent. Just over one in three consumers surveyed in the United States reported eating beef several times a week, and in fact, close to or more than one-third of respondents in 7 of the 14 countries included in Greendex 2008 said they eat beef several times a week. Just calculating the cost of water needed to grow the feed that a cow eats before becoming a source for burgers and steaks, beef eating takes a greater toll on our natural resources than eating fruits, vegetables, and grains.

Responses in this category that came from those living in India represent a distinctively different pattern, with 72 percent of consumers reporting that they "never" eat beef at all—a cultural phenomenon with its origins in religion, politics, and tradition.

SEAFOOD DILEMMA A common mantra offered the grieving party after an unpleasant breakup is "There's plenty of fish in the sea." Unfortunately, the adage is losing its relevance as habitat destruction and increasing consumption of seafood by a growing world population diminish many of the ocean's species, especially the larger fish we enjoy such as tuna, cod, and halibut. Overfishing is decimating what had previously been a renewable resource. While many reach for fish over beef for its health benefits, the trend toward eating more fish and seafood actually holds the potential for causing great risk to the world's oceans. For that reason, the prominence of fish and seafood on consumer menus played a role in our assessment of each nation's consumer sustainability quotient.

A majority of consumers in Japan and China eat fish and seafood daily, while consumers in Hungary eat the least: Only 9 percent of respondents there eat fish and seafood every day.

NO GENIES IN THESE BOTTLES When it comes to choosing the safest and most environmentally friendly way to acquire drinking water in the 21st century, it's clear the choices have become much tougher. Tap water may contain contaminants from old pipes, inadequate water treatment facilities, or bacteria-laden well water. Plastic bottled water creates environmental havoc because of the petroleum products needed to create the bottles, fill them, and transport them. The waste generated when consumers don't recycle the bottles is worse yet.

Water filters help consumers maintain individual control over their drinking water and don't add nearly the amount of cost per gallon that bottled water does. Pressure from consumers will raise the problem to an institutional and governmental level. In those places where tap water is not safe for drinking, a better long-term solution is to improve the municipal water system rather than to ship in more bottled water. This is one of those areas in which it would be better for the future of the planet if developing countries took the lead, finding ways to improve their water infrastructure rather than following the pattern in developed countries, where consumption of bottled water has risen too high and needs to be curtailed.

Survey results show 72 percent of German consumers—twice the international average—using bottled water daily, with only 2 percent reporting that they never use it. U.S. consumers are in the middle range but tilting toward more bottled-water purchases than not—36 percent of consumers in the States drink it daily. Only 15 percent said "Never." Among Canadians and the Japanese, the number of consumers who reported using bottled water nearly equals the number who said they do not. This is another area of high consumer choice that bears watching in future surveys.

Goods

Consumerism—it's everywhere you turn. Our streets are lined with stores. Our drawers filled with clothes. Our garages filled with almost everything but cars. Are we being as choosy as we should be when it comes to the things we buy, how they are packaged, and how often we replace them rather than repair them?

Think about it. The CD comes in a hard plastic shell, covered with another transparent wrapper, and the whole thing goes in a bag to get transported home. The clerk surrounds your new shirt in tissue paper and provides an oversize bag emblazoned with a logo and plastic handles, even though the shirt would fit in the bag with the CD.

Six disposable razors cost the same as one with refillable blades. The coffeepot is crusty and hard to clean; new ones are on sale. If you do buy the new one, do you toss the old one, put it in a yard sale, or donate it to a charity organization? Is there one TV per person at your house? More than one? What about computers?

THE GOODS, THE BADS, AND THE UGLIES The fourth major category in the Greendex survey queried international consumers about purchasing patterns, everything from everyday purchases to big-ticket items. Before you rush to judge consumers in Hungary or Mexico, where fewer than half of the consumers note they recycle regularly, think about the following variables in your own shopping habits.

Do you:

- ✓ Purchase (or avoid purchasing) specific products for environmental reasons?
- ✓ Avoid products with excessive packaging?
- ✓ Buy reusable products instead of disposable ones?
- ✓ Willingly pay a higher price for an item with environmental pluses?
- ✓ Buy used items rather than new ones at times?
- ✓ Try to repair your belongings rather than just buy new ones?
- ✓ Have more than one television or personal computer per person in your home?
- ✓ Have a garage or backyard full of recreational vehicles, lawnmowers, or other small engine-powered devices?

Greendex 2008 found that of the 14 countries' residents interviewed, Canadian and Australian, British, and German consumers were the strongest recyclers, in that order, with more than half surveyed noting they did so "all of the time." More than two-thirds of Russians said they do not recycle, a score that puts them at the bottom of 2008's ranking in the recycling category. Recycling behavior often indicates as much about institutions and governments as it does about consumers: If there are no community recycling programs, it's a harder habit to establish.

Consumers in China, India, and Brazil decisively top the goods ranking, thanks to a widespread preference for green products paired with ownership of relatively few appliances and expensive electronic devices. The Japanese, too, tend to own a modest number of "big-ticket" items and much prefer to purchase reusable items rather than disposable ones.

Only 8 percent of Mexico's respondents own one or more dishwashers, while 68 and 71 percent, repectively, of Americans and Germans do. The Greendex report concludes that consumers in the United States rank last in the ratings of goods purchasing patterns among all 14 countries because of "low levels of avoidance of environmentally unfriendly products and excessive packaging, infrequent selection of green products and a high number of televisions and dishwashers in the typical American household."

2008 AND COUNTING Each of the four indicators—housing, transportation, food, and goods—were summed up for consumers in each of the 14 surveyed countries. Consumers in the United States and Canada scored at the bottom when Greendex results were tallied: Despite information and conscience, North American lifestyles can make sustainable practices a challenge.

Although the survey found encouraging signs that individuals in all the surveyed countries feel empowered when it comes to the environment and are taking some action in their daily lives to reduce consumption and waste, it also found that those in developing countries are the most concerned, and that the behavior and personal choices of consumers in developing countries are more environmentally friendly than those in developed countries.

CONSUMER GREENDEX OVERALL RANKINGS

FOR BETTER OR FOR WORSE Consumers in developing countries feel more responsible for environmental problems than those in developed countries, and six in ten people in developing countries reported that environmental problems are negatively affecting their health—twice as many as in most developed countries. Moreover, consumers in developing countries said they feel strongest that global warming will worsen their way of life in their lifetime; are the most engaged when it comes to talking and listening about the environment; reported that they feel the most guilt about their environmental impact; and are willing to do the most to minimize that impact. The concern of people in developing countries is reflected in their behavior. They are more likely to:

- ✓ Live in smaller residences
- ✓ Prefer green products and own relatively few appliances or expensive electronic devices
- ✓ Walk, cycle, or use public transportation, and choose to live close to their most common destination.

By contrast, consumers in developed countries, who have more environmentally friendly options to choose from, often don't make those choices. Instead, they:

- ✓ Have larger homes and are more likely to have air-conditioning.
- ✓ Own more cars, drive alone, and use public transportation infrequently
- ✓ Are least likely to buy environmentally friendly products and to avoid environmentally unfriendly products

U.S. consumers scored worse than those in any other country, developing or developed, on housing, transportation, and goods. They are by far the least likely to use public transportation, to walk or bike to their destinations, or to eat locally grown foods. They have among the largest average residence size in the survey. Only 15 percent said they minimize their use of fresh water.

Without questioning why individuals choose to be more "green," the survey concludes that on average, individual consumers in developing countries are affecting our environment less than the average consumer in wealthy countries. Nevertheless, all measurable behaviors have environmental impacts, and individuals can make conscious choices at almost every turn to change their behaviors for the betterment—or the detriment—of our environment.

WHAT DO YOU KNOW?

Can you do better than the average respondent on the knowledge portion of the 2008 survey? In addition to the questions used to calculate their Greendex score, survey participants were asked to answer a series of multiple-choice questions to gauge their overall environmental knowledge. Across the 14 countries, the quiz-takers answered fewer than half the questions correctly. British respondents, followed by Germans, displayed the highest average number of correct answers; consumers surveyed in Brazil, China, Russia, and India demonstrated the lowest average knowledge levels. French and U.S. respondents also tended to fail the quiz.

1. What is the primary cause of recently measured increases in the Earth's temperature?
   - ☐ The atmospheric "ozone hole"
   - ☐ Increased output from the sun
   - ☐ Increased levels of carbon dioxide gas in the atmosphere
   - ☐ Changes in the Earth's orbit

2. In general, which fuel produces the most carbon dioxide gas when burned?
   - ☐ Wood
   - ☐ Oil
   - ☐ Natural gas
   - ☐ Coal

3. What is the projected population of the Earth in the year 2050?
   - ☐ Approximately 3.3 billion
   - ☐ Approximately 6.3 billion
   - ☐ Approximately 9.3 billion
   - ☐ Approximately 12.3 billion

4. Approximately what percentage of the world's mammals do experts believe are currently threatened with extinction?
   - ☐ 2 percent
   - ☐ 5 percent
   - ☐ 10 percent
   - ☐ 25 percent

5. What is nearly all plastic originally made from?
   - ☐ Crude oil
   - ☐ Rubber
   - ☐ Silicon
   - ☐ Corn

6. Which one of the following foods requires the most water to grow or raise for a typical serving?
   - ☐ Melons
   - ☐ Cereal grains
   - ☐ Beef
   - ☐ Leafy vegetables such as lettuce or spinach

CORRECT ANSWERS:

1. Increased levels of carbon dioxide gas in the atmosphere
2. Coal
3. Approximately 9.3 billion
4. 25 percent
5. Crude oil
6. Beef

How did you do? If you got four or more answers correct, you're doing better than most! When Greendex researchers posed these questions, the average number of correct answers was just over three in 8 out of the 14 countries surveyed. The United Kingdom and Germany scored highest, with Canada, Japan, and Mexico close behind. The United States ranked tenth in knowledge of environmental issues, with respondents averaging 2.73 correct answers to the 6 questions.

Knowledge is a key component in the commitment to making choices with the future of the planet Earth in mind. Beginning with this book and the Green Guide—both online and in print—and continuing to the many great resources listed in the next few pages, you can make a difference by reading, sharing ideas, and spreading the word. Every piece of information, every decision to make the world a little greener, will make a difference.

Take an online quiz and find out more about Greendex 2008 at http://nationalgeographic.com/greendex.

Take Action

You can adopt more sustainable consumption habits and raise your potential Greendex scores by doing any of the following:

- ✓ Eat less meat, more locally produced foods, and more fruits and vegetables; drink less bottled water.
- ✓ Improve the energy efficiency of their residences by sealing drafts, upgrading windows, and installing more efficient water heaters and other appliances.
- ✓ Keep the settings for home heating or cooling at levels that require less energy.
- ✓ Use only cold water to wash laundry and minimize water use overall.
- ✓ Drive alone less often and use car pools whenever possible.
- ✓ Drive less overall.
- ✓ Drive smaller or more fuel-efficient vehicles.
- ✓ Own fewer vehicles per household member.
- ✓ Walk or ride a bicycle when distance allows.
- ✓ Maximize the life span of household items and minimize disposal.
- ✓ Avoid environmentally harmful products and packaging and seek environmentally friendly alternatives.
- ✓ Recycle when possible.
- ✓ Use reusable shopping bags instead of accepting new ones.
- ✓ Have fewer televisions and personal computers per household member.

GLOSSARY

Acrylamide Acrylamide is a chemical produced during the baking, frying, and grilling of almost all carbohydrate-rich foods, forming chemically during the final stages of baking or frying.

Biodiesel Biodiesel is a diesel-equivalent processed fuel made from biological sources that can be used in unmodified diesel-engine vehicles. It's a renewable fuel that can be manufactured from algae, vegetable oils, animal fats, or recycled restaurant greases.

Carbon footprint A carbon footprint is the calculation of an individual's, factory's, or other entity's impact on the environment, measured as the total amount of carbon dioxide produced. See Greenhouse gases.

Carbon offsets Carbon offsetting is the act of mitigating the greenhouse gas emissions produced by your activities, from transportation to daily energy use, through payment of a fee to fund projects that reduce overall greenhouse gas emissions.

CFL Compact fluorescent lightbulbs (CFLs) are designed for home and office settings, with the advantage of using less power and having a longer life than conventional incandescent bulbs, hence being a more environmentally wise lighting solution.

CRT Cathode ray tubes (CRTs) are made of glass and used in electronics such as computer and television monitors to create a visual display. These tubes contain hazardous constituents that can leak into the ground if the tube is broken at the landfill.

CSA Community-supported agriculture (CSA) programs are farms that sell shares of their harvest to local residents. Members are assessed a fixed fee that helps pay for seeds, equipment maintenance, and labor in exchange for weekly shares of the farm's bounty.

DEET A common ingredient in insect repellents, N, N-diethyl-m-toluamide (DEET) is an eye irritant and may cause blisters or rashes; it has also been associated with more severe neurological symptoms including lethargy, confusion, disorientation, and mood swings. Non-DEET insect repellents are preferable, especially for children.

Dioxins Dioxins are organic compounds emitted during combustion, incineration, and various other industrial or chemical processes. They have been found hazardous to human health, even in minute amounts, and are believed to disturb human development, cause cancer, and affect the reproductive, immune, and endocrine systems.

EER The Energy Efficiency Ratio (EER) is a rating system for air conditioners that indicates how much heat is removed per hour for each watt of energy used. Heat is measured in British thermal units (Btu) and the rating is expressed in Btu per hour per watt.

Energy Star Run by the U.S. Environmental Protection Agency and Department of Energy as part of a national effort to reduce greenhouse gas emissions, the Energy Star program evaluates consumer products and buildings for their energy efficiency. Products meeting certain standards earn an Energy Star label.

EPEAT The Green Electronics Council's Electronic Product Environmental Assessment Tool (EPEAT) helps consumers review computers' environmental standards.

Ethanol Ethanol (or ethyl alcohol) can be used as a fuel. It can be manufactured from very common materials, such as corn, and can be mass-produced through the fermentation of sugars or the hydration of ethylene from petroleum and other sources.

E-waste Electronic waste refers to electronics that are no longer being used because they are broken, obsolete, or discarded. All electronic products will eventually become E-waste.

Fair trade Fair trade refers to products such as coffee, tea, and chocolate that are purchased directly from growers or their cooperatives. Fair trade importers ensure just business practices, including equitable pay, healthy workplaces, and environmental sustainability.

Formaldehyde Formaldehyde is an industrial chemical used to make other chemicals, building materials, and household products. A volatile organic compound, or "VOC," it vaporizes at normal room temperatures.

Fossil fuels So named because they are drawn from ancient underground deposits, fossil fuels include carbon-rich energy products such as coal, oil, gasoline, diesel, and natural gas. They are burned to generate power in many different applications, from electrical power plants to home furnaces to automobiles. When fossil fuels burn, they give off carbon dioxide, the primary greenhouse gas contributing to global warming.

GMO Genetically modified organisms (GMOs) are created by inserting a gene from one organism into another organism. This alters the recipient's genetic makeup to produce new and different traits, such as pest resistance or faster growth.

Greenhouse gases Greenhouse gases, which include carbon dioxide and methane primarily, trap heat in Earth's atmosphere. An increase in greenhouse gases is responsible for the so-called "greenhouse effect," a critical factor in global warming.

Heavy-metal dyes Heavy metals such as chromium and copper are commonly used to "fix" darker colors to cotton and other fabrics. While minute amounts of these elements are good for health, exposure to large quantities of any of them may cause acute or chronic toxicity.

HEPA High-efficiency particulate air (HEPA) filters are used in vacuum cleaners and air-handling systems in order to clean the air in residential and work settings. They are designed to trap particles as small as 0.3 micron.

HFCS High-fructose corn syrup (HFCS) is a modified form of regular corn syrup containing increased amounts of the sugar fructose. HFCS is made when cornstarch is treated with acids or enzymes, breaking down the starch into sugars. This process enhances sweetness and results in a syrup that dissolves at lower temperatures than unprocessed corn syrup.

Irradiation This process uses electron beams or radioactive substances to kill pathogens, retard sprouting or spoiling, and otherwise prolong transit time and shelf life in meat, eggs, grain, produce, and spices.

LEDs Light-emitting diodes, commonly called LEDs, are tiny lightbulbs that fit into an electrical circuit and are found in all kinds of household devices, from digital clocks to remote controls, watches, and appliances.

LEED LEED—an acronym that stands for Leadership in Energy and Environmental Design—is a voluntary rating system for commercial green design and construction and is becoming a nationally accepted benchmark for green buildings. Ratings reflect sustainable site development, water savings, energy efficiency, materials selection, and indoor environmental quality.

Low-VOC A label found on paints and finishes that indicates that a product contains low levels of volatile organic compounds (VOCs), as defined by the U.S. Environmental Protection Agency (EPA). See also VOCs.

Nanoparticles Mineral particles that have been fragmented to sizes below 100 nanometers; they are often used in sunscreens and mineral makeup products because they are less visible when applied to the skin.

Off-gas Off-gassing is the tendency of many chemicals to volatilize, or let off molecules in a gas form into the air. Many cleaning fluids, glues, and chemical treatments for building and upholstery materials have the tendency to off-gas, which means that some of the indwelling chemicals enter the air and may be inhaled. See also Low-VOC and VOCs.

Organophosphates Organophosphate insecticides are chemicals that disrupt the nervous system of insects, thus killing them. They are also toxic to animals and humans.

OVE Optimal Value Engineering (OVE) represents a coordinated effort to design, plan, and build in order to reduce the amount of lumber used in framing. Careful planning, redesign of certain elements, and use of alternative materials are key to the process.

Parabens A group of preservatives used in many kinds of toiletries and cosmetics, parabens demonstrate weak estrogenic effects in the body and may be linked to the development of breast cancer.

PBDEs Polybrominated diphenyl ethers, or PBDEs, are commonly used in upholstered furniture as fire retardants, although they are not chemically bound to the polyurethane foam itself. Like dust, the PBDEs are easily released into the air and inhaled.

PCBs Polychlorinated biphenyls (PCBs) are industrial pollutants that can persist in waterways for decades. They are probable carcinogens that have also been found to affect that body's cognitive and immune systems. PCBs accumulate in fatty fish like salmon, as well as in oysters and other shellfish.

PCW Post-consumer waste (PCW) is the paper taken by consumers to the recycling center when they have finished using it. Sustainable paper products are labeled with the percentage of PCW that they contain. That number also indicates the amount of paper that has been kept out of landfills and put to reuse.

Perchloroethylene A commonly used dry cleaning solvent, perchloroethylene (or tetrachloro-ethylene) has been named a hazardous air pollutant by the EPA, while the International Agency for Research on Cancer calls it a probable human carcinogen.

Petrochemicals Petrochemicals are chemicals that are made when petroleum is broken down and its building blocks are combined with other chemicals to create everything from polyester to plumbing pipes to household cleaning products.

PFOA Perfluorooctanoic acid, or PFOA, is one of the synthetic chemicals known as perfluorochemicals, or PFCs. It is used to manufacture fluoropolymers, including Teflon, as well as many other products, including stain- and soil-resistant coatings for carpets and clothing and grease-resistant films for food packaging and microwave popcorn bags.

Photovoltaics Photovoltaic (PV) technology uses solar cells to convert sunlight into electricity. PV installations may be ground-mounted or integrated into the building structure, for instance on a roof.

Phthalates Phthalates are a class of hormone-disrupting chemicals commonly used as solvents and fixatives in fragrances.

Processed chlorine-free Conventional bleaching uses chlorine, harmful to health and the environment. Chlorine-free processing helps to avoid those hazards.

rBGH Recombinant bovine growth hormone (rBGH) is a genetically engineered hormone injected into dairy cows to increase their milk production. Laboratory research results suggest that it may be associated with several cancers and with the rise of antibiotic-resistant bacteria.

SPF A sunscreen's sun protection factor (SPF) represents how quickly exposed skin will burn while wearing the sunscreen, compared with going without. This rating system takes into account the product's ability to reduce UVB exposure, which causes sunburn, but not the product's ability to protect against deeper-penetrating UVA rays.

Sulfate This classification includes several types of surfactants commonly used in skin and hair cleansers. Used in addition to or in lieu of soap, sulfates help to break up dirt and oil, boosting the performance of cleansers.

Thatch Thatch is a layer of living and dead materials that builds up between the soil and green grass caused by excessive fertilization and watering.

Vermiculture Vermiculture is the careful farming of worms in order to harvest their castings, which represent an excellent natural fertilizer for lawns and gardens.

VOCs Volatile organic compounds (VOCs) are chemicals that contain carbon and hydrogen and that evaporate easily, emitted as gases from solids or liquids. They include methylene chloride, found in paint strippers and adhesive removers; benzene, found in tobacco smoke and auto exhaust; and perchloroethylene, widely used in dry-cleaning clothes. Many VOCs cause significant health damage if they are inhaled.

RESOURCES

GENERAL INFORMATION

Center for Neighborhood Technology
2125 W. North Ave.
Chicago, IL 60647
(773) 278-4800
www.cnt.org

Center for Science in the Public Interest
1875 Connecticut Ave. N.W.
Suite 300
Washington, DC 20009
(202) 332-9110
www.cspinet.org

Centers for Disease Control and Prevention
1600 Clifton Rd.
Atlanta, GA 30333
(404) 498-1515
(800) 311-3435
www.cdc.gov

Columbia Center for Children's Environmental Health
100 Haven Ave., Tower III, Suite 25F
New York, NY 10032
(212) 304-7280
www.mailman.hs.columbia.edu/ccceh

Conservation International
2011 Crystal Dr., Suite 500
Arlington, VA 22202
(800) 429-5660; (703) 341-2400
www.conservation.org

Earth 911
Global Alerts, LLC
14646 N. Kierland Blvd.
Scottsdale, AZ 85254
(480) 889-2650
earth911.org

Environmental Defense Fund
257 Park Ave. South
New York, NY 10010
(800) 684-3322; (212) 505-2100
www.edf.org

Environmental Protection Agency
Ariel Rios Building
1200 Pennsylvania Ave. N.W.
Washington, DC 20460
www.epa.gov

Environmental Working Group
1436 U St. N.W., Suite 100
Washington, DC 20009
(202) 667-6982
www.ewg.org

Forest Stewardship Council—U.S. (FSC-US)
11100 Wildlife Center Dr.
Suite 100
Reston, VA 20190
(703) 438-6401
www.fscus.org

Global Exchange
2017 Mission St., 2nd Floor
San Francisco, CA 94110
(415) 255-7296
www.globalexchange.org

Global Green
2218 Main St., 2nd Floor
Santa Monica, CA 90405
(310) 581-2700
www.globalgreen.org

Greener Choices
Consumers Union
101 Truman Ave.
Yonkers, NY 10703
(914) 378-2000
www.greenerchoices.org

Greenpeace
702 H St. N.W.
Washington, DC 20001
(800) 326-0959
www.greenpeace.org

Marine Aquarium Council
P.O. Box 235878
Honolulu, HI 96823
(808) 550-8217
www.aquariumcouncil.org

National Audubon Society
700 Broadway
New York, NY 10003
(212) 979-3000
www.audubon.org

National Institute of Environmental Health Sciences, U.S. Department of Health and Human Services
P.O. Box 12233, MD NH-10
Research Triangle Park, NC 27709
(919) 541-3345
www.niehs.nih.gov

National Institute for Occupational Safety and Health
395 E St. S.W.,
Suite 9200
Patriots Plaza Building
Washington, DC 20201
(800) 232-4636
www.cdc.gov/niosh

National Recycling Coalition
805 15th St. N.W.
Suite 425
Washington, DC 20005
(202) 789-1430
www.nrc-recycle.org

National Safety Council
1121 Spring Lake Dr.
Itasca, IL 60143-3201
(630) 285-1121
www.nsc.org

Natural Resources Defense Council
40 W. 20th St.
New York, NY 10011
(212) 727-2700
www.nrdc.org

New American Dream
6930 Carroll Ave., Suite 900
Takoma Park, MD 20912
(877) 683-7326
www.newdream.org

Rainforest Alliance
665 Broadway, Suite 500
New York, NY 10012
(212) 677-1900
www.rainforest-alliance.org

Sierra Club
85 Second St., 2nd Floor
San Francisco, CA 94105
(415) 977-5500
www.sierraclub.org

United States National Arboretum
3501 New York Ave. N.E.
Washington, DC 20002-1958
(202) 245-2726
www.usna.usda.gov

Washington Toxics Coalition
4649 Sunnyside Ave. North
Suite 540
Seattle, WA 98103
(206) 632-1545
www.watoxics.org/

Water Environment Research Foundation
635 Slaters La., Suite 300
Alexandria, VA 22314
(703) 684-2470
www.werf.org

Worldwatch Institute
1776 Massachusetts Ave. N.W.
Washington, DC 20036-1904
(202) 452-1999
www.worldwatch.org

FOOD & AGRICULTURE

Chefs Collaborative
89 South St., Lower Level
Boston, MA 02111
(617) 236-5200
www.chefscollaborative.org

Food Alliance
1829 N.E. Alberta, #5
Portland, OR 97211
(503) 493-1066
www.foodalliance.org

Food & Drug Administration (FDA)
5600 Fishers La.
Rockville, MD 20857-0001
(888) 463-6332
www.fda.gov

Green Restaurant Association
89 South St., Suite LL02
Boston, MA 02111
(858) 452-7378
www.dinegreen.com

International Federation of Organic Agriculture Movements
Charles-de-Gaulle-Str. 5
53113 Bonn, Germany
+49 (228) 92650-10
www.ifoam.org

Local Harvest
220 21st Ave.
Santa Cruz, CA 95062
(831) 475-8150
www.localharvest.org

Marine Stewardship Council
2110 N. Pacific St., Suite 102
Seattle, WA 98103
(206) 691-0188
www.msc.org

Monterey Bay Aquarium Seafood Watch
886 Cannery Row
Monterey, CA 93940
(831) 648-4800
www.montereybayaquarium.org/cr/seafoodwatch.asp

National Organic Program
Room 4008-South Building
1400 Independence Ave. S.W.
Washington, DC 20250-0020
(202) 720-3252
www.ams.usda.gov/NOP

National Pesticide Information Center
Oregon State University
333 Weniger Hall
Corvallis, OR 97331-6502
(800) 858-7378
www.npic.orst.edu

Pesticide Action Network North America (PANNA)
49 Powell St., Suite 500
San Francisco, CA 94102
(415) 981-1771
www.panna.org

CONSUMER PRODUCTS

Alliance for the Prudent Use of Antibiotics
75 Kneeland St.
Boston, MA 02111-1901
(617) 636-0966
www.apua.org

Art & Creative Materials Institute
P.O. Box 479
Hanson, MA 02341-0479
(781) 293-4100
www.acminet.org

Campaign for Safe Cosmetics
www.safecosmetics.org

Clean Clothes Campaign
Postbus 11584
1001 GN Amsterdam
The Netherlands
+31-20-412-2785
www.cleanclothes.org

Coalition for Consumer Information on Cosmetics
P.O. Box 56537
Philadelphia, PA 19111
(888) 546-2242
www.leapingbunny.org

Consumer Product Safety Commission
4330 East West Hwy.
Bethesda, MD 20814
(301) 504-7923

Consumers Union
101 Truman Ave.
Yonkers, NY 10703-1057
(914) 378-2000
www.consumersunion.org

Cosmetic Ingredient Review
1101 17th St. N.W., Suite 412
Washington DC 20036-4702
(202) 331-0651
www.cir-safety.org

Green Electronics Council
121 S.W. Salmon St., Suite 210
Portland, OR 97204
(503) 279-9383
www.greenelectronicscouncil.org

Organic Consumers Association
6771 South Silver Hill Dr.
Finland, MN 55603
(218) 226-4164
www.organicconsumers.org

Organic Trade Association
P.O. Box 547
Greenfield, MA 01302
(413) 774-7511
www.ota.com

Skin Cancer Foundation
149 Madison Ave.
Suite 901
New York, NY 10016
www.skincancer.org

Skin Deep
Environmental Working Group
1436 U St. N.W., Suite 100
Washington, DC 20009
(202) 667-6982
www.cosmeticsdatabase.com

Sweatshop Watch
1250 S. Los Angeles St.
Suite 212
Los Angeles, CA 90015
(213) 748-5945
www.sweatshopwatch.org

BUILDING METHODS & MATERIALS

Builders' Websource
570 El Camino Real
Redwood City, CA 94063-1262
(888) 888-3111
www.builderswebsource.com

Carpet and Rug Institute
P.O. Box 2048
Dalton, GA 30722-2048
(706) 278-3176
www.carpet-rug.org

Efficient Windows Collaborative
Alliance to Save Energy
1850 M St. N.W., Suite 600
Washington, DC 20036
(202) 530-2254
www.efficientwindows.org

Energy and Environmental
Building Association
6520 Edenvale Blvd., Suite 112
Eden Prairie, MN 55346
(952) 881-1098
www.eeba.org

Green Roofs
3449 Lakewind Way
Alpharetta, GA 30005
(770) 772-7334
www.greenroofs.com

Healthy Building Network
Institute for Local Self-Reliance
927 15th St. N.W., 4th Floor
Washington, DC 20005
(202) 898-1610
www.healthybuilding.net

Healthy House Institute
13998 West Hartford Dr.
Boise, ID 83713
(208) 938-3137
www.healthyhouseinstitute.com

National Association
of Home Builders
1201 15th St. N.W.
Washington, DC 20005
(800) 368-5242; (202) 266-8200
www.nahb.org

Northwest Ecobuilding Guild
P.O. Box 58530
Seattle, WA 98138
(206) 575-2222
www.ecobuilding.org

The Shelter Institute
873 Rte. 1
Woolwich, ME 04579
(207) 442-7938
www.shelterinstitute.com

Solar Living Institute
13771 S. Hwy. 101
P.O. Box 836
Hopland, CA 95449
(707) 744-2017
www.solarliving.org

Sustainable Forestry Initiative
1600 Wilson Blvd., Suite 810
Arlington, VA 22209
(703) 875-9500
www.sfiprogram.org

U.S. Green Building Council
1800 Massachusetts Ave. N.W.
Suite 300
Washington, DC 20036
(800) 795-1747
www.usgbc.org

ENERGY & TRANSPORTATION

Alliance to Save Energy
1850 M St. N.W., Suite 600
Washington, DC 20036
(202) 857-0666
www.ase.org

American Council for an Energy-Efficient Economy
1001 Connecticut Ave. N.W.
Suite 801
Washington, DC 20036
(202) 429-8873
www.aceee.org

American Public Transportation Association
1666 K St., N.W., Suite 1100
Washington, DC 20006
(202) 496-4800
www.apta.com

Association of Home Appliance Manufacturers
1111 19th St. N.W.
Suite 402
Washington, DC 20036
(202) 872-5955
www.aham.org

Center for Sustainable Destinations
1145 17th St. N.W.
Washington, DC 20036-4688
(202) 828-8045
www.nationalgeographic.com/travel/sustainable

Coalition for Clean Air
811 West Seventh St., Suite 1100
Los Angeles, CA 90017
(213) 630-1192
www.coalitionforcleanair.org

Consortium for Energy Efficiency
98 N. Washington St., Suite 101
Boston MA 02114-1918
(617) 589-3949
www.cee1.org

ECO·CELL
2701 Lindsay Ave.
Louisville, KY 40206
(888) 326-3357; (502) 896-4398
www.eco-cell.org

Energy Efficiency and Renewable Energy
U.S. Department of Energy
1000 Independence Ave. S.W.
Washington, DC 20585
(877) 337-3463
www.eere.energy.gov

Energy Information Administration
1000 Independence Ave. S.W.
Washington, DC 20585
(202) 586-8800
www.eia.doe.gov

Energy Star Program
1200 Pennsylvania Ave. N.W.
Washington, DC 20460
(888) 782-7937
www.energystar.gov

International Ecotourism Society
1333 H St. N.W., Suite 300E
Washington, DC 20005
(202) 347-9203
www.ecotourism.org

League of American Bicyclists
1612 K St. N.W., Suite 800
Washington, DC 20006-2850
(202) 822-1333
www.bikeleague.org

My Green Electronics
Consumer Electronics Association
2500 Wilson Blvd.
Arlington, VA 22201-3834
(866) 858-1555
www.mygreenelectronics.org

National Biodiesel Board
3337A Emerald La.
P.O. Box 104898
Jefferson City, MO 65110
(573) 635-3893
www.biodiesel.org

National Energy Assistance Directors' Association
1615 M St. N.W.,
Suite 800
Washington, DC 20036
(202) 237-5199
www.neada.org

National Highway Traffic Safety Administration
1200 New Jersey Ave. S.E.
Washington, DC 20590
(888) 327-4236
www.nhtsa.dot.gov

National Pollution Prevention Roundtable
11 Dupont Circle N.W., Suite 201
Washington, DC 20036
(202) 299-9701
www.p2.org

Rechargeable Battery Recycling Corporation
1000 Parkwood Circle, Suite 450
Atlanta, GA 30339
(678) 419-9990
www.rbrc.org

Rocky Mountain Institute
1820 Folsom St.
Boulder, CO 80302
(303) 245-1003
www.rmi.org

Travelers' Philanthropy
1333 H St. N.W. Suite 300 East Tower
Washington, DC 20005
(202) 347-9203
www.travelersphilanthropy.org

SOCIAL & ANIMAL ISSUES

Adopt a Species, National Zoo
3001 Connecticut Ave. N.W.
Washington, DC 20008
(202) 633-4800
nationalzoo.si.edu/Support/AdoptSpecies

Alternative Gifts International
P.O. Box 3810
Wichita, KS 67201-3810
(800) 842-2243
www.altgifts.org

American Society for the Prevention of Cruelty to Animals
424 E. 92nd St.
New York, NY 10128-6804
(212) 876-7700
www.aspca.org

Born Free USA United with API
1122 S St.
Sacramento, CA 95811
(916) 447-3085
www.api4animals.org

Caribbean Conservation Corporation and Sea Turtle Survival League
4424 N.W. 13th St., Suite B-11
Gainesville, FL 32609
(800) 678-7853; (352) 373-6441
www.cccturtle.org

Center for Veterinary Medicine
7519 Standish Pl.
Rockville, MD 20855-0001
(240) 276-9300
www.fda.gov/cvm

Convention on International Trade in Endangered Species International Environment House
11 Chemin des Anémones
CH-1219 Châtelaine, Geneva
Switzerland
+41-(0)22-917-81-39
www.cites.org

Dian Fossey Gorilla Fund International
800 Cherokee Ave. S.E.
Atlanta, GA 30315-1440
(800) 851-0203; (404) 624-5881
www.gorillafund.org

Eatwild
P.O. Box 7321, Tacoma, WA 98417
(866) 453-8489
www.eatwild.com

Fair Trade Federation
3025 Fourth St. N.E.
Washington, DC 20017-1102
(202) 636-3547
www.fairtradefederation.org

Fauna & Flora International
1720 N St., N.W.
Washington, DC 20036
(202) 375-7766
www.fauna-flora.org

Humane Farm Animal Care
P.O. Box 727
Herndon, VA 20172
(703) 435-3883
www.certifiedhumane.com

Humane Society of the United States
2100 L St. N.W.
Washington, DC 20037
(202) 452-1100
www.hsus.org

National Wildlife Federation
11100 Wildlife Center Dr.
Reston, VA 20190
(800) 822-9919
www.nwf.org

People for the Ethical Treatment of Animals (PETA)
501 Front St.
Norfolk, VA 23510
(757) 622-7382
www.peta.org

RugMark
2001 S St. N.W., Suite 430
Washington, DC 20009
(202) 234-9050
www.rugmark.org

TransFair USA
1500 Broadway, Suite 400
Oakland, CA 94612
(510) 663-5260
www.transfairusa.org

Wildlife Adoption Center
Defenders of Wildlife
1130 17th St. N.W.
Washington, DC 20036
(800) 385-9712
www.WildlifeAdoption.org

Ableman, Michael. *Fields of Plenty: A Farmer's Journey in Search of Real Food and the People Who Grow It.* Chronicle Books, 2005.

___________. *From the Good Earth: A Celebration of Growing Food Around the World.* Harry N. Abrams, Inc., 1993.

___________. *On Good Land: The Autobiography of an Urban Farm.* Chronicle Books, 1998.

Arvigo, Rosita, and Nadine Epstein. *Rainforest Home Remedies: The Maya Way to Heal Your Body and Replenish Your Soul.* HarperOne, 2001.

Berthold Bond, Annie. *Better Basics for the Home: Simple Solutions for Less Toxic Living.* Three Rivers Press, 1999.

___________. *Clean & Green: The Complete Guide to Non-Toxic and Environmentally Safe Housekeeping.* Ceres Press, 1994.

___________. *The Green Kitchen Handbook: Practical Advice, References, & Sources for Transforming the Center of Your Home into a Healthy, Livable Place.* Harper Perennial, 1997.

___________. *Home Enlightenment: Practical, Earth-Friendly Advice for Creating a Nurturing, Healthy, and Toxin-Free Home and Lifestyle.* Rodale Press, 2008.

Brown, Lester R. *Eco-Economy: Building an Economy for the Earth.* W. W. Norton, 2001.

Clay, Jason. *World Agriculture and the Environment: A Commodity-by-Commodity Guide to Impacts and Practices.* Island Press, 2004.

Coperthwaite, William S. *A Handmade Life: In Search of Simplicity.* Chelsea Green Publishing, 2007.

David, Laurie. *Stop Global Warming: The Solution Is You!* Fulcrum Publishing, 2006.

Davis, Devra. *When Smoke Ran Like Water: Tales of Environmental Deception and the Battle Against Pollution.* Basic Books, 2004.

Davis, Rochelle. *Fresh Choices: More Than 100 Easy Recipes for Pure Food When You Can't Buy 100% Organic.* Rodale Books, 2004.

Diamond, Jared. *Collapse: How Societies Choose to Fail or Succeed.* Penguin Books, 2005.

Dolan, Deirdre, and Alexandra Zissu. *The Complete Organic Pregnancy.* HarperCollins, 2006.

Ehrlich, Gretel. *John Muir: Nature's Visionary.* National Geographic, 2000.

Erickson, Kim. *Drop-Dead Gorgeous: Protecting Yourself from the Hidden Dangers of Cosmetics.* Contemporary Books, Inc., 2002.

Fay, Mike, and Michael Nichols (photographs). *The Last Place on Earth: With Mike Fay's Megatransect Journals.* National Geographic, 2005.

Forbes, Alison, and Laura Forbes Carlin. *The Peaceful Nursery: Preparing a Home for Your Baby with Feng Shui.* Delta, 2006.

Francis, John. *Planetwalker.* National Geographic, 2008.

Gaynor, Dr. Mitchell. *Nurture Nature, Nurture Health: Your Health and the Environment.* Barbed Wire Publishing, 2005.

Goldbeck, Nikki, and David Goldbeck. *Healthy Highways: The Road Guide to Healthy Eating.* Ceres Press, 2004.

Gordon, Anita, and David Suzuki. *It's Matter of Survival.* HarperCollins, 1991.

Gore, Al. *An Inconvenient Truth.* Rodale Press, 2006.

Grant, Tim, and Gail Littlejohn. *Greening School Grounds: Creating Habitats for Learning.* New Society Publishers, 2001.

Gussow, Joan Dye. *This Organic Life: Confessions of a Suburban Homesteader.* Chelsea Green Publishing Company, 2001.

Halweil, Brian. *Eat Here: Homegrown Pleasures in a Global Supermarket.* W. W. Norton, 2004.

Harris, Lis. *Tilting at Mills: Green Dreams, Dirty Dealings, and the Corporate Squeeze.* Houghton Mifflin, 2003.

Heacox, Kim. *An American Idea: The Making of the National Parks.* National Geographic, 2001.

Helvarg, David. *Blue Frontier: Dispatches from America's Ocean Wilderness.* Sierra Club Books, 2006.

____________. *50 Ways to Save the Ocean.* Inner Ocean Publishing, 2006.

____________. *The War Against the Greens: The "Wise Use" Movement, the New Right, and the Browning of America.* Johnson Books, 2004.

Henson, Robert. *The Rough Guide to Climate Change.* Rough Guides, 2006.

Hollender, Jeffrey, Geoff Davis, Meika Hollender, and Reed Doyle. *Naturally Clean: The Seventh Generation Guide to Safe & Healthy, Non-Toxic Cleaning.* New Society Publishers, 2006.

Hollender, Jeffrey, and Stephen Fenichell. *What Matters Most: How a Small Group of Pioneers Is Teaching Social Responsibility to Big Business, and Why Big Business Is Listening.* Basic Books, 2005.

Jackson, Dana L., and Laura L. Jackson, eds. *The Farm as Natural Habitat: Reconnecting Food Systems with Ecosystems.* Island Press, 2002.

Johnston, David R., and Kim Master. *Green Remodeling: Changing the World One Room at a Time.* New Society Publishers, 2004.

Kerley, Barbara. *A Cool Drink of Water.* National Geographic, 2002.

Kerry, John, and Teresa Heinz Kerry. *This Moment on Earth: Today's New Environmentalists and Their Vision for the Future.* Public Affairs, 2007.

Kimbrell, Andrew, ed. *Fatal Harvest: The Tragedy of Industrial Agriculture.* Foundation for Deep Ecology, 2002.

Kolbert, Elizabeth. *Field Notes from a Catastrophe: Man, Nature, and Climate Change.* Bloomsbury Publishing, 2007.

Landrigan, Philip J., M.D., Herbert L. Needleman, M.D., and Mary M. Landrigan, M.P.A. *Raising Healthy Children in a Toxic World.* Rodale Press, 2002.

Liittschwager, David, and Susan Middleton. *Remains of a Rainbow: Rare Plants and Animals of Hawai'i.* National Geographic, 2003.

Linden, Eugene. *The Winds of Change: Climate, Weather, and the Destruction of Civilizations.* Simon and Schuster, 2006.

Lynas, Mark. *Six Degrees: Our Future on a Hotter Planet.* National Geographic, 2008.

McDonough, William, and Michael Braungart. *Cradle to Cradle: Remaking the Way We Make Things.* North Point Press, 2002.

McKay, Kim, and Jenny Bonnin. *True Green: 100 Everyday Ways You Can Contribute to a Healthier Planet.* National Geographic, 2007.

________________. *True Green at Work: 100 Ways You Can Make the Environment Your Business.* National Geographic, 2008.

McKibben, Bill. *Deep Economy: The Wealth of Communities and the Durable Future.* Times Books, 2007.

Meadows, D. H., Jorgen Randers, and Dennis L. Meadows. *The Limits to Growth: The 30-Year Update.* Earthscan, 2004.

Nelson, Willie. *On the Clean Road Again: Biodiesel and the Future of the Family Farm.* Fulcrum Publishing, 2007.

Nestle, Marion. *What to Eat.* North Point Press, 2007.

Newman, Nell, and Joseph D'Agnese. *The Newman's Own Organics Guide to the Good Life.* Villard Publisher, 2003.

Norbert-Hodge, Helena, Todd Merrifield, and Steven Gorelick. *Bringing the Food Economy Home.* Kumarian Press, 2002.

Parson, Russ. *How to Pick a Peach: The Search for Flavor from Farm to Table.* Houghton Mifflin, 2008.

Pennybacker, Mindy, and Aisha Ikramuddin. *Mothers & Others for a Livable Planet Guide to Natural Baby Care: Nontoxic and Environmentally Friendly Ways to Take Care of Your New Child.* John Wiley and Sons, Inc., 1999.

Petrini, Carlo. *Slow Food: The Case for Taste.* Columbia University Press, 2003.

Plotkin, Mark J. *Tales of a Shaman's Apprentice: An Ethnobotanist Searches for New Medicines in the Amazon Rain Forest.* Penguin Books, 1993.

Pollan, Michael. *In Defense of Food: An Eater's Manifesto.* Penguin Press, 2008.

_______________. *The Omnivore's Dilemma: A Natural History of Four Meals.* Penguin Press, 2006.

Ponting, Clive. *A New Green History of the World: The Environment and the Collapse of Great Civilizations.* Penguin, 2007.

Poole, Buzz, ed. *Green Design.* Mark Batty Publisher, 2006.

Pregracke, Chad. *From the Bottom Up: One Man's Crusade to Clean America's Rivers.* National Geographic, 2007.

Revkin, Andrew C. *The North Pole Was Here.* Kingfisher, 2007.

Rifkin, Jeremy. *The Hydrogen Economy.* Penguin Putnam, 2002.

Roberts, Jennifer. *Good Green Homes.* Gibbs Smith, 2003.

____________. *Good Green Kitchens: Ultimate Resource for Creating a Beautiful, Healthy, Eco-Friendly Kitchen.* Gibbs Smith, 2006.

___________. *Redux: Designs That Reveal, Recycle, and Redefine.* Gibbs Smith, 2005.

Ryan, John C., and Alan Thein Durning. *Stuff: The Secret Lives of Everyday Things.* Northwest Environment Watch, 1997.

Schor, Juliet B., and Betsy Taylor, eds. *Sustainable Planet: Solutions for the Twenty-First Century.* Beacon Press, 2002.

Sommerville, Annie. *Everyday Greens: Home Cooking from Greens, the Celebrated Vegetarian Restaurant.* Scribner, 2003.

Steinman, David, and Samuel S. Epstein. *The Safe Shopper's Bible: A Consumer's Guide to Nontoxic Household Products, Cosmetics, and Food.* Macmillan Publishing Company, 1995.

Stewart, Iain, and John Lynch. *Earth: The Biography.* National Geographic, 2008.

Walljasper, Jay. *Great Neighborhood Book: A Do-It-Yourself Guide to Placemaking.* New Society Publishers, 2007.

Weinstein, Jay. *The Ethical Gourmet: How to Enjoy Great Food that Is Humanely Raised, Sustainable, Nonendangered, and that Replenishes the Earth.* Broadway Books, 2006.

Winter, Ruth. *A Consumer's Dictionary of Cosmetic Ingredients.* Beaverton, 1999.

Wolverton, B. C. *How to Grow Fresh Air: 50 House Plants That Purify Your Home or Office.* Penguin, 1997.

Worldwatch Institute. *State of the World 2008: Toward a Sustainable Global Economy.* W. W. Norton, 2008.

For more titles, visit
http://www.thegreenguide.com/books/

CONTRIBUTORS

THE EDITORS

Seth Bauer is the editorial director of National Geographic's *Green Guide.* Prior to joining the National Geographic Society, Bauer served as editor-in-chief of several healthy lifestyle publications, including Martha Stewart's *Body+Soul* and *Walking*. He is an Olympic medalist and former world champion in the sport of rowing.

Wendy Gordon is the founder of National Geographic's *Green Guide.* She worked as a senior staff scientist for the Natural Resources Defense Council before co-founding Mothers & Others for a Livable Planet with actress Meryl Streep and serving as its executive director. Mothers & Others introduced the *Green Guide* as a monthly newsletter in 1994. Gordon has a B.S. from Princeton and an M.S. in environmental health from Harvard School of Public Health. She lives with her husband and two sons in New York City.

Editor and lead writer **Donna Garlough** (Chapters 4-7) regularly lends her green living expertise to national publications including the *Green Guide* and Martha Stewart's *Body + Soul* magazine. Currently a senior editor at *Boston* magazine, she covers dining, shopping, weddings, travel, and home design. She holds a B.A. in creative writing from Cornell University.

THE AUTHORS

Jessica Cerretani (Chapters 1, 2, and 11) is a freelance writer and editor specializing in health, wellness, and lifestyle issues. She has written for *Body + Soul, Natural Health,* and the *Green Guide,* as well as for the websites of Andrew Weil, M.D., and Mark Hyman, M.D.

Kristen Pakonis (Chapters 3, 10, and 12) is a freelance writer focusing on environmental and green living topics. Her articles have been published in *Sierra* and *Body + Soul*. She holds a master's degree in environmental education from the Audubon Expedition Institute.

Dave Wortman (Chapters 8, 9, and 13) is a freelance writer and senior consultant with TheBrendle Group, a Colorado-based sustainability consulting firm. A regular contributor to the *Green Guide,* he has also written for *Sierra, Mother Earth News,* and other publications. He is the co-author of the book *Engaging People in Sustainability.*

Catherine Zandonella ("The Science Behind It") is a science writer and frequent contributor to National Geographic's *Green Guide.* She has also contributed articles to *Nature, New Scientist, The Scientist,* and many other publications. She has a master's degree in public health with an emphasis in environmental health from the University of California, Berkeley. She resides in Princeton, New Jersey.

THE ILLUSTRATORS

Nigel Holmes ("The Science Behind It") graduated from London's Royal College of Art in 1966 and worked for newspapers and magazines in England until 1977, when he joined *Time* magazine in New York as graphics director. He remained in that position for 16 years, committed to the power of pictures and humor to help readers understand abstract numbers and difficult scientific concepts. He has written six books on aspects of information design. He lives in Westport, Connecticut.

Willie Ryan, who created the logos for this book, graduated from London's St. Martin's School of Art. He has been developing his linear less-is-more style for the past 15 years. He specializes in icons, logos, and symbols. He lives in Hastings, U.K., and has 10-year-old twins.

THE GREEN GUIDE

National Geographic's *Green Guide* magazine, available by subscription or on newsstands, offers simple tips and practical examples on how to make changes that add up to big benefits for your wallet, your family's health, and the planet. Visit the website at www.thegreenguide.com or subscribe to the magazine online at www.thegreenguide.com/subscribe.

THE ADVISORY BOARD

In the planning and completion of this book, editors benefited from consultations with the distinguished experts listed below, who served as an advisory board. Advisers provided general advice and direction. Specific recommendations expressed in this book, however, originate with the editors of the *Green Guide*.

Michael Ableman is a farmer, author, and photographer. He is also the executive director emeritus of the Center for Urban Agriculture at Fairview Gardens, a nonprofit organization located on one of the oldest and most diverse organic farms in southern California, where he farmed from 1981 to 2001. He has worked as an educator and consultant, inspiring dozens of initiatives in support of small-scale and urban agriculture. He has written three books, including *From the Good Earth: A Celebration of Growing Food Around the World* and *Fields of Plenty: A Farmer's Journey in Search of Real Food and the People Who Grow It.*

Annie Berthold Bond, named one of the top 20 environmental leaders by *Body + Soul* magazine, has worked for more than two decades as a writer and editor concerned with the environment, personal health, and well-being. She has written four books, including *Home Enlightenment, Clean & Green,* and *The Green Kitchen Handbook.* Bond was the founder and editor-in-chief of *Green Alternatives for Health and the Environment* and was a founding editor of the *Green Guide.*

Joan Gussow is the Mary Swartz Rose Professor Emerita of Nutrition Education and former chair of the nutrition education program at the Columbia University Teachers College. She is a member of the advisory board of the Center for Food Safety and a member of the board of overseers of the Chefs Collaborative. Along with numerous scholarly and policy papers, she has written the book *This Organic Life: Confessions of a Suburban Homesteader.*

Fred Kirschenmann is a distinguished fellow and former director of the Leopold Center for Sustainable Agriculture. In 1976, Kirschenmann returned to his family's 3,500-acre farm in North Dakota, achieved certified organic status for it over the next four years, and established it as a model of large-scale organic agriculture. He helped found Farm Verified Organic, an international certification agency, and served as its president for ten years. *The Progressive Farmer* named him Leader of the Year in Agriculture in 2002.

Philip J. Landrigan, M.D., is a pediatrician, epidemiologist, and world leader in the area of public health and preventive medicine. He is chair of the Department of Community and Preventive Medicine at the Mount Sinai School of Medicine in New York City. He is a specialist in the effect of pesticides on children's health, and his work inspired passage of the Food Quality Protection Act and establishment of a new Office of Children's Health Protection within the Environmental Protection Agency. He is the author of *Raising Healthy Children in a Toxic World.*

Frederica Perera, Dr. P.H., is a professor of environmental health sciences and director of the Columbia Center for Children's Environmental Health at Columbia University. A pioneer in the field of molecular epidemiology, she is internationally recognized for her research on environmental causes of cancer and developmental disorders, including the effects of ambient air pollution, environmental tobacco smoke, and pesticides on health outcomes, especially in children.

Jennifer Roberts is a writer, lecturer, and consultant who specializes in ways to improve the environment and enrich our lives by building better buildings. She has written about green buildings and green living for publications as varied as *Professional Builder, Body + Soul,* and the *Financial Times* of London. She holds a certificate in urban permaculture design and has professional LEED accreditation. She is the author of *Good Green Kitchens, Redux,* and *Good Green Homes.*

Jay Walljasper is a senior fellow at the Project for Public Spaces, a nonprofit dedicated to creating public places that build communities. He is also the executive editor of *Ode,* an international print and online magazine. He was the editor of *Utne Reader* from 1984 to 1995 and 2000 to 2004 and has written about urban planning and public place issues for many years. He is the author of Great Neighborhood Book.

INDEX

ILLUSTRATIONS CREDITS

1, Courtesy smart USA; 2-3, Taylor Kennedy/NG Image Collection; 4, Randy Faris/CORBIS; 7, iStockphoto.com; 8, Igor Dutina/iStockphoto.com; 11, Serhiy Kyrychenko/Shutterstock; 12, Trinette Reed/Getty Images; 14, Maceofoto/Shutterstock; 15, Stefano Tiraboschi/Shutterstock; 16, Jacob Wackerhausen/iStockphoto.com; 19, Eric Isselée/Shutterstock; 20, mashe/Shutterstock; 21, Robyn Mackenzie/Shutterstock; 22, s_oleg/Shutterstock; 23, Kapu/Shutterstock; 25, Kateryna Govorushchenko/iStockphoto.com; 28, Olga Shelego/iStockphoto.com; 30, iStockphoto.com; 32, iStockphoto.com; 33, eAlisa/Shutterstock; 34, iStockphoto.com; 37, Andresr/Shutterstock; 38, Leigh Prather/Shutterstock; 39, Hans Van Ijzendoorn/iStockphoto.com; 41, R. Gino Santa Maria/Shutterstock; 44, Yuri Arcurs/Shutterstock; 45, Angel Rodriguez/ iStockphoto.com; 46, Smit/Shutterstock; 49, Jaroslaw Wojcik/iStockphoto.com; 50, Victoria Alexandrova/Shutterstock; 52, Lana Langlois/Shutterstock; 53, Olena Savytska/iStockphoto.com; 56, Andrew Johnson/iStockphoto.com; 58, iofoto/ Shutterstock; 61, NatashaBo/Shutterstock; 64, yazan masa/Shutterstock; 65, Dan Bachman/iStockphoto.com; 67, kotikl/ Shutterstock; 68, Mecan/Anyone/amanaimages/CORBIS; 70, Andrew Dernie/iStockphoto.com; 71, Christine Balderas/ iStockphoto.com; 74, Sasha Davas/Shutterstock; 76, Glenda M. Powers/Shutterstock; 77, Thomas Pullicino/iStockphoto. com; 78, Marko Vesel/iStockphoto.com; 80, Konstantin Kikillov/iStockphoto.com; 84, Tatiana Popova/iStockphoto. com; 85, Claudia Dewald/iStockphoto.com; 86, Anatoly Tiplyashin/Shutterstock; 87, Andriy Dorly/iStockphoto.com; 88, Marc Dietrich/Shutterstock; 92, Dex Images/CORBIS; 94, ajt/Shutterstock; 97, Spectral-Design/Shutterstock; 98, Greg Nicholas/iStockphoto.com; 101, Bloomimage/CORBIS; 104, iStockphoto.com; 106, Emrah Turudu/iStockphoto.com; 109, Ivonne WierinkvanWetten/iStockphoto.com; 110, iStockphoto.com; 114, Maggie Molloy/Shutterstock; 115, Tatiana Popova/ Shutterstock; 116, iStockphoto.com; 118, Bakalusha/Shutterstock; 119, iStockphoto.com; 120, Bakalusha/Shutterstock; 122, Julián Rovagnati/Shutterstock; 123, iStockphoto.com; 128, Trinette Reed/Blend Images/CORBIS; 131, Brian McEntire/ iStockphoto.com; 132, Lisa Gagne/iStockphoto.com; 133, Aleksandr Frolov/iStockphoto.com; 134, Pamela Moore/ iStockphoto.com; 136, Dmitriy Kuznetsov/Shutterstock; 137, Carl Kelliher/iStockphoto.com; 139, Eric Audras/Getty Images; 141, WebstockPro; 144, Robert Payne/iStockphoto.com; 147, Margo Harrison/Shutterstock; 148, Mats/Shutterstock; 149, iStockphoto.com; 150, Valentin Casarsa/iStockphoto.com; 152, ikopylov/Shutterstock; 154, Marcelo Gabriel Domenichelli/ Shutterstock; 155, Gina Smith/Shutterstock; 156, Oktay Ortakcioglu/iStockphoto.com; 160, Oleksil Abramov/Shutterstock; 162, Rey Kamensky/Shutterstock; 166, Juriah Mosin/Shutterstock; 168, iStockphoto.com; 171, Paul Bodea/Shutterstock; 172, Mustafa Ilker/iStockphoto.com; 174, WebstockPro; 175, Nanka/Shutterstock; 176, Beata Becla/Shutterstock; 179, Monika Adamczyk/iStockphoto.com; 182, iStockphoto.com; 183, Alina Solovyova-Vincent/iStockphoto.com; 184, Eric Hood/ iStockphoto.com; 187, Carri Keill/iStockphoto.com; 190, semenovp/Shutterstock; 191, Hu Xiao Fang/Shutterstock; 192, Robert Madeira/Shutterstock; 194, 6493866629/Shutterstock; 196, iStockphoto.com; 197, Aleksandra Nadeina/Shutterstock; 199, Thomas M. Perkins/Shutterstock; 200, Dwight Lyman/iStockphoto.com; 203, LIttle Miss Clever Trousers/Shutterstock; 207, HomeStudio/Shutterstock; 208, Mika/zefa/CORBIS; 210, Alexander Zhiltsov/iStockphoto.com; 211, iStockphoto.com; 212, Kiraly Zoltan Ladislau/iStockphoto.com; 214, Leonid Nyshko/iStockphoto.com; 215, Siddligatta Viswakumar/iStockphoto. com; 216, Rafael Laguillo/iStockphoto.com; 220, Winston Davidian/iStockphoto.com; 222, matka_Wariatka/Shutterstock; 223, Andrew Barker/iStockphoto.com; 225, Krystian Nowak/iStockphoto.com; 226, Christoph Ermel/iStockphoto.com; 228, Sophie Louise Asselin/Shutterstock; 229, Andy Piatt/Shutterstock; 231, ultimathule/Shutterstock; 232, Kativ/iStockphoto. com; 234, Christine Balderas/iStockphoto.com; 237, Isabelle Limbach/iStockphoto.com; 238, Feng Yu/iStockphoto.com; 239, iStockphoto.com; 240, Stacey Newman/iStockphoto.com; 243, Eric Isselée/iStockphoto.com; 247, Susan Trigg/ iStockphoto.com; 248, Roman Barelko/iStockphoto.com; 249, Hasan Kursad/iStockphoto.com; 251, Richard Hobson/ iStockphoto.com; 252, Blend Images/Alamy Ltd; 256, iStockphoto.com; 257, Natalia Vasina Vladimirovna/iStockphoto. com; 259, Joas Kotzsch/iStockphoto.com; 260, Serg64/Shutterstock; 264, Image Source/Getty Images; 266, Kimberly Hall/Shutterstock; 268, Galushko Sergey/Shutterstock; 269, Michael Shake/Shutterstock; 272, J. Helgason/Shutterstock; 274, Monkey Business Images/Shutterstock; 277, Mladen Mladenov//iStockphoto.com; 278, Courtesy WMATA; 279, Franck Boston/iStockphoto.com; 281, iStockphoto.com; 282, Christine Balderas/iStockphoto.com; 288, Dana Neely/Getty Images; 290, iStockphoto.com; 291, efiplus/Shutterstock; 293, iStockphoto.com; 294, Emrah Turudu/iStockphoto.com; 295, David Lee/Shutterstock; 299, Petr Gnuskin/Shutterstock; 300, Yi Chen/Shutterstock; 301, fotoadamczyk/Shutterstock; 303, Yury Kosourov/Shutterstock; 306, melkerw/Shutterstock; 307, Ilya Genkin/Shutterstock; 308, Edward Shaw/iStockphoto.com; 310, Venus/Shutterstock; 313, Alanna Jurden/iStockphoto.com; 316, iStockphoto.com; 319, Tom England/iStockphoto.com; 322, kmss/zefa/CORBIS; 324, Nikolay Postnikov/iStockphoto.com; 325, Sean Locke/iStockphoto.com; 326, Simon Crinks/ iStockphoto.com; 327, iStockphoto.com; 328, Agata Dorobek/Shutterstock; 329, Eliza Snow/iStockphoto.com; 330, Kelly Cline/iStockphoto.com; 331, Luminis/Shutterstock; 333, iStockphoto.com; 334, Hagit Berkovich/iStockphoto.com; 336, marekuliasz/Shutterstock; 337, Abrie Viljoen/iStockphoto.com; 339, Giancarlo Polacchini/iStockphoto.com; 341, iStockphoto. com; 343, Anna Subotina/iStockphoto.com; 344, iStockphoto.com; 345, Roman Ivaschenko/iStockphoto.com; 346, Steve Snyder/iStockphoto.com; 347, Jill Chen/iStockphoto.com; 349, Vladislav Mitic/iStockphoto.com; 352, iStockphoto.com; 353, iStockphoto.com; 355, Rafael Angel Garcia Dobarganes/Shutterstock; 356, Anne-Marie Weber/CORBIS; 358, Serbey Siz'kov/iStockphoto.com; 359, Chirstine Balderas/iStockphoto.com; 361, Maria Bibikova/iStockphoto.com; 362, Oliver Sun Kim/iStockphoto.com; 364, Stefan Klein/iStockphoto.com; 365, Fortish/Shutterstock; 366, Jan Rysavy/iStockphoto.com; 367, Michael Chen/iStockphoto.com; 368, iStockphoto.com; 370, iStockphoto.com; 371, Eric Isselée/iStockphoto.com; 374, Cultura/CORBIS; 376, Skip ODonnell/iStockphoto.com; 378, Andresr/Shutterstock; 379, Christine Balderas/iStockphoto. com; 381, Tamás Ambrits/iStockphoto.com; 382, Olivier Vanbiervliet/Shutterstock; 384, Mariano N. Ruiz/Shutterstock; 388, Ariel Skelley/CORBIS; 391, iStockphoto.com; 392, Morgan Lane Photography/Shutterstock; 393, iStockphoto.com; 395, Courtney Weittenhiller/iStockphoto.com; 396, Suzannah Skelton/iStockphoto.com; 397, Bonita Hein/iStockphoto.com; 399, David Franklin/iStockphoto.com; 403, paulaphoto/Shutterstock; 404, Tan Wei Ming/Shutterstock; 408-409, Britt Erlanson/ Getty Images.

Illustrated Green Guide
by the Editors of the *Green Guide* Magazine

Published by the National Geographic Society
John M. Fahey, Jr., President and Chief Executive Officer
Gilbert M. Grosvenor, Chairman of the Board
Tim T. Kelly, President, Global Media Group
John Q. Griffin, President, Publishing
Nina D. Hoffman, Executive Vice President;
President, Book Publishing Group

Prepared by the Book Division
Kevin Mulroy, Senior Vice President and Publisher
Leah Bendavid-Val, Director of Photography Publishing and Illustrations
Marianne R. Koszorus, Director of Design
Barbara Brownell Grogan, Executive Editor
Elizabeth Newhouse, Director of Travel Publishing
Carl Mehler, Director of Maps

Staff for This Book
Susan Tyler Hitchcock, Editor
Vickie Donovan, Illustrations Editor
Linda Johansson, Contributing Illustrations Editor
Marty Ittner and Melissa Farris, Art Directors
Cameron Zotter and Linda Johansson, Designers
Heather Sisan and Kathleen L. Pond, Researchers
Mike Horenstein, Production Project Manager
Marshall Kiker, Illustrations Specialist

Jennifer A. Thornton, Managing Editor
R. Gary Colbert, Production Director

Manufacturing and Quality Management
Christopher A. Liedel, Chief Financial Officer
Phillip L. Schlosser, Vice President
Chris Brown, Technical Director
Nicole Elliott, Manager
Monika D. Lynde, Manager
Rachel Faulise, Manager

Founded in 1888, the National Geographic Society is one of the largest nonprofit scientific and educational organizations in the world. It reaches more than 285 million people worldwide each month through its official journal, *National Geographic*, and its four other magazines; the National Geographic Channel; television documentaries; radio programs; films; books; videos and DVDs; maps; and interactive media. National Geographic has funded more than 8,000 scientific research projects and supports an education program combating geographic illiteracy.

For more information, please call 1-800-NGS LINE (647-5463) or write to the following address:

National Geographic Society
1145 17th Street N.W.
Washington, D.C. 20036-4688 U.S.A.

Visit us online at www.nationalgeographic.com/books

For information about special discounts for bulk purchases, please contact National Geographic Books Special Sales: ngspecsales@ngs.org

For rights or permissions inquiries, please contact National Geographic Books Subsidiary Rights: ngbookrights@ngs.org

Illustrated green guide : a complete reference for consuming wisely / by the editors of the Green Guide ; foreword by Meryl Streep.
p. cm.
Includes index.
ISBN 978-1-4262-0308-4
1. Environmental responsibility. 2. Green movement. 3. Sustainable living. 4. Green products. I. Green guide (Mothers & others for a Livable Planet, Inc.)
GE195.7.I45 2008
333.75--dc22
2008041619

ISBN: 978-1-4262-0308-4

Printed in the United States of America

How can I stay current with the *Green Guide*?

Just about everywhere you look, you'll find National Geographic's *Green Guide*—your personal companion to green living.

SUBSCRIBE TO THE MAGAZINE

In Spring 2008, the National Geographic Society—known for inspiring millions to care about the planet and one of the most trusted brands in the world—launched the *Green Guide* magazine, a how-to resource chockful of simple tips, steps, and advice on how to tread lightly on the Earth and save money at the same time.

To learn more and to subscribe, visit www.thegreenguide.com/magazine. Or, to order by phone, please call 1-800-NGS-LINE (1-800-647-5463).

VISIT US ONLINE

Updated daily, TheGreenGuide.com has the latest in green tips, tools and news to help make being eco-friendly easy, understandable and practical.

Visit us online at www.thegreenguide.com.

RECEIVE OUR WEEKLY NEWSLETTER

Every Wednesday you can receive our weekly eNewsletter, the *Green Guide To Go*, delivered to your inbox, with links to the latest green news and information.

Sign up online at www.thegreenguide.com.